GO ANYWAY

*Go anyway
for your dreams!
Lyn Foley*

Sailing
Around the
World with
Parkinson's

Editors: Kurt Wilson and Jean Howze
Cover Design: Stephen Horsley
Cover sketch of Galle, Sri Lanka lighthouse: Lyn Foley

Parts of some chapters in this book have appeared in *Sail Magazine*, *Living Aboard*, *Flying Fish*, *Mid-Gulf Sailing*, and *Latitudes and Attitudes*. A serialized edition has appeared in *The Round Top Register*.

Publisher's Cataloging-in-Publication
(Provided by Quality Books, Inc.)

Foley, Lyn.
Go Anyway : sailing around the world with Parkinson's / Lyn Foley.
2nd ed.
p. cm.
ISBN 978-0-9854624-0-6
ISBN 978-0-9854624-1-3 (electronic version)

1. Foley, Lyn. 2. Foley, James V. 3. Travelers--Biography. 4. Parkinson's disease--Patients--Biography. 5. Sailing. 6. Voyages around the world. I. Title.

G226.F65A3 2012   910.4'5'0922   QBI12-600078

First Edition: ISBN:978-0-578-08016-1
First Edition, Electronic Version: ISBN:978-0-615-59014-1

© 2012 by Carolyn H Foley
All rights reserved. No part of this publication may be reproduced or transmitted in any form or by any means, electronic or mechanical, including scanning, photocopying, recording, or any information storage or retrieval system, without permission in writing from the publisher.

Round Top Books
Post Office Box 368, Round Top, Texas 78954
Phone: (979) 249-3358
e-mail: RoundTopBooks@RoundTopBooks.com

For my mother, Carolyn Harrell Kilgore,
and
for Jim's mother, Ina Young Hansen

They taught us to follow our dreams and loved us enough to let us go.

"On an ancient wall in China

where a brooding Buddha blinks,

deeply graven is the message——

'It is later than you think.'

The clock of life is wound but once,

and no man has the power

to tell just when the hands will stop

at late or early hour.

Now is all the time you own,

the past a golden link.

Go for it now my friend;

It's later than you think."

Anonymous

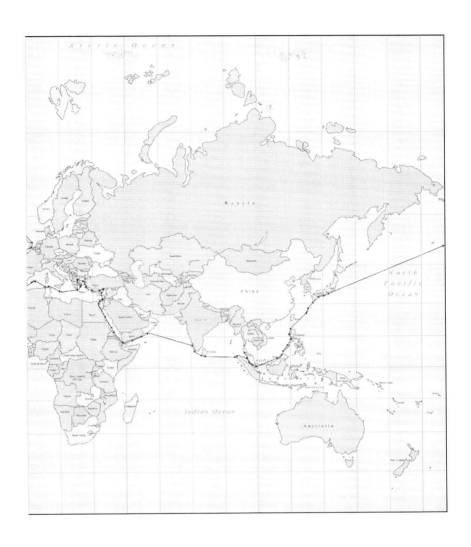

Sanctuary's Circumnavigation Route: 1991-2001

Table of Contents

Introduction 13
The Dream is Born 17
A Wakeup Call to Move Aboard 29
Small Craft Advisory 39
Shakedown in the Pacific Northwest 51
A Six Mile Lesson 59
Some Like It Hot 65
Back to the Beginning at San Patricio 77
Te-Wan-Te-Peckers 83
Ticos and the Zone 91
Off the Charts in Kuna Yala 101
A City, Some Islands, Tikal, and Malaria 107
Back in the United States 119
The Ditch 125
The Gulf Stream Dragon 133
Caught in a Gluepot 147
Letterboxing, a Tattoo, and the Burryman 155
Grounded in Spain 167
Morocco: Which One Would It Be? 179
Across the Mediterranean 187
The Turkish Spay and the Exiled Camel 197
From Mersin to the Suez 211
The Egyptian Pilots 221

The Gate of Tears	233
Halfway 'Round	247
A Banshee, Some Elephants, and Monkeys	265
Vegetarians and a King	277
The Point of No Return	289
Land of the Rising Sun	301
Crossing the Pacific	311
Tying the Knot	333
Epilogue: Swallowing the Hook	351
Glossary of Nautical and Foreign Terms	353
Sanctuary Layout	359
About Parkinson's Disease	361
Acknowledgements	363
About The Author	365

Introduction

Navigating around roadblocks, be they emotional, physical, or financial, becomes a normal part of life if you choose to undertake any adventuresome endeavor. For folks who want to sail across the oceans of the world, the challenges start long before they set to sea: earning the money to buy or build a boat, learning both sailing and seamanship, finding the right boat, convincing themselves and their partner to put aside careers, everyday contact with friends and family, and the security of life as they know it for the constantly changing life that lies beyond the horizon. Lyn and Jim Foley successfully navigated all of these hurdles. With their business and home sold, their skills honed, their boat outfitted and charts on board, they were literally within days of setting sail when one more seemingly insurmountable roadblock was placed in their way. Jim was diagnosed with Parkinson's disease. "Don't go," the doctor said. But as Jim and Lyn walked toward the doctor's door, his intern whispered the fateful words "Go anyway."

Larry and I had the pleasure of meeting Jim and Lyn when we sailed into Horta in the Azores, north bound from Brazil toward Ireland on board our 29 foot cutter, *Taleisin*. Their handsome sloop, *Sanctuary*, lay secured at the custom docks as Lyn and Jim considered their next moves. The problems associated with Jim's advancing Parkinson's symptoms were obvious. The heavy weather they would face if they continued towards Europe had them both concerned. But among the three or four dozen voyagers we met at these cross roads, none seemed more thrilled with the experiences they were having; none had more enjoyable stories of interacting with the people they'd met during their travels. Though they glossed over the hurdles they'd had to overcome, we eventually got them to tell us of the steps they took to safely cross oceans, the concessions they each made, and the coping mechanisms they used to keep their keen senses of humor. "Those two are real heroes," I remember Larry saying when we headed home after a laughter filled dinner on board *Sanctuary*.

There is inspiration to be found in this book. But there are also useful guidelines for anyone who wants to go out cruising.

It should be essential reading for anyone who has started a career then discovered the idea of cruising under sail. The steps Lyn and Jim took to go from sailing neophytes to coastal cruisers helped prepare them for the realities of choosing a cruising boat wisely. Once they'd chosen their boat, they undertook real sea-trials and a proper shake-down cruise before setting off into foreign waters. This logical and often enjoyable approach saved them from the first passage traumas that have ended many cruising dreams.

Those who have been sailing all their life can also take lessons from Lyn's story. She clearly shows the work that goes into keeping a cruising boat ready to cross yet another ocean- plus the difficulty of insuring that it is done properly if outside contractors are used. Their boat had relatively simple systems, not as simple as we ourselves have always preferred, but definitely simple by today's standards. Yet there were times when Jim and Lyn felt they were "repairing their boat in a series of exotic ports." The reality of cruising life is that you are the one who must insure that all the systems keep working: the sails, the rigging, the engine, generator, water tankage and pumps, ground tackle, and your shore boat. This takes time, patience, and a commitment to understanding and knowing how to maintain the gear you have on board. We surveyed several marine professionals then combined their suggestions to estimate the time it would take to maintain a 35 to 40 foot cruising boat, equipped with currently suggested equipment in top, ready to go to sea condition while it was being used for offshore voyages. This came to two or three days a week. Combine this with the time spent actually crossing oceans, plus time to clear into then out of various ports, time for basic people maintenance (laundry, shopping, provisioning) and in actuality, folks who take off cruising find they have little more true time off than those working at normal jobs on shore who get weekends and holidays free.

Here is the magic that Lyn's story shows. Those who do set off cruising, and then learn to slow down and take the time to savor this new life they've chosen, will spend all that free time surrounded by potentially enticing adventures. Then, as they sail onward, they will, as Lyn and Jim did and as Larry and I did, spend much of the time while at sea reminiscing about these encounters and wondering what magical happenings the next landfall will bring.

As much as Lyn's descriptions of moonlight nights at sea, magical landfalls or swimming in crystal clear tropical waters might entice you to go to sea, it is the stories of the people Lyn and Jim encountered, and the friendships they formed, that will encourage you to "Go Anyway."

Lin Pardey

Lin Pardey and her husband Larry are award winning sailors, two time circumnavigators and authors of eleven books and five video programs. Their books have been translated into four languages. You can learn more about them at www.landlpardey.com

The Dream is Born

1974

"The meeting of two personalities is like the contact of two chemical substances: if there is any reaction, both are transformed."

— Carl Jung (1875-1961)

I was born in Georgia, deep in the South of red dirt roads, barbed wire fences tangled with honeysuckle vines, and chickens scratching in the backyard under the pines. Growing up I drank water from our well, waded in creeks during hot summer days, jumped off rope swings to splash in muddy rivers, or fished for catfish and trout in lakes. A tomboy, I ran around in my overalls, half wild, catching mice in the fields and climbing mimosa trees to build tree houses. By the time I was eight, I could bait a hook, start an outboard, row a flatbed boat, or paddle a canoe, but sailing never occurred to me. During my childhood Alaska was a frontier wilderness and California, "that place with the weirdos," as distant as China. A yellow bus carried me 14 miles past cotton patches and herds of cattle to grammar school in Macon, the nearest town with paved streets and stop lights.

At home, I rode my bicycle by fenced-in fields to visit Gladys, my nearest friend two miles away. As a teenager I wore bobby socks, penny loafers, and poodle skirts and with a flashlight under my pillow, read at night well past my bedtime. I brought home "A's" on my report cards, twirled baton as a majorette, and played flute in the band. Three times a week our family drove to a white clapboard church down the road—twice on Sunday for preaching, and once on Wednesday for Prayer Meeting. The boys I knew pumped gas or played on the football team or drove their daddies' tractors. I went steady but didn't "do it" before I got married——that would have been a sin. I was raised to go to college (so I'd have "something to fall back on" if I ever needed to work), get married, and have two kids who would both say "Yes Ma'am," and "Thank you, Ma'am" and "Please pass the butter beans," just as my sister and I had.

Sometime between the prayer meetings and the college degree, the "place with the weirdos" called me like a siren, and I started leaning west. I pushed myself, working to pay for the Bachelor of Arts degree I earned in Art Education.

Where was the adventure in teaching in a small town with the red dirt gravel roads, chickens, pine trees, corn patches, and church three times a week? I yearned for something different. I turned 22 a few months before the tide of the 1967 "Summer of Love" receded and rode along into San Francisco on the crest of the next wave, one of the hundreds who migrated across country to the tune of the Mamas and Papas singing *"California Dreamin'."* With the Mississippi River behind me for the first time, I shed my tidy Jackie Kennedy pumps, straight prim skirts, and clean white gloves and threw out my girdle, my stockings, and my bras.

By 1974, after seven years in California, I'd dropped out of graduate school, tossed away a career teaching art, given up a responsible job (advancement possible) at an insurance company, and failed at "Marriage and Relationships 101." I entered my 29th year divorced—no children, no alimony. My Southern accent and manners still intact, I was strong, healthy, my blue eyes still bright, but my dark brown hair showed an early stripe of gray.

As a fiber artist, I created (and sometimes sold) large wall hangings for banks, offices, or private homes. I mostly sold crocheted clothing in art shops and at street fairs. With my wild hair cascading halfway down my back, I dressed in long, flounce skirts and crocheted tops, piled Janis Joplin type jewelry on my neck, ears, both arms, almost every finger, and even some toes, and kicked those toes in handmade sandals or knee-high Frye leather boots. With three cats for company, I lived in a small railroad flat down an alley called "Middle Street" in the heart of the

Fillmore district of San Francisco. I spent early mornings practicing Tai Chi at a park in Chinatown, and the rest of my morning crocheting, spinning or dying the wool and cotton I used in my art. Afternoons I baked bread, made yogurt, or cooked pots of soup. My nights I spent alone, or out at "Minnie's Can-Do Club" smoking weed, drinking red wine, dancing with friends or looking for company.

By 1974 I wasn't so much dreaming as floundering around trying to figure out what had happened to the first third of my life and what to do with the remainder. I had no inkling my star was about to collide with the orbit of Jim Foley's star—–or that we'd join hands for a wild ride that would include a ten-year sail around the world. While I was toddling back in Georgia, Jim was born 2,500 miles away in Oakland, California, three years and six days behind me. "Precocious, noisy, always into something," Lee, his mother, said. "Jim growing up was really a handful——especially since I already had a little girl. He was always into mischief; I never knew what the teachers would be calling me about next."

Eight year old Jim tap dancing

Two more children followed, so Jim grew up fast, with his older sister leading, and his younger sister and younger brother tagging along behind. He rode his tricycle around the block; he later walked on city sidewalks to Catholic school. By the age of seven little Jimmy sported a pint-sized top hat and cane as he tap-danced Saturday mornings on *King Norman's Kingdom of Toys*, a San Francisco TV show for children. At eleven years old, he played the drums. By fifteen he was pounding out Beatles and Rolling Stones tunes in a rock and roll band. And water, what water did Jim know? Only that the rolling ocean lay across the bay over by San Francisco. The water he knew was in the swimming pool, the one he lapped, day after day, as a member of the high school swim team. Sailing? Sailing never occurred to him.

Jim was headed for college, too—until his girlfriend got pregnant. Marriage came earlier than he had planned and just about the same time his dad died of cancer. A huge loss, a new wife, a new baby, holding down a job, and going to college, too—something had to give. And something did give—the marriage failed, and his wife left with their baby. Jim tried to keep up with college. He settled down to studying and working. One semester an art elective was required, so he signed up for jewelry making. "Well, there were a lot of fine-looking girls in the class," Jim told me later. "I thought maybe I'd meet someone new. After all, my wife had been gone a long time."

"But I forgot about the girls," Jim said, "when I discovered jewelry making. I took to it like a natural. I could see the design I wanted to make. Carving the wax, setting the stone, soldering the bezel, all of it was easy for me. And Horst Kampmann, a really good German goldsmith—a master really—taught the class and he liked me. Horst was just waiting for someone who really wanted to learn. I soaked up everything; I couldn't get enough. He paid me to be his teacher's aide, but I'd have done it for nothing. I even went up weekends to his studio in Sebastopol to learn more. So, I started making jewelry to sell on consignment to stores in Berkeley, and then I began riding my bicycle over to Telegraph Avenue every weekend and started selling along with the other street artists."

"Selling in Berkeley got really crazy! That Christmas in 1973, some big guy named Bear pulled a gun on me. Staring down the barrel of a large caliber handgun while he shouted at me, "Get out—this is my spot!" wasn't my idea of fair play. In spite of Bear and his gun, and all the other hassles of coping with a hostile atmosphere, I made some money. The college students were desperate to buy unusual gifts to take home for the holidays, so really the money was extra good. I had some cash in my pockets, and my friend Chris said, "Why don't we go to Hawaii? You'll love it there--it's wonderful. There'll be lots of beautiful women and you can sell your jewelry to the tourists. We can hitchhike around the islands and camp in the state parks, eat natural foods that grow wild, and man, the ocean fishing will be great." It sounded great, so we packed our backpacks, got plane tickets, said our goodbyes, and went."

"Hawaii was beautiful, but the police didn't like us camping, and the locals called us *haoles* and always tried to run us off the road. The girls were all stuck-up, and even though I earned money selling jewelry I made from pukka shells I found on the beach, I couldn't take that hassle either. Chris and I gave up and flew home to California after about three months. We got back, and I set up my jewelry workshop again. I heard that being a street artist was easier in the city, so I started lugging my display case onto the Oakland to San Francisco bus every weekend."

In 1974 Jim also was not so much dreaming as floundering around trying to figure out what had happened to the first third of his life and what to do with the remainder.

By 1974 I was one of twelve San Francisco artists who owned a crafts cooperative on Fillmore Street. I hadn't sold much at the store lately, so Saturday morning, April 6, 1974, I got up early thinking about raising money to pay the rent on my flat. After practicing a short set of Tai Chi in my tiny backyard, I ate a breakfast of tea, homemade yogurt, and granola, then gathered about two dozen of my crocheted hats, two crocheted sweaters, and a few woven belts I had made, stuffed them into a big slouch bag along with a small quilt, and got dressed for a day in the city. By 7:00 I had caught the California Street cable car and ridden it downtown. I got off at Market Street and walked the rest of the way to Justin Herman Plaza to sell my wares.

A sculptural fountain dominated "The Plaza." The fountain and its surrounding concrete park lay sandwiched between the tall, asymmetrical Hyatt Regency and the entrance to the Ferry Building across the way. Even though the fountain smelled like a broken sewer and looked like a broken freeway, hundreds of tourists passed by to view it as they crossed the plaza from the parking areas or sauntered from rooms or tours of the Hyatt, making their way to the next attraction—Fishermen's Wharf, Pier 39, or the ferry to Sausalito or Alcatraz Island. Those tourists meant money. So, every weekend without rain, street artists gathered to sell fiber art, leather purses, jewelry, wooden puzzles, pottery, photography, and paintings. With a few food stands, local musicians, mimes, and jugglers thrown in, "The Plaza" was a weekend street party, a way to make some extra money, or for the majority, a living.

Since his journey across San Francisco Bay took much longer than my inner city ride, Jim got up even earlier that morning than I did. After packing his portable display case, he walked about three blocks from the house he shared with Chris in Oakland to catch a bus to San

Francisco. He'd eat later at a place he liked in the city. He dozed on the bus, woke up as it pulled into the transit terminal, got off, and walked on to the plaza with nothing on his mind but putting down his case and going over to a café to order a Danish or eggs and home fries for breakfast.

Meanwhile, I'd arranged my quilt on the concrete in a likely looking place near the tourist walkway and placed my crocheted hats, belts, and sweaters on top in neat rows. As I sat back on my heels surveying the scene, I noticed a good-looking guy heading my way. He wore an embroidered jean jacket, some clean, well-fitting jeans, and a leather slouch hat atop his shoulder-length brown hair. His eyes were fiery, and a diamond sparkled in his pierced nose just above his full mustache and beard. Man, I liked the way he looked, but his boot-tapping, staccato walk signaled trouble—he clearly wasn't just out shopping. I stared at him—interested but with no inkling that in almost exactly three years I'd be married to him.

"What are you doing here?" the guy said abruptly, putting down a case he was carrying. "This is my spot."

"Well, I just set my blanket here to sell some crocheted hats and my friend's hand-painted eggs," I replied pointedly.

"This is my spot," he said again. "Everybody knows that."

"Your spot? I had no idea. There's no mark, and I don't see your name on it," I said, standing my ground.

"I always set up here to sell my jewelry," he said, as if he were San Francisco's Mayor Alioto.

"Well, today I am here." I decided to make peace and softened my tone. "My name is Lyn; who are you?"

"I'm Jim," he replied, looking at me and relaxing his stance.

"There's plenty of room for both of us; we can set up side by side, okay?"

"Well, alright, I guess. Just move over a bit."

And with that he began unpacking his case which folded out into a display with legs that raised it up to easy viewing height. I discovered then that Jim was a jeweler, and the rings in his case were beautiful— delicate replicas of flowers and leaves he'd first carved out of wax and then cast into silver or gold and set with gemstones such as opals, rubies, or sapphires.

Jim's artistry was impressive, and people liked my fiber work as well. We both made a lot of sales that day. Between customers he told me he lived in Oakland across the bay near Berkeley. I noticed he was really tan for so early in the year, asked him why, and also wondered why he wasn't selling on Telegraph Avenue in Berkeley—supposedly a great selling spot for artists. I heard the story about the trip to Hawaii and how the plaza was better than "The Ave."

Lyn & Jim at the Plaza - 1974

Later, as I took a break walking around and looking at the other art work for sale, I asked some of the other artists about Jim. One friend told me, "Yeah, Diamond Jim—that's what we call him—he's the best jeweler on the streets. He's a good man, but, ah, Lyn, you don't want any of that—Diamond Jim's married." Married?! He hadn't told me that! I liked him a lot, but I wouldn't fool with a married man. When Jim gave me his card at the end of the day, I tucked it into my bag but threw it away later thinking, "What a shame." He asked me for my number, but I didn't have to worry about that—I didn't have a telephone.

We danced around each other at the plaza and other Art and Craft shows for a few months. I learned more about Jim and finally heard the story about how his wife had left him. Yeah, he was still legally married but had been separated for over two years; his divorce would be final soon. So, one fine day in late September when I went down to the plaza not to sell but just to enjoy a day with my friends, I saw Jim set up there as usual. I really loved his jewelry and had some extra money, so I bought a beautiful ring of his made from a live casting of a plant named Baby Tears. I sat around talking with him for a while, and he asked me out to dinner after he was done selling. I said yes. And we both knew the yes meant more than dinner.

Around closing time Jim stashed his portable display in the coin operated lockers at the East Bay Bus Terminal, and we walked, holding hands, to San Francisco's Chinatown. As we studied the menu in the window of The Good Earth Chinese Restaurant, a waiter at the door noticed us, sensed our mutual infatuation, and called out, "Need private booth! You come." We ate the food but wanted to consume each other. We stared at each other wantonly and contained ourselves as we hiked the long walk to my apartment. When we got to my place the fireworks began. Jim kissed me on the back of my neck; I turned around, and we fell into bed not sleeping until sunrise, a George Harrison record playing over and over on the turntable, neither of us getting up to go change it, "Hare Krishna, Hare, Hare, My Sweet Lord...." Jim didn't go home for three days. After he left I saw my friend Margot and told her, "This is it." Jim went back to Oakland and told Chris, "This is the one." Our faded dreams of love sparked, flamed, and burned. We were a couple by Thanksgiving and living together by Christmas. All of my earthly possessions—including my piano, my rocking chair, my spinning wheel, my yarn, and my three cats—fit into one load in the back of Chris' pickup truck. I set up my studio-workspace in the same room as Jim's jeweler's bench. While Chris was off doing his thing, Jim and I worked, talked, stopped and made love, worked some more, talked some more, stopped and made some more sweet love...

By the end of 1974, we sat together every weekend at "Our Spot" bundled up, keeping each other warm from the cold Northern California winds that sweep through the streets of San Francisco and The Plaza. Jim sold his jewelry and I sold my hats, and holiday business and sales were good that season—maybe because we were in love.

We pooled our profits and planned our first trip/business venture together to Mexico in January of 1975. We'd buy inexpensive Mexican textiles, hand crafts, fire opals, and fire agates. Jim would set the gemstones into his jewelry to sell at The Plaza, and I'd place the textiles and crafts on consignment at a store on Union Street. We'd have an adventure, a nice vacation in a warm wonderful climate, and pay for the trip by reselling our purchases for a profit.

We bought a beat up old VW bug and started driving from Oakland to the Mexican border. The Bug stalled going over the mountains outside Los Angeles. We coasted over to the side of the road, the wind generators whirring on the hills in the background. I got out, kicked the tires, screamed and yelled, "Don't stop now you stupid car, we've got to get to Mexico!" Jim calmly examined the engine but could find nothing wrong. We flung ourselves back inside in frustration. "What are we going to do now?" I wailed. Jim said, "I'll try the key one more time, then we'll see." "It started!" I yelped. So on we puttered.

We finally made it to the border, parked the Bug in a lot on the United States side, and took out and put on our back packs. I said to Jim, "Maybe somebody will steal the car." "You wish," he replied. Then we walked across the border to the train station at Mexicali. As we sat in the station waiting room, the *Federales* stopped and asked to see our money and papers. We cautiously pulled them out and handed them over. They flipped through everything, shook their heads, gave us our stuff back, and walked on mumbling something in Spanish. "Wonder what they really wanted," I said, "I couldn't understand the Spanish, could you?" Jim said, "No, but I guess we have to have money to get into the country—they don't want us broke and causing trouble, they're just like the cops in Hawaii. Well, I'm glad the tickets are cheap." With that we boarded the train and settled into the second class section with the Mexicans for the ride south.

South: through the tunnels of the tropical canyons and hillsides. South: to discover the markets with inexpensive gemstones and crafts. South: to the isolated villages and beaches about which we had only read. Two days later we arrived in Guadalajara with backsides aching from the hard seats of the *Segundo Clase* train.

Guadalajara offered big-city sights and a fascinating inner city market. However, we wanted a beach, so after a few days we caught a bus to the coast. On our map Manzanillo looked terrific, but when the bus pulled into town at the end of the line we were disappointed. Drifts of papers blew in the breeze, and old tires, broken bottles, and unidentified bits of rebar and sheet metal lay rusting along broken fences and half-finished houses. Menacing-looking dark smoke poured out of chimneys attached to scruffy buildings with boarded-up windows. Where was the beach or the market with fresh fruits and vegetables? Looking at each other uncomfortably, we got off and lugged our backpacks out of the belly of the bus. As we hauled them over to the side by a wall with crumbling plaster and mishmashed paint colors, a money changer with greasy hair and black fingernails caked with dirt, crooked his finger at us, calling "*Señores, Señores*," trying to hustle us with a high exchange rate— U.S. Dollars to Mexican Pesos. We calculated the *cambio* and as we declined his offer, he spat to the side and turned his back.

Earlier, on the bus ride south, we had both noticed a small town on the coast with a plaza surrounded by bougainvilleas. Goats, chickens, and children had played by the bus stop. Through the bus window we had also glimpsed a bay with sparkling, clear water and a beach with few people and no visible trash. The bay was ringed with small cabanas, palm trees, and open-air stands advertising fresh coconut and fruit juices. I asked Jim, "Do you remember that little town we saw that looked so wonderful?" "Yes," he said. We gulped simultaneously: "Let's go back and find it!"

The bus driver threw his hands up in a quizzical gesture as we tried in limited Spanish to explain that we wanted to reboard the same bus we had just gotten off of to return to a town we didn't know the name of since it wasn't on our map. The driver, obviously puzzled, finally let us back on the bus, and we returned to what we discovered was San Patricio—the little bus stop that changed our lives.

We got off the bus. As we sat catching our breath by the side of the road at San Patricio's dusty bus stop, a couple approached us speaking English—accented English, but English. Hubert and Laura, a Canadian couple who told us they were wintering in warm Mexico, said, "We noticed you sitting here looking distressed. Do you need a place to stay?" "We do," we replied, and with that they took us under their wings. They introduced us to Señor Malacho, San Patricio's unofficial mayor and owner of a family restaurant. Sr. Malacho rented cabanas behind his restaurant overlooking Bahia Navidad. His little rooms were still under construction, and he said we could have an "almost finished" cabana for just 8 *pesos* a day (about $4 U.S. in January, 1975). We'd cook for ourselves in the tiny kitchen next door or eat in his small restaurant. We paid him for one week. The next morning we settled into our new routine— towels out to the beach to sit on the sand or swim in the warm bay or go up to the beach bar to sip *cervezas* or snooze in the hammocks suspended under the bamboo *palapa*.

We sat and watched the local boys throwing fishing nets into the bay competing with the pelicans diving for the same fish. The fish jumped out of the water to avoid being scooped up by the big beaks and pouches of the pelicans or the encircling nets thrown by the boys. Unlike the soon tired and bored fishing boys, the large birds took flight again and again to dive into the schools of fish, emerging with their beaks overflowing with fish whose tails flapped as they tried to escape before being swallowed whole. Later in the afternoon, after *siesta*, the boys played soccer in the sand using beer cans as goal posts. They even let the *gringo* with long hair and bushy beard play "football" with them, yelling "*Mano, mano, mano!*" when Jim let his hand touch the ball.

One morning as we sat on the sand, we noticed a small sailboat approaching. It sailed lazily into the bay first one way and then the other. As the boat got closer to the shore, the two people on board went into action. The woman lowered the sails as the man dropped the anchor off the bow. The little boat stretched out on the anchor line and began rocking gently back and forth in the light breeze and slight swell that entered the bay.

We continued to watch the harmonious movement of the boat just as we had watched the pelicans earlier. The boat, anchored in perfect viewing distance from our spot on the beach, fascinated us. After a while the sailors assembled a small inflatable boat. They pumped it up and lowered it into the water. They climbed in and rowed toward the beach—right to where we sat taking it all in. We got up and waded out into the surf to help them drag the dinghy past the tide line.

"Can you tell us where the market is?" the couple asked. We pointed in unison toward the fresh market where locally grown avocados, papayas, lettuces, onions, oranges, coconuts, and other produce was sold. "Thanks. Will you watch our dinghy while we shop?" "We'll be glad to," we said. "That way the kids won't play on it."

When the couple returned, we struck up a conversation and learned that they lived aboard their sailboat enjoying "coastal cruising." They explained that a small group of sailors plied the coast of Mexico living on sailboats. These boaters sailed along the coast from port to port staying a long time or a short time in each anchorage—drifting or sailing as they fancied or as the weather allowed.

With gleaming eyes, they described "ocean voyaging" as sailing to distant shores, isolated islands, exotic places, and other countries. Ocean voyagers sailed long distances sometimes taking many days to cross bays, seas, or oceans. Those who sailed farther took more chances but were able to visit and see more of the world. The ocean voyagers used the wind, followed charts, and were guided by the stars.

The couple became really excited telling us about "circumnavigators, the most accomplished of sailors." Circumnavigators sailed vast ocean expanses using refined sailing skills, navigational expertise, and command of instruments. Circumnavigators took even more chances, faced unforeseen, possibly death defying events: rapacious pirates, boat-destroying flotsam or jetsam, or hurricane-force storms. Circumnavigators dealt with the ocean in an entirely different way, continuing their voyaging until they made it all the way around the world. We imagined the countries and cultures they might experience, the physical stamina required, the navigational and sailing skills needed, and how mentally strong they surely were. What an accomplishment circumnavigating would be!

We enjoyed the company of the sailing couple for a few days until they pulled up the anchor and sailed away. The idea had snared us like fish in a net. Wouldn't it be incredible to live aboard a boat, to cruise, to voyage, to sail around the world? What if we could? What a wonderful dream! Sailing around the world!

Then reality set in. We had little or no money, and neither of us knew anything about sailing. Jim said, "I've never been on a boat other than a fishing boat or the ferry to Sausalito."

"Well, when I was a Girl Scout I learned how to paddle a canoe, swamp it, and rescue myself. I also used to fish for catfish with my Dad and Uncle," I replied.

"Oh, well, we'll learn somehow." We were young, we were in love, and we were creative: one minute the idea didn't exist, the next minute it was born. We created it together, because the world was there to be seen, because we wanted a challenge, because we had a zest for adventure, and well …just because.

A Wakeup Call to Move Aboard

1977—1990

> "The sea that calls all things unto her calls me, and I must embark. For to stay, though the hours burn in the night, is to freeze, and crystallize, and be bound in a mold."
> —*The Prophet,* Kahil Gibran

Our catch-as-catch-can existence shifted. Back at the border, our vacation over, we dusted off our old VW bug, cranked it up, and nursed it home. We'd been gone only a month, and when we drove up to our rented house in the Oakland foothills it looked just as we had left it. Yet everything was different because now we reached for something. We had a goal and a dream.

In a quest to earn money to finance our adventure, we pooled our resources and became focused. Jim began taking custom orders for his jewelry. After a while Chris moved out of the house we three shared, so we turned his former bedroom into an "Appointment Only" jewelry show-room. Meanwhile, I began managing a shop that sold my fiber work, so I had a paying job in addition to the sales of my artwork. We turned our business partnership into a life partnership when we married in 1977.

Life threw us opportunities and we caught almost all of them. By 1979 we had cleaned up our act (including cutting our long hair) and opened a fine jewelry store. By the 1980s we owned two greeting card stores as well. Jim took more classes and became a certified gemologist and appraiser as well as a jewelry designer. Our three businesses thrived. We'd been able to buy a house and had squirreled away some savings for our dream. But we still hadn't ever been sailing!

Then Jim met a sailing teacher, delivery captain, and ocean voyager with lots of experience. A fellow named Jim Marco wandered into our jewelry store shopping for wedding rings. In the process of buying the rings, the two Jims learned a little about each other. Eventually Jim Mar-

Jim & Lyn 1989

co, the sailor and delivery captain, said, "Would you like to trade sailing lessons for wedding rings?" "I was just about to ask you the same question," Jim Foley replied.

"Marco Polo," as we called him, started Jim off in a sailing dinghy on Lake Merritt in Oakland. Marco Polo gave both of us lessons as we sailed on San Francisco Bay aboard *Intention*, his 37-foot sailboat. Later we joined a sailing club at the Berkeley Marina and took more lessons in boat handling and navigation. Jim joined a racing crew, and we enrolled in night classes in celestial navigation and coastal piloting at Alameda College. Soon we qualified to rent sailboats from the school's fleet and squeezed as many days off from our stores as we could to go sailing.

The first time we managed two free days in a row, we sailed to Angel Island and docked overnight. We were so excited and proud of ourselves until we realized we had forgotten to bring food for the next day aboard and therefore ate saltine crackers for breakfast.

That, and other mistakes we made, prompted us to enroll in a two-day "Cruising Seminar" led by John Neal, an experienced ocean voyager. We learned how to plan for long voyages, prepare for bad weather, stow food and supplies, and repair sails. We garnered information on how to live comfortably aboard a small boat while crossing oceans or holed up at anchorages in remote locations.

By 1981 we had chartered a 32-foot sloop in The British Virgin Islands and skippered it on our own for 10 days. Every vacation we could squeeze in, we flew to islands in the Caribbean to continue chartering and sailing.

In the fall of 1987 we boarded sailboat *Vanessa*, harbored in Bora Bora—a Tahitian island of French Polynesia. The charter boat captain, Jerry, a cantankerous old sailor and high seas veteran, took us out in a gale, went below, and said, "Handle it. I'm going to sleep." We "handled it." After the two weeks of Jerry's training on *Vanessa*, we felt technically ready to tackle our dream. But back at home, our cycle of owning, operating, and occasionally selling retail stores consumed us again. The money to finance our dream sat socked away accruing interest. However, we let objections stand in our way. I said, "We don't have enough money to go." Or Jim said, "How can we leave now, just when our businesses are thriving?" We kept dreaming about "someday."

Then, one morning three days before Thanksgiving of 1988, I began hemorrhaging. I'd been trying to ignore some abnormal spotty vaginal bleeding and a swelling in my abdomen for months. That Monday, however, I started bleeding profusely and called my gynecologist in a panic. He saw me right away, examined me, and sent me for x-rays and a sonogram. His news was not good.

He explained, "You have a fairly large ovarian tumor. Since you are over 40 and not planning to have children, I recommend surgery immediately. The tumor may be malignant or benign. We'll do a biopsy, and if the tumor is cancerous, we'll get it out and start appropriate therapy. If it's benign, I recommend a complete hysterectomy anyway. I'll schedule surgery for day after tomorrow, Wednesday."

Thursday was Thanksgiving, and I wanted a reprieve. I said, "Let's schedule the surgery for Friday. I want Thanksgiving with my family—especially if I am confronting cancer." He agreed. So, the Friday after Thanksgiving I lay on a hospital gurney waiting for surgery while alternately crying and talking with Jim who held my hand. I asked him, "What will you do if I have cancer or don't survive?"

Jim answered softly, "I guess I'll sell everything and go sailing."

I braced myself up on my elbows and said, "Like we always planned to? Without me?"

"I guess so," he said. "I would rather you survive this thing and come with me."

"You're not going without me," I mumbled as they wheeled me off to the operating room.

I survived the surgery. The tumor was benign, and with that all our considerations about going cruising "someday" fell away. My cancer scare provided the wakeup call that jolted us into winding down our materially rich lives.

Just after 5 p.m., January 26, 1990, I sat on the oatmeal-colored Berber carpet in the empty dining room, leaning against the wall. The only things belonging to us that remained in the Spanish style two-story bungalow were a box of food, a bucket of cleaning supplies, a mop, broom, and vacuum. I'd cleaned the house we lived in and loved for the last eight years for the last time, and the keys were off my key chain ready to give to the new owners. What remained of our limited clothing, kitchen utensils, and personal possessions was already aboard the new "house," our 40-foot sailboat, *Sanctuary*.

Earlier in the day a crew had packed a large crate with items we would keep in storage: a dining room table, a bed with mattress and box springs, a set of leather living room furniture, a couple of lamps and tables, some large framed lithographs we hoped to sell at the end of our voyage, and 27 boxes of miscellaneous small possessions precious to us (mostly photographs, and family memorabilia). Everything else accumulated in 40 plus years of our lives had been sold at a giant New Year's Day invitation only garage sale.

Meanwhile, Jim and his son, Jim Jr., were moving *Sanctuary* from the boat yard in Alameda's estuary to the new berth we had rented in the south bay at Ballena Isle Marina. Looking around at the empty walls of the house, I reminisced about all the years we had enjoyed the lovely home, sighed, and glanced at my watch—6:30 p.m.! Where were Jim and Jimmy? They had promised to pick me up at 6:00. It was my 45th birthday, and we three were going out to dinner to celebrate. Afterwards, Jim and I would go home to *Sanctuary* and officially be "Living Aboard."

After agonizing, pawing over, and looking at sailboats in various conditions for weeks, we ultimately had rejected them all and had been discouraged. A new boat was not in our budget, and boats we liked didn't seem to be on the used market. Our yacht broker, Jill, an old salt who had sailed single-handedly from Great Britain to the West Coast of America on a 27-foot sailing vessel said, "Why don't you come down and look at the Valiant? If you like the Esprit, you will love the Valiant."

We were ready to see something we might love. That particular Sunday was our day off, so we said, "Let's go" even though the invite sounded like a sales pitch. However, the moment we stepped aboard the Valiant 40 we noticed that she barely moved. Other boats tipped or rolled when we walked about, or a passing wake rocked them back and forth with ease. The Valiant was stiff and solid and felt settled in the water. Her rigging was heavier, the winches were larger, and the teak was thicker and in much better condition than other boats we had seen of the same size. The sails were in excellent condition. The gleaming interior seemed well cared for. The equipment list was long and listed just about all we wanted or could imagine. She had been outfitted for cruising, and everything we tested was working. We had found our boat at last and knew it even before taking her for a sail. After a trial and an official inspection, we made an offer and settled on a fair price.

When the previous owner came aboard to give us her history and a rundown on how all the systems worked, he sat on the companion way stairs and wept as he told us of his dashed dreams of sailing his pride and joy on an extended ocean voyage. We wiped our own eyes as well, hoping we could fulfill the dream of an extended ocean voyage.

Port side settee with salon table

By January 1990 the lockers were packed. There were medical supplies in the head which consisted of a toilet, sink, hand-held shower, mirror, and two tiny shelves. Food lined the galley and filled the small refrigerator. A wealth of books about sailing and cruising were stowed on one of the starboard side shelves. The "bed" in the aft cabin was made, ready for our first night's sleep aboard.

As I sat on the carpet in the house waiting for my birthday dinner, I pictured the berth and wondered what it would be like to sleep on its barely double size mattress after so many years on a queen sized bed. Actually, the mattress wasn't even strictly double sized—it was an odd shape that conformed to the boat's curving hull, and it got bigger at the bottom down where our feet would be. That width at our feet didn't do us any good since we couldn't turn around and sleep at the bigger end. The aft end had an overhang, caused by the shape of the cockpit, and the crawl space wasn't even high enough to sit upright.

I planned to sleep on the side of the mattress next to the hull. I had practiced lying there, and it didn't bother me that the port side deck configuration meant I would have only about 18 inches of breathing room. In fact, I felt secure knowing I couldn't roll out—even though I'd have to use gymnastics to get up in the night. I found out later just what this meant. First, while on my back, I'd gradually rise up on my elbows, tuck my head under so I wouldn't hit it on the cabin top (the ceiling formed by the deck above), reach out and up for the handle/safety bar just above me, scrunch my legs up and out of the covers, then turn over to my stomach. Trying not to kick or disturb Jim, I'd kneel, raise my right leg over Jim, again without kicking him, and find the berth step (if it were down) with my toes. Otherwise, I would reach over Jim's head to unlock the berth step and lower it into its notched holder. Putting my right foot on the step, I'd reach with my right arm over to the other side of the tiny cabin using the wall as a brace. Now I'd be astraddle Jim still hoping not to wake him. As long as the boat didn't rock at this crucial moment, I'd then shift my weight to the right, balance on my right foot and knee, swing my left leg over, shift my balance to my left leg, get my right foot down onto the cabin sole, and I'd be out of the berth without his waking or knowing. In the beginning I woke him up a lot, but as the years went by these contortions became a practiced ballet, and I didn't even think about it even when the boat rocked and rolled.

I was far from understanding life onboard as I sat daydreaming—my reveries wore thin. I had taken the day off from work at the jewelry store to accomplish all the packing; I was tired, hungry, and wondering what was keeping Jim. Lateness was not like him—something was wrong. I had no way to call him. There was no phone aboard the boat, and in 1990 we didn't have a cell phone.

The phone at the house, sitting on the floor upstairs, was still connected. As I picked it up to see if there was still a dial tone—there was—I remembered the other two telephones downstairs. I'd forgotten to pack them, so I hung up the upstairs phone and went down to get them. I looked around to make sure I hadn't forgotten anything else. The downstairs deck was empty except for the built-in hot tub. We'd sold all the patio furniture and giant potted plants. Our bedroom and bath were empty; the only things left were memories—and the indentations in the carpet where the bed and bedside furniture had been for the last eight years.

The other bathroom, the den, and all three of the downstairs closets were empty. I hadn't forgotten anything but the telephones. I took them upstairs, put them in the box with the bucket of cleaning supplies, and checked my watch again: 7:30 p.m. Jim was almost two hours late. Where was he? I could walk down the hill to Orinda's shopping area. There were a few restaurants there including a really good Chinese one where we often went. I was hungry and imagined their delicious shrimp and snow peas. What if I missed Jim? Did I have any paper in my purse or a scrap of packing paper on which to write a note? No, the house was really clean. I'd done a good job. Anyway, I didn't relish the idea of a walk down the hill in the dark, and I wanted my birthday dinner! I could go over to a neighbor, but that didn't appeal to me.

So, I leaned back against the dining room wall and eventually fell asleep. I was startled out of my nap by the ringing of the remaining plugged-in phone. As I picked up the receiver I glanced at my watch and was shocked to see that it was 10:30.

"Jim," I practically yelled, "Are you okay? Where are you?"

A female voice said, "This is the Marine Operator. Will you accept a collect call?"

"The what? The who?"

"This is the Marine Operator, you have a ship-to-shore call, and will you accept the charges?"

"Yes."

"Go ahead, sir."

I recognized Jim's voice over the scratchy, hollow-sounding connection. "What's wrong?"

"We went aground in the entrance to the marina and won't be able to get off until high tide around midnight."

"Midnight? Oh, there goes my birthday, and now the Chinese restaurant is closed. Well, I'm glad you're okay."

"Yeah, I'll tell you the whole story when I see you."

"Well, bring me something to eat when you get here. Okay, talk to you later."

Jim finally picked me up around 1:30 a.m. He'd already taken Jimmy home to his place in Berkeley. As we loaded the cleaning supplies and box of food into our BMW, Jim explained what had happened. He didn't have a chart of our new marina, so before he and Jimmy began motoring *Sanctuary* from the boatyard he called the marina and inquired about the depth at the entrance channel. The woman in the marina office said, "Sure, there's plenty of depth at the entrance. Just swing around the piling keeping the green light to port, keep the red buoys to starboard, and come on in."

As Jim and Jimmy motored *Sanctuary* over to our new berth, they were having a fine time aboard. Everything was going perfectly. The bay was flat calm and there was no wind to hinder Jim's inexperience in handling and docking our new boat. They rounded the Naval Air Station, and the green entrance light became visible about a mile ahead. Suddenly the depth alarm beeped. Jim looked at the gauge, and it read six feet. Just then the boat pitched forward and stopped as it pushed into the soft mud of San Francisco Bay.

Jim tried to power out backward to no avail. *Sanctuary* was hard aground. He called the Coast Guard for assistance hoping they could send out a skiff to pull *Sanctuary* into deeper water. The answer he got was straightforward: "Captain, be advised that there is a minus two foot spring tide this evening with a high tide starting to flood at 2100 hours (9:00 p.m.). I would suggest you drop your anchor so that you don't go any further aground and wait until there is sufficient water to continue over the bar and into the marina." Jim, chastened after his hasty call to the Coast Guard when there was actually no danger, declined the offer to be taken off the boat or towed off the mud bar by a marine salvage company for an exorbitant fee.

"No thanks, we'll wait."

Jim left the VHF radio tuned to Channel 16. A fellow boater who had overheard the conversation with the Coast Guard called Jim a few minutes later: "Hey *Sanctuary*, that channel is really narrow. Call the marina security using the Marine Operator. The security guy knows the channel. Just wait 'til you float off the mud."

Jim knew I was waiting in the empty house probably exhausted from packing and cleaning and impatient for my birthday dinner. He hadn't thought of using the Marine Operator before, so he called me first promising to make amends for my missed celebration. Then he called marina security and got the Harbor Master, who happened to be working late. Together they worked out a plan for high tide.

At 11:00 p.m. *Sanctuary* unstuck from the mud snubbing up on the anchor chain. Jim reached the Harbormaster on VHF radio and got better directions. After jigging and jogging in the very narrow channel, Jim made it into the marina, and the security guard and the Harbormaster, waving their flashlights, greeted him. The long dock lines Jim had prepared and left on the cleats at the space assigned to us had been stolen; only short stubs were left. Jim quickly substituted our jib sheets and tied up. The security guard held up a skimpy five foot long dock line that wouldn't reach the dock cleat, shook his head, and chuckled at the inexperience of the new boat owner.

Days later we laughed over our inauspicious beginning to cruising life. Perhaps it was an omen after all since five months after moving aboard, physical problems Jim's doctor had been unable to diagnose for the past two years intensified. Jim's left hand, elbow, and shoulder became stiff and rigid. His doctor thought the symptoms were those of arthritis. When a slight tremor began in his left hand, the good doctor conceded that the symptoms and the tremors came from some kind of deeper, darker problem—a neurological disorder. He referred Jim to a neurologist. After numerous tests, including a claustrophobic MRI, the neurologist concluded, and in his report stated, "The patient's symptoms indicate the early stages of Parkinson's disease."

Jim was only 42 years old—surely Parkinson's was an "old man's disease" not one he could have. However, his doctor confirmed "Early Onset" of PD, a progressive, degenerative neurological disorder with no known cure. The three cardinal symptoms for PD are rigidity or slowness of movement, tremor, and postural instability or imbalance. In other words, Jim sometimes could barely move, sometimes would go rigid or "freeze" in place, sometimes shake uncontrollably, or sometimes fall over unexpectedly. Jim had already experienced the symptoms to one degree or another for many months prior to diagnosis.

Still, in spite of glaring evidence, we were in denial and didn't want to believe the diagnosis. We were afraid our dreams of sailing around the world were shattered before they'd begun. Even living aboard a sailboat would be challenging or dangerous—never mind sailing. In quiet desperation we looked for a second opinion, a better diagnosis, or even a possible cure. We did some research and found that the most knowledgeable neurologist on the west coast was the Chief of Staff of the

Neurological Department at the University of California School of Medicine in San Francisco.

There was no better diagnosis and no possible cure. The more experienced neurologist confirmed Jim's symptoms as definitely being those of Parkinson's disease. Jim had told the doctor and his intern about our plans to begin ocean voyaging in the near future. The doctor's final report stated: "The patient has plans to sail a boat on an extended voyage. I highly recommend, for obvious reasons, that this not be undertaken."

As the neurologist reviewed the report with Jim, the intern stood behind the doctor reading over his shoulder. The doctor, looking over his reading glasses at Jim, said sternly, "Having Parkinson's disease and sailing a boat is a foolish idea, and I don't recommend you go off on this crazy idea of sailing around the world on a sailboat." When he turned his back, looking for a book or chart on the shelf, the intern leaned over to Jim, cupped her mouth, and whispered, "Go anyway."

Later, after the eminent doctor left the room, the intern went on to say, "Parkinson's disease is not a death sentence. Don't let Parkinson's stop you from doing whatever you want in life. Things may become more difficult for you as time goes by but stay as active as possible, do the things you always dreamed of doing, and go for it—go anyway."

Small Craft Advisory

January, 1990—May 1991

"Sustained winds of 21 to 33 knots. A Small Craft Advisory for Hazardous Seas is issued for seas 10 feet or greater."
—Warning issued by the U.S. Coast Guard, Western Washington and California coasts

After 15 years of dreaming, we were living aboard with a foot in the door on our five-year "Sail around the World" plan. The house and the two greeting card stores were sold. We continued to work at our jewelry store and had planned on another year of saving money to add to the cruising kitty.

Jim's diagnosis changed that plan. He lost his ability to hold small objects, and gemstones shot wildly out of his hands and flew into space. His hands often shook as he talked to customers about jewelry designs. His handwriting deteriorated, so he couldn't write up sales slips or orders or draw designs for rings. His voice softened causing people to say, "What? Speak up!" They didn't realize that, due to PD, he couldn't speak any louder. His ability to solder or make delicate wax models was severely impaired. The jewelry store customers didn't know or understand that Jim had Parkinson's and often thought his symptoms, including his unsteady gait, were those of a drunk or worse. Attempts to hide or minimize symptoms that medicines could not mask or aid became a daily strain on both of us. The neurologist in San Francisco warned, "Jim will probably live about five more years. That's about it before PD either incapacitates him or ends his life."

We were stricken and frightened. Even if we did not go cruising, we needed to sell the jewelry store since Jim could no longer function successfully as a custom jewelry manufacturer, designer, and salesperson. Jim was the heart of the business. I could not foresee running it without him. We stepped up our efforts to sell the store. Throwing caution to the winds, we decided to live for our dream. We would go anyway.

We vowed that if the effects of Parkinson's disease made it necessary to end our voyage somewhere along our route, we would sell the boat and abandon the cruise. I could do most of the physical work aboard *Sanctuary* by myself if need be, and Jim could direct me on things such as repairing the diesel engine or mechanical items if he couldn't hold tools. After all, he was still functioning fairly normally, and most people probably would not notice or care about his shaking, unsteady gait, soft voice, or other symptoms. "Exercise all you can" was one of the prescriptions the doctor had given Jim along with lots of pills. Sailing would give him plenty of exercise. So we fast-forwarded our plans, learning curve, and departure date.

We sailed *Sanctuary* every chance we got, practiced maneuvers, and learned to use the auto-pilot and other onboard systems. We took classes in piloting, navigation, medical preparedness, storm tactics, sail repair, and diesel engine maintenance and read all the books we could find pertaining to world voyaging on a sailboat. I learned Morse code and got my Amateur Radio License so that we could contact other worldwide cruisers via our ham radio. We purchased tools, generator and engine spare parts, tested all of our sails, and organized our provisions. For three months I kept a log of everything we purchased and consumed so we would know what food and supplies to have aboard for long passages. We worked daily on items from the pre-departure list. The tally seemed endless. As we completed one project two more were added.

The universe aligned with us. The jewelry store sold, and we set a departure date of May 1991. We optimistically planned to sail through a window of good weather "uphill" to Puget Sound, Washington. Once in the sound we'd gunk hole (hop from harbor to harbor) through the Gulf Islands, the San Juan Islands, Vancouver Island, areas in Desolation Sound, and other nearby areas. Spending our first leg in an area where English was the native language and supplies were easy to obtain seemed prudent. Sailing north along the California coast would be a significant challenge to our novice skills, and we would find out early on if we were capable of continuing. If the "shake down" cruise went well, we'd retrace our route south to San Francisco Bay for final adjustments and good-byes to our California family and friends then continue towards Mexico, Central America, and beyond.

Pulling our dock lines aboard, we blithely left Alameda on Sunday, April 28, 1991, and *Sanctuary* headed for the Golden Gate. Surprisingly, the bay was crowded with traffic: sail, power, small, large, even jet-skis and wind surfers. We knew they weren't there to see us off, and belatedly we realized that opening day of the San Francisco Bay yachting season was in progress complete with boat parades, races, and the blessing of the fleet. Friend and sailing mentor Jim Marco, who had come along with us for moral support on the first leg of our voyage, said, "Maybe some of the blessings will drift over to us."

The U.S. Coast Guard weather forecast, broadcast on the short wave radio, called for: "Point Reyes to Big Sur; A small craft advisory is in effect; west to southwest winds 15 to 20 knots and seas to six feet." It was the wind direction we were waiting for, and six feet of ocean swell didn't sound so bad to two greenhorns. We looked forward to a beam reach to round Point Bonito and sail northwest up the coasts of California, Oregon, and Washington.

As we headed out under the Golden Gate Bridge, with the sun setting on the Pacific Ocean, the winds increased to 25 knots. Furthermore, they had clocked around to the northwest—right in the direction we wanted to sail. We could sail close hauled west through the busy shipping lanes with traffic coming in and going out of San Francisco Bay. To keep our course, we would soon have to turn to starboard (short-tack) and recross the shipping channel continuing in this zigzag pattern northwestward, or we could start the diesel engine and motor sail, powering into the wind and seas. Jim Marco had sailed this route several times either in his own boat or while delivering boats. He said, "It's always like this going around Point Reyes." We took his respected recommendation and started the 36 HP diesel engine.

By midnight *Sanctuary*'s bow crashed into (as it seemed to us) high winds and seas. Jim was terribly seasick and yelped, "The pounding will damage or destroy *Sanctuary*! We'll die at sea before we even begin!" Conditions seemed bad to me, too. Winds were much stronger than winds during any of our practice sails–even the one in Tahiti. Jim Marco calmed us saying, "The conditions aren't that bad. And besides, this boat can take it a lot longer than you can."

We continued with Jim Foley on the first night watch. He sat in the cockpit under the dodger scanning the horizon for other vessels and occasionally looking up to admire the bright full moon. He heard a strange hissing sound just as the boat dropped as though falling into a hole. He glanced upward wondering why the moon had turned green. A towering rogue wave suddenly broke on *Sanctuary* from the southwest and over the port beam. Tons of cold sea water crashed upon our little boat flattening the canvas dodger and bending the one-inch stainless steel pipes of the dodger frame as if they were soda straws. The cockpit, filled to overflowing with sea water, sent a deluge cascading around Jim Foley and surging into the cabin below.

Jim Marco, hearing the wave crash and feeling *Sanctuary* lurch, jumped up from the navigation station and rushed to the bottom of the companionway stairs where he was knocked off his feet by the surge. Off watch, I was asleep on the port side berth. The loud, crashing sound woke me just as the plunge and roll threw me out of my sea bunk. I bounced onto the main salon table, and groggily watched sea water splash through the cabin all the way to the "V" berth in the bow. I cried out crazily, "What happened, did we hit something?"

Nothing major was damaged. We slogged on toward Point Reyes, rounded the headland two miles off, and wearily headed for the fishing port of Bodega Bay. We arrived at dawn, wet, cold, and exhausted. *Sanctuary*'s interior cushions were soaked with sea water, the spray hood lay in ruins, and Jim F. had a bloody knot on the top of his head from the crashing dodger. We had been through hell our first 24 hours at sea.

Muffin, our 16-year-old cat, was the only one aboard unruffled. When we sold our house Jim Jr. took her to live with him—we thought life at sea would be too difficult for an older cat. We missed her terribly, and she seemed unhappy without us, so she moved aboard shortly after we did. Sailing didn't bother her, and during the "Big Crash" she remained safely tucked into her favorite berth amidships on the port side.

The next day we cleaned the salt water stains off the cabin teak, washed and dried out the interior cushions, and jerry-rigged a dodger repair with some expandable curtain rods we bought at a dime store in Bodega Bay. The harbor was crowded with veterans preparing to go out the next morning for the opening of the salmon fishing season. As Jim cleaned up in the harbor's shower room and shaved at the sink, a fisherman, obviously excited about the opening of salmon season, commented, "I see you're getting all pretty for them fish."

Three days later we motor sailed in light air to Brookings, Oregon. We tied up at the fuel dock at 0700, and waited for the attendant to arrive. As we lingered a shrimp boat came in and the crew began offloading the catch. After we topped up our fuel tank and tied up at the guest dock, Jim Marco said, "Let's go see what they've got and buy some fresh shrimp. Fishermen give you the best price and the shrimp are still alive." The shrimp were still flipping and snapping as a crewmember handed us a five-pound bag simply saying, "Enjoy." I offered to pay for what they had given us but was refused. I never much liked fish or seafood. However, fresh shrimp marked the beginning of my love of both, and Muffin wildly wolfed down some she snagged even before we could peel them!

Lyn & Jim Marco with crab pots in Oregon

The Pacific coasts of Mexico, the United States, and Canada can have dangerously unpredictable weather. I tried my best to second guess what weather was coming. We needed a three or four day weather window in order to make our next port of call, Newport, Oregon, without another rock and roll passage. Our fateful first night out had definitely jump started my desire to become a good forecaster. I listened faithfully thereon to the daily VHF weather forecasts and taught myself how to obtain the more detailed weather information available via SSB (Single Side Band Radio). A special modem allowed us to use our laptop computer as a receiver. I saved the broadcast faxes in a computer file, and we studied them trying to decipher weather patterns.

The weather window we wanted appeared, and we enjoyed a bouncy, albeit nice, three day sail to Newport. The winds picked up just as we approached the outside channel marker for the harbor entrance. Jim Foley declared, "Take down the sails, start the engine, and we'll motor through the narrow channel to the marina on the south side of Yakima Head Bay." Jim Marco agreed but said, "Don't cover the sail or untie the halyard." Just about the time we crossed the entrance bar and entered the channel, the engine died. Jim Marco, a master of boat handling, started giving directions, "Jim, you get the main sail back up— now! Lyn, you put dock lines on both sides of the boat and put out all the fenders. We're going to sail her in; we don't have time to bleed and restart the engine!"

We looked up the long, narrow entrance to the harbor and saw a dredge coming out to dump her load of mud and sand. Her skipper noticed *Sanctuary* hugging the north side of the breakwater and called us on Channel 16 (the hailing and emergency channel) of the VHF radio. The rule of right of way for oncoming ships is to pass one another port side to port side as two cars would pass each another on an American road. We obviously were breaking protocol, and Jim Marco answered the call explaining that we were engineless and therefore hugging the windward shoreline in case we needed sea room in which to maneuver. The dredge captain called back and agreed we would pass "Starboard to starboard— and good luck skipper."

Jim Marco masterfully maneuvered 40-foot *Sanctuary* under sail into an open slip at the end of a marina dock. He instructed me to step off as soon as I could to secure the bow line. Jim F. was to do the same with the stern line. We had no other way of stopping *Sanctuary*'s 12-ton forward progression (which would lead us into the breakwater wall) except by Jim Marco's expert command of the sail trim.

As we approached the selected dock, Jim got a sick feeling in his stomach when he noticed that the dock was half sunken with a crushed and waterlogged pontoon. He yelled at me, "Watch out! The dock's listing!" Anxious and nervous, I didn't hear him since I had already jumped and didn't see the broken dock until it was too late. I hit the edge of the dock on the cantilevered, wobbly high side and careened head first into the frigid water wearing my full foul-weather gear and boots. I surfaced, waterlogged, bow line in hand, worried about *Sanctuary* but facing two Jims worried about me.

Several fishermen came over to help haul me up onto the derelict dock. As I poured water out of my boots, they saw I was okay and congratulated us on a job well done. One fisherman gave us three live Dungeness crabs of fairly good size. He showed us how to clean them, told us how to cook them, and lent us a crab trap to use as long as we were in port. During our entire stay in Newport's south side fisherman's harbor, we were showered with fresh seafood.

As soon as we secured *Sanctuary* to the slanting dock, the two Jims squeezed into the engine room to solve the stalling engine problem. The fisherman next to us suggested we check the fuel filters, saying, "You sailboats sail around these bays and don't get out in the rough stuff enough. And when you do, all that junk sittin' in the bottom of your fuel tank gets kicked up and sucked up into the fuel filters. Plugs 'um up and engine goes down. I would check there first." Right he was. Both water-separating fuel filters were so plugged with sludge off the bottom of the fuel tank that they could hardly be removed from their bowls.

A few days later we sadly said goodbye to Jim Marco. He had held our hands and guided us through our first three difficult weeks giving freely of his time, patience, and expertise. It was truly a gift from him and his wife, Marilyn. We had interrupted their cruising, and Marilyn was waiting back in Hawaii aboard *Intention*, their 37-foot sailboat, for him to return. Jim Marco had built their vessel from the bottom up and outfitted the bare hull by himself with a few volunteering friends. Jim and I had helped on many a workday and Jim Marco took me for my first sail.

The wind howled and gusted in the rigging as we waited in port for the winds to lessen or shift so we could progress without taking a beating. We enjoyed the port with fishermen docked around us. When working they trolled for salmon, netted shrimp, or hooked albacore, halibut, or cod. Their boats were a maze of poles, lines, leaders, cannon ball weights, and hooks with names like hoochies, spinners, and flashers. They too waited for lighter winds. They gathered on different boats to swap stories, stood on the docks setting out crab pots, worked on their engines, did laundry, or went shopping—just what we were doing. Jim serviced our filters, tuned our diesel engine, and checked the halyards, sheets, and sails to make sure *Sanctuary*'s drive train was in top condition.

Fishermen Bill from the trawler *Columbian* and Russ from *Clipper* helped us catch more crabs than we could eat. They gave us halibut and lingcod along with tips on how to catch salmon, repair diesel engines, and clean oil out of jackets. They pointed out on the charts where to run to along the coast if a big blow caught us unaware. I traded them paperback novels and answered questions about whether a woman liked living aboard a sailboat. Most of their wives tended house inland and rarely appeared at the docks. The fishing life was wet, cold, sometimes lonely, backbreaking, rough, unpredictable, and generally not very monetarily rewarding. They went out day after day searching for fish because they loved it. Those big men with raw red hands, black, oil-encrusted plaid shirts, and well-worn rubber hip boots told me they couldn't wait for "a g'ud day out ther'." The boats' decks were a maze of equipment, and many had tires on the side for fenders, but the organization of their lines and hooks was precise. The boats were sturdy, and the men matched them. It was an arduous way to earn a living, but the fishermen we met would not trade the life. Encountering these men and seeing how they worked gave me a new appreciation for the fish we consume.

People all along the way cared for and befriended us. The diesel engine needed a part, so we walked over the Yaquina River Bridge into town. After a long hike to several auto parts stores, we trudged into another one that also did not have what we needed. After some discussion the owner said, "Well, I guess Newport Auto Parts will have what you want—it's about a mile or so that way." When we replied that we were walking and needed more specific directions, he said, "Come on out to my truck—I'll take you over." We, with our recent Bay Area hustle and bustle mentality, were taken aback by the offer to drive us to the competition but humbly accepted the ride (and found the part). We were frequently treated with generous humanity. It was a joy.

Left on our own, we were a little nervous and apprehensive about our next encounter with the ocean. However, our zeal for adventure never abated. I carefully watched the weather faxes and listened to the coast guard reports for a weather window we could squeeze through and continue north. I asked one of the salmon fisherman how he judged his weather. His answer, whistled through a dearth of teeth, was, "When I wake up in da mornin' I sticks me head out da winder. If da wind don't blow me hat off—then out I goes."

In late May 1991, we again untied *Sanctuary* from the security of a dock. We slowly motored out of the fishermen's harbor waving to the friends we had made. Some shook their heads as if they didn't understand why we would brave, for "pleasure," unpredictable life-threatening elements of the open ocean: the cold water, large unobservant ships with oblivious crews, flotsam, jetsam, rocks, wind and seas, or any number of hard items that could punch a hole in a fiberglass hull and immediately cause us to sink and die. Yet out we goes.

As *Sanctuary* left the protection of the breakwater that had protected us for two weeks, I gave Jim a course. He adjusted *Sanctuary*'s auto pilot accordingly, and *Sanctuary* lifted and rolled over the gentle Pacific swell and came around to the heading for the next port. Suddenly, we saw a medium-sized whale on what seemed to be a collision course. The whale took shallow dives as it swam straight for *Sanctuary*. We both sighed with relief when, at the last moment, the whale dove under *Sanctuary*'s bow and easily cleared our six-foot draft. A light breeze filled our sails, and we shut down the diesel engine and listened to the sounds of slapping water going under the hull as we sailed north at about four knots.

The route we chose took us out into the Pacific enough to miss the effects of the Columbia River delta. The delta's far-reaching churn of surf was notorious, and many small craft and fishing vessels had been lost in its surge. Yet we did not venture so far out that we would be caught if bad weather headed our way. Astoria, nicknamed "Graveyard of the Pacific," is the first port inside the river delta. Astoria's bar is rough to cross even in mild conditions and is dangerous in moderate conditions. When the Coast Guard deems safety is at risk, the port is closed to keep foolish mariners from endangering lives—their own or others.

The Brookings Coast Guard station officer said:

> U.S. Coast Guard stations are strategically placed along the west coast. They give excellent weather forecasts using information gained from their weather buoys. Their SSB reports are designed to give mariners an idea about how much time they have to seek a sheltered port. The most meaningful report for a slow moving sailboat like yours is from the weather buoy 250 miles off the coast. The buoy report tells you what weather is coming at you, and just how soon. Check the charts and judge which port or protected cove you can run to, and how fast you can get there.

His advice continued,

> Stay five nautical miles off the coast except Astoria where you should stay 25 miles off. This will keep you out of the main shipping lane and fishing operations. At five miles out, moving at the average speed of five knots, you are within an hour or so of the coast where there is a port within a day's run which is usually all the time you have if the 250-mile buoy is

reporting the weather is about to "blow up" along the coast.

Heeding his advice, we stayed offshore to avoid dangerous tidal effects of the Columbia River delta. The radio forecast stated that the bar at Astoria was closed to small craft. In addition, the 250-mile buoy reported gale force winds. Gray's Harbor at West Port, Washington, was the next available port for us. At our current position and speed, we'd make the bar crossing at the end of the flood tide and just before the gale started its swell and "stink." (The ocean takes on a particular odor just before a blow. The sailor's jargon, "It's blowin' like stink" started to make sense.) We'd learned in class that the best time to cross the sand bar that builds up in front of coastal ports, especially if seas are breaking, is the end of the flood tide or slack high water when the most water covers the bar. We had no firsthand experience and were worried about our computations.

We definitely wanted to arrive at the bar before the flood, so we motor sailed as fast as possible hoping to make the open port. We were a little late approaching the bar, and bay waters had begun to ebb. The pre-gale ocean swell was already breaking on the bar as the water flowed steadily out of the bay. Soon the waves would be breaking steeply, and the port would be closed. As we drew closer we could see the breakers and knew crossing was not going to be a cakewalk. We heard nothing from the Coast Guard, so we hailed them on Channel 16.

The conversation went like this:

Sanctuary: "Calling the U.S. Coast Guard, U.S. Coast Guard, U.S. Coast Guard, this is sailing vessel *Sanctuary*, can you copy *Sanctuary*? Over."

The Coast Guard: "This is the United States Coast Guard. We copy you *Sanctuary*; do you have an emergency? Over."

Sanctuary: "No sir, we need information regarding crossing the bar. Over."

Coast Guard: "*Sanctuary* switch to, standby, and answer channel six eight. Over."

Sanctuary: "*Sanctuary* going to six eight and standing by."

Coast Guard (after a long pause): "This is the United States Coast Guard calling the sailing vessel *Sanctuary*. How do you copy the Coast Guard *Sanctuary*? Over."

Sanctuary: "Yes, this is *Sanctuary*; I copy you loud and clear. Over."

Coast Guard (in curt tones of annoyance): "What is the information you need, *Sanctuary*? Over."

Sanctuary (Now feeling kind of stupid for calling the Coast Guard with such a trivial question): "We are approaching the entrance to Gray's Harbor, Washington, and would like to know if the bar is safe to cross. Over."

Coast Guard (after a long pause): "What is the size of your vessel, *Sanctuary*? Over."

Sanctuary (now feeling intimidated and my voice shaking): "*Sanctuary* is a 40-foot sailing vessel. Over."

The Coast Guard: "What is your gross tonnage, *Sanctuary*? Over."

Sanctuary: "*Sanctuary* weighs 12 tons unladed, sir. Over."

The Coast Guard: "How many adults and how many children do you have on board *Sanctuary*? Over."

Sanctuary: "We are two adults. Over."

Coast Guard: "Do you have life jackets for two adults on board? Over."

Sanctuary: "Yes sir, we do and we have them on. Over."

Coast Guard: "Do you have any firearms, ammunitions, weapons, or anything you consider weapons on board *Sanctuary*? Over."

Sanctuary: "No sir, nothing like that at all. Over."

The swell lifted *Sanctuary* up and down, higher and higher, as we closed on the port entrance. I waited nervously by the radio. After a long pause, the Coast Guard radio operator returned to the air and read a statement that would totally absolve the U.S. Coast Guard of any responsibility if we didn't make it over the bar:

Coast Guard: "Captain of sailing vessel *Sanctuary*. Please be advised that vessels of your size and weight, at this time, are successfully crossing the entrance to Gray's Harbor. Over."

Sanctuary: "Thank you, sir. *Sanctuary* is clear on six eight and going back to channel sixteen."

We hovered just outside the breaking bar studying the timing and watching for the third wave to roll under *Sanctuary*. Jim revved the diesel engine up to 3,500 rpms and *Sanctuary* surfed in through the harbor entrance. I looked astern calling out wave positions as Jim clutched the wheel with white knuckles. At one point *Sanctuary* slewed and was almost pushed around sideways by a breaking sea. If *Sanctuary* had lost engine power and been beam to the seas, she would have rolled in the surf—sinking our ship and ending our lives as well.

The tension of crossing the bar slowly drained away as we (chagrined) tied up in a safe, protected port. We gradually learned about the coastal California weather and how to handle its effects. (Later we applied our hard-learned weather forecasting knowledge to coasts and ports all over the world.) We'd picked up the meaning of another sailor's motto: "When in doubt, stay out." Vowing to practice the art of self- sufficiency, we never called the Coast Guard again.

Shakedown in the Pacific Northwest

June 1991—August 1991

"Courage is being scared to death - but saddling up anyway."
—John Wayne

After a week resting in Gray's Harbor, we conferred with new friends Al and Sandy on sailboat *Jubilación* (Spanish for retirement) and decided to "buddy boat" for awhile. This was an often-followed routine among worldwide cruisers. Al Butler and Sandy Olsen, longtime cruisers, were moving their boat from the Sea of Cortez up to the Pacific Northwest. They provided a wealth of information about anchorages and the port captains in Mexico. Sandy also gave me suggestions about provisioning and cooking aboard. We'd read a lot of journals from a sailing club we'd joined. However, *Jubilación* was the first boat we'd met with actual cruis-

Lyn receiving a weatherfax

ers living the life aboard. We pooled weather information, made a prediction, and both boats sailed from Gary's Harbor the same morning bound to Neah Bay, Washington.

We called it right. With winds a perfect 15 to 20 knots, the seas less than six feet, and the sun shining, we scooted up the last leg of the Washington coast and then turned starboard to sail around Cape Flattery and Tatoosh Island. After a 20-hour passage, we reached Neah Bay just before higher winds and rains engulfed us. Snug at anchor, we toasted the success of our journey with glasses of wine.

We launched our inflatable dinghy later and motored ashore with Al and Sandy to visit a village at the Makah Indian Reservation. At the excellent museum, we learned that the Makah had inhabited the Washington coast for over 2,000 years. For centuries the Indians had tamed the rugged shore and built large longhouses for the tribe who lived off whale, salmon, beaver, seal, and various fish. Some of the hand-hewn cedar canoes the Indians used for fishing were displayed. Battling winds and ocean in a powerful 40-foot enclosed vessel challenged us, yet the Makah had put to sea in 20-foot open canoes and had caught whales!

Even though we were around the corner in the Strait of Juan de Fuca, we still had to consider the weather even though its effects would be lessened. We left Neah Bay and proceeded to Port Angeles enjoying the first day in the cockpit without having to wear full foul-weather gear. It was pure pleasure to be on deck with only a sweatsuit and one jacket between me and the weather.

The strait also was enjoyable because we sailed within one mile of the shore and could watch the coastline. The snow-blanketed peaks of the rugged Cascade Mountains filled the background, and cedar-dappled hillsides ran to the foreground. Granite cliffs dropped blackly down to pristine coves—Agate Beach, Crescent Bay, Whiskey Creek, Eagle Point, and Pillar Point. It was an idyllic day's run and a reward for the offshore journey. We reached Port Angeles, a city which logging built and still supports. *Sanctuary* dodged log booms on the way to the harbor, and as we later walked into town, we passed lumber mills. Signs in stores and yards proclaimed, "This family is supported by the timber industry."

Al and Sandy became our good friends. Talking with them over the VHF in the middle of a starless, moonless night filled with fishing boats had been so comforting. We'd enjoyed exploring shoreside museums and restaurants with them. From Port Angeles we were heading in different directions, so they cast us off and we sailed over to the San

Juans, an archipelago of over 170 islands. We pointed toward San Juan Island itself with Friday Harbor our goal. The guidebooks listed it as a popular destination, and they were right. After enjoying the comforts of ice cream and a much-needed Laundromat, we quickly left. There was constant ferry and seaplane traffic, and we wanted tranquility. We found it farther up the island.

We anchored in Roche Harbor, a beautiful bay overlooked by a small resort built in 1879. The buildings hadn't changed much and looked as if a girl from *The Great Gatsby* would appear, stroll through the flower gardens, duck under the arbor by the picket fence, and walk out to the weathered docks with her parasol twirling. She would carefully step into a canoe, swans swimming alongside, never getting her dainty white shoes wet or dirty. After the canoe ride, her beau would escort her to dinner in the white clapboard restaurant by the bay with gaslight flickering on the water. Echoes of church bells ringing in the twilight, the couple would slowly walk up the hillside to a cabin nestled under maple trees.

The romantic setting remained, and my white tennis shoes didn't even get damp in the calm dinghy ride to shore. We, however, skipped the clapboard restaurant and walked around the point to an oyster farm where we dug oysters in the mud flats. Jim starred in his own romance as the light from our stern barbecue flickered over his freshly grilled oysters.

Serene Roche Harbor was difficult to leave, but a date with my mother called us to Seattle, so we set sail again. Our Seattle arrival was not quite the one we planned. As we motored toward the entrance to the Chittenden Locks in order to proceed into Lake Washington, we heard a strange, ominous CLUNK accompanied by a little jerk. Hmmm! Nothing was visible in the water; we had not hit anything, so why did *Sanctuary* slow down? Suddenly Jim realized what had happened and said, "Quick! The transmission's gone; prepare to drop anchor!" I ran frantically to the bow and untied and dropped the anchor just in time to save us from grounding. In mere minutes we had drifted out of the main channel and, by the time the anchor grabbed, were afloat in a scant eight feet of water near shoals and the shore.

"What do we do now?" I asked Jim. "We don't have any power, there's no wind, and we're on the edge of a really busy channel." "I know," he said. "Lots of boats, even freighters, will be coming by in order to get to the Seattle piers on Lake Union. We're in the way, and the tide may ground us. We'd better fix this quickly."

Jim went below into the engine room and discovered that the

transmission was no longer attached to the propeller—the bolts had sheared off. We didn't have the parts we needed, so we radioed for a tow to take us into nearby Shilshole Harbor. Once in the harbor, we bought the needed parts, repaired the transmission shaft, and then sat, once again watching and listening to the weather forecasts, hoping for a clear, fogless day for our first encounter with canal transits, locks, and bridge openings.

    I spent a restless night worrying about entering and negotiating the lock. My job as line handler involved lassoing a bollard (a large iron post on the side of the canal). I would need to tighten or release the line as water flowed into the lock raising *Sanctuary* from sea level to the higher freshwater of Lake Washington. After the water level was obtained and the lock gates opened, I would (merely) flip the lines off the bollards so we could motor out of the lock chamber.

    We did not know if we would be directed to the large or small lock. Therefore, I had to have four lines of either 25 or 50 feet ready to go at a moment's notice as well as side fenders to keep our hull off the slimy moss-covered concrete walls which were waiting, in my imagination, to scrape *Sanctuary*'s tender fiberglass topsides to shreds. Also, in my mental movie the lines tangled, the walls of the lock moved up and down at a rapid pace, the current jostled us backwards, and the large tugboat in the lock with us rammed us as it left. The fact that hundreds of ships and boats transited this lock daily meant nothing to me. I was, as Jim called out to the lock tender as we finally approached, "A virgin! Never been through a lock before!"

    As it turned out, the night before was far worse than reality—although the crowd of sightseers lining the shore of the lock gave me a round of applause when I finally roped the first bollard after five nervous attempts. I was so intent on my job that I looked up in surprise to the cheers and saw that we were going to be stars in sundry home movies. We were too busy to get many photos for ourselves. We exited gracefully, due to Jim's steering, without a scrape or a (wayward tugboat) ram.

    After the canal we headed toward the second of five bridges which needed to open so *Sanctuary* could pass into Lake Washington. My nervousness gradually diminished as bridge after bridge opened for us. I blew our large brass horn with long and short hoot-like blasts to "knock" on the bridge doors. The bridge tender replied with his own deep mechanical blasts usually signaling "Yes." Our one "No" necessitated a circling wait while a train passed nearly overhead.

The waterway gave a distinct view of the interior shores of Seattle, lined as it was with barges, freighters, float planes, houseboats, and pleasure craft. The Montlake Bridge, spanning the cut from Lake Union to Lake Washington, was elegant. A greening copper Art Deco structure, the bridge was surrounded by willows with their limbs dipping into a narrow fresh-water canal. Canada geese honked on a grassy shore with University of Washington buildings on one side and Seattle on the other. We motored past canoes and an Irish Setter swimming for a tennis ball thrown among the water lilies. The lazy motoring brought us to Lake Washington, a civilized body of water on the edge of the city with genteel looking suburban homes set on small knolls above the lake. Their manicured lawns sloped down to the shore, and most had private docks for the resident "runabout."

On we headed to Kirkland, a lakeside community which reminded us of Piedmont Avenue (the street our stores had been on): a friendly, funky but classy neighborhood. After tying up at the public dock, just one short block from the main street, we walked ashore for lunch complete with a Berkeley-type waiter, homemade pasta, and microbrewery beer. My 80-year-old mother, in Seattle honeymooning with her new husband, met us at a nearby hotel, and together we embarked on a fast-paced tour of Seattle. We met my new stepfather Morris for the first time and enjoyed getting acquainted. Our whirlwind visit with eating, sightseeing, and chatting breezed by all too quickly, and they flew back to their home in Houston.

After the touring and visiting, we caught our breaths and sailed north again, out of Puget Sound to Canada, our sights set on the Gulf Islands of British Columbia. We stopped en route at tiny Penn Cove on Whidbey Island, made a rainy pass through the Swinomish Channel on the way to Anacortes, anchored a few quiet days at Clark Island where, nestled in with eagles and Great Blue herons for company, I nursed a sprained ankle and then crossed Boundary Pass for our entrance into Canadian waters.

We cleared customs at Bedwell Harbour on the Fourth of July celebrating our freedom to travel by being in another country. We weren't too far from American waters and watched distant fireworks from our quiet Canadian anchorage, a Provincial Marine Park. Fir trees lined the shores, waters were fathoms deep, and cliffs stood black against vast cloudless skies.

After our first Canadian anchorage, we visited many others. Old-timers who had sailed the waters for over 30 years shared secret tips about hidden oyster-filled coves. We learned to negotiate rapids with currents up to six knots, walked in fern and moss covered forests, picked fresh blackberries, dug clams, or sat in the cockpit and watched glowing pink sunsets. We walked ashore in tiny Canadian towns barely bigger than large marinas, bought fresh raspberries, sailed over inland waterways of deep black-blue, spotted eagles, loons, grebes, murres, herons, geese, mergansers, kingfishers, otters, and seals. Each day revealed its own surprise. One day a mule deer swam across the bow of our dinghy as we both made our way to shore.

We also swatted mosquitoes, were drenched by cold unexpected rainstorms, worried about reefs and currents, complained about, but paid, high Canadian prices for food and fuel, battled a recalcitrant autopilot, repaired an alternator, spent a lot of time sitting in Laundromats, and looked hard to find anchorages which weren't full with boats. The scales, however, tipped far in favor of the "It was terrific" side.

We ventured farther north to Desolation Sound and at Lund, British Columbia, picked up friends Paul and Melissa Coupin, who joined us aboard for a portion of our journey. The Coupins had driven from California on 101, the highway that winds all the way from its southern-

Sanctuary - Princess Louisa Inlet, B.C.

most point in Castro, Chile, up America's entire coast all the way north to one last town, Lund: "The End of the Road." In 1991 Lund consisted of one little hotel with a small marina, a drinking lounge, and a dirt parking lot.

Having friends aboard was a treat, and the care package they brought, which included California wines, was a bonus. We took off from Lund and enjoyed isolated spots accessible only by boat. We picked oysters, swam in a freshwater lake encircled by three-foot-diameter sun bleached logs, and then sat in a mountain stream that whirlpooled and cascaded down to our saltwater anchorage.

Conifer forests again soared up to granite cliffs. Intense purple starfish dotted moss-covered shorelines. Skies stripped of clouds were bright and stunning in their majesty. Sometimes we simply sat in the cockpit gazing and craning our necks to view snow-capped peaks. Sea birds dipped and whirled into view, and seal heads popped up like peppercorns. July floated by on days full of imposing scenery and peaceful interactions with each other and the people we met.

We sailed back to Lund to drop off Paul and Melissa and then began inching our own way south. In Anacortes *Sanctuary* was hauled out; we painted the bottom and made repairs in preparation for the return passage down the Pacific Coast. We savored the last few days in the Gulf Island anchorages. We slowly sailed across the Strait of Juan de Fuca to return to Port Angeles in order to purchase fuel and food before setting out for Cape Flattery and our passage to San Francisco.

The Port Angeles harbor was crowded with salmon fishing boats, so the Harbormaster instructed us to raft up to a small sailboat named *Tarpon*. Its name was written in different-looking lettering, and it flew a red communist flag on its stern. Russian? Yes. Sign language with the gaggle of men on *Tarpon's* deck got *Sanctuary* tied up. Two days of point and tell began with all of us looking up words in a double language dictionary provided by the eight Russian sailors.

Yuri and Zigmas spoke enough English to keep us going. We learned that the eight men had sailed from Petropavlovsk Kamchatka (near western Siberia) across the Aleutian Trench to Dutch Harbor and Kodiak, Alaska, then down the Gulf of Alaska and the North Pacific outside Vancouver Island to the Strait of Juan de Fuca and into Port Angeles. Their vessel, a 30-foot homemade wooden sailboat, carried old canvas sails, a compass, a sextant, and very few charts. They had used an American road map of Washington State to sail into Port Angeles!

We gave them some charts and pored over them together to trace their journey and ours. Hearing their story reminded us of the freedom and abundance Americans have, which we usually take for granted. *Tarpon* and crew had been allowed to leave Russia only under strict sponsorship. Their return date was governed by permits, not weather, and the pressure of the looming deadline showed in their telling. They were not looking forward to a hasty return across very treacherous, icy seas.

Their voyage was one of peace symbolized by small blue flags and pins they carried. We were honored to receive a set. The pins and small flags, with the image of a globe covered by an umbrella of unity, were made of metal from a destroyed missile. Their Russian dictionary had no word for "sanctuary." After much cross-referencing they finally understood the meaning of our boat's name. We understood they felt safe in America and the comprehension of the translation suited the occasion.

The Russians' home port, a nuclear submarine base, was "off-limits" to foreigners. None of us were aware during the days of our meeting that the U.S.S.R. was in a process of dissolution. We later learned of the social and political changes which took place in the fall of 1991 in the Soviet Union. The eight sailors would return under an outdated red flag to an altered homeland. Meanwhile, unaware of what was afoot at home, *Tarpon* quietly sailed for Seattle, and we slipped away to the west towards the Pacific and our sail south. We sighted whales in the strait near Neah Bay and took it as a good omen.

A Six Mile Lesson

August 1991—October, 1991

"An inch of a miss is as good as a mile."

— Old Proverb

It was 3:00 a.m., and we were sailing south along the coastal waters of California. Jim, wedged into the port side settee, was resting and trying to sleep. I sat at the navigation station on watch. A cold, heavy fog dripped outside, enveloping *Sanctuary*. Every fifteen minutes I climbed the four companionway steps to the deck, clipped my harness onto a safety line, and hung onto the binnacle stanchion as I stood on the cockpit locker tops. I poked my nose over the dodger and peered toward *Sanctuary*'s bow hoping to see through the fog. I couldn't. Each climb into the cockpit raised a hope the fog had lifted. It hadn't.

My watch dragged on, and Jim's had been the same. Most of the hours that stretched into days sailing south from Neah Bay, Washington toward San Francisco Bay had been similar. The radar slumbered on standby to conserve electricity. I activated the screen every six minutes, scanned the ranges up to 24 miles for signs of vessels, reset standby, checked our course, and then sat either reading a book or dreaming of sunshine. It was six minutes on and six minutes off for three hours at a time. I would climb to the cockpit, peer into the night, listen to the slapping of the waves and gurgle of the wake, check the sails and wind, climb below, and start over again. I was bleary eyed. *Sanctuary*'s heel and motion were steady with only an occasional big wave changing the routine: rock, pause, surge, pause, roll.

We were three-quarters of the way toward our Golden Gate goalpost, and *Sanctuary* galloped at six knots with a reefed mainsail and staysail—fast for our vessel on her dark, foggy passage. I turned on the radar again. Suddenly a blip on the screen broke my routine. The glowing green speck was large and indicated an enormous vessel only six miles away. I nervously calculated the size of the vessel and our combined speeds. We were moving directly toward each other at an astounding 30 knots! While not fast in freeway terms, at that moment in our watery world, *Sanctuary* equaled a race car speeding straight at a steel wall as long as two football fields. I hailed the vessel on VHF but got no reply.

As a sailing vessel we technically had the right of way. Technicality, however, does not keep a boat afloat. By the time I roused Jim, the approaching vessel was a scant four miles away and still on a collision course. He groggily rechecked my calculations about speed and said, "Oh, wow, you're right. Something big like the Exxon *Valdez* is on a constant bearing and closing at a combined speed of 30 knots. That's one mile every two minutes. We've got to change course now!"

Jim, scrambling into the cockpit in stocking feet and thermal underwear, knocked the auto pilot switch to off, unlocked the steering arm, grabbed the wheel, and turned 90° while cranking in the main sheet to keep the speed we needed to escape certain death. Meanwhile, I unlocked the propeller shaft so we could start the diesel engine if necessary. (We kept the shaft locked while sailing so the motion of the spinning prop wouldn't wear out the transmission or slow us down.)

Jim trimmed the sails perfectly, and we began to sail away from the collision course at six knots—one mile every ten minutes. I checked the radar screen again and yelled to Jim, "We're barely going to be out of the way! They'll cross our stern at less than a quarter of a mile!" We both peered into the fog looking for the ship's lights. Not even a glimmer was visible—only a distant rumble from the vessel's huge diesel engines penetrated the leaden fog.

As the vessel passed astern, we reset our course. I went below and stared at the glowing blip as it moved north and we sailed south wondering if her crew had seen us on their radar or heard our radio call. Was the ship on autopilot with no one on watch? We'll never know. I was thankful we kept a careful watch and had radar. I wasn't bleary-eyed anymore.

Most of our southward passage was not as eventful. We paralleled the shore about 20 miles off easily dodging the fishing vessels we encountered. With light winds from five to twenty-five knots, accompanied by moderate seas from flat to fifteen feet, only the heavy fog caused tension. A glimpse of the sun in midday gave us an excuse to celebrate.

We hove to five miles outside the entrance bar to Eureka, California, and took turns napping while we waited to cross the bar at slack high water. ("Heaving to" created a slick so that waves would not break on us and lessened the motion of the sea and the screaming of the winds. Basically, we jogged in one place, perhaps drifting downwind at less than one-half knot.) Our "Call the Coast Guard" bar crossing on the trip north had taught us well, and after heaving-to we crossed Eureka's bar without incident.

After we tied up at the small boat marina, I noticed an older couple aboard a sailboat with a barnacle and seaweed encrusted waterline. In the middle of what should have been the sailboat's cockpit stood a makeshift cabin with a huge TV dish antenna on the top. Jim commented, "What is going on with that sailboat? It looks like it has been at the dock a long time and has turned into a houseboat or something."

Later we walked down the dock and met the couple. Like us, they had wanted to test their skills and had sailed their brand-new boat north up the notorious California coast from Los Angles to Eureka. Caught in a storm they, like us, had panicked and crossed a breaking bar in a nasty blow. However, their spirits had broken, and there they sat 20 years later, never having ventured forth again. They befriended cruisers though, offered rides into town, gave advice on where to shop, and shared their still-vivid memories of barely surviving crossing the Eureka bar.

We timed our exit from Eureka and sailed on easily to San Francisco Bay where we made a rhumb line for Ballena Bay Marina in Alameda. I radioed the security guard (the same guard who had witnessed Jim's first late-night entry and short dock lines) who remembered us and assigned us a slip. He had followed our progress as we prepared to go cruising and left to go north. He came over to congratulate us as we returned to our old marina and said proudly, "You really did it. Y'all are real sailors now."

We weren't sure we were "real sailors," but our shakedown had done its job. Our teamwork, sailing and anchoring skills, and general big boat handling ability had all improved in our first five-month voyage. We had (for the most part) quit yelling at each other and developed some hand signals and sign language we used during docking and anchoring.

We had also fallen into some natural routines about who did what aboard. Each of us (more or less at this point) was capable of sailing *Sanctuary* alone. However, life aboard was easier, and Jim with his Parkinson's-induced problems was safer, if we divided duties. Jim therefore spent most of his time steering and managing a light wind sail configuration from the safety of the cockpit. The roller-furling jib could be handled from winches mounted on the coamings. Our mainsail traveler track was at the stern, so either of us could change tacks without the other, and more importantly, without leaving the cockpit. When winds picked up and the mainsail needed reefing, which required going out on deck, I went out while Jim stayed in the cockpit to tail the lines. I did most, and as the years went by all, of the foredeck work such as raising and lowering the mainsail, setting and reefing the staysail, changing the staysail to storm staysail, rigging the cruising spinnaker, raising and lowering the main anchor, and—worst case scenario—setting and deploying the parachute sea anchor.

We refined the rigging on the set of high safety lines we strung from bow to stern on both sides of the boat each time we left port. We religiously clipped our safety harnesses to one of these lines anytime we were underway. At times our caution seemed like overkill, but as the years passed and Jim's balance and grip worsened, he was saved more than once by his harness and the lines. Jim needed to be aware of his balance at all times. We had another strict rule: "One hand for you, one hand for the boat." Jim Marco also recommended Jim keep a one-handed knife on him at all times: "One with a big hole in the folded blade, so you can flip it open with your thumb if you only have one hand available. You never know when you might need to cut something free using one hand and hang on to the boat with the other."

We resumed pre-departure preparations aboard *Sanctuary* anticipating a worldwide voyage—hopefully a circumnavigation. Therefore, we scrutinized all our equipment more closely than we had initially. Jim rebuilt *Sanctuary*'s refrigerator/freezer and added a new 12-volt DC charging and monitoring system. Even though we knew how to navigate using a sextant, we purchased a Global Positioning System (GPS) and a spare. We ferreted out electrical or schematic diagrams for every important system aboard and ordered spares for our auto-pilot so we could rebuild it ourselves from scratch. We had spent a good part of the shakedown cruise without a functioning autopilot; hand steering and watching for three or four hours at a time had worn us out.

We upgraded our interior lights and fans. I sewed wind scoops, sail bags, and a waterproof laptop bag. Together with a local canvas shop, we designed and made a "storm proof" dodger with sturdy one-inch stainless steel handrails and supports. I sewed lee cloths to enclose the cockpit and keep out some of the wind and water spray as we sailed. The life raft was professionally checked and repacked. Our "grab bag" (a collection of lifesaving items we could snatch in a hurry if we had to abandon ship) was reviewed. Along with emergency rations, we stuffed it with a small, hand operated water maker, reading glasses, a compass, paper, pencils, sunscreen, three weeks' worth of Jim's medicines, matches, knives, fishhooks, fishing lines, flares, and more.

We purchased charts covering California to Central America and the South Pacific. I sewed courtesy flags for every country along our planned route. We bought spares for every fuse, every light bulb, and every boat part we could imagine needing for the next five years. I logged all the spares into a spreadsheet inventory system I maintained on our laptop and printed hard copies to keep in a three-ring binder where we logged items out or in as we used or purchased them.

We had already set up a mail-forwarding service over the summer. Service it was, since our good friends Mary Claire and Robert Blakeman-Neuman did the job out of love for us. All of our mail, including Jim's very necessary prescription medications, was sent to a post office box they maintained in all of our names. Robert and MC filtered the junk mail, condensed the rest of the mail into as small a package as possible, and shipped it to us after we supplied them with an address such as a boat yard or marina that would accept mail for us.

We repacked all 50 of *Sanctuary*'s lockers. I made a diagram and labeled each locker with a name related to its location such as: "Navigation Station, under seat," or "Main Salon, Starboard Middle, behind settee." We prioritized items according to several criteria: What would we need most frequently? What would we need in a hurry? What absolutely must stay dry? What would we probably never use but had to stow anyway? What was heavy and should go low to the centerline? Binoculars, for example, were always needed, so they stayed in a special rack near the companionway. Light bulbs didn't get changed too often, so they were in an awkward locker under the aft cabin mattress.

Once we figured out all the priorities, we packed what we could in waterproof plastic boxes, labeled the boxes, logged each item into our system, and vowed always to return each thing to its designated location after use. Now we didn't have to remember where obscure items were located; we could use our cross-referenced notebook system.

For common items such as food, we developed a "grocery store" and "food warehouse" approach. Most of the lockers in the galley were designated "grocery store" lockers, and the food in them could be used anytime, by anyone, without logging it in or out. However, items taken or added to the "food warehouse" lockers had to be logged off or on the master list. Each time before a passage of more than three days' duration, I checked the master list and created a shopping list of items to purchase to bring our spares up to acceptable minimums.

Sanctuary's galley with "grocery store" lockers behind the tea kettle

Almost 10 months had passed since Jim's PD diagnosis. So far Jim's iffy balance and weakening muscle system were the two symptoms not fairly well controlled by the meds. We therefore decided to ignore the "five years to live" warning and renewed our sailing vows determined to continue our dream as far as we could, as long as the money lasted, and as long as the journey was fun and we were safe.

Sanctuary tacked under the Golden Gate Bridge one last time on Friday the 13th of October, 1991. We brought her about and set our sights toward Baja, Mexico. As the sun set, its golden light reflected off the windows of houses along the California coast.

I asked Jim if he missed our house. "Well, not really," he replied. "If we say we miss something, let's always say next what we don't miss." "Okay," I agreed, "I don't miss the house payments." He laughed and we yelled out fast what we didn't miss: the freeways, the car payments, and the worry over whether we'd sell enough at the stores to pay the employees. The long hours we'd worked. The dressing up in suits and fancy clothes. The bills always piling up. The sometimes fussy customers or the employees who didn't show up to work on time—or at all. We calmed down and finally said yes, we'd miss our family and friends, but new friends were out there waiting for us to arrive and discover them.

Some Like it Hot

October 1991—October 1992

"Those hot, dry winds that come down through the mountain passes and curl your hair and make your nerves jump and your skin itch. On nights like that every booze party ends in a fight. Meek little wives feel the edge of the carving knife and study their husbands' necks. Anything can happen."

—*Red Wind*, Raymond Chandler

After an unruffled overnight sail, a raucous gang of sea lions announced our arrival to Monterey Bay. The barking, smelly sea lions wreaked havoc in the marina by sinking docks and destroying small boats. The tourists loved them, but the harbormaster didn't. He and the city installed an expensive underwater sound system that emitted "cricket" noises believing the sounds would drive the heavyweight sea lions away. It didn't work. The sea lions figured out how to avoid the underwater chirping. They simply left the water and lounged on the docks. Our trips to shore and town were gauntlets run between the lions curling their lips, swinging their whiskery snouts toward us, and growling as we tried to sneak past them.

We left the sea lions and Monterey Bay behind to harbor-hop farther south arriving at Oxnard in the Channel Islands in time for Thanksgiving. We berthed at the Pacific Corinthian Yacht Club where we enjoyed the club's hot tub and restaurant. For the first time we were without at least part of our family on Thanksgiving and quietly ate our turkey in a restaurant. Where were the new friends we hoped to meet?

San Diego, our last port in the United States, buzzed with Coast Guard, military aircraft, and harbor police. Sailors from all over the world were also in town preparing for the start of the America's Cup race which would take place early in 1992. Sleek sailboats, sitting high in the water with no engines but outfitted with deep, up-to-the-minute designed keels and huge Kevlar or light sails, were towed out of the harbor into the Pacific for practice trials.

Sanctuary's waterline, on the other hand, rose as we hauled more provisions onto our 12-ton cruising sailboat. We rented a car and drove across the border to Mexicali to get Mexican visas, a Mexican fishing license, Mexican insurance for our boat, a reciprocal Mexican ham radio license, and tetanus, diphtheria, and hepatitis shots. All the rushing around made us nervous. We itched to get away from land and back out to the Pacific. By December 1991 *Sanctuary* ambled along the Baja coast, and finally, away from town and underway, we breathed deeply.

The offshore boundary between the United States and Mexico is a thin line on the chart; however, we experienced a physical difference immediately. The warmer waters were lighter, clearer, and cleaner. Pelicans held court as we sailed past long stretches of craggy, uninhabited coastline. There were no military vessels or planes; in fact, we counted only two fishing boats in ten days. We navigated effortlessly without offshore oil rigs, freighters, fishing fleets, and other hazards we had contended with on passages along the California coast. The few cruise ships we passed were easily spotted and glittered like electric wedding cakes at night. Otherwise, our night passages were illuminated only by a bright moon, stars, and the streaks of dolphins in the water. The dolphins played alongside *Sanctuary* and in our bow wake fishing for the krill we disturbed as we sailed. At night the friendly mammals glowed like sleek torpedoes leaving bright green phosphorescent trails as they reeled and spun around us.

We anchored when we could—Islas Todos Santos, Punta Cabras, Isla San Martin, Bahia San Quintin, and Isla Cedros. We tumbled into the harbor at Cedros on the leading edge of a gale and anchored as the winds built. A 50-knot gust tugged us so strongly that our 45-pound CQR anchor dragged through the harbor. After resetting with three anchors, we still maintained anchor watch throughout the night. Between the smelly fish plant on shore and the gusty winds, Cedros was not a good anchorage. The next morning we checked both in and out with the Port Captain at the same time.

The first anchor came up heavily laden with stinky, slimy, guano-encrusted mud, and a tire was tangled on anchor number two. By the time I got to the third anchor, I was breathing hard and thought perhaps my exhaustion was the reason I couldn't raise the last hook. After enlisting help from some other cruisers, we realized it wasn't me. Our 45-

pound main anchor was definitely hooked on something other than the bottom. We hired local Mexicans to dive on it, and they surfaced shortly. We finally understood, after a charade of hands combined with their broken English and our broken Spanish, that the anchor had fouled on the concrete base of a defunct mooring ball. After the divers unhooked the last anchor, we raised it and sailed a short distance to Bahia de Las Tortugas, a wide calm bay with clear waters. A small village lay nestled among the sand dunes and copper-colored hills and plateaus surrounding the bay. I could clearly see the anchor buried 20 feet below in clean white sand. Even so, I swam over it to make doubly sure we were safely hooked—a habit I continued all the way around the world each time we anchored in warm waters.

Eighteen other sailboats were anchored in Turtle Bay. We chatted with each other on a morning VHF radio net discussing the weather or future anchorages. Cruisers called each other by boat name over the net and in person, too. We, for example, were Lyn and Jim *Sanctuary*. If we didn't want company, we'd turn off the "phone." Company usually happened, though, and the dinghies whizzed back and forth from boat to boat, or in the case of purists, were slowly rowed to and fro. *St. Leger*, with Mike and Doreen Ferguson aboard, organized a scavenger hunt which essentially involved cleaning up the beach. I won a lime squeezer and limes and put them to good use making margaritas.

Christmas Eve we went ashore with some of the other cruisers ("Yates" the Mexicans called us) to the church on the hill for midnight Mass. Most of the 150 inhabitants of the fishing village appeared to be there as well. We "Yates" stood in the back listening to the service and trying to understand the mixture of Spanish and Latin. Most of us recognized the songs the choir sang accompanied by four guitars. After the service we dragged our dinghies down the beach and back into the water. Our anchor lights winked us home and, in some cases, 12-volt Christmas tree lights strung on masts and backstays blinked at us as well. The next day we celebrated Christmas with new friends on sailboats *Aquarius* and *Genie* with fresh lobster as the main course for dinner.

Our home for New Year's was Man-O-War Cove in Bahia de Magdalena. Ashore, at the center of a few small fishing huts, stood a big hall with a concrete floor and no roof. Why were people stringing strands of regular household-type light bulbs from pole to pole? Some passing fishermen pulled up to *Sanctuary* and the other sailboats and invited the "Yates" to a New Year's party. Ah, that's what the lights were for!

Mexican partygoers began arriving by boat. I watched as a local woman, wearing a gold satin dress and tall, bright-red spike heels, alit from a *panga* (the seven- to eight-foot-long flat-bottomed, blue and white fishing boats that just about all the Mexican fishermen used) and tiptoed across the sand without getting her dress or shoes wet or dirty.

I, however, was a damp and sandy mess by the time we rowed over and hauled our dinghy out of the tide line. Never mind; I dried my feet, put on my shore shoes, and along with the other cruisers, Jim and I joined the party to dance and drink beer. Children played games on the dance floor between music sets, and we did the best we could to chat in Spanish with our Mexican hosts. Mario, an enterprising 10 year old, spoke excellent English and became our emissary helping us complete conversations, buy beer, or get party food. At midnight one of the locals, in drunken hilarity, pulled out a pistol and began shooting it off like a firecracker. Luckily, his friends and some of the *Federales* got it away from him before injuries occurred. We cruisers released our held breaths and, after sharing New Year kisses, hugs, and *Feliz Ano Nuevos* with our neighbors, beat a retreat to the relative security of our anchored boats.

In the new year, we moved on around the Cape to Cabo San Lucas, staying there longer than planned to repair a broken engine-starter motor. Repairs made, we headed up into the Sea of Cortez. Days passed like the tones of a watercolor painting where only a suggestion of the whole filters through. We sailed, we anchored, and we went ashore walking among the shells and sand or hiking inland past cactus and desert flowers. We swam or fished for Dorado and lobster. Coyotes howled at the moon during the nights. *Sanctuary*, rocking at anchor, swung with the breeze as we lounged on our cool decks gazing at the stars and listening to the bats diving for insects.

Sometimes we met Mexican fishermen and their families ashore. They lived in makeshift *palapas* (semi-permanent huts with palm-frond roofs used as homes during fishing season). The children and dogs played and rolled in the sand; the women cooked tortillas on grates over open fires or sometimes over propane grills. At the end of the fishing day, the men steered their flat-bottomed boats to the surf line opposite their camp. Idling casually to study the wave train, they gunned their engines at exactly the right moment, quickly flipping the outboard engine out of the water, plowing onto the shore in a burst of sand and sea water. Then, with *panga*s all in a row above the high tide mark, they cleaned their catch, throwing the fish heads in a pile to the side. Pelicans and other sea birds hovered waiting for the toss.

We cooked the fish we caught on our propane grill which hung on *Sanctuary*'s stern rail. We'd pull anchor every few days lazily sailing on to explore other bays or small islands. Then we discovered La Paz and spent five weeks in its grip.

La Paz: City of Peace. La Paz lulled. It mesmerized. We met cruisers who, after stopping on the way to the South Pacific, lingered, and anchored there for years—and are still there as far as we know. Its huge bay had only one wistful town on part of the shore. Ancient palms with the bottom half of their trunks painted white lined a wide paved bay front walkway, the *malecon*. Adobe houses crumbled next to '50s style glass-front shops, and taco stands jostled with ice cream carts for selling space. *Panga*s lined the shore, fisherman sat in the sand mending their nets, and dogs (always the dogs) and children played on makeshift swing sets and jungle gyms. Disco music blared on top of guitar music on top of *banda* records. Dented, rusty cars parked next to shiny, new trucks. Everything leaned and heaped together in a jumble of pink, blue, red, and orange—a blaze of sounds and colors against a sizzling sky. Shopping began daily (except Sundays) at dawn in the market, *El Mercado*. Piles of avocados, papayas, and limes jockeyed for space with glassy-eyed fish lined up in neat rows. There was raw, red beef hanging on hooks, stacks of cheeses, loaves of bread, bright baskets hand woven out of plastic strips, leather belts, leather shoes with recycled rubber-tire soles, machetes, cassette tapes, polyester shirts, tee shirts, makeup, and dishes. Vendors with food stands sold slices of pineapple on a stick or cups of cubed watermelon. Guys with blenders made fresh fruit smoothies. Women hawked tacos, burritos, or tamales in buckets under cloths to keep off flies. Oh, the flies were everywhere all the time; we grew used to listlessly, endlessly brushing them away. And the people, the patient people, the loving people, were willing to listen carefully to the *gringa* and offered slow smiles at the recognition of the Spanish word finally found in the English/Spanish—Spanish/English dictionary.

There was no air conditioning and, as the sun rose, dogs, children, vendors, and shoppers retreated. Even the flies retreated indoors. By noon it was so hot rivulets of sweat dripped into eyes, clothing stuck to bodies, and walking seemed a chore. It was too hot to move except into a patch of shade. *Siesta* stretched from noon to 3:00 p.m., or 4:00 p.m., or even 5:00 p.m., depending on the brightness of the sun or the level of heat. After sunset people reappeared to eat, drink, walk the *malecón*, visit by the lapping bay waters, or dance late into the night in discos and clubs.

In March *Carnaval* arrived. It was a week of more: more colors, more sounds, more vendors, more music, and more dancing in the streets. Drinks were sipped from special bisque-fired cups made to be tossed away at the end of the night. Flashing lights, sweets, games, balloons, a King and Queen of Joy, floats, and people in costumes surrounded a precarious-looking Ferris wheel. The weeklong celebration was a cross between a county fair, a mild-mannered Mardi Gras, and a neighborhood block party. "Confetti Bomb," the crowd's favorite game, involved bombarding any off-guard suspect with a handful of confetti from a little bag. A toss down a neck or into a talking mouth won the game. We all played with glee since on the first day of the carnival a costumed "Bad Humor" was burned at the stake. Up in smoke went last year's sins, all was forgiven, each slate wiped clean, and no bad feelings were allowed.

During *Carnaval* we also played a bingo-like game called *Juego de Lotería*. *Juego* involved matching numbers and names of objects to pictures on a large board as they were called out. With help from table mates, and pointing to the pictures, I learned a lot of Spanish. I had also been taking les-

"Carnaval" float
La Paz

sons three times a week from Lourdes Ayala, a doctor's wife with huge, flashing eyes, dancing earrings, flowered dresses, and a sprightly spirit. I missed my visits with Lourdes when we left La Paz and realized Jim and I had learned more than Spanish words. We'd absorbed the generosity of the culture.

We slowed down our pace in the heat and absorbed the *mañana* attitude. (It didn't really mean "tomorrow"–more like "not today.") We sailed slowly on to Puerto Escondido and hung around waiting for a big batch of missing mail. We purchased most of Jim's Parkinson's medications in Mexico, but the ones not available were shipped from the USA, and he needed them. Never mind, we still had a three-month "emergency supply" aboard; the meds would arrive *mañana*. Pulling up *Sanctuary*'s hook, we headed out to Isla Carmen to explore a ghost town at Salinas Bay. In Caleta San Juanico we captured lobsters and stared at the moon-like desert landscape reflected in the still, turquoise waters.

Muffin, our 17-year-old (92 in cat years) fur baby, had adapted to cruising, but her thick black coat didn't help her in the 95° or more Mexican heat. She hunkered below decks, hugged the teak floors, and lay with her belly exposed and paws akimbo hoping to catch a breath of air. Only cool evening breezes enticed her into the cockpit.

From Juanico we entered Bahia De Conception—so grand some cruisers spent months exploring its many coves and tiny islands. With its varied birds, scallops, Dorado, clams, lobsters, and shells, it captured our attention, too. At a Fourth of July party, we and other cruisers celebrated with fireworks and a potluck on the beach. Cruisers shared stories of acquiring their boats, quitting their jobs, and selling their possessions. The stories varied yet were woven of similar cloth. Conversations were threaded with tales of years of hard work coupled with desires to check the pace and follow dreams instead of dollars. We smiled, hugged ourselves, and raised beer toasts to our particular, fortunate freedom saying, "Somebody has to do it!"

After scouring a shell beach at Santa Domingo, we halted at Isla San Marcos. Seals and whales milled around nightly along with manta rays that flung themselves out of the water, splashing the surface loudly, and stirring up krill to eat. Some brave friends swam with sharks, but I stayed on the beaches and searched for spindle shells. We went on to Santa Rosalia still looking for our lost mail which did not surface. We re-ordered the medicine, reprovisioned, and left behind the hot desert winds that blew red dust and sand onto our decks. Since June, butter left out of our small refrigerator melted immediately. Even the sea water was 86° or hotter. We sweltered through *siesta* time each day lying in the cockpit under our sun awning. Our "poor man's air conditioning," a bottle of water we regularly sprayed on each other, cooled us down a little especially if there was a breeze. It was too hot to read. The running sweat clouded our eyes, and the pages of books clumped together from our damp, salt-encrusted finger marks. We moved towels around to sit on so we didn't drip sweat on our cabin settee when we did go below. We and other cruisers joked that our sex lives consisted of "tips of two wet index fingers touching for less than one second." Any further activity produced a river of sweat and was too exhausting.

We pointed *Sanctuary*'s bow north heading farther up into the Sea of Cortez in search of relief. We uncovered a cooler anchorage at San Fransisquito, settled in, and called it home for over two weeks. Jim hooked a prize 40-pound yellowtail, a 20-pound Dorado, and captured lobster, grouper, and triggerfish. Our daily diet of fresh fish, fruits, vegetables, and rice suited us. We looked and felt healthier, and each of us had lost over 10 pounds since we'd started cruising.

By early August we found a hurricane hole and prepared to leave the boat for a trip back to the States. Chores included pulling out sweaters and cold-weather clothing, charts, and books we no longer needed aboard. We listed repair parts and supplies obtainable only in the States and reorganized and inventoried foodstuffs. To make *Sanctuary* safer while we were gone, we cleared the deck of anything high winds could catch. We removed sails, stripped the fenders off the safety lines, and put them and the life sling, sheet bags, and all other deck gear below. We cleaned out the refrigerator and turned it off, closed the sea cocks, and battened down the hatches. Larry, the skipper of *Ocean Angel*, would watch *Sanctuary* and take care of Muffin while we traveled by land from Baja, Mexico to San Lorenzo, California.

That past May we'd purchased a 1973 red VW van and planned to drive it to California. The red van had transported groceries, diesel, gasoline, water, us, and many other cruisers all summer. We shared the cost and took turns hop-scotching the van from port to port by riding a bus back to the old anchorage, retrieving it, and driving to the new anchorage. Jim, three friends, and I would drive the van back to the States and haul along *Ocean Angel's* bulky life raft which needed repairs. We'd return in a month with the life raft, bottom paint, and other supplies from California.

Or so we thought. Thirty miles down a lonely road from our anchorage, loaded to the gunnels with 23 bags, boxes, and the large, heavy life raft, the old red van clunked and rolled to a halt. Cactus prickled to the right of us, cactus lined the road to the left of us, and not another car was in sight. The sun beat down relentlessly as we and our friends discussed the possibilities and probabilities. Jim was depressingly sure the engine had blown. Two hours later, after he had torn into the greasy, hot engine (under the 23 bags, of course) we found he was right. We were in the boonies of Baja and knew we were in for a long wait before anyone would come along. Finally, after two and a half sweltering hours, a car going the wrong way, back to the bay where the boats were anchored, came along. We hailed it, and a friend and I hitched a ride in hope of arranging a tow. We knew a few Mexicans who owned a small cabana hotel and some trucks and lived at the bay. Once there we met Ricardo, whom we hired to tow us and the VW van to a Pemex service station on Highway One.

Jim and the station mechanic figured out that the van needed a new piston. It wasn't available in Baja, so we left the van in the mechanic's care vowing to return with the part in a few weeks. All five of us piled the awkward life raft and our collective bags over to the side of Highway One so we could flag down a bus going north. Much to our dismay a drunken Mexican, also waiting for a bus, befriended us. Thinking we were all drunk, the driver of the first bus that came along would not take us. When a second bus arrived about an hour later, I quickly jumped ahead of the Mexican brandishing his tequila bottle to get to the door of the bus first. My language skills had much improved, and I was able to beg the driver in Spanish, "Sir, we're not with the drunk. Our car is broken; we desperately need to ride the bus, please let us on."

We had left our boats at 6:30 a.m. so by 10:30 p.m., when the driver of the second *Tres Estrellas de Oro* (Three Gold Stars) bus to Tijuana reluctantly let us onboard, we were very thankful. The bus was full, but a kind Mexican woman moved her child into her lap so we five could share one seat. We took turns sitting in that one seat, or standing in the aisles, for the four-hour ride. The bus floor was so sticky and dirty that, in spite of our exhaustion, none of us would sit on it. The drunk, however, lay down in the middle of the aisle and promptly passed out. We watched as one by one the busload of Mexicans turned to look him over. The next time the bus stopped, a few of the men took his tequila bottle, rifled his pockets, and then rolled him out of the bus and onto the side of the road. We *gringos* exchanged looks but didn't dare say a word.

We straggled into San Diego early the next day. After counting and sorting the 23 pieces of luggage, we parted company with our friends. Jim and I could not face another bus, so we rented a car and drove straight to a motel room where we took two consecutive showers each and then fell into bed for our first night sleeping on land in over two years.

After about a month in the USA visiting family and friends, seeing Jim's doctors, having the life raft repaired, and buying bottom paint and other supplies we couldn't find in Baja, we returned to *Sanctuary*. The symptoms of Parkinson's disease were progressing–especially the head shaking, hand trembling, bad balance, and stiffness of movement–but we just made sure we had Jim's extra three-month buffer of meds and continued.

Jim's brother Dennis and his girlfriend Cathy came aboard for a visit. We sailed up farther into the Sea of Cortez anchoring at Bahia Alcatraz with its rookery of sea lions. We launched the dinghy, put on snorkel gear, and motored over to investigate the many pups in what seemed to be a nursery with a few mothers. The pups were very inquisitive and, after we got into the water to snorkel, they boldly swam along with us. The mothers remained on the rocks barking occasionally. In the water the lions were sleek and graceful—not bulky and threatening as those on the docks in Monterey. However, as we continued snorkeling with the pups, two bulls suddenly barked aggressively and barreled off their perches towards us. Playtime was clearly over; we climbed back into our dinghy and left immediately!

Sanctuary needed her yearly bottom painting. The haul-out in La Paz was expensive, so we decided to sail across the mouth of the Sea of Cortez from Baja to a small, inexpensive facility in Mazatlán about which we had heard. Mazatlán, on the mainland of Mexico, was a two nights and three days passage away. *Santa Anas* were mentioned on the weather report and we didn't know what they were. We should have asked since they were forecast for the three days of our passage. (*Santa Anas* are gale force winds that sweep down the Southern California valleys and through the deserts. They funnel into the Sea of Cortez causing havoc and destruction all along both coasts as they blow, terrorizing novice and seasoned boaters alike.) Oblivious to their meaning, Jim and I raised *Sanctuary*'s anchor and, with 10 knots of wind behind us, started our sail.

By nightfall, with *Sanctuary*'s main sail reefed to a sliver, we began to figure out *Santa Ana* winds. Leaving the safety of the last port had been a bad decision. The wind picked up to 45 knots and gusted to 60 knots. *Sanctuary* surfed down steep and dangerous 12-foot seas at more than 10 knots (her hull speed of 7.6 knots plus a 3-knot current). After being pooped by waves that crashed unexpectedly over the stern several times, I frantically pored over the charts searching for a safe anchorage we could reach quickly.

The strain was too much for the autopilot, so Jim hand-steered, doing his best to keep *Sanctuary* from a knock down or a pitch-pole. Salt water blew off the tops of waves and soaked Jim who continually spit out seawater as it drained over his face and into his mouth. I found a good-looking anchorage on the chart and yelled so Jim could hear me above the maelstrom going on outside the cabin: "Isla Guanaha is 35 miles away! At our current speed we could be there in about four or five hours! Let's go for it! We can't take these conditions much longer!"

Four grueling hours later we rounded the point of the sheltering bay, with still two miles to the safe holding ground. As we turned into the bay the seas immediately calmed. Yet the wind continued to blow—now straight at us over the bow. Even with her engine fully revved, *Sanctuary* could only push one half mile per hour through the 45 knots of wind. Four tiring hours later we finally made the anchorage.

I dropped the anchor, letting out 200 feet of chain. *Sanctuary*'s anchor grabbed, and the heavy chain snubbed up with a jerk. We were anchored. We plopped down in the cockpit completely exhausted and hoarse from yelling for the last eight hours in order to hear each other above the howling winds. I saw Jim clearly without the blowing spray, and he looked so old, so white, and so tired. Then I started laughing. "What are you laughing at?" Jim asked, "Nothing's funny." "Yes there is," I replied. "Look in the mirror. Now I know what an 'Old Salt' is. Your face, especially your eyebrows and beard, are completed encrusted and white with salt!"

Back to the Beginning at San Patricio

November 1992—January 1993

"A journey of a thousand miles must begin with a single step."
—Lao Tzu

We washed the salt off ourselves and *Sanctuary*. We recuperated, the winds calmed to 15 knots, and we sailed leisurely across the Sea of Cortez to Mazatlán, our first port on the Mexican mainland. Mazatlán's small harbor teemed with cruise ships droning in and out, and shrimp boats churned its waters. After anchoring, we flitted from boat to shore to town like dragonflies lighting on the huge market, the restaurants, tourist shops, and ice cream stands. The palms, parrots, and balmy breezes of the mainland surprised us after the months we'd parched on the edges of the Baja desert. The haul-out facility we anticipated turned out to be defunct, so after a few days we left Mazatlán and headed out to Isla Isabella looking forward to a remote anchorage again.

During the 85-nautical-mile passage, I cleaned *Sanctuary*'s topsides of city soot while Jim navigated and tended to the sails. Then I read aloud to Jim from our guide to Mexico about the wild island refuge of Isabella, a warden-regulated shore access. All visitors had to stay on paths. The nesting boobies (with their electric blue feet), the frigates, nor any other wild life was to be disturbed. The waters were also protected and no fishing was allowed. Snorkeling was okay though, so after we arrived and anchored, down we went. In the clear waters we easily spotted Moorish idols, blue boxfish, reef comets, and other exotic-looking fish at more than 30 feet away.

The anchorages at Isabella were dicey with poor holding and fluky winds. A few days later we upped and left in the middle of the night when shifting winds turned our anchorage into a lee shore. We couldn't delay our dreaded boat haul-out much longer anyway, so we nosed *Sanctuary* to Puerto Vallarta and a boatyard there. After we got our bearings for a few days in Marina Vallarta we gritted our teeth and paid for a week on land. *Sanctuary* was pulled out of the water onto the cradle—"the hard."

We dug out of the deepest lockers the special anti-fouling paint we brought and set to work. The project called for removal of old, flaking bottom paint, then application of one coat of primer and two coats of anti-fouling. We couldn't afford to hire workers and could only pay for one week in the boatyard. Our 40-foot sailboat, small in a big ocean, suddenly seemed very large as we approached her from ground level with sandpaper and paint brushes in our hands. Jim and I labored steadily from sunup to sunset each day, barely completing the work in time to reenter the water a back-breaking seven days later.

Back at the Marina Vallarta docks, we cleaned the remainder of the boatyard dust off the decks and prepared to leave *Sanctuary* for the second time in 1992. In August we had visited Jim's family in California. This time we planned to ride bus and train across mainland Mexico to Texas to visit my family in December. *Sanctuary*, with Muffin aboard, would stay safely tied to the marina dock. Friends would feed her and check on the boat daily. We were unexpectedly offered a car ride, so we adjusted our route and headed off to Texas via Guadalajara, a city we had last seen 17 years earlier, just before our dream to sail around the world was born.

Guadalajara did not disappoint us; we fell in love with the city and each other all over again. We stayed in a 400-year-old home converted to a small hotel, walked the *paseos*, and toured the ancient Government buildings and the Cabanas (an orphanage-turned-museum). The market was better and bigger than we remembered it, and somehow the bustle of the people in the city of more than four million didn't bother us. The streets were decked out for Christmas with tall, tinseled angels. Candles and stars hung from the lampposts. In front of the cathedral, a nativity scene, strangely complete with kangaroos and seals, attracted viewers. We quickly got into the spirit of the season and joined the coursing city crowds looking and Christmas shopping.

Diane, a friend from Canada, lived in Guadalajara, teaching English to young Mexicans. We visited her classroom and enjoyed conversing with the students who invited us to a pre-Christmas "Virgin of Guadalupe" celebration at a small church in Tetlán. Once a pueblo, Tetlán had been engulfed by Guadalajara's skirts. The students said some of Tetlán's residents had never been into "The City" and that no other *gringos* had attended this special festival. We were certainly an attraction, and groups of wide-eyed little boys followed us around.

The church was decorated, a band played, and food and game booths lined the square. The fireworks were piled to the side as several men lined them up in some semblance of order. We pressed into the mash of humanity. Chatting in Spanish as much as we could, we joined in the eating and drinking. We didn't attempt the dance which was an elegant but fast cross between a rumba and a polka. We milled around with the crowd, then looked alive at the start of the fireworks.

Replicas of white bulls had been constructed out of bamboo, wire, and papier-mâché, all overlaid with a frame of fireworks. The strands of fireworks led to the *torrito's* tail which served as a fuse. We stepped back as a brave soul lifted a *torrito* onto his back, and as soon as the tail was ignited, took off around the square at a fast clip with fireworks popping and spraying behind him. Laughing, screaming boys followed closely—daredevils running with the sparks. The rest of the crowd parted in waves as the "little bull" approached.

The intermittent *torrito* runs were a lead-in to the main event at midnight. A freestanding bamboo tower, about 30 feet high with nine stars protruding at intervals along its height, was topped with an elaborate bamboo crown. The *castillo,* wired with fireworks from top to bottom, dominated one side of the square. People had circled and admired it all evening. As midnight approached we jockeyed along with everyone else for position. We wanted to be close enough for a good view but far enough away to escape burns, so we checked to see which way the wind was blowing.

The fire master touched cigarette to fuse, and the show began! The bamboo stars twirled, sending off rockets. As sparks flew, brave boys danced in a waterfall of white light, smoke, and heat. The crowd gave a last gasp as the glowing crown blew off the top of the *castillo*, lighting the midnight sky. The fire-lit crown whizzed past the cathedral, raining green sparks on the cross at the apex.

A brave soul runs with a "torrito" on his back, Tetlan, Mexico

The fireworks were a fitting finale to our stay in Guadalajara. We bounced onward by bus to Texas and arrived in time to be with my family for Christmas. We celebrated with visiting, eating, partying and whizzing around Houston. As usual, we shopped for boat parts and made a route decision by buying charts for Panama and the Eastern Caribbean. We would be going against the grain, as the most accepted or usual sailing routes for circumnavigators led west around the world, downwind (in theory), most of the way. We chose to sail east about, or "the wrong way" as lots of sailors repeatedly told us.

We had our reasons. In 20 months of cruising, our longest offshore passage had been five days. Even though we couldn't see land, we had always been less than 25 miles from shore. If we continued west from Central America to the South Pacific, a passage would take us anywhere from 19 to 24 days. I was not mentally ready for a passage like that. Furthermore, symptoms of Parkinson's disease were increasing at a disturbingly steady pace. Worsening balance, loss of grip, hesitation of movement, shaking, and general malaise were all bothering Jim in spite of medications. Therefore, we wanted an easier (we thought) route that would allow us to harbor-hop until we reached the Eastern Caribbean. Also, if we sailed east, we would still be relatively close to the United States. When we reached the Caribbean, we'd see if we felt up to a long ocean crossing.

Weighing down the airplane with seven pieces of luggage, we flew back to Puerto Vallarta. Even though we drew the black bean (which meant "stop") from the customs inspection lottery can, the Mexican customs agents did not want to plough through our water maker parts, charts, material for flags, videos, paperbacks, navigation books, diesel parts, tax forms, pressure hoses, mast lights, clothing, and prescription medicines. With half-closed eyes they patted everything and waved us through. We struggled back to *Sanctuary* and Muffin.

Glad to be aboard our home after more than a month away, we rounded up food and took *Sanctuary* out of the marina in a flash. I was itching to swim in an anchorage with clean water and welcomed the hot sun after some very cold, wet days in Houston. We had maintained a hectic pace since November and wanted to slow down a bit. However, we knew, due to the weather patterns, that if we wished to proceed along our chosen path to the Panama Canal, we needed to march steadily southward. We could not linger as we had over the summer in Baja.

We continued southward, from Puerto Vallarta to Chamela to Tenacatita, and finally, Bahia Natividad, a significant stop. In 1975 we had arrived at the coast and rented a little bungalow with the beachfront *palapa* restaurant in San Patricio, the village on the shore of Bahia Natividad, from Señor Malacho and his family. We remembered it easily: the swimming, sitting on the beach, watching the pelicans dive, being in love, staring out at Bahia Natividad and the one picturesque sailboat anchored there, how one dream had led to another, our whispered vows, and how we'd sworn to stay together and one day, someday, return by sailboat.

Ever good to our word, we kept our vows and 18 years later, sailed into the small bay at last. Our sleepy little bay was sleepy no longer. The beach was ringed with hotels, shops, and restaurants, and Señor Malacho's *palapa* restaurant and bungalows were gone. The "one picturesque sailboat" had multiplied. The day we sailed into our dream bay, 22 sailboats anchored there rocked by the wakes of jet skis, fishing tour boats, and a big, *panga*-pulled inflated plastic banana with four people riding in its garish curve. "Well," Jim said, "everything's surely changed." "Yes," I replied, "We had to change things to get here too, didn't we?" We surveyed the bay from *Sanctuary*'s cockpit and toasted our continuing relationship, love, dreams, and promises—all the while wondering if anyone on shore was watching us and making plans.

Te-Wan-Te-Peckers

February 1993—May 1993

"Any fool can steer a ship, sir. It's just knowing where to take it."
—Sailor, *The Bounty Mutiny*, William Bligh and Edward Christian

Squeaky clean Zihuatanejo (nicknamed "Z-watt"), our favorite Mexican town, served up tamales we drooled over, excellent native crafts, provisions, and an anchorage filled with cruisers. We arrived there a week after leaving San Patricio and enjoyed beach parties with crews from sailboats who would soon be striking out in all directions. Some were sailing to the South Pacific, Hawaii, Central America; others were heading back to the States. Copy machines in town clicked away as yachties shared notes and anchorage information. The cruising family we'd created during 14 months in Baja and Mexico was scattering in the wind. The changing season served as taskmaster, and we pored over pilot charts and cruising guides discussing winds and routes.

The pilot charts, valuable tools to the offshore sailor, provide data on prevailing weather patterns, winds, currents, wave heights, and more. We studied the wind arrows, tracing their circles and feathers with our fingers. Each crew looked for a quick, safe route balancing the probability of perfect prevailing winds against the least chance of bad weather. I was teary-eyed as we pulled the hook to leave Z-Watt. We'd made our choice though, and since we were heading southeasterly toward the Panama Canal and most others were heading west, we would not see the majority of them again.

Acapulco, one of our next stops, proved to be a noisy, dirty port. Even though Acapulco was well known as a beach getaway, as cruisers we saw another side of town and endured a few grimy days checking in and out. Afterwards, we filled *Sanctuary*'s fuel tank with diesel and exited as quickly as possible bound for Puerto Huatulco. Huatulco, in the state of Oaxaca, tripped up our tongues, our tempers, our timing and our budget.

Huatulco hosts the last secure anchorage on the northern edge of the Golfo de Tehuantepec, a very windy body of water dreaded by cruisers. The Mexican mainland narrows there, and mountains spill over to a low, narrow waist of sand flats cinched on the eastern side by the Gulf of Mexico and on the west by the Tehuantepec. The sailing directions state:

"In the vicinity of the Gulf of Tehuantepec, northers are particularly strong because of the damming of the N flow of air by the mountain ranges both to the E and W of the gap which lies immediately N of the head of the gulf. These gales, known locally as Tehuantepecers (Te-wan-te-peckers) generally prevail from October through April and at times blow with a force that exceeds Force 8 (34-40 knots or 39-46 miles per hour) on the Beaufort scale. The gales may last several hours to several days. They are liable to raise a high sea and may be felt up to 100 miles offshore. The barometer cannot be relied on to give any prior warning."

Seasoned sailors who had crossed this treacherous gulf before warned: "Keep one foot on the beach." In other words, stay really close in, follow the shoreline curve, and sail the two-meter water line all the while. Do not try to shorten the journey by cutting straight across to your destination because the farther from shore the more fetch the seas and the more funnel the winds. All will conspire into fierce, gusty winds and seas of short, steep, and dangerous proportions.

So, we hung tight in Huatulco waiting for good weather. When we thought the forecast was good, we gritted our teeth, set our shoulders back, and then, in the company of three other boats, sidled out to cross the Tehuantepec. To our dismay *Sanctuary*'s autopilot quit working about an hour after our departure. The marvelous autopilot (nicknamed "Otto") allowed *Sanctuary* to maintain a set course without a person steering. Otto relieved us of long, tedious, back-breaking hours standing before the wheel in the cockpit, and afforded us "one person on, one person off" watches. The person "on watch" could semi-relax in the cockpit, getting up every 12 to 15 minutes to scan the horizon or change the set of sails if needed. Technically, Otto was not essential, but for 20, 30, or more hours at sea, we deemed an autopilot essential for our well-being and comfort. We turned back to Huatulco to repair it, leaving the three other boats sailing on to meet the Tehuantepec.

We re-anchored in Huatulco assuming we'd make a quick repair. Otto had broken before, back in 1991, during our first leg of sailing to

Canada. Hand steering all that summer had been an uncomfortable, hard lesson, and we had since maintained spares aboard for every part of the contraption we imagined could break.

Located underneath the steering binnacle, Otto's "arm" resided in a cramped slope-sided locker in *Sanctuary*'s stern. I could barely fit my hips and shoulders through the locker hatch to reach the controls. I crammed into the awkward space and, with Jim directing me from on deck, we spent the next two days troubleshooting Otto. We took the pilot apart, checked and tested everything, and put it back together—twice. Every cycle of repairs involved a convoluted climb into and out of the cavernous locker. No joy. Another cruiser, with a similar autopilot and with more electronic experience than we, offered to help. He came over to *Sanctuary*, and together we took the pilot apart a third time. The third set of eyes helped us figure out what we needed—of course it was the one part we didn't have.

Ordering the part and getting it to Huatulco turned into a "you can't get there from here" disaster. We began with round-robin daily telephone calls to the States and to Mexican and American customs officials. We endured "lost" shipments, more telephone calls, mistakes by the auto-pilot manufacturer, and a lot of waiting. Finally, after four weeks of frustration, we gave up on having the pilot part shipped. Deciding to cut our losses, I flew back to the United States hauling a 50-pound box containing the dismembered autopilot. Jim stayed in Huatulco caring for Muffin and *Sanctuary* and longingly watching other cruisers sail in, stop a while, and then head out to conquer the *Golfo*.

By the time I returned with the repaired autopilot and more spares, we had been anchored in Huatulco so long people had nicknamed us "The Mayors." We reinstalled "Otto," reset our shoulders, and five weeks after our first departure, marched into the Tehuantepec for *Sanctuary*'s second attempt. During our enforced wait, we'd listened to many radio reports chronicling uncomfortable—even dangerous–passages. Boats had suffered through 60-knot winds with shredded sails and decks awash. One single-hander had been reported as "missing at sea," (and to our knowledge was never found). Our two-day crossing, however, was textbook perfect, and we sailed into Puerto Madero wearing grins and sighing thankfully. The repaired autopilot had performed flawlessly, and our most dreaded passage to date was safely behind us.

From Madero we hired a truck and driver and took a whirlwind trip inland to Tapachula netting fresh fruits and vegetables. We departed

Mexico on April 17, 1993, our rubber-stamped *zarpe* for Costa Rica in hand and visions of nearby Quetzal, Guatemala, on the horizon. We didn't stop on the west coast of Guatemala after all. The 15-knot winds were too good, so we kept sailing.

Late on the day after we passed Quetzal, the winds built to 30 knots, switching directly onto our nose. Acajutla, El Salvador, lay abeam as we pounded into sloppy seas with forecasts predicting more of the same. A night at anchor looked enticing. Should we chance stopping? We knew El Salvador's long civil war had ended in 1992. The cruising grapevine said all was peaceful, the political climate stable, and visitors from the U.S. were welcome. On the other hand, the United States Department of State had issued travel advisories and warnings for almost all of Central America, so we weren't sure. We decided to chance it anyway.

Our first surprise: "Acajutla Tower Control" spoke fluent English and, after welcoming us to El Salvador, cheerfully directed us by radio into the commercial harbor. Then out to the anchorage came a Naval Captain accompanied by an English-speaking ships agent. They expertly boarded *Sanctuary* without scraping our hull with their launch, glanced at our documents, and politely issued us special passes for our Sunday night arrival with full clearance to be secured during business hours on Monday.

The next day Jose Ortega, the ships' agent, while chatting in beautiful, grammatically correct English, took us to his home and introduced us to his family. For his job as ships' agent, Jose needed to buy provisions for a large cargo vessel. He offered to take us along on the shopping trip to Sosonate, a city 15 miles inland. I wanted help learning Spanish, so Jose and I struck a deal. I would speak Spanish to him and he would speak English to me. We would correct each other's mistakes, and that way we could each learn. (I got the better of the deal by far, as his English needed few corrections.)

Before we were allowed to go to Sosonate with Jose, we had to pass clearance out of the port area which was under the military control of the government, the "Reforma" party. The day before, Jim and I had been required to leave our passports with the Port Control and stop at Military Checkpoints throughout the town. We noticed armed soldiers and guards most places we went. Before we left the United States to sail around the world, Jim and I discussed several issues of attitude, prudence, and safety. We declared ourselves "Ambassadors of Good Will" and followed the edicts of a sailing organization we belonged to, the Seven Seas Cruising Association (SSCA). We pledged to uphold certain tenets, such as maintaining a clean wake, in order to be members. Not only would we respect the environment by not throwing trash overboard and the like, but we would respect the peoples we met so that anyone following in our wake would be warmly welcomed.

With this goal in mind, we carried no weapons aboard. Also, with the same goal in mind, we had declared we would not discuss religion or politics with the people we met. If pressed, we would be circumspect. Telling people we were retired jewelers and jewelry store owners might also raise a few unnecessary red flags, so we decided to stretch the truth a little. Both of us had been teachers at various times in our lives and had taught occasionally while we owned the stores. So, when locals we did not know in El Salvador (and elsewhere) asked us what we did, we replied, "We are retired teachers."

Vegetable vendor
Sonsonate, El Salvador

On the way to Sonsonate, we passed men working in fields of banana trees. Road crews hauled bricks in wheelbarrows, and workers were crammed by the dozen in flat-bed trucks. Old yellow school buses had been repainted wild red and blue, named "Jocelena," "Maria," "Wendy," or the like, and served as city buses. Big trucks lumbered by, piled with sugarcane. Simple-looking dwellings and piles of rubble lined the roadsides. However, at the market, with radios blaring in the background, we shopped among small hillsides of fruits and vegetables of all kinds. Buckets overflowed with herbs and flowers, including yucca blossoms. Pails of churned butter sat covered with cloth to keep out the flies. Cheeses were stacked like building blocks. Meat spilled off counters black with dirt. Naked children played in tubs. So many people were shopping in the inside part of the market that we had to walk mostly sideways or with our bags on our heads.

In spite of all the activity and apparent rebuilding, Jose said, "The war ended almost two years ago, but tourists are slow to return, and the economy is only creeping along. The Reforma Party rules now, but the Christian Democrats will win next year." What that meant for the daily life of Salvadorians I didn't know.

Jose piled the rations he bought for the *Fujisan* (a container vessel from Bangkok at dock in Acajutla) into his pickup, and we rode back to Acajutla atop burlap bags and crates of vegetables. Jose dropped off the goods for *Fujisan* then took us back to his house for another visit with his family. It had been a long, hot, dusty day, and his wife invited us to use their cool, green-tiled bath for showers.

We carried 150 gallons of fresh water on *Sanctuary*. An American household easily squanders that much water in less than a day, but we could make the amount last a month or more. At anchor we typically consumed 10 gallons a day when we knew we could easily refill our tanks, and on passages we used only five gallons of fresh water daily.

Showering aboard, therefore, involved careful water rationing. We used less than two and a half gallons each by first wetting our bodies, then turning off the water while we soaped. We'd turn the water back on to rinse, then turn off the water again for a second soaping—if needed. Rinsing involved aiming the spray directly on the part being rinsed. Sometimes we'd use clean salt water for all washing and rinsing until the last fresh-water rinse. We did not have the luxury of standing under bountiful running water unless we were in a marina with shoreside showers or a dock water hookup. The offer of long, hot showers in a beautiful, large, cool, green-tiled bath was a gift joyfully received. Afterward Mrs. Ortega served slices of cold watermelon. Heavenly!

After our shower and a visit, Jose drove us and our fresh vegetables back to the harbor. *Sanctuary* was moored in the company of some very impressive vessels in Acajutla's working harbor. The rusty, barnacle-encrusted docks were a danger to our inflatable rubber dinghy, so Juan, a local dockworker, ferried us to and from shore in a wooden dugout.

Seven-foot hammerhead shark
Acajutla, El Salvador

Each trip required climbing up and down a precarious iron ladder that swayed on dock pilings 20 feet to water level. Each time we went ashore we gingerly raised and lowered ourselves and our purchases in and out of Juan's long, leaky dugout, which was powered by a recalcitrant Yamaha. One evening at the docks I scuttled up the ladder, got to the top, and almost fell backward into the water as I came face to face with a very freshly caught and still moving seven-foot hammerhead shark.

We left Acajutla with documents allowing us entry into other Salvadorian ports. At Isla Meanguera (in the Gulf of Fonseca) we settled into a quiet bay with only three huts ashore—one of which overflowed with a family of fourteen. La Union, a city of more than 40,000, was a short day-sail away, so, we continued to explore.

Disembarking in La Union, another commercial harbor, challenged us again. The great tide, the rusty metal docks, and the mud flats with hidden sharp projectiles were too much of a risk for our rubber tender. I finally arranged transport by chattering in Spanish with men who replied reluctantly, thinking they should speak only to the male captain.

Freddie Cooper, wide-faced with a silver-toothed grin, manned a dugout and didn't mind talking to a woman. He helped us haul water, fuel, and more groceries including the very good Salvadorian beer "Pilsener" with an ace of hearts on its label. Two days was enough in muggy La Union. It was time to tackle the last leg to Costa Rica. We hoisted *Sanctuary*'s sails and clawed down the Nicaraguan coast against the prevailing winds and currents, arriving two and a half days later in Bahia Cuajiniquil, Costa Rica.

Quiet Cuajiniquil surprised us with 40-knot gusts that piped each afternoon over the hills into the bay. We danced around on the anchor chain in clear, silky water hoping *Sanctuary* wouldn't drag. Wild animal calls echoed from the shore. Our guidebooks said we were surrounded by jaguars, margays, ocelots, pumas and jaguarondis, 60 species of bats, green macaws, howler monkeys, coyotes, and a long list of birds. The calls and screeches were intense; however, we couldn't see anything through the thick jungle. I longed to spot a margay or a jaguarondi, so one morning at 5:30 a.m. we lowered the dinghy and slid into the mangroves with binoculars at the ready. I knew we had become seasoned cruisers when I felt disappointed that we "only saw parrots and macaws."

Ticos and the Zone

May 1993—October 1993

"For those onboard a ship in transit, the effect for the greater part of the journey was of sailing a magnificent lake in undiscovered country."

—*The Path Between the Seas*, David McCullough

May in Costa Rica marked the beginning of the rainy season, and it rained on us every day for two months. It was a mixed blessing. Our water tanks were always full, our decks were clean, our clothes were clean, but our interior teak mildewed, the clean clothes never dried completely, and in the 85° heat and high humidity, we and our cat looked and felt slightly matted.

In spite of Costa Rica's reputation as an ecologically minded and cleanliness conscious country, we found it to be just the opposite. Most of the Pacific waters near the shores of Costa Rica were filled with sewage, plastic trash, scum, and generally nasty looking stuff. When we anchored in warm waters, I usually swam laps around *Sanctuary* for an hour or more every day. However, the filth and sightings of numerous highly poisonous yellow-bellied sea snakes kept me from swimming much in Costa Rica.

Receiving our mail in a foreign country was always an adventure. In Costa Rica, even though we knew our mail was sitting at the post office, getting the officials to hand it over took two days of traipsing from Customs to the Free Zone to the Post Office, back to the Free Zone, to the bank, then back to the Free Zone (which was not "free"). Each office required pieces of paper, in triplicate. In the "Duty Free" office we forked over the equivalent of seven dollars and were allowed to have our mail. Included in the bundle was the "lost" mail from Mexico. It had surfaced in California as "returned to sender," so our two-day struggle garnered two large packages of mostly old news.

Costa Ricans, or "Ticos" (as they called themselves), were neutral, neither rude nor helpful. Encounters with exuberant, loving Mexicans had spoiled us, the hospitality of the Salvadorians had overwhelmed us, but the neutrality of "Ticos" left us looking for an intrinsic characteristic or personality which we did not encounter. Nothing much stood out except the extraordinary beauty of the rainforests accompanied by the rain, the rain, and the rain.

Along with another couple, we rented a car and drove inland to the capital city of San Jose and toured the Gold Museum. The three-story underground vault of the Central Bank (an architectural delight) housed over 1,600 pieces of fine gold jewelry created by the Maya and Aztec some 2,000 years ago. The small, intricate iguanas, quetzals, frogs, people, bells, and other images made of gold rivaled anything Jim or I had ever created at our jewelry store, yet the ancient artists had fashioned their masterpieces using only primitive hand tools and casting methods. We left knowing why the Spanish had come to conquer, and we felt mortified when we saw the last display case. It contained some strands of plain glass beads the Spaniards had given the Indians in exchange for their priceless gold workmanship.

We learned from displays at the Jade Museum and the Museum of National History that, because of its central location on the isthmus between the Americas, Costa Rica had been a pathway for peoples and trading for many centuries. *Sanctuary* followed in the famous (or infamous) footsteps of Cordova, Coronado, Ribera, and Drake—Columbus had remained on the Caribbean side. The gold was long gone; coffee and tourism were the kings in 1993.

We visited coffee plantations, volcanoes, and toured a butterfly farm where we saw the spectacular, iridescent blue morpho butterfly. Back at the hotel, as I babbled on enthusiastically about the more than 220 species of butterflies at the farm, a Tican lady laughed saying, "Costa Ricans have no need to visit the farm. We simply sit in our gardens." She was right. I started to pay closer attention and realized that butterflies abounded. As we later sailed offshore, some even flew out to light on *Sanctuary*.

Flowers, dripping off flowing vines, pushing up through jungle undergrowth, poking out of lava boulders, and bursting off of trees were prolific. The blooms served nectar for the butterflies, and we saw howler monkeys eat whole blossoms. The screams of the howlers echoed out of the jungles and across the waters of most every anchorage. One day, as we hiked in the jungle, a pair swung from branch to branch following above us as we walked to a mountain stream. As we stripped off our clothes and sat luxuriating in a pool in the middle of the clear stream, the big-eyed faces of the howlers peered through the overhanging trees and vines. They draped over the branches watching and chattering at us as if to say, "What are you doing in our bathtub?"

We sighted scarlet macaws, roseate spoonbills, tropicbirds with their long white tails, boobies of all descriptions, yellow throated vireos, cattle egrets, white herons, king buzzards, orange-chinned parakeets, hummingbirds, green kingfishers, trogons, and tropical kingbirds. We heard the elusive toucans, with their bills making a sound like two wooden balls clicking, but couldn't spot them.

We discovered all the above birds in the wild. Some Tican families practiced an unusual, yet appealing way of enticing wild birds to be pets. They fed them, providing handy food containers nailed to branches near their patios, and the birds became live-in yet "fly-away" residents. There were no cages or clipped wings. The birds were free to depart, yet they roosted near the food containers. We observed several scarlet macaws sitting around terraces in this manner. They were wild, and we were warned that they would bite, yet they remained perched when we approached. One family we met had enjoyed several green parrots in this fashion for more than 14 years.

We hopped *Sanctuary* along from Playa del Coco, Potrero, Carrillo, Ballena, Isla Gitana, Leona, Quepos, Drakes Bay, Jiminez, and Rincon, to Golfito, where we anchored in a beautiful (but dirty water) area called the "Golfo Dulce" (Sweet Gulf). Once the center of extensive pineapple and banana exporting, Golfito had lapsed, due to strikes and problems with the soil, into a languid, somewhat seedy atmosphere. The rotting docks tilted dangerously; we sailors seemed to be the only foreigners around. At pot lucks and information swaps, we enjoyed the company of cruisers we had not met before. Sailboats just up from the Panama Canal filled us in on what to expect for our upcoming canal transit.

Expatriate Americans Whitey and Barbara ran the "Jungle Club," a cruisers social center/compound ashore on the edge of the jungle, their home and our home away from home for a time. Three months after we entered the waters of Costa Rica we exchanged our remaining *colones* for dollars, gave the Port *Capitán* a hearty handshake, and left Golfito on July 21, 1993, bound for Panama, with visions of perfect, clean beaches drawing us onward.

Our overnight passage led us to Isla Gamez, Panama, where the vision materialized! We dropped the hook in clean turquoise water off a sparkling, white beach lined with coco palms, colorful parrots squawking amongst the fronds, and wild purple orchids growing in the shade. No people were around—we heard only the sounds of nature. We couldn't put the boat to bed fast enough. Without bothering with swimsuits, we dove into the pristine water we had been longing for and swam to the beach. Gamez was the siren island, the island I imagined when dreaming about cruising. Our afternoon ended with red cheeks, rosy not from the sun but from embarrassment.

A local family surprised us as they appeared quietly, having paddled up in their dugout canoe to bring us lobsters, avocados, limes and mangoes. When I suddenly heard and saw them, I dove into the water thinking to conceal my nakedness. Chagrined, I realized the water was so clear I needn't have bothered. Oh well, the family was nonchalant and chatted away as if it were normal.

We traded and visited with Jose and his island family during the next few days and went swimming, fishing, and snorkeling. It truly was the island of my dreams, and we left it very reluctantly. We'd planned to travel quickly through the Panamanian islands on the Pacific side, stop a few days in Panama City/Balboa to refuel, flash through the canal, and then start our Caribbean cruising with the San Blas Islands on the Atlantic side. However, as we sailed away from Isla Gamez, we looked over our shoulders saying, "Hmm, maybe we should re-assess the timeline." One beautiful island led to another, and we didn't arrive at Balboa until a month later, finally giving up the islands in order to reprovision.

Islas Gamez, Cevada, Insolita, Cebaco, Roncador, San Jose, Bayoneta, Chapera, and others are impressed in our memories of Panama with their jungles stopping at white sand's edge, waterfalls flowing over dark lava rocks to clear, clean salt water, and very friendly, neat people who did not throw their plastic oil cans into the ocean. Our encounters and adventures included an inland river trip. We hired an experienced local pilot, Wenceslaus, to guide *Sanctuary* over the shallow six-foot river sand bars. We gathered wild limes and grapefruits from the jungle and lounged in freshwater pools at the base of waterfalls. Once back aboard *Sanctuary*, we heard local families chattering and singing, bright as parrots, as they glided by in their dugouts. We anchored near an island teaming with white ibis and storks and met a family who taught us how to cook yucca. At another we went ashore on a hike with three little girls who led us through the jungle to the egg lady. As I started the trade, the egg lady said, "Only five eggs today." As we were talking, I recognized in the background the distinctive "cluck, cluck, cluck" of an egg being laid, so we got six. The moments shared with the Panamanian people we met in the islands sparkled like the waters.

Bromeliad
Bahia Honda, Panama

One anchorage in particular stands out: Bahia Honda. The land surrounding Honda is part of the mainland, but by virtue of geography, the area remains as isolated as an island. A few families maintained small farms at the jungle's edge. They constantly hacked the encroaching vines away with machetes and supplemented their diet of fish, fruit, yucca, and garden vegetables with trips upriver to small pueblos for staples. As we anchored, a man and three young girls paddled a *cayuco* out to *Sanctuary*. Trading ensued, with *Sanctuary* offering soap, coffee, powdered milk, fishhooks and other staples. The man, Domingo, and his three daughters offered limes, coconuts, yucca, tomatoes, cilantro, bananas, *guanábana*, and crayfish. Days drifted by and we "shopped" daily with Domingo. We chatted and visited, enjoying his cheerful patience with our Spanish, and learning a lot about the local plants, produce, and way of life. Finally, after digging into the lockers for a dress for his wife and finding some galvanized nails and marine paint for him, we gave all our trade goods away. Domingo's garden was running out of tomatoes; but his heart was still full. *Sanctuary*'s lockers had run out of staples to trade, yet our hearts were full too.

One final day I shared my watercolor drawings with him. The drawing of Bahia Honda and his *finca* (little farm) that sat on the edge of the bay was all we had left to offer. That day he showered us with flowers. Domingo and his daughter rowed back and forth to *Sanctuary*, trip after trip, with buckets and pails of flowers flowing out of his dugout. Domingo had gathered the flowers from the surrounding jungle and, as he presented them to me, he named them in Spanish:

La Danza del Amor (The Dance of Love), *El Corazón Blanco* (The White Heart), and *La Flor Estrella* (The Star Flower). Some I recognized: hibiscus, begonias, poinsettias, bromeliads, shrimp plant, ginger blossoms, gardenias, lilies, sweet clover, and wild orchids. Others I didn't know. On and on the flowers came, with Domingo identifying each one and detailing the special leaves used for brewing and healing. Jim photographed and I drew as some wilted in the heat. *Sanctuary* was dressed for days with bouquets. Muffin sniffed and inspected each one.

The anchorages in Panama offered up treasures of both the sea and of the spirit. We talked of settling there and found an island for sale for only $20,000. "Oh, we've only just begun cruising. We don't want to stop now and sell *Sanctuary* to buy an island," we said while tucking the tempting thought away for future reference.

A new aspect of Panama was soon revealed as we approached the canal entrance, radioed "Flamenco Control" and prepared *Sanctuary* for transit.

We sailed on to The Balboa Yacht Club, situated almost under the Bridge of the Americas near the entrance to the Panama Canal. Anchoring was not allowed, so we hooked *Sanctuary* to a mooring. After settling in we blew our horn for the club's launch which ferried us to shore. We hired a taxi driver for the day and first checked in with Immigration. Then we were taxied to another office to obtain a cruising permit and made a third stop for an appointment with the "Admeasurer" who later come aboard to measure *Sanctuary* for our transit. As the day wore on, we visited the Port *Capitán*, Traffic Control (who scheduled our transit time) and a bank to withdraw the cash required to pay for it all. Our fees were $393 (which included insurance)—a mere pittance compared to the average transit fee of $29,000 for most ships in 1993. As we dashed from office to office, we discussed the maintenance *Sanctuary* needed and the items necessary to replenish the lockers.

We liked Panama and what we were seeing of Panama City. "It surely seems like we're going through here too fast," I said to Jim. "Let's see if there is a marina somewhere." We asked around and discovered a tiny, well-liked marina in the heart of the canal. The pocket-sized Pedro Miguel Boat Club lay hidden behind one arm of the Pedro Miguel Locks. It served as a temporary home for vessels less than 70 feet and, even though it was almost full out to the mooring balls, we secured a spot. Ah, a perfect place to rest a bit from our travels and repair and restock *Sanctuary* while enjoying the sights and shopping pleasures of Panama and the canal area. After making a date with the club, we prepared for the first leg of our transit.

The canal consists of three sets of locks in about 50 miles of waterway. It was not designed for small boats. The scale is immense. Each lock is 85 feet deep, 1,000 feet long, and 110 feet wide. The locks work 24 hours a day every day. They act as water elevators that raise ships to the level of Gatun Lake, 85 feet above sea level, and later lower them to sea level again on the other side of the Isthmus of Panama.

Forces inside the locks are huge and currents boil like river rapids. Cruising boats were required to be in the locks along with other cruising boats, fishing vessels from around the world, container vessels, and other bulk carriers. Since we were on the Pacific side, *Sanctuary* would travel astern of bigger ships ahead of us. I began worrying as soon as I learned about the requirement. We'd heard accounts of the ship in front starting her huge engine and thus wreaking havoc with the prop wash on the small boats behind.

Sailboats transiting the canal are essentially treated like cargo ships. Therefore, the Admeasurer was sent to measure *Sanctuary*'s length and beam and calculate her interior volume. We were then handed a printed schedule, given a strict time for our transit, and told in no uncertain terms to be ready at 0822 hours on 08/23/1993.

Sailboats had four potential choices for their placement in the lock: center tied, side-tied to other sail boats, nested with other sailboats, or side-tied to a canal tugboat. We requested side-tied to a tug thinking the tug would protect *Sanctuary* from the potentially dangerous canal walls. In any event, sailboats were required to have aboard four lines of at least 125 feet each, and four dedicated line handlers. The captain was required to do nothing but steer the vessel. A Panama Canal Pilot would be put aboard to handle all communications with the lock controllers and give us instructions. It was also advised, however not required, that one crew of the sailboat act entirely as a liaison between the pilot, the captain, and the four line handlers.

Photographs of Sanctuary's transit of the Panama Canal

By 6:00 a.m. on the appointed day our lines were ready. To protect *Sanctuary*'s tender fiberglass hull, four big truck inner tubes, wearing tee shirts so they would not blacken our white paint, hung topsides. Friends from sailboats *Manotic* and *Cindy* were aboard as line handlers, Jim was prepared as captain, and Rudy had been dropped aboard to pilot. I was the liaison. I also had cooked lunch for all aboard. Since we were not allowed to use radios during the transit, I ran frantically and nervously back and forth from bow to stern, worrying all the while, as I relayed the pilot's instructions to the two line handlers on the bow.

Even though we had requested that *Sanctuary* be side-tied to a tug, it didn't happen. As we entered the Miraflores Lock, we nosed in behind cargo vessel *Esmeraldas* and were ordered to center-tie. A canal line handler, high on the walls 80 feet above us, threw down a monkey fist. I didn't dare run to catch it since its weight could have knocked me cold. The first fist rounded our spreader and hit our dodger with a thump. I struggled to untangle it from around the spreader and then ran the fist up to the bow where my cruising friend/line handler and I attached it to the first bow line. The canal employee up on the wall then hauled up the attached fist and untied it from our line and then wrapped our first line around the huge canal bollard.

The monkey fist hauling up process was repeated for each line until *Sanctuary* was centered in the canal—strung out like a spider in the center of a four-legged web. Meanwhile, Jim jockeyed *Sanctuary* to keep her from drifting forward into the stern of the *Esmeraldas* ahead of us or over to the jagged, filthy, dangerous walls of the canal lock before the lines were secure. Once the water started rushing in, and we floated upwards, our line handlers evenly and steadily took up the slack in the four lines to keep *Sanctuary* centered. By the time we exited the Miraflores lock and motored across Miraflores Lake over to the Pedro Miguel Boat Club, I was exhausted from tension. I gradually lost my nervousness about locks though, and by the time we left the canal, Jim and I had served as line handlers for various sailboats seven times!

Our berth at The Pedro Miguel Club was literally only feet from the second set of canal locks. *Sanctuary*'s stern lay toward the dock and her bow was mere feet from the buoy marking the starboard side of the lock entrance. Day and night, 24 hours around the clock, freighters, cruise ships, fishing boats, and cargo vessels passed in parade. Instead of bird calls, we woke to "toot, toot, whistle, whistle, beep, vroom, tweet," the sounds of communication between lock personnel, line handlers, "mule" drivers, and tugboat pilots as they guided the big boats entering the lock.

Between watching the ships slide by, we bought groceries and boat parts. I sewed new cushion covers. Together we repaired the water maker, generator, oil cooler, hatches, and mosquito screens. We washed our teak cap rails. We washed clothing. Between acting as line handlers for friends, we watched movies in the club house, enjoyed restaurants, and, last but not least, shopped. I loved the baskets made by the Wounaan and Embera Indians, the exquisite beads carved from nuts of Taguoa palm, the intricate *chaguira* (tiny bead necklaces made by the Guaymis Indians), and especially the famous reverse appliqué *molas* made by the Kuna Indians. I caught "*Mola* Madness." It was difficult not to blow the budget, because the quality and beauty of the crafts in Panama were outstanding.

Serendipity led us to set up a booth at a crafts fair! After we sold our jewelry store, I kept my bead collection and packed my beads and small tools aboard. I continued to make necklaces and bracelets which I shipped to two small shops in California to sell. I purchased special beads along our route. So, when we were invited to a crafts fair I jumped at the chance to sell some of my creations without having to ship them to California. I worked like crazy making necklaces, bracelets, and earrings. Jim helped on fabrication and created a terrific display. We rode the bus to the one-day fair where we set up with the *mola* makers and basket weavers. We felt a sense of "déjà vu." The jewelry was a hit. Jim was a master salesman (even speaking Spanish), and our sales helped replenish the cruising kitty.

After more than two months at the Boat Club, we dug out the 125 foot lines and enlisted four cruising friends to line handle for us to complete the last two sets of locks that would lead us to the Caribbean and the Atlantic. The remaining paperwork was easily done. Already at the mouth of the Pedro Miguel locks, we motored the short distance into the chamber where *Sanctuary* was instructed to nest next to another sailboat, again in the center, again behind a large cargo vessel. Sailing was not allowed in "The Zone," so we exited the lock to motor long miles through the Culebra Cut and the Rio Charges into Lake Gatun. At the Gatun Locks, *Sanctuary* was stepped down to sea level. She burst out into the mud flats at Cristobal (now part of Colon) and anchored off the Atlantic Panama Canal Yacht Club.

Off the Charts in Kuna Yala

October 1993—December 1993

> "For believe me! The secret of realizing the greatest fruitfulness and the greatest enjoyment of existence is: to live dangerously! Build your cities on the slopes of Vesuvius! Send your ships out into uncharted seas!"
> —Friedrich Nietzsche (1844 - 1900) German philosopher, poet

Friends of ours were robbed at knifepoint in Colon (the town surrounding the Port of Cristóbal). Another cruiser had his pants (and the wallet in them) cut off his legs while he was in town. We skipped the town and didn't tarry at the Panama Canal Yacht Club. We wouldn't taste ice cream again for a long time, so after a final cone each, from a stand near the club, we left Cristóbal. We pounded on a close haul into the Caribbean to Portobello, a Panamanian harbor the Spanish used in the 14th century during their pillage of the "New World." The remains of Sir Francis Drake, an explorer who circumnavigated the globe in 1580, are said to lie deep in the ocean off the harbor entrance.

Centuries-old fortress walls and turrets stand guard over Portobello, their rusty cannons aimed at the narrow entrance to the natural harbor. After anchoring in the shadow of a fort, we went ashore to explore. Climbing across moats, we poked through a powder house, turned on our metal detector, and dug when it beeped. We hoped to discover a stray doubloon. No such luck. We only unearthed cannonball shards. The 14th-century treasure house, which had stored plunder until galleons hauled it over the Atlantic to the Spanish queen, lay across the bay surrounded by the village itself. (I didn't dare take our metal detector there.)

"The Festival of the Black Christ" was in full swing in the village, so we crossed the bay in our launch to see what that meant. Near the steps of the cathedral a man selling souvenirs explained: "Long ago, Spain sent a gift to the Viceroy of Peru. The gift sank in a shipwreck near Portobello and was salvaged by my ancestors."

We peered into the cathedral and discovered the gift—a large, carved wooden statue of a black Christ. The carving looked remarkably like the local people, the first blacks we had seen in Panama. The townspeople are convinced that the relic has special powers, and each October believers flood into Portobello from all over Central America to see the "Black Christ." In fact, the village was swollen to bursting with people camped all around the church steps and in the fields and forts nearby. The unsanitary conditions had already reached horrible, smelly proportions, and flies plagued us during our walk. The souvenir salesman said, "At midnight the Black Christ will be decorated with flowers, raised onto the shoulders of the strong, and a large parade will happen."

After looking at the crumbling old treasure house, empty except for rotting fruit skins, flies, and debris, we decided we'd seen enough. We scurried back to *Sanctuary* and used our binoculars to watch hordes of believers as they walked the winding roads and filed into town. As the sky darkened, the walkers lit candles that formed a snaking chain of tiny flickering lights as more and more people poured into the village. Loud disco music and sounds of a drunken (religious?) uproar echoed off the hillsides out toward *Sanctuary*, who swung safely on her hook. We were glad to view that bit of history from a distance. We departed the next morning while everyone ashore was still asleep and proceeded to our actual destination, the San Blas Islands.

The Archipelago of San Blas, a broken chain of more than 350 islands gracing the fragile neck of Central America, stretches for more than 100 miles along the coast of northeastern Panama. The coral reefs and islands of the San Blas guard a narrow area of the Panamanian coast that is barely accessible even by boat. The islands and strip of jungle at the base of the cordilleras are owned by the Kuna Indians, who claim to be the only Indians in the world still inhabiting their land. Some Kuna live on the mainland of Panama, but most of their 40,000 population dwell on the San Blas islands, land of the Kuna, Kuna Yala.

History of the Kuna is debatable. Some anthropologists declare them descendants of the Maya; others say they migrated and wandered from Southeast Asia more than 6,000 years ago. Whatever the true past, when we arrived we saw that the Kuna maintained a unique and fascinating realm by closely guarding a way of life little changed for centuries.

Technically part of Spanish-speaking Panama, the Kunas are nonetheless independent. They negotiated the Porvenir Treaty with Panama in 1925, gaining a Bill of Rights and control of their government and civil affairs. Some learn Spanish, but most speak only Kuna. Patriarchal, with a *cacique,* or tribal ruler, leading the nation, each populated island also has a chief or *sahile*. Matrilineal, the Kuna trace ancestral descent through the maternal line. Upon marriage, the man moves in with his wife, her mother, any of her sisters, and all their families. The women also control the money.

After carefully negotiating the entrance, we anchored inside the protective reef of Chichime, our first island in the chain. *Sanctuary* floated calmly on turquoise water, our anchor clearly visible 30 feet below. On the surrounding islands of the cay, bamboo huts peeked out beneath towering coconut palms. A clothesline strung between two of the palms advertised a wealth of *mola* waving in the gentle breeze. Bright October sunlight reflected off bone-white sand lining the shore. A *cayuco* full of Kuna women, chattering like parrots and rowing effortlessly, pulled up alongside. In spite of language problems, I understood we were welcome ashore and learned my first words of Kuna: "*Igi mani Mola?*" You want to buy a *mola*? Yes, I did.

We rowed our dinghy ashore. The Chichime inhabitants looked like other Kuna we had met in Panama City where we had also purchased a book that gave us some insight into their history and lives. Very small in stature, almost as small as pygmies, the Kuna are stocky and sturdy with coconut brown skin and sculpted facial features topped by a head of short but thick, straight, jet-black hair. The women, especially, were arrestingly beautiful with aristocratic features: wide eyes, aquiline noses, and high cheekbones. An ear-grazing haircut is adopted at a puberty ceremony and maintained

Kuna woman chopping coconuts, San Blas

for life.

Females adopt traditional dress at the puberty ceremony along with the haircut. A red scarf, with contrasting yellow patterns, is loosely worn over the short black hair. Big earrings, nose rings, necklaces and breastplates of 22-karat gold sparkle in the sun. A black line tattoo stripes the nose. Black stars or half moons mark the high cheekbones. Bright red circles, made of a paste from a native plant, paint the cheeks as well and complete the facial adornment. Wrist to elbow, ankle to calf jewelry called *winis* replaces ancient arm and leg tattoos. The orange, black, red, or yellow beads are painstakingly counted, then woven in geometric patterns and wrapped tightly to the body. As these are applied at puberty to be worn for life, a weight gain is easy to spot: fat hangs over the beads in telltale fashion. Skirt lengths of brightly printed cotton fabric are wrapped once around the body and tucked at the waist. The overall effect of the color and pattern of the traditional female dress is spectacular. The men, wearing plain trousers or shorts and shirts, look positively dull by comparison.

The most striking article of clothing worn by the women is the *mola*. Over 100 years ago, missionaries to the islands badgered naked and tattooed Kunas into wearing "proper clothing." The Kuna women complied but replicated the complex geometric tattoo patterns in stitchery. The designs evolved and copies of animals, birds, words, even magazine ads, adorn the blouses or *mola* made today. Two panels, one for the front and the other for the back, are created using three to four layers of cotton. The intricately cut material is hand sewn with almost invisible stitches, by a method called "reverse appliqué." Puffy sleeves added to the panels complete the blouse. A market for this handiwork developed, and now sale of *mola* is second only to the sale of copra as a cash crop for the Kuna.

Ashore at Chichime we looked at the *mola* for sale. The women, quiet and solemn while discussing the price of a chosen *mola*, smiled and giggled once the deal was done. The shrewd bargainers were clearly elated at having skunked the *merki*, the American lady. I had cheerfully paid only $10 for a well-sewn *mola* with a complex eagle, so we were all satisfied. Jim and I visited with the families at Chichime for several days. Wanting a change of pace, and remembering that there were more than 350 islands in the chain, we decided to move to a new anchorage. With the sun high in the sky so that we could see the reef clearly, we negotiated the pass and headed in search of an uninhabited island.

There were no houses, only coconut palms, on nearby Gunboat Island. We enjoyed the swimming, fishing, and reef diving, but did not take any coconuts; all the trees were private property. Copra trade with Colombia was the Kuna's main source of income. If we wanted a coconut we paid for it (about 10 cents). All the land belonged to all the Kuna. There was no division of "have" and "have-not" among them. They lived in thatched bamboo huts built on the sand, slept in hammocks, and cooked on open fires. Most of the islands had no fresh water. The Kuna, therefore, farmed a narrow strip of the adjacent mainland jungle.

We grew accustomed to the daily pattern of Kuna life. At daybreak the procession began as Kuna after Kuna rowed or sailed a *cayuco* to the mainland to cultivate yucca, rice, plantain, corn, or other crops. Some men paddled among the islands to fish or gather coconuts. The women and children worked as well by washing the laundry in a pure mainland river or fetching fresh water. Returning from the mainland around noon, the women would complete chores and then sit in hammocks sewing on *mola* with the children playing nearby. At mid-afternoon the men streamed homeward in their *cayucos* for rest or family matters. The rhythms of Kuna life were ancient. We were suspended in time.

Sailing to a new anchorage, *Sanctuary* passed islands crossable in ten paces while others accommodated a teaming press of humanity. Etiquette required obtaining permission to go ashore, and on larger islands this included a preliminary visit to the *sahile*. He was usually found lounging in the congress, a centrally located thatched meeting house. Accompanied by a Spanish-speaking islander as interpreter, we chatted and presented the *sahile* in question with a small knife as a gift. The *sahile* invariably conferred blessings to tour the island, visit with the people, take photos, and buy *mola*. Even though we had permission, taking photographs was a tricky business. Some Kuna were extremely shy and believed we were "taking their souls." Others, worldlier, demanded money. It was best to ask each time we raised the camera.

Progressing eastward from Cayos Chichime, our log comments include: *"Scary reef," "High anxiety looking for reef,"* and *"Many uncharted coral heads and reefs."* Clear visibility was imperative for reef spotting, and we did not move *Sanctuary* unless the sun shone brightly with no possibility of rain. As we tiptoed through the maze of islands, the day came when we sailed off DMA Chart #26042, the last available chart of the area. Armed thereafter with only simple sketch charts, we stretched our navigational ability and pressed deeper into the Kuna world. Foamy breakers outlined most of the reefs. Thin, upright bamboo poles marked a few channels. The Kuna had placed the poles for their own use or to aid the Colombian boats plying the waters trading for copra and bringing supplies. Sometimes we hovered en route tacking and circling until we judged the water ahead coral-free and deep enough. Always we maintained a sharp lookout. Many times I stood high on the stanchions of the bow pulpit hanging onto the forestay to get a better view of the water ahead. Each time we anchored, we sighed with relief.

Yet as we prepared to leave our last anchorage at Isla Pinos, or Dupuk as the Kuna call it, we felt that the rewards were well worth the challenges. We had met many Kuna including Embierto from Tigre, who took us to a special parade and celebration. On Ciedras was Diego, a rare male *mola* maker, with the best *mola* of all. Long out of money, we traded him our ship's kerosene lantern for a special *mola*. The *mola* depicted the birth of the Kuna nation. Three Indians, with stars on their foreheads, descended from the hand of God in the heavens as he lowered them to earth in a basket. With Clemencio, the jeweler, who made nose rings, earrings, and breastplates worn proudly by the women, we traded some of Jim's old tools for some gold eagle earrings. There was Florina, wife of the school teacher on Pinos, who talked with me about the history of the Kuna. We gave our remaining school supplies to her husband.

As I write this I see their faces, and others, and am flooded with memories of these unusual people. At Pinos, while waiting for satisfactory weather to cross to Cartagena, Colombia, we helped repair a leaking *cayuco*. The repair was successful, and the owner, Enrique, rowed out to *Sanctuary* with a gift of limes as thanks. We needed no thanks, for the pleasure had been ours. As we raised anchor with one last reef to carefully negotiate, Brigillio on shore blew into a conch shell in farewell. We turned off the engine to begin sailing, and I heard the conch echo ring across the world off the charts—the world of Kuna Yala.

A City, Some Islands, Tikal and Malaria

December 1993—May 1994

"Mosquitoes remind us that we are not as high up on the food chain as we think."

—Tom Wilson, American actor

When the winds shifted west, we set off for Cartagena, Colombia, 30 sailing hours away from Isla Pinos, San Blas. We did not have a chart for the first leg—there weren't any. Before leaving I talked with a copra boat captain who traveled regularly between Colombia and San Blas and compiled another sketch chart. For two tense hours, using only a sketch chart, we tiptoed through the shallows surrounding the island looking out for reefs and dodging them. Finally, *Sanctuary* crawled 12 miles off shore into deeper waters, and we breathed easier, settling down to enjoy the passage and prepare for a new country. Limes, coconuts, bananas and potatoes were the only fresh foods left aboard, so we really looked forward to a produce market. After arriving in Cartagena, we walked into a fancy grocery store and felt we had emerged from a time machine. The sight of rows and rows of fresh vegetables had me gibbering.

Thanks to the American news media and their "drug wars" talk, we were a little leery of stopping in Colombia. However, Cartagena, except for the automobile traffic, was almost sedate. As we walked around the town, we felt far more in danger of death by speeding taxi than by any other means. The well-preserved old town sat inside the walls of yet another Spanish fort while the newer part, at Boca Grande, was a high-rise haven. Salesmen hawking emeralds accosted us on every corner trying to hijack us into jewelry stores to look at gemstones. They didn't convince us to buy. Jim, a gemologist, knew the prices were high and the quality low.

Cartagena seemed safe enough even though the Manager of Club Nautico did warn us and other cruisers that we risked "losing" items off the boat itself. We heeded his warning and removed most everything of value from *Sanctuary*'s deck and locked all the hatches, ports, companionway, and deck lockers every time we went ashore. At night we raised our outboard and dinghy out of the water and locked them. Things we couldn't take below decks, we lashed to the boat with a steel cable. All the daily locking and unlocking was new to us and exasperated us and the other cruisers who followed similar routines.

One morning we woke to hear excited chatter over the VHF radio net: "What did you lose?" "Oh, no! All your fenders!" "What? You lost your dinghy! Didn't you lock it?" We quickly looked out to see if everything on *Sanctuary*'s deck was still in place. The outboard and dinghy were both okay. Suddenly, remembering I had forgotten to bring our fenders below, I glanced at the fender lines which were still there. The fender bag, however, looked flat and funny. I leaned over the stern rail for a better look and discovered the fenders were all missing. Their cut lines waved in the breeze. Another boater, who had spent the night in his cockpit hoping to catch the water-borne thief in the act, had lost gear as well. The boater had slept through the entire episode. True stealth in action!

Sketch of a Diego Mola

Most of the 30-plus cruising crews we met in Cartagena were westbound heading toward the San Blas Islands and the Panama Canal. We and the other two sailing crews who had just arrived from the islands, gave a "*Mola* Show and Tell." We had taken lots of photos and promised to send copies back to the islanders who had not been afraid of the camera. After the pictures were developed, we made up a few small albums, wrote down the names and island addresses of the recipients, and gave the albums to some cruisers headed to the San Blas Islands and the Kunas. We included some flip-flops, powdered milk, and other things we knew they needed. Years later, news floated back to us via the cruising grapevine. The islanders we'd photographed had received their pictures, remembered *Sanctuary*, and proudly showed off the pictures to those who sailed in after us.

Also in Cartagena, I was treated for an ear infection, and Jim endured a root canal. So, with the doctor bills and the cost of buying replacement fenders, we racked up a lot of expenses in just over two weeks. We had also gotten used to lettuce—a sure sign that it was time to pull the hook and get moving. "Northers," winds that sweep the Caribbean from the Gulf of Mexico and blow continuously throughout the winter, were about to start. We needed to make for Honduras before they began. We looked over the charts, chose our route, checked our food, gear, deck, and mast fittings and looked for a weather window. As it turned out, we picked a good five days to make the leap.

Because of land configurations, the first 24 hours out of Cartagena were lumpy with confused seas. The beam reach we settled into was lively, and we anchored at Isla Guanaja, Bay Islands, Honduras, about five days later. The routine of that passage was typical: Jim kept watch daily from 0700-1300 while I made and served breakfast, cleaned up, rested a little, then in a few hours made lunch and washed dishes again. Jim slept while I was on watch from 1300-1700 when we switched again. At 1700 Jim watched for two hours while I checked into the Pacific Maritime net, reported our position, listened to weather reports, cooked dinner, then cleaned up again. After dinner, from 1900 to 2200, I was on watch. Usually Jim wasn't sleepy, so we both relaxed in the cockpit in a casual double watch as night fell.

We'd discuss the weather, look over the charts, and pinpoint any possible hazards or shipping lanes along our route. Every time we changed watches we briefed each other about any wind shifts, traffic we had encountered, or traffic still in the vicinity. Every 12-15 minutes (more often if in the midst of traffic) the person on watch scanned the horizon 360°. In theory, when under sail, *Sanctuary* had the right of way in the majority of situations with motor vessels. In spite of the rules of the road, we operated under the assumption that freighters and large motor craft did not see *Sanctuary* at day or her lights at night. The "might makes right" assumption saved us numerous times in 10 years at sea.

As night fell we usually shortened sail since the winds typically picked up as the sun went down and the temperature dropped. We followed a safety rule that no sail changes requiring deck work were done solo, so shortening sail in the evening helped prevent "Chinese Fire Drills" in the middle of the off-watch person's sleep. With Jim set for 2200-0200, I slept until he woke me at 0200. I loved the 0200-0700 watch which included sunrise, my favorite time of the day at sea. This also gave Jim five hours of sleep in a stretch, and he usually slept soundly after hours in the cockpit. We'd start the routine over for the next day at sea.

Our watches were not the typical "Four On, Four Off" used by most sailboats with a two-person crew. However, the rhythm we set up worked for us with Jim taking longer watches during the day. He struggled with seasickness and erratic sleep patterns due to the side effects of Parkinson's medications. Sitting in the cockpit with the horizon visible helped waylay seasickness. His balance was so affected by the boat motion that he could not cook underway, so I did all of the cooking and cleaning during passages. However, Jim did enjoy cooking and had done all of the cooking in our household on land. Jim was the chef when we were in port.

Watches were over for awhile after we reached Honduras. The anchor was down and set by 10:30 a.m. the day we arrived, so we swam in the clean, clear waters off Isla Guanaja, showering afterward in the cockpit using our sun shower. The sun shower, a sturdy plastic bag (black on one side) with a shower nozzle attached, held two and a half gallons of water. We laid it on the foredeck to heat up in the sun. When the water was hot, we hung the contraption from the boom which extended over the cockpit well. Since we had spray cloths port and starboard around the stern, we could sit in the cockpit well and shower in privacy. We had a shower in the head, but it was awkward and the teak had to be dried each time we used it. The fiberglass cockpit was much easier to clean than the head, so I really preferred our "outdoor" shower.

During the afternoon we relaxed on board. Now that we were in port, and not rocking and rolling, Jim cooked a dinner of chicken breasts with potatoes, carrots, green tomatoes, and rice. It was great to have a meal again without having to brace and skidproof ourselves and our dishes to keep everything from sliding. Later I checked into the Maritime Net, gave our anchorage position, and we both fell into the "V" berth early.

The San Blas Islands had required a lot of energy. Both navigating without charts and the daily attention from the Kunas had been stressful. Life in Cartagena had been packed with socializing, medical work, and lots of city activities. In Guanaja we claimed a nice, clean anchorage to ourselves for the first time since the west coast of Panama. Even though we saw a small settlement on the island, we didn't go ashore to visit tiny Savannah Bight until three days later. The village didn't offer much in the way of supplies. Barbecue chicken was for sale, but there was no ice cream—my yardstick for a "real" town.

A ham net participant informed us that our mail was in French Harbor. We really needed to check into Honduras properly, so we took one step toward check-in and the mail. We moved *Sanctuary*, anchored off Guanaja settlement, and went ashore to complete our paperwork with the Harbor Master. After a few more stepping-stone anchorages, we arrived in Old French Harbor, Roatan Island, before Christmas, 1993.

We tied up at the smallest marina we had yet visited, only six slips. Our mail included a holiday care package with fudge from Jim's mom. After decorating our mast with lights, we shared Christmas dinner with old friends Ken and Mary Jones on sailing vessel *Vision II*. Mary cooked a turkey, we provided pie and trimmings, and the four of us celebrated and stuffed ourselves with good food just as we would have at home.

On New Year's Day we ate traditional Southern black-eyed peas and ham hocks. We were thankful to be in one piece, since for New Year's Eve the locals on shore around us randomly shot off rifles, handguns, and automatic weapons (Uzis or AK-47s) most of the night. I guess it was fun for them. Jim and I spent a sleepless evening and night cowering in the v-berth, hoping no stray bullet would find us or *Sanctuary*. Happy New Year 1994—Whew!

Daily rain and the seawater dirty with sewage and trash curtailed snorkeling or swimming, so we washed the decks, filled our water tanks, then read and bided our time waiting for a weather window to proceed. We tiptoed toward Guatemala, stopping at Islas Barbaretta, Utilla, and Puerto Cortes. Anchorages were generally uncomfortable since the northers had started blowing, and even though we were protected, swells rolled in night and day. We finally made it to Ox Tongue Bight, Guatemala, by January 17th, where we peacefully anchored in calm waters off the headland. We caught two sierras along the way. Ah, how nice to have fresh fish to cook for dinner and anchorages clean enough for swimming.

After a bit of a rest at Ox Tongue, we proceeded to Port Livingston, set on Guatemala's scant 50-mile eastern seaboard and tucked tidily between Belize and Honduras. Port Livingston marked the mouth of the Rio Dulce. A meandering river, Rio Dulce flowed down from high mountains through Lago Izabal into El Golfete where it spilled at last into the Caribbean Sea. Our entry fee to this freshwater road through the Guatemalan jungle was a bump across the bar at the river mouth. The bar had a maximum depth of barely six feet and slim tides. *Sanctuary* had a draft of six feet: any deeper and we would have to be heeled drastically and towed over sideways. After anxiously awaiting the small rising tide, we picked our time and plowed through the soft mud bottom from the sea to the river. We checked into Guatemala to the tune of $60 and a chorus sung by five officials who all trooped aboard: Port Captain, Customs, Immigration, Medical, and Police.

After negotiating the tricky river bar and enduring the legalities, we judged the trials worth it as we motored upriver and rounded its first bend. The sight of 300-foot cliffs dripping with jungle vines, bromeliads, orchids, and other flowers left us awestruck. Flocks of cormorants, snowy egrets, blue herons, and parrots disturbed by our intrusion scattered and flew before us through the river canyon. Mayan Indian fishermen paddled their *cayucos* silently along the banks. Their small canoes were piled with yucca, firewood, or animals whose weight left scant inches of freeboard. Trails of smoke drifted up, pinpointing palm huts otherwise camouflaged by the encroaching jungle. The river twisted and turned. We sensed that Mayan life had flowed along its course in the same way for centuries.

Then—whoosh! Up on our stern surfed a powerful 25-horsepower driven *panga*. It sped around us, rocking the illusion and *Sanctuary* with its wake. Well, yes, the Maya were in Guatemala, and so was the 20th century. It proved true throughout our three-month stay in the tiny, fascinating country. Many of the Maya or Indian population still dressed, farmed, and lived as they had for centuries. Yet, other Maya or Indians we encountered in the large cities appeared at home there as well.

Our introduction to Guatemala continued as we anchored in the lower river bay of El Golfete. Here, amongst water lilies and water hyacinths, we sat on *Sanctuary*'s deck at jungle edge watching toucans eating orange flowers from the trees. Later, while riding in our dinghy, we watched shy manatees surface and dive. I gulped when I spotted a six-foot boa constrictor sunning calmly on a log. Jim captured a photo of the huge snake. He would have taken more photos, but my excited comments, "Oh, Jim, don't get too close! No! Look out!" caused the boa to slither away.

Occasionally farms dotted the river shore. Otherwise, we passed rich, verdant jungle. Hours drifted away as we sat in the cockpit watching birds and listening to their calls. We lollygagged until we ran out of fresh food. The next section of the river contained a road, a bridge, and a town. Instead of Mayas lost in time, that part of the lake was ringed with the grand vacation homes of Ladino Guatemalans complete with power boats, jet skis, swimming pools, satellite dishes and more. We changed our money to *quetzals* (named after the shiny, shy, long-tailed bird that is now endangered), bought some veggies, and proceeded up the lake. After leaving town we once again traveled by scarcely populated shores.

We went ashore to Casa Guatemala, an orphanage on the shores of the lake. The privately owned orphanage was staffed mostly by volunteers and depended totally on donations. They raised their own food on their nicely maintained farm. We met the staff and some of the children, and we took a tour. We returned later to contribute everything we could spare from *Sanctuary* including fabric, powdered milk, medicines, and canned goods.

We proceeded to the shores of *Finca Paraiso* (Paradise Farm) nestled at the base of the jungle on the northwestern edge of the lake. Ashore the next day at 8:00 a.m., we paid a five-*quetzal* entry fee (about 85 cents) to Señora Blanco, got directions, and started walking. We passed chickens, roosters, pigs, dogs, cattle, and horses all intermingled with fields of runner beans, corn, and orange groves. We stopped for breaks along the way, watching birds and spotting finches, hummingbirds, parrots, turkey vultures, egrets, herons, and trogons. We could hardly continue our walk for stopping to look at the birds and the butterflies, including blue morphos, such as we had seen in Costa Rica. The road followed a shallow meandering river and gradually gave way to a footpath. Then, as the footpath gave way to a single-file trail through the encroaching jungle, we encountered Señor Santiago, a small man barely five feet tall, dressed in long trousers tucked into calf-high waders, a long-sleeved shirt, and a straw hat. As he swept the narrow path with a plaited twig broom, he identified the plants, flowers, and birds and offered to lead us to the waterfall.

Even though the path was easy to follow, Señor Santiago came with us toting his broom, a flour sack, and a machete. Upward we climbed, and as the jungle thickened, the path changed to a root stairway. We heard a hissing, took a few steps down, and discovered the cause. A sulfur stream flowed over a cliff into a natural river pool. As the steaming sulfur hit the cold pool of water, it hissed and gurgled. Ferns, brackens, bromeliads, orchids, philodendrons, and vines cascaded from tall jungle trees. We got into the cool pool, which was just big enough to swim a few laps, and then, screwing up our courage, stood under the hot sulfur water. It was indeed paradise.

We enjoyed our jungle hot tub, then got dressed and followed Santiago along the river bed higher up the mountain and deeper into the jungle until the strong noon sunlight barely penetrated the gorge. At the mouth of the cold waters we swam in another pool—dark, secret, deep in the cliff. Here we listened and peered through the jungle shadows as bats squealed and flew out of the cave where the river was born.

We loved *paraíso* so much we returned again and again. Lago Izabal offered even more to explore. There was a small Mayan town near an abandoned nickel mine, more rivers, more birds and monkeys, and always the Mayas to see in their *cayucos* fishing with throw-nets as they had for centuries. On the other side of the lake, we filled our tanks with fresh spring water. At that spring we met Señor Gomez and his two sons, who later drove us to the Mayan ruins at Quiriquá near the lake shores. Preserved sandstone stele there told tales about Cauac Sky, Scroll Sky, Imix Dog, and the Black Bat Woman. I drew watercolors of the ruins and noticed that the Gomez children had faces like the ones on the 2,000 year old temples.

Our appetite whetted for inland travel, we hired the pilot of a little four-seated "Moonie" to fly us to Tikal, site of extensive Mayan construction and civilization. We stayed two nights at the "Jungle Lodge" nestled in the middle of the park. For two days we climbed and traipsed around some of the 40 or so uncovered and excavated temples, palaces, monuments, and stele.

Tikal's population was estimated to be 55,000 during its heyday some 2,500 years ago. The ruins cover an area of 16 square kilometers. The sheer size of any one monument overwhelmed us. Because of his waning strength and bad Parkinson's disease balance, Jim couldn't climb many of them. I struggled almost to the top of one temple Jim wanted to photograph. I watched him far below me backing farther, farther, and farther away trying to get the entire temple in the viewfinder of his camera. The developed photo pictured a tiny red dot barely visible against a massive gray structure. I was the dot, in red shorts, about 200 steps and 200 feet up in the clouds. No one knows why the civilization died. After I climbed 10 temples in two days, I decided they must have plain tuckered out!

Wild animals roamed Tikal fearlessly. We saw (closely): silver fox, oscillated turkeys, howler monkeys, spider monkeys, keel-billed toucans, parrots, trogons, black penelopinas, hummingbirds, warblers, hawks, woodpeckers, egrets, and herons. I regretted not wearing long pants, and more insect repellent, since after tramping around the ruins I also saw, too closely, hundreds of bugs and mosquitoes. I counted 42 mosquito bites on my right leg alone.

One afternoon about 10 days after we flew back to the Rio and *Sanctuary*, I returned from a walk so tired I could barely climb over the life lines to get onto the boat. I ached all over. The next day I suffered from a terrible headache. My joints and glands were swollen, my lower stomach hurt, even my eyeballs hurt. I alternated between chills and fever and lost my balance control. We thought I had a flu or intestinal infection. Nothing helped. My symptoms didn't fit anything we read in the medical books aboard *Sanctuary*. After six days I was so weak we knew we needed expert advice and soon. We were miles from a city, and the nearest doctor was a long, dusty, bumpy two hour bus ride away.

I was too weak to talk above a whisper, so Jim put out a call for help on the morning cruisers' radio net. A woman's voice with an English lilt broke into his transmission. She identified herself as an M.D. from England, who was volunteering for a year at the orphanage we coincidentally had visited when we first entered the lake. She thought I had malaria and told Jim to bring me to the orphanage immediately for an exam. Since there were no roads from where we were to the orphanage, we needed to cross the lake and fast. Jim hired a *panga* with driver. I could barely crawl so the driver and Jim rolled me over *Sanctuary*'s cap rail into the small, fast boat. The doctor determined I did have malaria. After about 10 days of taking the chloroquine pills she gave me, I felt much better (none too soon for my nurse, Jim).

The three-week bout with the parasite left me minus 15 pounds, weak, and shaky. Malaria had attacked our time in Guatemala as well, leaving us with the opportunity to visit only Antigua. I recovered enough for a little exploring, so we bussed inland and checked into a lovely B & B inn. The old city of Antigua, built in the mid-1500s, was preparing for Easter, and Indians poured into town from the highlands. They came to celebrate and to sell their wares: *huipiles* (hand woven embroidered blouses) blankets, cloth, and baskets. The town swirled with a feast of color, smells, music, and foods. We wandered looking, sampling, and shopping.

We enjoyed a classical guitar concert and toured museums and ruins. The most dramatic event of *Semana Santa* (Easter Week or Holy Week) was the procession of the Christ statue over the intricate flower carpets, or *alfambras*. The day before the procession, the families of Antigua accumulated fresh flowers by the hundreds. The next day they rose at dawn to interweave onto the cobblestone streets intricate carpet patterns made of sawdust and flowers. The event began around noon. We arrived early and wandered through the streets watching as the carpets were created. We were careful not to disturb or step on the flowers. Fascinated, we scratched our heads when we noticed that the hordes of children and dogs running around didn't disturb anything either.

Citizens of Antigua making alfambras

Mere minutes after the flower carpets were finished, the local believers appeared dressed in elaborate purple robes that looked like Klu Klux Klan outfits. Led by a priest, the robed believers marched forward bearing an enormous platform with a statue of Christ. The platform, so large it took more than 80 men to carry it, was slowly paraded over the carpets and through the city. The thousands of perfectly placed flowers were trampled and scattered while more purple robed acolytes lined the route swinging burners that blanketed the scene in incense and smoke. A phalanx of more believers, a statue of the Virgin Mary (carried by women) a contingent of Roman soldiers, a group of thieves bearing crosses, and a brass band paraded after the Christ statue. Crowds of locals brought up the rear, gathering up what little remained of the flowers. We gave up around 4:00 p.m. and by 7:00 p.m. retired to a restaurant for dinner. As we sat eating, we looked out the window. There in the dark, carrying lights and lanterns, the purple-robed believers still marched the flower-strewn streets.

We loved Guatemala. Many cruisers loved it so that they lingered in the "Sweet River" for a year or more. I was weak after my fight with malaria and longing for home, so we exited after three months waving goodbye to those who might never leave. *Sanctuary* bumped back across the bar at Port Livingston and by April turned north for Belize to weave through some of the outer barrier reefs. Shifty weather made most of the anchorages untenable.

México—ah, México was next. We enjoyed it on the west coast and looked forward to it on the east. Ascension Bay protected us from northern winds, and in calm, secluded waters we swam with no worries about safety. While we sat waiting for a wind shift, I used our ham radio to patch a call through to my mother on her 83rd birthday. She sounded very chipper and happy to talk to us but didn't quite understand the limits of the ham radio and had difficulty remembering to say "over" after she completed each part of the conversation. We both missed our families very much, and I was especially looking forward to visiting Mother in Houston. So as soon as weather allowed, we proceeded to Isla Mujeres. Mujeres, an island near the Yucatan peninsula, was our last stepping stone before crossing the Gulf of Mexico to Galveston Bay.

We swam and snorkeled in the island's lovely clear bay. The nice markets in town, and restaurants with great tacos and roasted chickens, provided a perfect interlude and spot to prepare for our passage across the gulf. Once again we would part from friends. Boats anchored at Mujeres would scatter with the wind: some to Cuba, others to Trinidad, many to the Florida Keys, and one or two boats, like *Sanctuary*, would make for Texas. Hurricane season was fast upon us, and we sailors in that pot of water all looked for a safe hidey-hole. Most of us were taking cruising a season at a time, tentatively making plans, and hoping to see each other again somewhere in a pleasant anchorage.

April 1994 marked exactly three years since Jim and I had started our voyage. We felt the tug of home. We'd sailed more than 10,000 miles, visited 10 countries including the United States, migrated from the

Pacific to the Atlantic, touched numerous islands, and met numerous people including many cruisers. We'd learned to converse in Spanish, compiled a dictionary in Kuna, tasted a volume of new food, spent a purse full on crafts, tested and improved our sailing skills, and seen all types of wildlife and natural delights. We'd gained new insights into our abilities to cope with ever-changing environments including those reflecting glittering wealth or glaring filth and poverty. We'd also pushed Jim's Parkinson's-afflicted body to the limit. I was worn down by my bout with malaria. We needed and wanted a break.

We wanted a dose of the "old used to be": old friends, family, familiar faces, and familiar places. I wanted clean restrooms, big bookstores, fresh lettuce, good mail service, and the ability to take long, hot showers. So, we would head to Galveston Bay and the Houston area where we planned to repair and refit *Sanctuary* and plan the next leg of our journey.

Back in the United States

May 1994—March 1995

"The best laid plans of mice and men oft go awry."
— Robert Burns

I plotted our route: 621 nautical miles from Isla Mujeres to Galveston Bay. With southeast winds and a favorable current we estimated a five-day passage, so we bought one last roasted chicken from our favorite Mujeres restaurant and set off early on April 26, 1994, for the crossing. About 12 hours out of the harbor, our bilge pump broke. Jim rigged up a spare we had aboard and put it on, never minding the heel of the boat. The old motor was clogged with oil and became another repair item added to the "While We Are in Texas" list.

On our second day out, a cattle egret landed on the foredeck and hunkered near the starboard bow, with feathers ruffled in the wind. We were 288 miles from land at that point and wondered if the egret was lost. A house martin also stayed aboard for an hour or two and then suddenly flew away. Our watches were easy with no traffic and, with steady winds at about 15-20 knots, no sail changes were needed. Jim was on watch from 6:00 to 9:00 p.m., I managed 9:00 p.m. to midnight, Jim midnight to 3:00 a.m., and I enjoyed my favorite sunrise watch from 3:00 a.m. until Jim got up at 6:00 a.m. The watches began getting chilly, and we dug our sweatpants and sweatshirts out of the deep clothes locker and ploughed around for our foul weather gear. We hadn't used either since, um, let's see, the coast of California?

Jim slept soundly on his off watches on the passage maybe because we had calm winds and were sailing downwind. Three years into our voyage, we had become used to passages. In the easy sailing, we had time together on deck to speculate, and we talked a lot about "What is next for us?" Should we venture up the east coast and across the Atlantic, or sail down to the Caribbean, Venezuela, and around South America?

Then what? How much longer would we be able to keep cruising? The symptoms of PD were marching steadily, if slowly, onward. Jim tired very easily simply from the effort it took to stay in balance and upright. On many shore excursions, I left him sitting and resting while I walked around town shopping for necessities. His grip was not dependable, due mostly to moments when his arm froze or his fingers moved slowly. How would the long list of PD woes affect both of us? Should we, or could we, keep heading around the world? We tossed ideas around and made lists for the work we would do on *Sanctuary* while in Texas then drifted off into silence as we watched the clouds and stared down into the hypnotic waters more than 1,900 fathoms deep.

"Edgar" the cattle egret made himself at home. We put out water and flying fish remnants for him, but didn't know what else to do. He'd become somewhat used to us and jumped down into the galley. As he walked elegantly around below decks, our cat Muffin looked at him stonily. I needed to use the galley and herded him out, wings flapping. He ensconced himself in the cockpit squawking if we sat too close to him. We ran out of flying fish and hadn't caught anything larger. What, if anything else, could we feed him? We needed to make sail changes and couldn't use the winches with him underfoot in the cockpit, so Edgar moved out to the side deck, tucked his long neck under, and hunkered into a tight, low profile.

Edgar - the cattle egret who stayed aboard across the Gulf of Mexico.

As we sailed closer to Texas, oil rigs rose from the mist like creatures from an alien planet. In four days we'd passed only one freighter and a lonely-looking sailboat heading south. Neither answered my radio call. The traffic and oil wells increased, however, and as we dodged the wells and ships we decided to sail just outside the designated "Safety Fairway." *Sanctuary* would be safer out of the big boys' lanes. It turned foggy, cold, and gray. Underneath overcast skies, rain pelted the oily- looking gulf waters. As I peered out toward the bow in the rain and fog at dawn, I noticed a lump on the side deck. I went forward and saw poor Edgar, stiff and unmoving. Dead. We theorized that the cold had been too much for him. Also, he essentially ate insects, not the fish we had provided, and there weren't any aboard. We'd tried cat food, coconut, hamburger, bread, and vegetable scraps—all to no avail. Survival of the fittest, we supposed.

A scant 15 miles out from the ship channel, a norther hit hard, bringing up lumpy, choppy seas in its 30-knot headwinds. We gave up bashing and short tacking and anchored in the deep water anchorage outside the main harbor. Deciding to wait for better light and hoping the winds would die down as well, we tucked *Sanctuary* as close as we dared in the lee of a huge freighter and sat rocking and rolling in the strong winds, taking turns on anchor watch. The next morning the winds weakened a bit. Our anchor was mired in the mud and came up heavily laden with silt and debris. In order to sail into Galveston on the flood tide and before the channel clogged up with big boat traffic, I skipped the time-consuming process of cleaning the anchor and the foredeck.

At the customs dock, we easily checked back into the United States with just a phone call and then motored over to the Galveston Yacht Basin. As we set about putting the boat to bed, snubbing up the dock lines, putting the sail covers on the sails, and washing the salt water off the rigging, a family walked up the dock toward their boat. *Sanctuary*'s anchor was still clogged with mud and the staysail sat on the foredeck lumped in a hastily tied bundle amongst the silt and debris. As the family stopped by our bow to greet us, the boy said, "Look Mom, they've been somewhere!"

Yes, we had, and we were glad to be home. My mother, and most of the rest of my family, lived within about a 100-mile radius of Galveston and Houston. The comfort of their welcome and love was enormous. My sister and brother-in-law sold us their old '77 Plymouth station wagon so we'd have some transportation. As we clunked around the Houston area, driving to and fro visiting and shopping, we noticed a lot of impoverished people who appeared to live or camp under the freeways. At traffic lights near the underpasses, beggars approached the stopped cars asking for money. If the windows didn't need cleaning, the beggars splashed dirty water on the windshields and then demanded a dollar to wash it off. We laughed since not one homeless person ever approached our rattletrap car. We looked as scruffy as they did.

Back ashore, it was time to paint *Sanctuary*'s bottom again! We found a boat yard, hauled out, and after the bottom job, moved over to a marina on the west shore of Galveston Bay. Here, we would be closer to Houston where we planned to sell jewelry at art shows to replenish our depleted cruising kitty. Shortly after a telephone was installed, my mother called. Morris, her new husband of just three short years, had suffered a severe stroke at age 85. A few days later we all realized that the stroke had severely debilitated him. My 83-year-old mother could not care for him alone, so we sadly helped Morris move into a full-care facility. It was a heart breaking time, and all we could really offer my mother was a shoulder to lean on.

Meanwhile, back on *Sanctuary*, Muffin, our dear 19-year-old cat, was not well either. At 133 in cat years, Muffin must have lived her entire nine lives because the vet said she would not recover from her varied ailments. We didn't want her to continue to suffer, so the vet put her to sleep.

Sanctuary was not the same without her. Muffin slept a lot in her elder years aboard the boat; however, she always ventured into the cockpit when we anchored in order to look around her new "home." She appreciated Jim's fishing talents, and the fresh fish he caught probably kept her alive some extra years. Jim gave her to me before we were married, and one of her nicknames was "The Fur Baby." Long after she was gone, we'd think we saw her curled up in her favorite spot on top of a basket on the port side, or we'd expect her to wake us up if we overslept. We imagined the fur baby telling wild cruising stores in cat heaven.

In August we closed up *Sanctuary* and flew to Oakland to visit Jim's mother, Lee, his step-father, Don, and his son, Jim, Jr. We squeezed in visits with the rest of Jim's family and our California friends. Then Jim, Lee, Don, and I piled into Lee's car and drove from California to Missouri and Arkansas for more good food and good times with more of Jim's kin. After a whirlwind month, we were back aboard the comfort of *Sanctuary*.

The comfort lasted only a few days then bad news struck again. My mother, still reeling from Morris's stroke and his move to a full-time care facility, had developed physical problems and needed knee replacement surgery. Jim and I checked mother into the hospital and, in order to be nearby, moved into her empty apartment anticipating a two-week stay. One thing led to another, and Mother was hospitalized for a month until some scary after-surgery complications were tracked down and tamed. My sister and I took shifts while Jim fed us and ferried us back and forth to the hospital. Finally, Mother was able leave the hospital, and Jim and I brought her hobbling back to her apartment. After she began steadily recuperating, we reboarded *Sanctuary*.

Being far away from our elderly parents always concerned us while we were sailing. Our return to the United States brought all of those concerns dramatically to the surface. Each time we visited and then left to continue our voyage, we drank in their love and made sure they received our love in return. Should we quit cruising? Was it selfish to follow our dream? Time would march on whether we were at sea or not, and obviously our presence couldn't prevent the effects of aging. Our dream called us forward even though that meant long times apart from the family we loved.

We spent more money than anticipated in our years of cruising. In order to replenish the cruising kitty, we designed, produced, and sold beaded jewelry in between caretaking and hospital and veterinary visits. Fishing tackle boxes full of beads were squirreled away throughout *Sanctuary*'s lockers. I strung necklaces from my voluminous bead collection while Jim made matching earrings and built a simple booth that collapsed and fit in the back of the funky station wagon. We signed up for a series of craft fairs and took the show on the road every other free weekend from September to December, managing to sock away a tidy profit by the end of the year. Déjà vu.

After a lot of soul searching about Jim's health and long talks about leaving our families, we decided to continue our cruise. We'd enter the Intracoastal Waterway (ICW) in January and follow its trail around the edges of the southern states. Midway up the east coast we'd take off across the "the big pond," as cruisers call the Atlantic Ocean.

Between stringing and selling beads, we continued researching, planning, and working on *Sanctuary* with both of us doing at least one chore daily from our long maintenance/repair list. We installed a new generator and tore out and sold an undependable water maker that gobbled up a lot of space in the engine room. The entire teak interior was refinished. In mid-December we declared ourselves retired and packed the remaining beads deep into safe lockers aboard *Sanctuary*. The displays were sold to other vendors, and we traded the car to a contractor in exchange for new mosquito screens for our hatches. We planned to enjoy Christmas and New Year's with my family and then depart in mid-January. Plans changed.

Morris, while slowly recovering in the nursing home, was hit by a brain hemorrhage. Mother's replacement knee simultaneously began exhibiting ominous clicking sounds accompanied by excruciating pain. After X-rays and office visits, her doctors determined that the new miracle knee was broken. Mother's knee problem and Morris's brain hemorrhage both occurred between Christmas and New Year's, and Mother entered the hospital for revision knee surgery on January 3, 1995. We didn't do much holiday celebrating.

Morris, bless his heart, died on January 6, 1995, sliding into death to suffer no more. Mother, on the other hand, was anguished. After two very intense weeks, she turned a bend on her road to well-being and was released from the hospital. Jim, my sister Mary, and I once again took turns with caregiving of various kinds including arranging Morris's quiet funeral. We shifted our departure date to late February to give Mother some at-home assistance until she could walk. It was a difficult and sad time for all involved.

An unexpected boost to our own physical cares occurred as a by-product of all the time we spent living in mother's Houston apartment. We met her next door neighbor, a woman with Parkinson's disease. Jim accompanied the neighbor to some PD support group meetings and met Dr. E., a neurologist who had left a fine position at Baylor University to devote his life and skills to finding a cure for Parkinsonism. Dr. E. and his research assistants dealt only with a select group of patients willing to try experimental PD treatments. Because Jim had contracted the dreadful disease at such an early age, Dr. E. added him to the group.

Jim consulted with Dr. E., and after a battery of tests was prescribed some newly marketed and experimental drugs. Jim's worsening symptoms quickly abated due to Dr. E's treatments, and we sighed with relief as Jim's shaking, freezing, and lurching diminished. We'd head across the Atlantic with a refurbished boat and a rejuvenated Jim.

So much activity, so many heartaches and crises happened during our 10 months back in the U.S.A. But we continued to nurture our dream to sail around the world—especially after the wrenching reminders of the shortness, preciousness, and unpredictability of life. We reboarded *Sanctuary* and reconfirmed our mission: to demonstrate that you can live your dreams (even if not on schedule).

The Ditch

March 1995—May 1995

"Twenty years from now you will be more disappointed by the things that you didn't do than by the ones you did do. So throw off the bowlines. Sail away from the safe harbor. Catch the trade winds in your sails. Explore. Dream. Discover."

—Mark Twain

Sanctuary stirred up the mud as we plowed out of our slip in Clear Lake on February 21, 1995. My sister, Mary Reeves, and nephew, Abraham Armer, joined us aboard for a unique reintroduction to cruising. First stop: the fuel dock to fill our tanks with 90 gallons of diesel in preparation for a long motor in the Intracoastal Waterway from Texas to New Orleans.

The "Ditch," as the ICW is called, is just that—a 9- to 12-foot-deep and 125-foot-wide ditch. The long series of manmade canals connects major shipping ports along the Gulf of Mexico. Navigated primarily by barges transporting oil and other products vital to Southern commerce, we, in our small deep-draft sailing vessel, were an anomaly. We chose the route as protection from the choppy waters of the gulf, which is filled with oil rigs and adverse winds and currents. Protected, but unable for the most part to sail, we aimed eastward avoiding the barges and watching the depth-sounder as we edged along the narrow ICW channel.

Motoring about 55 miles a day, we steamed past bayous, swamplands, farmlands, and industrial wastelands. In a week's travel, we passed only two sailboats. Otherwise, we encountered barge after barge after barge. They ran to 60 feet wide and sometimes were a "six pack" long (towboat lingo for six barges cabled two wide and three long, like a six pack of beer). We learned to call the vessels steering the barges "towboats" even though it was confusing since they pushed—not pulled—the barges. The waterway is charted and tracked with mile markers beginning with Mile Zero at Harvey Lock, Mississippi River, New Orleans. The radio chattered constantly as each tow captain sang out his approach— especially on the numerous blind curves. It took the tows more than a mile to slow their speed or come to a halt, so relative mile position was crucial when communicating. We assiduously avoided them by slinking over to the edges to allow the tow a clear passage.

It was too hazardous for *Sanctuary* to travel the ditch after dark. Finding a nightly home in the narrow, shallow passageway was an additional challenge. Since the barges marched along the water highway 24 hours a day, we nosed into abandoned pier areas, sniffed out capped-off oil well sites, snuggled into crooks in the waterway, or ferreted out holes beyond the traffic lanes to spend the night out of harm's way. Not all likely looking anchor spots were deep enough, and we had several tense periods unsticking *Sanctuary*'s keel-foot from the Southern mud which was black as sin, and twice as heavy, when glued to and hauled up on the anchor the next morning.

Towboat captains, with Cajun accents, spoke their own language: "I got a lit'le ol' sailboat up heah at mile 130; I'm breakin' up and my east is wild." Translation: A tow was approaching *Sanctuary* at mile 130. One of his barges had become uncabled from its group and had drifted in the current out into the channel to the east. We slowed, hovering and anxiously watching with binoculars, as the crew wrestled the wild barge back under control and reattached it within the row.

"A handkerchief comin' down the middle. Ah'm all up in them crab traps and can barely hod it from crossways. Pass me on the one." Translation: *Sanctuary*, in the middle of the Mississippi River and heading downstream, was approaching a northbound tow battling the downstream current and slewing sideways across the river. The captain was worried about snagging some crab pots set in the river. An overtaking barge, also coming upriver, would pass the tow talking on the radio starboard side to port side. Both were aware of us—the "handkerchief" ahead. "The one" referred to navigation rules and the use of one blast of a whistle to signify intentions regarding passing or overtaking vessels. Whistles were still used; however, radio communication has superseded the old whistle signals. Clear as that black Mississippi mud?

Each lock, ferry, and bridge had a specified station, channel, or unique call. Black Bayou Bridge, for instance, would not answer the call "Black Bayou Bridge" nor would it answer Channel 16—only Channel 13. Communications in the Panama Canal were easy compared to those approaching the Mississippi River and New Orleans. The two locks and ten bridges we passed and cleared on our final approach and crossing of the Mississippi all required a particular radio contact. The lock keepers were easy on us though. One said as we approached, "Just come on in and jockey around, and I'll blow ya' on thru." With Galveston a week behind us, we slipped down and across the Mississippi River in the fog and rain navigating by radar and radio contact with Gretna and Governor Nick Lights, the two river traffic control stations. Of course, by the time I figured out and remembered all the channels and slang, we completed the hurdle and no longer needed the special radio lingo.

We motored into Lake Pontchartrain on the morning after Mardi Gras. In spite of tension due to poor visibility, we were just as glad for the obscurity the fog and rain provided since we'd been warned that people in New Orleans living along the edges of the ditch used sailboats for target practice! We put Mary and Abraham below decks, and both Jim and I slouched as low in the cockpit as we could. Maybe the shooters were sleeping it off since we arrived without incident at South Shore Harbor near the Star Casino in Lake Pontchartrain.

Mary and Abraham provided good company for our first ICW leg. Needing to return to their normal lives, they disembarked in New Orleans. My brother-in-law, Charles Reeves, drove from Texas to pick them up and treated us all to some of New Orleans's famous oysters then left us to our own devices with *Sanctuary*'s sick transmission. Meanwhile, Jim's cousins, Hollis, Alsira, and Larry Young, who lived in New Orleans, eased the pain of an expensive repair with more Southern hospitality.

Other friends took us to a New Orleans jazz funeral, complete with a marching jazz band, singing, and dancing in the streets of the French Quarter. After enjoying some more Southern cookin' with dockside friends, we rode out a late winter storm, then left Lake Pontchartrain with rebuilt transmission, and reentered the ICW. The next portion of the "Ditch" crossed Mississippi Sound. The sound's wider vistas and deeper water made

Jazz Funeral in New Orleans

evening anchorages easier to find.

    The shores and islands of Mississippi and Alabama looked so inviting with stately Southern homes set among tall pine forests edged with pristine white beaches. Eagles soared above oyster boats plying the flats. The string of our Atlantic crossing pulled us forward, keeping us from lingering. Meanwhile, the supposedly repaired transmission began leaking oil, and we limped into Pensacola, Florida. The beautifully restored homes and downtown of Old Pensacola lay near our marina. Between blustery showers and bluster in the engine room with the transmission, we walked old town. At least we were in a spot to find parts we needed and once again remembered that cruising was the art of repairing your boat in exotic locations.

Jim in St. Petersburg

We left Pensacola feeling optimistic, checking the transmission every few hours. No leaks, so we leapt out into the gulf for a three-day passage to St. Petersburg. With seas lumpier than we had anticipated, we slogged back into sailing and passage making—something we hadn't done in pure form in many months. We didn't use the transmission in near-gale winds—only our foul-weather gear and storm sails. The sloppy conditions reminded us we needed to begin preparing for the Atlantic crossing, so we wrote "To Do" lists while underway.

    We stopped

briefly in St. Petersburg to visit Ken and Mary Jones, cruising friends of several years and many locations, who had settled in Florida after selling *Vision II*, their 44-foot sailboat. We couldn't linger long; our Atlantic-crossing weather window continued to draw downward. In order to arrive on the east coast for a timely departure date, we skipped several enticing anchorages and harbor-hopped briefly around the Keys, hightailing up Florida's east coast to West Palm Beach, our Atlantic jump-off point.

"Sunfest," a huge music festival, was under way in West Palm Beach just a short block from the marina where we berthed *Sanctuary*. Over 250,000 people attended the five-day event enjoying food, music, and crafts on the edge of the Intracoastal Waterway. On May 7, the area was a hotbed of activity with a crowd of 50,000 listening to one of two bands. The music reverberated over the water, battling with the clatter from two helicopters buzzing overhead. Golf carts zipped from parking lot to dockside dodging sunburned walkers and Rollerblade skaters and ferrying boating revelers and their party supplies to and fro in the busy marina.

Jim and I were overheated and over stimulated. My temples throbbed from the activity and decibel level. We spent the day searching for boat parts and trudging in the hot sun from hardware store to marine outlet. Straggling back to *Sanctuary* at day's end, wrestling a roll of over 50 charts and loaded with other parcels, we wove through the crowds to find the boat oven hot, our toilet malfunctioning, and the noise blaring.

We postponed the toilet repair, grabbed cold beers, and sat in the cockpit to simmer down and remember what we were doing there. We looked at our new chart of the Azores and ignored the noise to talk about our upcoming passage. Around May 15 we planned to strike out to cross the Atlantic. The Azores, a small group of Portuguese islands, were 2,300 miles–and at least a 19-day sail–from frantic West Palm Beach. Their beckoning shores were *Sanctuary*'s only planned stop on our way from the United States to Ireland.

We looked forward to the European leg of our journey, with old world history and cooler climes. *Sanctuary,* a proven passage maker, was seaworthy. However, our longest crossing to date had been just six days. So, for an anticipated three weeks at sea, we amplified our normal pre-departure routine and started by examining our safety equipment.

The life raft was professionally inspected, repacked, and re-lashed on the deck just forward of the mast. Our Emergency Position Indicating Radio Beacon (EPIRB) mounted below deck was tested and fitted with a new battery. Fire extinguishers, life sling, and personal safety gear (life vests, whistles, strobes, and harnesses) were all in good condition. We'd examined the "Ready Bag," a waterproof pouch of abandon-ship items we kept near the cockpit, and replaced the expired items. The small hand pump water maker packed in the ready bag was working. We reread our "Mayday/Abandon Ship" instructions, and I then added the emergency radio frequencies pertinent to the Atlantic and replaced the list in its plastic container at the navigation station.

Next we inspected *Sanctuary* herself. Thru hulls, sea cocks, hoses, hose clamps, exposed wiring, and worn or corroded fittings were cleaned or replaced. We flooded the bilges and tested the bilge pumps. Safety latches were installed on all the lockers that didn't have them already. Loose gear that normally sat out in calm conditions was stowed.

Moving topside, we checked the mast, tricolor, and rigging. The standing rigging was tuned and examined for cracks or rust. Other deck gear, the remaining navigation lights, safety lines, and stanchions and their fittings were scrutinized. We gave our jib, staysail, mainsail, and running rigging a once-over. All were in good shape, and we were satisfied.

We cleaned the cockpit lockers, and while they were empty, I climbed inside to inspect the steering and autopilot gears. Our spare anchors, spare anchor chains, heavy-duty dock lines, extra sheets, and our least-used spare sails were repacked low to the waterline. We greased the swivel fitting on the parachute sea anchor and reviewed the complicated deployment instructions and then stowed it in the locker next. Near the top were two sails we could need right away—the storm staysail and the cruising spinnaker. Which one would get used first? Only the winds would tell.

The propane tanks were full, and we'd bought new European type fittings for them. Fuel and water would be topped off before we left. We'd already checked the spare-parts log book, taken inventory, and replenished anything in short supply such as light bulbs and fuel filters. Jim serviced the engine, and we declared *Sanctuary* ready to depart. I'd counted canned goods, medical supplies, and other consumables and packed them all.

We still needed fresh foods, the final things to come aboard. I'd buy fruits and vegetables such as tomatoes or avocados in groups of ripe, barely ripe, and green so they'd ripen and last as the days sailed by. I cooked and froze several quick "pop in a pot" meals. The first 48 hours underway, adjusting to sea conditions and watch schedules, were always the most difficult for me. Having a few preprepared meals eased me into the tilting galley routine. I also shifted a few days' provisions from our harder-to-access deep lockers into the more reachable galley lockers. I packed high-energy snacks such as granola bars, raisins or nuts into one serving plastic bags. The snacks, along with a cup of hot chocolate or tea, would help us through the long night watches.

Assembling the navigational supplies was a fun part of the "To Do" list. We had accumulated sailing directions and more than 240 charts for the Azores, Ireland, England, Wales, Scotland, France, Spain, Portugal, and Gibraltar. Poring over the charts reading harbor and anchorage names, we imagined what the Azores and Ireland, our first two stops, would be like. As we planned timing, anticipated the weather and sea conditions, and read about the places we planned to visit, our visions sprang to life. We studied the pilot charts and reread the notes and sailing articles we had collected for years with tips gleaned from other cruisers. A couple from Spain were berthed a few boats down the dock from us. They had sailed across the Atlantic three times, and they shared a wealth of information I added to my notes.

Using the Defense Mapping Agency (DMA) Regions publications as a guide, I typed our chart list into our laptop and put the first few needed in the chart table. The remainder were sorted, labeled, and stowed in order of our anticipated journey. We would be using a Great Circle chart for the first time, plotting our rhumb line on it, and transferring the waypoints to the Atlantic crossing charts.

We planned to sail north along the eastern edge of the Gulf Stream and then turn for the Azores at about 38° north, aiming to get a kick from the stream as it meandered toward Europe. I plugged the new frequencies for Atlantic weather forecasts into our SSB band radio. I also plugged in the ham frequency for my daily call to our friends on shore in St. Petersburg, Florida. Ken and Mary would track our progress and relay messages to our families.

We had one last item to buy: a set of waterproof paints. We needed the paints to draw our ship's name and logo on the famous harbor wall at Horta, Faial Island, Azores. How fun it would be to join the ranks of sailors who'd made their mark there after crossing the Atlantic.

Even though we prepared all of our gear and took extra precautions in case of rough sea conditions, we fervently hoped that most of the systems would never be used. As the official *Sanctuary* optimist, I anticipated the good times of passage making. I remembered the best of our other passages and the joy I experienced when we and the boat sailed in tune with the winds and seas. Jim and I were both nervous. The passage would probably take three weeks. Anything could happen. What would happen? We didn't know. We had done everything we could to make our crossing safe, so we checked out of the marina and anchored out at Jupiter Inlet. Ready, set. The wind shifted to the SE, and at 0900 on the morning of May 17, 1995, *Sanctuary* nosed out to sail across the Atlantic Ocean. Go anyway.

The Gulf Stream Dragon

May 1995—July 1995

"Force 10 Storm: Winds, 48-55 Knots: Very high waves with long overhanging crests. The resulting foam, in great patches, is blown in dense white streaks along the direction of the wind. On the whole the surface of the sea takes on a white appearance. The "tumbling" of the sea becomes heavy and shock-like. Visibility affected."

— The Beaufort Wind Scale

A weather fax we received the morning we departed showed a large high covering most of the southwestern Atlantic. Destination: Azore Islands; Range: 2,690 nautical miles; anticipated time at sea: Three weeks. You take what you get.

We headed *Sanctuary* for the eastern edge of the north-setting Gulf Stream planning to use its one- to five-knot current to push us along faster. Flying our jib, stay sail, and main in light winds from the south or southeast, *Sanctuary* trundled along, and we sailed 415 nautical miles in the first three days. We were off and running. A large school of ancient-looking pilot whales swam past our bow, a good omen.

The morning of the fourth day began eerily. Our main compass, mounted on the binnacle in the cockpit, showed a heading of 035° north while the GPS said our course over the ground (COG) was 090° east. This deviation was huge. Were we really being set 55° off course? Our wake looked normal. Were we caught in an eddy? If we believed both instruments, we were sailing backward! (Of course, since we were out of sight of land, we had no reference points other than the direction of the winds and seas.)

I went down below to double check our heading by looking at a second, smaller compass mounted at the navigation station. As I looked at it, I shook my head thinking my vision must be blurry because the needle on the small compass did not point to a heading. The compass arrow was free spinning! My heart lurched just as *Sanctuary* took a strange jog. I turned and jumped up the companionway stairs just as Jim yelled, "The autopilot has lost its heading!" (It had an internal compass as well.) We both looked down at the main cockpit compass—its needle was swinging freely, too. We were scared.

Jim hand-steered us back on a course in tune with the wind and set of the sails. We sat down and discussed our options, trying to find a logical explanation for the erratic behavior of the three compasses. We knew *Sanctuary* wasn't turning circles. Jim steered and kept her sails flying full and steady. Maybe we were sailing over a huge submarine or some strong metallic object deep below? Nothing, not even a fish, registered on our combination fish finder/depth sounder.

I said, "Maybe we are near something on the surface of the water that has an enormous magnetic pull." We searched the horizon 360° with our binoculars but saw only empty ocean. I went below and turned on the radar and, after it warmed up, called up to Jim, "There's no return at all on the radar for 24 miles in any direction. I'm scared. Something really weird is going on. What is it?"

"I'm just as baffled as you are. Let's just stay calm; we're not in any danger that I can see," Jim replied. We were nervous, though, and like rats in a dead-end maze, we kept checking both compasses to see if the needles were still spinning. They were. We knew we were not willing to hand steer all the way across the Atlantic. The autopilot couldn't work without a compass. Even if we decided to hand steer, we would still need a boat's compass.

Suddenly we heard "click," then "whirr."

"What was that noise?"

"I don't know—it sounds like the camera." I picked up our little Instamatic from the companionway shelf and, as I stared at it, the camera clicked and whirred again, taking a picture. I was sure I had not touched any buttons. I almost dropped it but instead threw it like a hot potato toward Jim crying, "What's going on? The camera is taking pictures; I'm not doing this!"

Jim looked it over to see if the buttons were jammed or something when it clicked again. We were really scared then. "Okay, let's just calm down; there has to be an explanation for all of this," Jim said.

Then, as suddenly as the needle spinning had begun, it quit and the compasses returned to a heading we deemed normal. We discussed the strange behavior off and on for hours. After scanning the horizon carefully and repeatedly checking the depth sounder, we still saw no evidence of anything or anyone. Finally, to save energy, we turned off the radar and the depth sounder and decided to pass the anomalies off as "something weird on the ocean bed." Later, when the camera film came back from the developer in the Azores, there were three unexplained pictures in the group: picture one was a black fuzzy blur, the second a weird, blurry photo of the top of my head, and the third, also out of focus, was a strange elongated photo of Jim's face and part of his arm.

Lyn plotting the location of the Gulf Stream

After our fright, we replotted our position using dead reckoning, GPS, and compass headings. An updated weather broadcast gave the Gulf Stream eddy's locations and sizes, and we discovered that *Sanctuary* lay smack dab in the grip of an eddy 60 miles in diameter. Winds from a cold front were upon us, and we were trapped. Our only option: sail before the front and with the eddy—south—the wrong direction! A long day later, we broke free of the eddy and the front passed, leaving behind confused seas and no wind. In 24 hours we'd logged 120 miles over the ground; however, only 33 of those miles were to the good. Putting our heads down, we returned to the stream, grudgingly accepting the risks accompanying the one-to five-knot boost.

Sanctuary marched onward. Each degree of latitude inched us closer to Cape Hatteras, known as the "Graveyard of the Atlantic." We eyed the impending shape of the cape on the chart with trepidation, discussing and plotting our passage past the dreaded hook of land. Should we stay in the stream? When exactly should we strike east? At Hatteras or Chesapeake or continue on to 40° north as so many before us had recommended?

Feeling overwhelmed, we vacillated, finally deciding to stick to our original plan. We stayed in the stream until 36° north and then turned east passing Hatteras at about 100 miles offshore. We angled northeasterly, hugging the edge of the Gulf Stream. Our established routine included listening to high seas weather broadcasts three times a day after which I plotted the winding, shifting location of the stream including the warm and cold eddies. We were determined to avoid another eddy encounter, and I plotted forecast weather events as well.

The area above 40° north, from the coast of the United States all the way to Europe, was riddled with high seas and high wind warnings, gales, and storms. Yet, below 40° north, conditions were benign with forecast highs producing 15-knot southeasterly winds. These were not the westerly winds we expected, but they would do. We continued to track northeast.

I realized later that we'd overlooked an important weather report, the one including weather approaching from farther west coming at us from the United States mainland. We needed to scan the weather horizon 360°, just as we scanned the horizon for traffic only on a much larger scale. I concentrated on the weather ahead of us to the northeast, or from the Caribbean to the South, neglecting the weather on the U.S. mainland. It was a big mistake—the storm hit us on the 11th day.

The beautiful azure of the Gulf Stream lulled us into complacency. Wearing shorts and tank tops, we sat under an awning jury-rigged under the boom to protect us from the blazing sun. I painted watercolors while Jim read. The stream ferried us along at five to seven knots. We'd had no sight or sound of any traffic for more than 48 hours. There was just *Sanctuary*, dolphins, birds, and the clear skies. Man-o-war jellyfish floated by shining in the sunlight on the almost flat seas. Weather reports predicted a low above 40° north. We sailed below 39° north and felt safe.

Then we noticed a swell which, in such light winds, was unusual. By the time we said, "Hmm, better take down the sun awning" the clear sky way off in the distance had turned an ugly-looking purple-black. Previously calm winds increased within 15 minutes to a consistent 30 knots from the northeast in direct opposition to the steadily flowing Gulf Stream. We hurriedly furled the jib and put one reef in the main. By the time I got the staysail changed to storm staysail, the winds were gusting 40 to 50 knots, so I went back to the mast to wrestle the mainsail down farther while Jim manhandled the wheel. As I struggled to pull down the mainsail, gusts of 60 knots lifted me off the deck. My safety harness and tether saved me from going overboard. Drenched by blasting rain and wind-driven salt water foaming off the tops of the waves, we were shaking in our shorts from cold and from fear.

The sun had disappeared and rain poured from the dark clouds surrounding us. Winds intensified and the choppy seas rose to 14 feet, breaking angrily. The Gulf Stream current held us in the trough. Heaving to did not work. Neither did towing warps since the seas headed west and the current set east.

Still wearing the shorts we had on when the storm hit, we finally crawled below one at a time to dry off and pull on foul weather gear. Normal conversation was impossible; we yelled to hear each other above the howling, shrieking winds. We battled the storm for over five hours as it increased in intensity. A weather report confirmed our analysis of a Force 10 storm, and a plot of the storm's position indicated many hours yet to endure. Exhausted, we decided to set our parachute sea anchor, our "storm tactic of last resort."

Sanctuary rocked and rolled in the winds and seas as I struggled to dig the parachute contraption and its long heavy line out of the cockpit locker. While Jim grappled with the wheel in the cockpit, I crawled to the bow to lead the line for the sea anchor. Breaking waves threatened to snatch me off deck. My hands shook and my heart pounded fiercely. After I crawled back to the cockpit, we double checked with each other that the rode ran free to the cockpit winch and then threw the parachute over. We couldn't really see it due to the blowing seas, yet we could sense the change in motion as the parachute inflated. Beautiful. It worked perfectly, turning our bow to the now 24-foot seas. Riding up the wave faces as if on an elevator, *Sanctuary* punched through their monstrous tops as they slid under our hull. We looked at the wind indicator and saw that the arrow was pegged out at 70 knots. With the sea anchor set and the boat stabilized, we staggered below to rest.

We had never set or used a sea anchor before and belatedly realized that, in our anxiety-ridden inexperience, we had left off the chaff guard. We decided to let a little rode out every 20 minutes so the boat's motion wouldn't saw through the line. Also, though we doubted that any other foolhardy vessel was caught in the storm near our location, we decided to continue watchkeeping. Visibility was zero. The rough, high seas made our radar useless, so we hailed into Channel 16 on the VHF every half hour stating our position and inability to maneuver. The sea anchor should have slowed our progress to a knot or less. However, the GPS indicated *Sanctuary* set northeasterly along the curving Gulf Stream at over four knots.

We hunkered below, lying on the cabin sole near the foot of the mast, and took turns sleeping fitfully. At 2:00 a.m., some four hours after deploying our sea anchor, we both lurched awake to a sharp gunshot like sound. We groggily realized the rode had parted. We'd slept through the "let the sea anchor rode out" schedule. With our sea anchor gone, *Sanctuary*, instead of riding up and over the oncoming waves, slewed sideways in the troughs.

Lying ahull was perilous, yet in the black of night, with confused seas and no visibility, we decided steering would not be any safer. It might be more dangerous and cause us to pitch pole. As we talked, breaking waves slammed and crashed onto the cabin top. The seas rocked *Sanctuary* heavily from side to side, but none knocked us completely down. Holding our breath, we lurched into the aft cabin thinking we would be more protected there if *Sanctuary* were knocked down. There we cowered listening to the violent screaming winds and crashing seas. We talked about selling the boat and buying a farm. If only we survived until daylight, we'd work on controlling the boat again. We held tight and lived a long night.

At first light, as soon as the monstrous seas were visible, Jim began steering. We carefully timed our first move of shifting *Sanctuary* from her trough position to one of running before the seas. I stood in the companionway facing aft toward the oncoming seas and warned Jim of potential sideswipers or especially high rollers. As *Sanctuary* surfed and skittered down the huge breakers, we angled her south, desperate to escape the storm's fury as it veered to the north. We wearily realized we had reached the back side of the counterclockwise circling winds as the seas shifted and moved with the Gulf Stream. We ran before the seas towing 100 foot warps rigged with fenders and a milk crate tied in the middle. Soon the warps stabilized our motion enough that the autopilot could steer, so Jim staggered below exhausted. I sat in the cockpit mesmerized by the sight of the wave trains marching toward us. In the troughs I looked up, and up, and then up again measuring their mammoth heights against our spreaders and estimating them at 24 feet high. Later, after the huge seas calmed to 15 feet, they seemed like placid hillsides in comparison.

Twenty-six hours after the storm hit, I went below and cooked our first meal. We assessed the damage. We'd lost a dorade, I had whip marks and rope burns on my legs from a flaying staysail sheet, we were both covered with bumps and bruises, our hands were chaffed raw from grabbing lines encrusted with salt water, and we had lost our parachute sea anchor and about 400 feet of rode. The cabin was littered with nasty, wet piles of salty clothing and towels. We had made it. We were alive.

Eight hours later, as we used some precious diesel fuel to run the engine to charge our batteries, we motored on a flat sea with foul weather gear barely flapping on the stern rigged clothesline. The storm had blown itself out, and we took turns sleeping around the clock. A few days later a gale blew up. The winds seemed mild in comparison to the storm, and we simply towed warps to keep the breaking waves out of the cockpit. This time we avoided the Gulf Stream, having learned that lesson the hard way. Riding before gale winds was uncomfortable, yet we proceeded in the desired easterly direction.

The remainder of the journey was a mixture of sun, cold, rain, fog, seas, winds, and calms. We slogged hazily along, days blending into gray until on day 16 we heard another sailboat on the VHF radio. What a thrill to discover *White Trillium*, a British boat returning to England after a sail to the U.S.A. We hailed them and discovered they had left West Palm Beach two days before us on May 15. Also slammed wildly by the nasty weather, *White Trillium's* wind-vane steering had broken, and the four aboard were taking turns hand-steering. We did not envy them that job and were thankful that, other than the lost sea anchor, *Sanctuary* had sustained no real damage.

The presence of a buddy boat lightened the journey immeasurably. We jogged along at about the same speed chatting via VHF, comparing weather notes and dinner menus, and instigating an afternoon "anything goes" radio net. At one point we maneuvered within camera distance, hooted and hollered, and each crew took photos of their neighboring vessel under full sail. We identified each other easily by voice once we met days later on land in Horta.

On we plugged, anxiously awaiting sight of the Azore Islands. The islands, mere dots on a map of the world, are hard to find even when searching the charted blue area west of Portugal to whom they belong. Known as "The Disappearing Islands," sailors relying on sextants often missed them completely, for sun sights are difficult to take when rain and fog cloud the sky day after day. We, however, with the aid of GPS satellites circling the globe, would, or should, find them easily. Still, I continually plotted and replotted our position, checking and rechecking my computations. I updated my dead reckoning. Closer and closer we crawled to our destination with my dots plodding across the chart. I upped my fixes to hourly as we drew within 60 miles (half a day) away.

Raising the courtesy & quarantine flags for the Azores

The sailing directions said that the Azore island of Pico, crowned by a 7,000-foot volcanic mountain, was visible from over 100 miles away, yet at 60 miles, we saw only clouds on the horizon bringing cold winds and more rain. We drew within 24 miles, which was radar range. Ghostly images appeared on the radar screen—land! Still, we saw nothing. Closer and closer we sailed, hearing VHF radio conversations and watching land birds fishing in our wake, but there was still no sight of land. We drew even closer, with our radar showing just 12 miles to the harbor at Horta. Fifteen minutes later there was still no sight of land. The rain diminished, and we searched with binoculars. We knew the islands were there. The radar images were clear, yet no island was visible.

A sweet, rich odor wafted around *Sanctuary*. As we realized we smelled the island of Faial, the clouds lifted and beautiful purplish blue hillsides rose from the mist. The Disappearing Islands had appeared. Our journey had ended after 25 days at sea. Tucking into a corner of the yacht harbor, we jockeyed for position among more than 100 boats from many ports of the world. We quickly slid into the joyous atmosphere pervading the international sailing fleet at harbor. We were one of only five United States vessels. Flags flew on yachts from Ireland, England, France, Canada, Sweden, Norway, Germany, Denmark, Spain, and Portugal. The list was as varied as the size, shape, and demeanor of the hulls and their crews.

We discovered the source of the wonderful smell: hydrangeas. The island was paved with them in gardens and hedgerows. The hydrangeas' vibrant color draped the island in a chimera of purple-blue, and the scent of thousands, no millions, of blossoms sweetened the air. The islands are also known for their wines, cattle, and dairy products. Once ashore we celebrated the end of our passage with a good bottle of wine, some cheese, a steak, and ice cream for dessert. The entire meal was produced locally. Ah, arriving in port was just too good! The dreams of two sea-weary sailors were fulfilled.

Traditionally, ships' crews arriving in the Azores paint their boats' names on the quay wall. We followed suit, picked a spot for our sign, and added *Sanctuary*'s and our names and date along with some palm trees signifying California. We'd first heard of the wall in 1980, and in June 1995 we left our mark alongside the crazy elite who have crossed an ocean under sail. We joined the nightly routine of strolling along the jetty, meeting and greeting other sailors, and enjoying the artwork on the wall. The sun played peek-a-boo with the clouds, and we enjoyed our taste of Portugal. The ambiance of the two islands we visited, Faial and Pico, was restful and gracious and the inhabitants helpful. We bought fresh vegetables in the local open-air market, learned a little Portuguese, sampled "September Water," tramped over the hills with the sheep and the cows,

Lyn adding Sanctuary's name to the quay, Horta, Azores

went to volcanic black-sand beaches, and when we could tear ourselves away from delights ashore, caught up on sleep.

The small marina was tightly packed with vessels, and we became a bit tired of the fishbowl atmosphere. The constant chatter of sailors carousing on the docks at all hours of the day and night grew tiresome. But later, I changed my tune: One evening I sat reading and idly wondered where Jim was when I heard noisier than usual commotion on the dock. Poking my nose out the companionway to see what was happening, I discovered Jim soaking wet and being helped aboard *Sanctuary* by several of our neighbors. "What's going on?" I asked. Jim replied, "Well, the safety line broke just as I grabbed it to climb aboard, and I fell into the water. That damn PD. I just can't grip stuff or climb. Luckily, our neighbors were out chatting on the dock. You didn't hear me hollering. They did, and hauled me out of the water. I just missed drowning!" We got Jim dried off and counted our blessings. Later we took our neighbors some special desserts as a small token of thanks for a big rescue.

A few days later, as we prepared to leave Horta, we moved *Sanctuary* to the customs dock where we waited for fuel and our departure papers. We noticed a small sailboat flying a red and white flag, short-tacking past the breakwater into the harbor. "I'll get the fenders ready," I said to

Jim. "That Canadian boat will need to side-tie to us for check-in with the Post Captain."

A couple sailed the trim vessel on a harbor pass. Weaving her around several moored fishing boats, they came about, and instead of approaching the dock, they anchored and raised a yellow Q flag. "What a perfect approach and anchor under sail alone," said Jim. "Why anchor instead of tying to the check-in dock?" I asked. "Why sail in such tight quarters? Don't they have a motor?" "Maybe they have an engine problem," Jim replied. We watched as they launched their dinghy.

A few minutes later a woman rowed the bright dinghy alongside *Sanctuary*. "Hello" she said, "This is the customs dock, right?"

"Yes, bring your sailboat over, and you can side-tie to us."

"We don't have an engine, so we'll wait until the Port Captain gives us a berth. That way we'll only move once." she said.

"The Port Captain is still at lunch; he'll be back at 2 o'clock," I told her.

"We'll row in then. Do you have any tomatoes? Could I possibly have one?" she asked. "We've been at sea 45 days from Brazil and have eaten most of our fresh food. Larry would love a tomato sandwich for lunch."

"Must have been quite a passage. I'll gladly welcome you to port with a tomato." I brought her a tomato from our galley asking, "What's your name?"

"Lin."

"So is mine. How do you spell it?"

"L-i-n."

"Mine is "L-y-n." As we discussed the spelling I thought of Lin and Larry Pardey, a seasoned cruising couple and authors of nine well-written books about voyaging, seamanship, and boatbuilding. They communicate their love of sailing and adventurous cruising via magazine articles as well. "Are you Lin Pardey?"

"Yes, and that's Larry out there on *Taleisin*."

"Your writing has made such a difference in my life," I told her. "Thank you for putting your experiences on paper."

"Oh, sharing is what it's about," she said, adding, "We all learn from each other."

Off she rowed with the tomato. I recalled reading *The Care and Feeding of the Offshore Crew* in 1989, as we began preparing to fulfill our dream of sailing around the world. Lin's account of their 4,600-mile crossing from Japan to Canada aboard 24-foot sailboat *Seraffyn*, with no engine or electronics, inspired me. Vivid descriptions of their 49-day passage, and her organized approach to provisioning, guided me as we readied *Sanctuary* for life offshore. I learned a lot about cooking at sea, stowage, and passage making. "What a good idea. We could do that," I said time and again as I read. She put trials and discomforts into manageable perspective and laid many of my fears about cruising to rest. I owed her a debt of gratitude. We sat in the Azores due in part to what we had learned from Lin and Larry's books, and here they were!

Remaining in Horta due to the weather, we visited with the Pardeys, sharing meals, trading books, and swapping sea stories. They had circumnavigated twice and sailed more than 130,000 miles to 68 countries. They'd sold *Seraffyn* and built 29-foot *Taleisin*. They graciously shared their knowledge of boats and sailing with us. Larry's terse remarks and Lin's pithy, sharp comments punctuated our encounters. Their engaging tales were told with ready wit.

Lin and Larry had weathered many conditions during their countless hours at sea, including a typhoon in the Bay of Bengal in 1977 during which they hove-to. We bemoaned the loss of our para-anchor, and while discussing storm maneuvers, we learned that the Pardeys had recently completed a book: *Storm Tactics Handbook: Modern Methods of Heaving-to for Survival in Extreme Conditions.*

Lin and Larry led a group of seminars sponsored by *Sail Magazine*, and the participants swamped them with questions. How did you gain experience to cope with extreme conditions at sea? What works? What doesn't? How do you deal with the high waves and high winds? Have you been pooped, broached, or rolled? What about running bare poles or lying ahull? How do you heave-to? Does it work? What else can the crew of a small sailboat do in the face of an unavoidable storm at sea? Discussion of a 1994 storm off New Zealand (one boat sank and seven were abandoned in 70-knot winds and extreme conditions) raised the questions again. The answers weren't readily available or taught, so their book was born, and it provided the answers.

After talking with Lin and Larry and reading *Storm Tactics Handbook*, we devised a new heaving-to plan for *Sanctuary*. Armed with the plan and their loan of a spare para-anchor, we were encouraged and less jittery about our impending passage to Ireland across the often storm-strewn North Atlantic. Feeling fortunate that we had met the knowledgeable yet unassuming couple, we parted company saying, "Maybe we'll see you in Ireland."

Sanctuary left the Azores early one morning in July with forecasts promising fair winds. Five days later, sailing close hauled in 35-knot winds with waves breaking on us, the rigging pumping, and the bow plunging, we decided to heave-to. Exhausted from hand-steering, we needed a rest. Equipped with new knowledge gleaned from the Pardeys and their book, we hove-to using only the triple-reefed mainsail. This was a different tactic for us. It worked! The noise level immediately dropped, the motion became bearable, and waves no longer broke on board. I wrote in my journal: *"We are "parked" in the middle of the ocean. We'll take a shower, relax, and get some rest. Watchkeeping will be easy. What a blessing to properly heave-to!"*

After eight restful hours of heaving-to, we continued sailing. Upon approach to the marina in Dingle, Ireland, we saw two familiar-looking people on the dock near a boat that looked like *Taleisin*. "Wait a minute. That is *Taleisin*! That's Lin and Larry waving to us," I yelled. "How did they get here ahead of us? They were planning to stay in the Azores awhile." Jim joked in reply, "Maybe they secretly have an engine after all!" We later discovered that Lin and Larry left the Azores nine hours after us yet arrived in Ireland a full day before us. With years of experience behind them, they had sailed through the gale, its strong winds filling their sails.

The Gulf Stream Dragon

The Gulf Stream dragon wends his way
from Caribbean Sea past Biscayne Bay.
Ever northward his belly flows
winding by Atlantic shores.
Leaving Savannah, Charleston, Beaufort, too,
he bids the South a fond "Adieu."
Climbing, snaking, with eddies as claws
he grabs and shakes Cape Hatteras in his jaws.
Flinging it out with a sharp eastward breath
the dragon strikes past the New England shelf.
A tiny boat rides upon his back
leaping and lurching as he makes his track.
The dragon sleeps at 40 degrees north
a cold wind wakes him with a snort.
He wheezes and puffs, yet the boat hangs on,
bound for islands beyond the storm.
Together they journey day after day
pressing onward come what may.
At last the dragon with a wink of his eye
bears the boat to the Azores High.
The boat with a nod shouts back to the beast,
"We'll miss you. We thank you. It's been a rare treat."
They were happy, their journey near done,
to see the islands how they shone in the sun.
The dragon remains though for any who dare
to greet him and join him there in his lair.
He frames the Atlantic with a sinewy tail.
Trust him—it could be he'll help you to sail.
Still I'd say, watch the dragon's eye.
Follow his glance, study the sky.
Listen to weather. Read the clouds.
Shorten sail early. Don't be too proud.
The Gulf Stream dragon is a powerful beast
with many moods: South, North to East
Sailors never know what they will meet
in crossing to Azores—a noteworthy feat.

Caught in a Gluepot

July 1995—October 1995

"The trouble in Ireland is not the getting to a place but the getting from it. I once dropped in on a stranger for a cup of tea and I stayed with him for a fortnight. In 1944 I went to Gougane Barta for a fortnight and I stayed there seven months. What with the lake and the island and the mountains, I seemed to get anchored"
—*Lovely is the Lee*, Robert Gibbings, Irish Author

We "seemed to get anchored" in Ireland. Fall came and strong winds blew, yet we postponed leaving. "Just one more anchorage, one more village," we said. The trouble was in the getting from it.

It started with Dingle on the west coast. We approached the marina late on a Sunday afternoon in early July. Our passage from the Azores had been wet, rolling, and foggy. We were tired after 10 days of coping with strong north and northwesterly winds and an incessant swell. Along with the Pardeys, two smiling men stood on the dock, pointed to a slip, and handled our dock lines. "Welcome to Ireland," they said, introducing themselves as Harbor and Dock Master. "Glad to see you. Make yourselves at home. Go on ashore. Customs will find you later." "How did you know we were arriving?" we asked, amazed at personal greetings from any Harbor Master and on a usual day off work. "Ah! 'tis a sixth sense I 'ave." said Dock Master Johnny Murphy.

Unused to "going on ashore" before being cleared by customs, we trusted the Harbor Master and went with Lin and Larry to Maire de Barra's pub for dinner. One old fellow we met was so intrigued that we had sailed over 3,500 miles of ocean—America to Ireland—that he raised his glass and broke into verse:

"There was a ship named *Sanctuary*,
Come sailin' round the rocks,
To find her crew to Danny's place,

And meetin' all the folks."

The da-di-da went on for six or eight verses 'til someone yelled, "Oh, shut up, Murphy, and let the folks enjoy themselves." When our waitress appeared, Jim asked, "What kind of beer do you have?" She yelled to the bartender, "Do we have any beer?" He scowled and answered, "No, we've got no beer." Then Larry said, as though he had been there all his life, "Bring us a coupla' jars of the black stuff" (two pints of Guinness stout). Two glasses appeared. We'd learned our first lesson ashore. In Ireland you'll find stout, lager, and pilsner but no beer.

After dinner we moved up to the bar and chatted with the bartender who steadily "pulled pints" with ease and finesse as he talked with us. We mentioned the cheerful welcome we had received from the Harbor Master and our amazement at being allowed ashore without a customs inspection. The bartender replied with sanguinity, "Ah, lads, in England, and Amerikey the law 'tis the law; in Ireland 'tis only a guide."

A few days later a short, stocky fellow walked down the dock leading a short, stocky Jack Russell dog. The man and the dog hovered on the dock near *Sanctuary*. The dog sniffed around our boat, and the fellow didn't say anything. Jim and I went on deck, asking, "Hello, can we help you?" "Oh, just looking. Where have you come from?" Jim went on to tell him, and as they talked, the little dog became very interested in my leg. I spent most of the time they were talking trying to shake the humping dog off my leg and was just getting to the point of real annoyance when the fellow introduced himself as the Customs Officer. We were "cleared" and I was glad I hadn't kicked his Jack Russell.

And so it went. From the "victualer" behind the meat counter who remembered our names after the first meeting, to the lady at the "post," to the grocer who offered "a lad to take y'er bags to the ship," people in Dingle acted as friends, not strangers. Most expressed amazement that, "You've come over the sea, 'ave you?" for few cruisers visit Ireland. We met sailors from Great Britain and France but saw only two vessels from the United States and two from Canada during our three-month stay. Anchorages were shared with Irish cruisers, fishing vessels, a rare charter boat or with no one at all. Crowded it was not.

Yes, Dingle—with pubs housed in 200-year-old buildings; with fiddle, guitar, bodhran (an Irish drum) and pennywhistle music seeping out of every pore; with lace curtains gracing bed and breakfast inns; and with the fishing vessels called "hookers" (old sailing workboats) and currachs (open canoes made of hides or canvas) plying in and out the harbor, provided the perfect introduction to Ireland. The pubs (more than 50 in Dingle) served as meeting place, eating place, political forum, and music hall and cropped up everywhere.

Looking for bicycles to rent, we were directed to a hardware store. Poking my head in the door, I saw the now-familiar Guinness tappers for "pulling a jar of the black stuff." We turned away thinking it the wrong site. "Can I 'elp you?" someone called. Coming about, we discovered we were in the hardware store—and bicycle rental—and pub! One might as well take a wee drop before or after a home repair or a hearty ride.

Jim weaved and wobbled on his bicycle due to bad balance from Parkinson's, but with little or no traffic we were safe enough to ride around the Dingle peninsula and disturbed only sheep or cows grazing if we veered off the road. Forts and oratories built 5,000 years ago were lined with hedges of fuchsias. Chattering starlings punctuated our route as we pedaled past cottages snuggled beside fern-covered stone walls. Gaelic names such as Dun Chaoin, Baile an Fheirteataigh, Gallan na Gille Brice, testified to a Gaeltacht area with Irish Gaelic the spoken language. Signs throughout Ireland were posted in English and Irish Gaelic, but we heard mostly the lilt of the Gaelic on the west coast. Putting on our newly purchased rain coats, we discovered the real meaning of "Celtic Mist." Riding back to the hardware store, we returned the bicycles, dried off, and the clerk "pulled us a pint."

The sun broke through the drizzle after a few days, and temperatures rose. Locals and weather men alike declared it, "The driest, fairest summer in Ireland for 187 years." Breezes were perfect for sailing, so, tearing ourselves from Dingle, we set off to explore other of Ireland's west coast harbors. "It's so hard to leave. It's so nice here." Our hue and cry of the summer had begun.

An overnight sail north, past the Aran Islands guarding the bay's entrance, brought us to Galway, once a small fishing village at the mouth of the River Corrib, now the third largest city in Ireland. Tides ran to 20 feet, so the locked city harbor only opened near high water in order to keep the docked vessels afloat. The tide tables, our constant companion while in Ireland, gave us the correct time to enter. There were no facilities for yachts, so we side-tied to an out-of-commission lifeboat resting along the quay wall. Freighters and fish boats came and went timing their work to coincide with the tidal gate opening.

Ashore we followed the old harbor Long Walk into the city and stopped under the Spanish Arch where grandees in their cocked hats mingled in times past with the Claddagh womenfolk selling their fish. Continuing, we passed a 1,600-year-old monastery. Craning our necks, we viewed Norman churches, Tudor Age stone houses, 17th-century Catholic churches, and an 18th-century theatre (where we later attended a very modern play). Relics of the medieval walled city, and other physical echoes of Ireland's past cohabitated with 19th- and 20th-century shops and pubs in happy disarray, all outlined by the meandering River Corrib. Galway's cobble streets were festooned with banners and crammed with singing, partying people—we had stumbled upon the 18th Annual Galway Arts Festival. The festival, held each summer in mid-July, captured us, and we fell into a net of music, theatre, parades, art shows, poetry readings, dances, and films.

After a busy festival week, we sailed out of Galway Bay on the ebb tide to wander down the west coast in search of a secluded anchorage. Possibilities abounded. Convoluted mouths of rivers and bays offered many a hidey-hole: some with shoreside villages, some with a pier for the fishing fleet, others with only the sheep, cows, and birds to watch us set our hook. We kept sharp lookout for rocks, minded the wide-ranging tides, and took our pick.

The gentle winds of the mild Irish summer led us to places such as Carrigaholt, Kilrush, Smerwick, Valentia Island, Derrynane, Castletowne, Berehaven, Glengarriff, Schull, Castletownshend, Glandore, Kinsale, and Crosshaven. Each displayed merits from the homemade bread and scones in the bakery, to the night in the pub singing with the locals, to a swim (an unexpected pleasure). The mild summer had warmed Ireland's usually frigid waters just enough for me to swim for about 10 minutes.

Swans greeted us in several anchorages and startled us early one morning with an insistent, pecking beg on *Sanctuary*'s hull. Fishermen surprised us with gifts of monk fish, cod, and mackerel. We tramped past purple heather to castle ruins and ancient cemeteries with Celtic symbols carved in the stones. I picked blackberries and wildflowers. Gannets, plovers, kittiwakes, guillemots, fulmars, and fat puffins, hardly able to fly, provided entertainment. Bottle-nosed dolphins swam lazy circles around our anchored boat. Irish cruisers, out sailing for their "holidays," greeted us, and we joined them for excursions and chats. If weary of seclusion we sailed a few miles to a town. If weary of town, we sailed a few miles to a secluded anchorage.

Plying past Mizen Head, with infamous Fastnet Rock in the distance, we remarked on our good fortune at the perfect sailing winds we had enjoyed all summer. Passing another shoreside castle, we anchored in Crookhaven with its church of St. Brandon the Navigator on the hill. Hiking the headland, we paused at Barley Coves beach. Ducks put on a show in the clear waters, diving for fish many feet below.

Walking on to Mizen Head, Ireland's most southwesterly point, we braved the 99 steps and suspension bridge to visit the old signal station. Live-in lighthouse keepers used to set explosive charges as a fog warning. No longer manned, the lights and signals are automated now. The station stands as testimony to the treacherous conditions the Atlantic dishes up along Ireland's southwest coast, for gales typically blow every week. Nearby Fastnet Rock is the first landfall the Atlantic makes after America. The mild summer of 1995 hadn't produced a gale—yet.

Summer drifted on. Our contentment in each spot made raising the anchor more and more difficult. Securing *Sanctuary* in a marina, we toured inland using inexpensive "Irish Rover" bus tickets and got a view of life in the broad lowlands. Women signed the cross as the bus passed a church. Bus drivers stopped to chat or drop off packages to cottage dwellers along the route. Neighbors greeted each other by name with lilting cries of "Lovely day, how 'yer lads?" One day as we rode the bus, the driver was listening to a sports broadcast on his radio. The passengers grew silent, listening too, and then buzzed with excitement as the announcer tracked Sonia O'Sullivan running the last stretch of the women's 200-meter race in the International Games. A great cry rose up when Sonia won. Her victory belonged to all the Irish.

More than 10,000 Foleys claim Ireland as homeland, so foraging for information about Jim's great-grandfather was a challenge. My great-grandfather was Irish as well, so the search for genealogical data led us on a great chase around Dublin, and we visited the Trinity Library and the Book of Kells in the process. Forgetting about same-name ancestors, we looked at the Viking and Bronze Age gold artifacts. Our heads swam with the thought of the generations of conflict and struggle visited on Ireland. The living, breathing Irish, however, welcomed and took care of us at every turn. Even the summer's record million tourists, one more influx in a long line of invaders to Irish soil, didn't ruffle the temperaments of the unspoiled Irish we met.

As we sailed from anchorage to anchorage and village to village, we'd often stay ashore for dinner and visit a pub. A cry would ring out when someone we chatted with raised his pint, saying, " 'Tis the Foleys sailed all the way from Amerikey. Send 'em another jar." So many patrons would host a toast that we'd have to leave early just to get back to the boat sober and not fall in the water climbing aboard.

Jim and I are both from good Irish descent which includes a reputation for love of the brew. Over the summer we joined a lot of people in putting away our share of pints. Somehow we'd avoided drunkenness, and reputations notwithstanding, we had never seen anyone else really drunk. A meeting with some serious drinkers, however, convinced us that for an Irishman "hardly been drinking lately" is a relative term. It could be "I hardly been drinking a fifth a day" or "I hardly been drinking lately— only three drinks a day instead of five or six."

Late one afternoon, as *Sanctuary* swung on the hook in a quiet anchorage, a fishing boat came alongside, bumping soundly into our hull as it arrived. Getting up from the main salon where we sat reading, we looked through the portholes and saw two obviously drunken fishermen. One man seemed to be barely functioning, and the other appeared to have a wet brain. I stayed below, listening, while Jim went up on deck to see what they wanted.

The slightly sober man held up a mackerel, saying: "You got ur fish?" Jim said, "We don't care to eat mackerel." The fisherman replied, "Oh my! Ladie, we 'aven't caught anathin' but mackerel. What kinna fish ya lookin' for?" Jim: "You got any cod?" Fisherman: "Nae ladie, we hawn seen cod for a fortnight. You'll haw ta eat the mackerel."

So Jim bought a couple of mackerel to use later as bait. Then, as he paid the guy, his companion muttered something in Gaelic. The fisherman then asked Jim, "You wouldn't haw a wee dram a whiskey on board for me brother would ya mate?" Jim looked at the brother sitting there in a stupor, lied, and said, "Sorry, I'm fresh out." The fisherman countered, "Ya must haw a wee pint of somethin' lad." Jim said, "None to give away." The fisherman says, "Me fine brother here has to have a wee drink."

Jim, annoyed by his persistence, decided enough was enough and said, "Your brother looks like he's had a wee too much to drink today."

The fisherman looked at his brother, took a moment to focus, then slowly turned and looked toward Jim, took another moment to uncross his eyes, refocused as well as he could, and said, "Me brother hasn't hardly been drinkin' at all lately." He gave Jim a big smile hoping that would work. It didn't, so they left.

Sidestepping for a while in Cobh, we visited the site of departure for thousands who left Ireland in search of a new life around the time of the potato famine. We looked for the names of our great grandfathers on the emigrant list, and our research confirmed that the Patrick Foley named there was Jim's relative.

Motoring *Sanctuary* across Lough Mahon, we wended our way up the River Lee into the heart of Cork and side-tied to Penrose Quay. At low tide we could not reach the quay wall ladder, making it necessary to time shore excursions very carefully. We spent high tides ashore shopping in the vegetable and meat stalls of the centuries-old English Market and envisioning the ghosts of our great-grandfathers. As we walked the streets of Cork, I often made double-takes, thinking I had glimpsed my father rounding a corner or believing the buxom lass offering me my change was Jim's sister. Our descent from Irish blood was clear—we looked like those around us and felt we had come home.

Sanctuary tied to the quay in Cork, Ireland. We could only go ashore at high tide.

Snug miles inland on the River Lee, we ignored the increasing rain showers and "blustery winds" mentioned by the weather forecasters. Summer was long gone. Still we lingered, taking some of the new friends we made aboard *Sanctuary* downriver for a day sail on Cork Harbor. As *Sanctuary* bounced on choppy whitecaps under dark gray skies, we looked at each other over the heads of our Irish friends and said sadly, "It really is time to go."

Jim decided to honor his link to Ireland with a shamrock tattoo over his heart, so visiting a skin artist was one of the last things we did in Cork. After provisioning the boat, we slipped downriver to Crosshaven near the mouth of Cork harbor. We'd decided to winter on the south coast of England and wanted settled weather for the crossing. It was so late in the season we thought maybe we'd winter in Ireland. Saying to each other, "No, if we don't leave now, we'll never leave," we set about listening to the weather reports in earnest.

"All ships, all ships, all ships. This is Valentia Radio, Valentia Radio with gale warnings for all Irish coastal waters and the Irish Sea." Day after day the forecasts were the same: "gale warnings." Late October cold fronts swept daily across the Atlantic, stalling over southern Ireland. The fronts brought high winds and a high Atlantic swell. Hoping for a passage with conditions milder than a gale, we lingered in Crosshaven enjoying the small village and the world's oldest yacht club, the Royal Cork. "Ah, 'yer may be 'ere for the winter, lads. Ah, Ireland, 'tis a gluepot," a yacht club member told us. We were honored when the club presented us with a Royal ensign bestowing honorary membership upon us.

Late ashore at Buckley's Pub listening to Irish folk songs, we stayed another day. Helping close the pub as the Irish do with the singing of the national anthem, we raised a last pint. With a lull in the gales, we finally let go the mooring the next morning. Using the gale's tail feathers, we snuck across the temporarily calm Irish Sea to England. We had enjoyed a special Irish summer. Truly, "What with the lake and the island and the mountains," and we added "the people," the trouble was "in the getting from it."

Letterboxing, A Tattoo, and the Burryman

October 1995—August 1996

"From there to here, and here to there, funny things are everywhere."

—Dr. Seuss

Weeks of gales left lumpy swells in the Irish Sea pummeling Jim with seasickness during our passage across it to the south of England. Seasickness usually whacked him at the beginning of any passage, and his myriad Parkinson's medications only made it worse. Way back in the beginning of our journey, we discovered that seasickness-prevention pills didn't help him. Adding any additional meds to the chemical soup already in his body was a prescription for disaster.

The symptoms of PD had crept relentlessly onward since 1990. By 1995, Jim could no longer rely on his grip; his hands would not always open or close at will. His left leg locked or froze unexpectedly, so when walking normally, he would suddenly stumble or trip as his leg refused to move. The same thing happened to his left arm which he'd begun to hold behind his body in an attempt to cover up the contorted hand and awkward, shaking arm movements. His digestive system didn't work correctly nor did his salivary and lachrymal glands. Assorted tremors that moved to different parts of his body on different days plagued him, and due to the "on-off effect," sometimes his medications worked to alleviate his symptoms, and sometimes they didn't. Altogether we were very discouraged about his physical safety, comfort, and ability to continue life aboard a sailboat.

During free moments in the passage to England, we discussed whether we would, or should, continue pursuing our dream of sailing around the world. The Atlantic crossing, Azores to Ireland crossing, and now the Irish Sea crossing had all extracted a high toll from Jim. The physical demands of sailing in even "normal" weather called for extraordinary measures of concerted effort from Jim, and the extra work needed in gale conditions pushed his PD physical limits drastically. His Parkinson's-affected brain did not always send the needed signals automatically anymore, and many times he had to will his shoulders, arms, legs, or hands to move. We jokingly called the situation "The Hesitation Blues" —black humor, since it wasn't a joke. Just a second's hesitation at a crucial moment onboard a ship underway could mean "man overboard" or worse.

In 1990, Jim's first neurologist had declared, "Most patients diagnosed with Parkinson's live about five years." After initial upset, anger, and a period of, "Why me, Lord?" pity, we got over that insensitive prognosis and decided to fight for Jim's life. Parkinson's would not define who he was or how he lived his life. Certainly, having a progressive, currently incurable, degenerative disease was a severe blow. We took a strong stance and declared that we would approach his diagnosis from the following point of view: Jim was Jim—a healthy, alive, loving, and magnificent person. He had been thrown a ball named PD with which to play the game of life. Until the rules changed or we discovered how he could drop it, he was destined to carry the ball. However, the PD ball was not Jim; he just carried it. We would accommodate, but not surrender to, Parkinson's.

We felt that the physical activity involved in sailing, and the rowing, walking, and lifting Jim did when we were ashore, helped keep him functioning and slowed the progression of the symptoms. Some days, though, I looked at Jim and almost burst into tears—either tears of sadness as I watched him struggle with what used to be a simple task or tears of admiration and awe at his unrelenting courage against the brick wall of the terrible disease. In spite of our positive attitudes, carrying the Parkinson's ball had worn us both down.

Luckily, my health was excellent, and I had developed strong arms, legs and shoulders thanks to all the winching, lifting, hauling, and sail management. Following Jim's instructions, I handled tools and made boat repairs that Jim's body wouldn't allow him do anymore. Still, we nibbled around the edges of quitting our journey. Would it be safer or easier to sell the sailboat and continue cruising by trawler? Should we hire a crewmember to help with the physical labor involved in sailing? As we tossed options back and forth, they all fell flat like lead ballast. We didn't want to quit or give in to the disease. We made a decision by not making a decision and simply carried on.

We made landfall in Plymouth, England, and chose Sutton Harbor Marina as home for an anticipated long, harsh winter. The next nine months were a period of "make and mend," some forward progress, and some in other directions.

Sanctuary's diesel-powered forced-air heating system worked well but was not ideal for continuous use, so after arrival in Plymouth, we bought a small electric heater and a large dehumidifier. We plugged them into shore power, and tucked under the main saloon table, they remained running until we got underway again in May 1996.

With a warm, dry boat to come home to, we bundled up in our Irish wool sweaters and full rain gear and set out exploring. *Sanctuary* was berthed near the Barbican, a historic part of Plymouth that survived the bombs of World War II. Sir Francis Drake departed Plymouth in 1577 for his world circumnavigation, becoming the first Englishman to sail around the world. Drake's statue guarding the green of the "Hoe" overlooked the harbor entrance. Flags marked steps where Pilgrims boarded the Mayflower in 1620 to sail for America. (Their landfall rock in Massachusetts was named for the soil they left in Plymouth.) Captain James Cook also set out from Plymouth. We "Yanks" ferreted out a fish and chips shop and munched our very British lunch as spirits of the famous seafarers ghosted around us.

Much of Plymouth didn't survive the bombs of WWII. The "new" city was rebuilt in the 1940s and sensibly designed for foot traffic with walking tunnels under the main automobile thoroughfares. We used the footpaths and tunnels, hiking just about every day to the big market with its cheese, dairy, meat and vegetable booths.

Friends Lin and Larry were wintering over in Falmouth a short bus ride from Plymouth. *Taleisin* was out of the water on "the hard" while they worked on a complete refit and lived ashore in a cottage. We visited and planned a Thanksgiving celebration. Pumpkin was difficult to find (the English do not grow it) but Lin and I rounded up a turkey and other suitable ingredients and together produced a scrumptious feast introducing a tableful of English sailors to a very American tradition.

I sold our handmade jewelry in Central America, and a shop in Ireland also purchased some. Our cruising kitty needed supplementing again, so we signed up for a Christmas Arts and Crafts show. Turning our cozy main salon into a jewelry-making factory, we worked on our designs every day. We rented a table for the three-day event, bought some tablecloths, and used found objects for display. The December craft show was a success. Pocketing our earnings, we left *Sanctuary* with a boat sitter and flew across the Atlantic to relatively warm Texas.

We visited Jim's neurologist in Houston first, and he adjusted Jim's medications, cautioning us that it would take at least a month for improvements (if any) to appear. We hoped for the best. After Christmas and New Year's with my family in Houston, we flew to California to visit Jim's family. The Texans and the Californians remarked on cold, wet weather, but to us, fresh from ice-covered docks and the sleety winds of Plymouth, the two climates were heavenly. The visits with those we loved so much were equally warm.

Tearing ourselves away from California, we returned to London in mid-March 1996. As the train sped from London toward Plymouth, magpies peppered the sky above snow-covered hills, and sheep, heavy with wool, hunkered in the icy fields. Winter in England was in full force. We skidded along docks covered with frost to reboard *Sanctuary*. We were "home" after four months in the States.

Thanks to the heater, dehumidifier, and boat watcher, *Sanctuary* was dry and warm, and her dock lines had held through the winter gales. We unpacked. As we put away groceries, including fresh milk for our coffee, we discovered that our refrigerator wasn't working. "Oh, well," I said as I put the milk outside, "We can just use the cockpit as a fridge until we make repairs. After all, the outside temperature is 38°!" Meanwhile, filling the kettle with water to make coffee, I turned to the stove—it wouldn't light. Searching for the cause, we found that both of our five-gallon propane tanks had rusted through and all of the propane had leaked overboard. (The refrigeration unit had lost its Freon due to corrosion, also.)

British propane parts wouldn't work on our American vessel nor would British parts work for our refrigerator/freezer. After much to-do, we ordered two propane tanks and new refrigerator parts from the United States. While we waited for parts, Jim jerry-rigged a British propane tank so we could cook. The tank sat temporarily in the steering well, and the milk, cheese, and other perishables lived in a box in the almost-ice-cold cockpit outside.

Most of my journal entries from March 15 onward began: *"Miserably cold and wet. Bitter gale winds."* No matter what else needed to be done, any day without rain was a day for a long walk, so one sunny day we discovered, and poked our noses into, the Royal Plymouth Corinthian Yacht Club. Friends we made there were matchless, and Tony Corrigan, especially, went out of his way to welcome us to Plymouth. Tony and his spry

Westie, Pippin, joined us on some walks. Even though Pippin was a dog, he provided me with a much-needed dose of animal love. I still missed our cat Muffin even after a year without her.

Stuck below on one of the bitter cold rainy days, I noticed a throwaway line in a travel magazine: "Letterboxing in Dartmoor will provide an amusing introduction to the moor." What on earth was letterboxing? Tony had never heard of it, but another Yacht Club member had, so we got organized and, on the next sunny day, set out on a treasure hunt.

In 1854, a guide to the moor stuck his calling card in a bottle and left it semi-hidden in a cranny. When a search for his bottle led to another, and another, a hobby was born. By 1995, more than 10,000 hidden waterproof containers mushroomed throughout The British National Park of Dartmoor. Each secret box contained a rubber stamp, stamp pad, and guest book.

Letterboxing enthusiasts hide their weatherproof gear in remote or scenic places in the moor and then distribute clues to its location in newsletters or on internet websites. The fun begins as other "letterboxers" set out to collect as many stamped impressions as they can find. "Letterboxers" even have clubs such as "The Five Hundreds," "The One Thousands," etc. We enrolled in the sport, found a grid-marked map of the moor, dug out our handheld compass, bought a current newsletter with clues, and with Tony and another friend, drove to Dartmoor to discover as many letterboxes as we could in one day.

Armed with our ships stamp, usually soundly stamped on documents required by Customs Officials, Immigration Agents, and Port Captains, we tramped the moor for hours, laughing and deciphering clues such as: "Take a regal step back in time, and from a granite post next to St. James Chapel, go 40 paces on a bearing of 121° to the royal lounge. Then nine paces 321° to the box." After discussing and pacing, we'd find a letterbox, stamp the guest book with our stamp, and add the date and a note about ourselves. In turn we stamped my journal with their stamp and name. We ferreted out eight letterboxes the last of which was in the bar at Forest Inn, Hexworthy. At the end of the day as we sat with our drinks, Tony said, "Letterboxing is a bloody daft game!" "Well, you Brits invented it," we hooted!

On a more normal note, Jim created a "How to Make Jewelry Using Lost Wax Casting" slide show for a local arts college. His PD voice was too soft for an audience to understand, so I manned the microphone to present the program. The art teacher, Caroline Lawrence, was added to our cumulative list of generous people we met around the world who took us under their wings. Meanwhile, the parts arrived, and we repaired the propane and refrigeration. The winter winds abated. I gladly unplugged the heater and dehumidifier (which had run continuously from November to May) and sold them to a secondhand store up the road.

The change in meds had helped Jim, so we decided to continue on to Scotland where we would haul *Sanctuary* out (again!) and replace our aluminum water tanks which were leaking. We were always working on the boat, thinking about working on the boat, or buying parts to work on the boat. Before we left Plymouth to sail to Scotland to work on the boat, we made plans and worked on the boat.

We bought or borrowed charts organizing and logging them into our inventory system and separating the borrowed ones from ones we owned. We revarnished the interior of the cabin and sanded and re-varnished the dinghy oars. I sewed courtesy flags for the next six to eight countries we planned to visit, a new autopilot cover, and a waterproof laptop carry bag. We cleaned and painted the engine room. I updated our medical log, cleaned out all expired meds, and relabeled their plastic containers with waterproof ink. In the process of cleaning the bilge and main bilge pump, we put in a new water-level sensor and reseated the pump. Tony gave us French lessons, and we bought language dictionaries for Norwegian, Swedish, Finnish, and German.

Leaving friends we made along the way continued to be difficult. In mid-May we cast off the dock lines and said tearful goodbyes to Tony and Caroline and other friends. Thoughts of discovery tempered the tears. What new friends and delights awaited us around the next headland? We were bound to Scotland to find out.

In any event, it was great to be out of the marina and underway again. We hung on a mooring in Falmouth, then, after a few days, rounded Land's End and pointed north up the Irish Sea. Strong winds with accompanying rain kept us in full foul-weather gear for the passage. We arrived at an all-weather harbor in Wales just ahead of a gale. Milford Haven, at the mouth of the Bristol Channel, proved a pleasant, safe place to wait out the winds, and wearing our full rain gear, we toured a museum, art galleries, and light ship.

The remaining passage north to Scotland was challenging. Currents ran at up to seven knots with tides of up to 16 feet. Wind against tide produced waves referred to as "square." *Sanctuary*'s bow jarred and pounded into what felt like solid walls—we turned back twice. The third time was the charm. Fair winds blew; we put up three sails and ran hell-bent up the rest of the Irish Sea. *Sanctuary* flew past Holyhead, the Isle of Man, and everything in between as fast as we could push her in a three-day race against the tides and changing winds. We tacked through the North Channel between Scotland and Ireland on the second night as the lights of hydrofoil ferries doing 45 knots blurred past us.

We sailed into protected waters among the fingers and lochs that form part of Scotland's convoluted west coast. Up the Firth of Clyde we slid, passing the Isle of Arran (Aran is the Irish one) just visible at 3:00 a.m. in the early Scottish dawn, then past Bute and Cumbrae, with a nuclear power plant looming on the starboard, the 3,000-foot hills of Dunoon towering to port. Pressing through the mist, rain, and fog to the Gareloch near Glasgow, we saw sheep grazing on green spring hillsides. Purple heather, yellow grouse and bluebells fringed the shores. The cold gray waters of the firth bounced off our bow as we hit the wake from the ominous black conning tower of a passing nuclear submarine.

Ferries ploughed from one loch to another. As we rounded the mark to Rosneath, our first port of call in Scotland, a local sailboat crabbed past us. A fellow in full foul-weather gear manned the exposed helm in the pouring rain. Meanwhile, a rain drenched, obviously cold and unhappy woman shivered at the boat's stern, not enjoying the "Sunday sail." Out broke the sun. Jackets came off, decks dried, and we moored at Silvers Marine, our home for the next month.

We sailed to the Silvers Marine boatyard especially for a haul-out. A long way to go to haul out, 'tis true, but we had a special reason—the Collinses. We met Bryan and Dorothy Collins in the Azores in 1995. During their vacation, they sailed their boat, *Caitlin of Argyll*, back from the Canary Islands, toward Scotland by way of the Azores. While we were both in Faial Harbor, they enticed us with details about Scotland, their home. Bryan described his job as manager of a boatyard. *Sanctuary* needed a haul-out and Bryan ran a boatyard, so one year later we arrived.

After a reunion with Bryan and Dorothy, *Sanctuary* was hauled out and installed on a cradle. Our list of maintenance and repairs began the next day: paint the bottom, install new lifelines, replace the sea cocks, repack the stuffing gland, and most dramatically, replace our water tanks with two new stainless steel ones. The entire main saloon was disassembled to remove the rusted and leaking aluminum tanks from under the settees. Once out, the tanks were duplicated in stainless. The new tanks were installed, and the saloon reassembled. Man-handling the tanks from the ground, up the ladder, and then down the narrow companionway and into the boat was a difficult part of the daunting job. Only Bryan and the Silvers crew kept it from being overwhelming.

Between coats of paint and rainstorms, Bryan and Dorothy showed us their neighborhood from the pub at Knockderry Inn to Loch Lomond, Helensburgh, and Glasgow. Jim pretended to be Scottish, rented a kilt, and with Bryan in full regalia too, the four of us stepped out on the town. We were graciously invited to a wedding reception for Duncan, one of the Silvers' crew. Most all the men wore kilts, and after a few toasts, I asked one of them what a Scotsman wears under his kilt. He answered with the following tale: "Two lassies were walking on the road after a fine party and saw lad John passed out in the field. They looked at each other and said, "I've all'as wanted to know what the lad wears under his kilt, hadn't you?" "Ah, yes, I tav'—let's see." So, they quietly lifted up his kilt and saw his organ peacefully lying there. One of the lassies took a blue ribbon out of her hair and tied it round his penis. Giggling, they went on their way. When John staggered to his feet the next morning and pulled aside his kilt to pee, he found the ribbon and muttered, "Ah, me lad, I dunno where you've been, and I dunno what 'ouve done, but I'm glad to see you've taken first prize!"

More tearful good-byes were said in June when Bryan and Dorothy flew off to the Azores to collect their sailboat and complete their transit to Scotland. *Sanctuary*, after a month on the hard, was plucked off the cradle and plopped back into the water. With our boat repaired and spruced up, we waited on a mooring for friends Jim and Marilyn Marco to join us. When they arrived, we set off to explore Scotland's west coast.

John and Sarah McCann, whom we met at the boatyard, lived nearby. Each summer they launched their sailboat, *Tamara of Lorne*, to cruise throughout the season. John and Sarah's 1996 vacation coincided with the Marcos' arrival, and we accepted their generous offer to introduce us to their favorite nearby anchorages. Off we went with John and Sarah aboard *Wee Tam* and four of us aboard *Sanctuary*.

Our only problem was trying to understand John's Scottish brogue over the VHF radio. *Sanctuary* almost missed the first anchorage at "What's that you say?" "That's Ten-a-what?" "Ten-a-brew-ah?" You'll get it. We finally got it—Tighnabruaich. We learned to have coaching, and careful reiteration of instructions the day before, and thereby made it to the rest of the anchorages without further difficulty. Or should I say we made it from pub to pub? A Scotsman (and Californians, too) needs a "wee dram" at the end of the day. As John said when offered another brew, "Seems a shame not to."

The farther north we headed among the islands and lochs of Scotland's west coast, the longer the day. Early light often woke us at 4:00 a.m. and at 11:00 p.m. we could still easily see our way across an anchorage and back to *Sanctuary*. Braving rainy weather, we explored Tarbert, Loch Melfort, Tobermory, and Oban. Shaggy Highland "coos" (cows) with their big horns watched us as we warily picked wildflowers from their fields. We took showers at the Mishnish Hotel, ate a gourmet dinner at Showers of Herring restaurant, sipped cider at numerous pubs, poked through castle ruins, learned about the pipes and the whiskey, and transited two canals.

The Crinan Canal, nine miles long and 200 years old, provides a shortcut across the narrow isthmus at the top of the Mull of Kintyre. Fifteen locks raise and lower boats 64 feet above sea level, and boaters must operate the locks themselves! Luckily, John and Sarah, old hands at transiting the Crinan, were with us. They taught us to lean into the big bars that open and close the huge wooden gates without hurting our backs. Sarah cranked the sluices perfectly so that the entry of the water into the

Wee Tam and Sanctuary in the Crinan Canal

lock caused minimum turbulence. John knew exactly when a crew member needed to disembark to walk to the next gate to start the process again. We'd open the gate, drive the boat into the lock, secure the boat to the canal walls, close the gate, open the sluices to raise or lower the water level, open the opposite gate, untie the boat, then exit the lock leaving the gates closed for the next boat coming either direction.

White stone cottages lined with roses, tall foxgloves, fuchsias, or pansies stood guard on the canal banks. Sheep and pigs barely blinked an eye as we glided past. We lingered in mid-canal at Cairnbaan, near the site of a Bronze Age burial mound. We didn't find the mound but did find ice cream at the Post Office and beers after dinner at a canalside pub. In the early years of the canal, "Clyde Puffers" moved sheep, cattle, coal, and whiskey. Few "puffers" remain today. Most canal craft are yachts enjoying the shortcut from one cruising area to another.

Parting from John and Sarah was another sad occasion, and proceeding without our sailing buddies on *Wee Tam* seemed strange. *Sanctuary* headed alone toward the Caledonian, a 60-mile canal seven times longer than the Crinan. Vessels are raised and lowered over 106 feet from sea level. As we cut across Scotland from Loch Linne at the western entrance, the canal would dump us into the Moray Firth on the east. Thank goodness the 29 locks of the Caledonian were automated as line handling was enough. Our friends the Marcos were still aboard, and with our month-long canal "ticket" we leisurely explored along the route, touring the Abbey at Fort Augustus and Urquhart Castle in Loch Ness. "Nessie," the famous monster, must have been sleeping in the thousand-foot depths of the loch, because we didn't see her. A few days of bright sun cheered us, and we docked in Inverness in time to attend a "tattoo," stumbling accidentally upon a prize Scottish experience.

Contrary to what we imagined, the tattoo was not a convention of skin artists but a military ceremony complete with Highland dancers, bag pipes and drums, military bands, Scots Guards, RAF dogs, and Scottish country dancing. The name "tattoo" derived from a drum roll used to call the troops out of the pubs and back to military business. The tattoo participants wowed us with music, dance, pomp, and circumstance kitted out in kilts of various tartan colors. Jim and Marilyn disembarked to fly back to California, and our "mend" saga continued, for we were off to a marina near Edinburgh to repair the boat again.

Our 1995 generator, still under warranty, had many problems. The manufacturer declared it a lemon and shipped a replacement to Port

Edgar Marina, Queensferry, Scotland. While we berthed there and Jim worked with a technician on installing the new generator, I wandered around the small village of Queensferry. A very strange manikin in the window of a two-room museum stopped me dead in my tracks. I went inside, chatted with the attendant, and burst out laughing. Hooting goodbye, I went back to the boat to prepare Jim for something even stranger than letterboxing.

Early the next day we walked into town to a pub for the event I'd learned about at the museum. Out walked the Burryman, a green apparition looking like a skin-diseased robot on his wedding day. A local man arose at the crack of dawn, dressed in a thin muslin bodysuit, and a team of townsmen covered him from head to toe in big green prickly sticker burrs leaving only holes for his eyes and a straw hole for his mouth. A

The Burryman, Queensferry, Scotland

yellow and red Lion Rampart flag cinched his prickly waist and a garland of fresh flowers was affixed like a bowler hat atop his sticker-covered head. He couldn't move his burr-encased arms, so attendants held them stretched out with a floral staff tied to each of his immobile hands. The attendants supported the Burryman along his way since he could hardly see, couldn't talk, and due to the stickers, could only walk in a stiff-legged robot-like shuffle.

The stickers were not the only reason he could barely walk— there's the amount of liquor he consumed as well. It was considered lucky to give him money and a drink. When we saw him at 9:00 a.m., the Burryman was already well lubricated from drinking whiskey through a straw. As he staggered on to the next place and the next, crowds of children and onlookers trailed behind him singing a "Here comes the Burryman, the Burryman" ditty.

The museum guide said that the Burryman followed a tradition from the 1600s and brought luck to the yearly fair. It was something akin to appeasing the gods for a good bounty, or representing good vegetation and fertility. It made no sense at all to us, but he'd surely added good cheer to an otherwise usual day. We followed him for a block or two, put a bit of money into his cup, and returned to our boat chores. About eight hours later, at 6:00 p.m., we walked back into town for a bite to eat and spotted the Burryman still staggering fitfully along, with attendants and crowd in tow. Ah, it must have been a long, difficult day, and a very odd job, walking all that way, having all those "wee drams" of whiskey, and not even a stop at a loo!

Grounded in Spain

August 1996—May 1997

"When men come to like a sea life, they are not fit to live on land."

—Dr. Samuel Johnson

It was cold and wet when we left Port Edgar and sailed out toward the North Sea to make our way past the Scottish headland, where we poured further offshore to the southeast for the rounding of the British headland at Great Yarmouth, then on across the Thames Estuary to Ramsgate. All log entries in that three-day passage start with the same word: Fog.

Crossing the Thames estuary at night in the fog challenged all of our navigational skills. The shipping traffic, which had been almost non-existent further north, increased to horrific proportions. We passed fishing vessels, ferries, hydrofoils, freighters, oil tankers, cruise ships, and a dredge. In one six-mile stretch, we encountered more than 100 vessels. It took both of us to navigate safely, and three times we flashed our strobe light on our sails and took evasive action to avoid being run down. *Sanctuary* floated like a chip of cork in a sea of hurtling dodge balls. Even wakes of the passing vessels were dangerous. Neither of us slept for more than 24 hours, and I had time for only the one log entry: *"8/12/96: 1346 hours; Winds NNW 25-30, Fog, weather deteriorated. Crossing the Thames Estuary at night, in the fog, 24 hours of hell."*

After docking in Ramsgate, we covered our portholes and, exhausted, crawled into our berths planning to fall dead asleep. We didn't. Race week was in full force. The harbor was noisy and jammed with fast boats and their macho, buffed-up crews coming and going. Race guns blasted at each high tide, and at low tides the boats' crews milled around on the docks, flip flop mashed to flip flop, slugging beer and rehashing the rounding of each mark. Music boomed over the speakers from sundown to 2:00 a.m., and then the loudspeakers began anew at 7:00 a.m., blaring: "Wakey, wakey, time to rise and shine. Breakfast in the tent."

Sanctuary, weighing in at a laden 14 tons, lumbered at the dock like a dear old Saint Bernard while all the sleek whippets charged out twice daily to run around the block. We got a modicum of rest and met the only other non-racing sailors around, June and Rosemary, a lovely pair who had been together 21 years. They kindly and timidly gave us a "Red Duster," the proper British courtesy flag.

It is a standard rule of the seas that visiting sailors fly the flag of the foreign nation on their boat when entering and operating on its waters. We adhered religiously to the rule, and I followed the scale drawings from an international flag booklet when I sewed our courtesy flags. We were surprised by the "Duster" and didn't know what it was. We had sailed in and out of English waters since November 1995, and no one had told us we flew the wrong flag on our starboard spreader. June and Rosemary explained to us that the one we flew indicated that "The Queen" was aboard. Jim quite seriously replied, "She is."

After a rest, such as it was, at Ramsgate, we continued westerly in the English Channel, making way to Falmouth. Entries again stated "Fog." Log entry: *"August 16, 1996: 0747: Fog. No wind, motoring. Just passed the white cliffs of Dover and could barely see them."*

With no wind, we plodded along under power, sitting on watch below in the navigation station staring at the radar. Visibility sometimes barely extended to our bow just 40 feet away. The fog broke just before our dawn arrival at Falmouth where we picked up a mooring in the outer harbor and then reconnected with friends we had made the previous year. While waiting for our mail that was sent to their house, we foraged around "boot sales" and used stores for books. (We didn't expect to find any in English in Spain, Portugal, or Morocco.)

The mail arrived soon enough with Jim's medications and the Mediterranean charts we had ordered. Unsure whether we could trade other boaters for new full-color charts, we ordered half-price black and white reprints from the United States. I organized each chart by area and number and then used waterproof pencils to color in the shoal waters, highlighting the lights, off-lying land masses, and any other navigational hazards. I marked shipping routes, buoys, and potential anchorages.

By the time I finished the coloring, I knew the charts well and the route was planned. Jim and I then discussed the first leg together, pinpointing any potential problems. Preplanning served us well. Many times, due to a change in the weather or fishing nets smack in the middle of an anchorage or some other uncharted hazard, we had to abruptly abandon the planned anchorage or planned route "A" and make for a second-choice anchorage or route "B."

Sanctuary sailed a perfect beam reach on our three-day passage from Falmouth across the Bay of Biscay. Nice winds, warm temperatures, and very little shipping traffic in the English Channel or the bay gave us a smooth sail. After uneventful watches, we arrived in Cariño, on Spain's northern coast rested and wearing shorts! Even the sea water I pumped in the galley for washing dishes was noticeably warmer. Seeing the sun thrilled us. It seemed we'd been wet and cold since July 1995, and our bones needed warming. Guidebooks described Cariño as a "dirty fishing village," so we were doubly thrilled to find Cariño clean, with a pleasant anchorage, friendly people, and a tidy little beach.

We checked into Spain, traded our British pounds for *pesetas,* and then sailed on to La Coruña, a much larger city that served as a watering hole for cruisers. Together with some yachties we'd met in the Azores, we enjoyed the town and its night life. The tradition of *siesta* lives on in Spain especially in August, a "hot month." All shops except restaurants closed in the heat of the day from 2:00 p.m. to 4:00 p.m., when the town awoke, stores reopened, and shoppers again filled the streets stopping to gossip, chat, or show off their babies. Groups of old men stood in the *bodegas* (wine bars) eating *tapas* (plates of seafood or snacks). Children rode bicycles or played behind the store counters. Girls, strolling arm in arm, flirted, making eyes at the boys. Music blared. Motor scooters wove precariously through the crowds, and we watched the action from a sidewalk cafe.

La Coruña had its share of old buildings, and we toured an ancient lighthouse, The Tower of Hercules. Built by the Romans in the second century AD, the 1,900-year-old tower is the oldest functioning lighthouse in the world. Modified slightly in 1790, its light still provides warning to mariners along Coruña's coast.

Leaving La Coruña, we harbor-hopped along Spain's Atlantic coast, anchoring overnight. We lingered at Camariñas, which is famous for handmade lace. Women and girls sat outside their houses or shops plying lace shuttles full of white thread. Some followed a pattern attached to a padded board. Others moved the pins by memory, their shuttles flying in the sun. They rolled up the completed lace on the back of the pillowed work forms and later applied the finished lace pieces to napkins, sachets, tablecloths, and clothing.

The houses of Camariñas, built of gleaming white stucco with red tile roofs, climbed the hillsides from the harbor. Palm trees and pots of red geraniums punctuated the narrow, winding streets. We roamed around looking for more lacemakers but found instead Señor Mariano Jerfe, a retired fisherman. He sat on his patio sanding his partially-completed model of a sailing work boat. He described with pride how he used to fish under sail, a skill no longer used in Spain. We realized then that the hull shapes of the Spanish fishing boats hadn't changed over the years; only the mast and sails were gone, replaced by a wheel house and engine. Sr. Jerfe's models were perfect, down to the handsewn sails and tiny, to-scale oars. We spent our souvenir money on a sailing work boat model instead of lace.

After Camariñas, we sailed around Cape Finisterre and pushed farther south. We stopped in Bayona where a replica of Columbus's caravel, the *Pinta*, towered over the anchorage. Castles (turned into museums, restaurants, hotels, or sometimes private homes) looked similar to ones we had seen in Central America. We had hiked around castles in Central America, South America, Ireland, England, Scotland, and now Spain. I'd mostly dragged Jim along. He was a bit fed up and finally said, "If I never see another castle, I'll be happy." I didn't promise him that, but I secretly was getting tired of them myself.

Sanctuary slid from Spain into Portugal where we crossed the bar at the Rio D'Ouro. The river valley is celebrated for its climate, soil, and grapes. Well-known port wine, produced as it had been for centuries, flows out of Portugal along the Rio D'Ouro, and is named after the town that controls the flow, Porto. We anchored in the river in the heart of Porto near the remaining *barcos rebelos*, curved-prow sailboats used to ferry the casks of port wine downriver. The wine is still aged in oak casks, but world distribution no longer depends on the river boats.

Porto crumbled down cliffs to the river with paint peeling off doorways, blue-glazed tiles yellowing and wet laundry dripping onto cobblestones. Every inch was crammed, packed, and salted with life like the sardines sold in countless shops and restaurants. We wondered how the ancient plumbing worked and discovered the answer as we rode our inflatable back to *Sanctuary*. Effluvia flowed into the river as it probably had for centuries. We were careful not to touch the water and watched horrified as many local children swam in the river near the mouths of the drainage pipes.

A bridge of lacy steel designed by Eiffel (of the tower in Paris fame) spanned the river. The south bank proclaimed the famous wine house names of Sandeman, Croft, Taylor, and Borges spelled out above red-tiled roofs. Tasting port in an ancient cellar was a soothing way to spend a rainy day. Rain indicated changing weather, so we upped anchor instead and headed *Sanctuary* downstream toward the bar, not wanting to be caught in a stormy, rain-swollen river.

By the time we reached the bar, the seas were up to 12 feet. We were very nervous about crossing the bar in such conditions but even more nervous about staying in the river with winds and rains increasing. We had to get out before we were trapped, so we put up three sails, turned on our engine for insurance, and took the roller-coaster ride with Jim's knuckles turning white as he gripped the boat's wheel. Our stomachs churned as we slewed across the bar entrance. We slid past it with no damage, and plying through lumpy seas, we sailed south in plenty of wind tiptoeing into and out of rivers with wide bars, entering and exiting at slack water, and watching for weather all the while.

Cabo Sao Vicente marked Portugal's south "corner." We anchored near this cape close by the school of Henry The Navigator, where astronomers, cartographers, and navigators Magellan and Vasco de Gama had studied. Ashore we poked around the faded remains of the 15th-century school and uncovered the barely visible old stone compass rose. Lagos, farther east, offered a modern marina and a chance to get together with other cruisers. We parked in the marina, replenished our water and fuel, washed clothes, and relaxed around a swimming pool in the October sun. A group of us rented a car and toured part of the interior of Portugal. We left Lagos to explore more rivers along the southern coast of Portugal. We met our downfall in the last one.

The River Guadiana forms the border between Portugal and Spain, and after crossing the bar we anchored first at Ayamonte on the Spanish side. The tallest church steeple in town, sitting on the highest hill, was taller still thanks to a stork and its large nest atop. More storks nested inland, so we motored gingerly upriver hoping to see them. We found the storks and then anchored about 25 miles inland in mid-river between Spanish San Lucar to starboard and Portuguese Alcoutim to port. Days drifted by, but we never lost track of time. Church bells on the Portuguese side rang out each hour while the Spanish church bells, with a different cadence and tone, echoed from the other side of the river. One extra "dong" echoed from Spain because of the one-hour time difference! Roosters, donkeys, dogs, goats, and sheep joined in the hourly chorus.

Enchanted by life on the river, we were tempted farther inland toward Pomarão. We never made it. We began motoring upriver at slack water. After going about five miles, slack ended and the flood tide was with us. As we slowly motored in about 15 feet of water, the depth in the middle of the river abruptly dropped to nine feet. As we began backing up, *Sanctuary* slewed sideways, and due to the current and the weight on, swiftly set into a sand bar. The depth dropped quickly on the bar, and *Sanctuary* went hard aground in five feet of water and heeled over in the current. As the current flooded, *Sanctuary* did not rise with the tide but was set harder aground on the sand bar.

We launched the dinghy and hauled the bow anchor into deeper water as fast as we could, then went back and set the stern anchor to use as a kedge. Back onboard and still fighting the current pushing us onto the bar, we tried to winch *Sanctuary* off. Then we tried to push *Sanctuary*'s bow around using the dinghy. Neither winching nor pushing worked. We were not strong enough. High tide had past. We worried about sinking lower into the silt as low tide came since there was not a predicted higher high tide for a month!

Then in our impatience we made a big mistake—we turned on the engine. We thought engine power added to our winching would kedge us off. It did. With the added power of the engine, *Sanctuary* popped off the bottom and slewed out into 15 feet of water, but as she moved the stern line was sucked up and wrapped around the prop. With the wind blowing and the current shifting, the full weight of *Sanctuary* rested on the stern anchor line caught on the prop.

We spent four hours trying everything we knew to untangle the line and finally gave up, deciding to cut the anchor loose. Jim didn't dare get into the river. We knew the current was much too swift and strong for his Parkinson's-impaired arms, so I struggled into my wet suit and went overboard to do the job. Once in the water, I couldn't see through the dark silt and could only work by feel. With the current dragging me away from the boat, I took deep breaths and dove under toward the prop and the line struggling to hang onto the hull while sawing at the line one-handed. I was uncertain and afraid of how the boat would swing when the line parted and didn't want to trap myself. The current and my fear quickly exhausted me. The job was more than I could handle.

I climbed back aboard to catch my breath. Looking ashore with our binoculars, we saw two young, strong-looking fishermen. Maybe they would be willing to help. I wrote down a few key words in Spanish and Portuguese (Please, need help, rope twisted, can you cut it?) and did a quick drawing of the hull and twisted anchor line. Jim took the note and rode the dinghy to shore. I waited onboard, changing out of my wetsuit and watching anxiously as he talked to the two men. They got into a small boat and followed him back to *Sanctuary*.

After some conversation in garbled Spanish and Portuguese (they were from the Portuguese side of the river) and the drawing of the boat, hull, prop, and anchor line, we finally knew they understood. They agreed to help, no problem. The smaller of the men put on my wetsuit, took his big fishing knife, and dove effortlessly under the hull. He cut the line but was unable to grab the other end to save the anchor. (Of course later as we bemoaned our fate and went over all of the "shouldas, wouldas, and couldas, we knew we "shoulda" tied a buoy on the anchor line.) We gave the kind fisherman the wetsuit and some money in thanks and payment and re-anchored *Sanctuary* in a deeper spot for the night, listening to the crickets singing as we licked our wounds. We had reacted too quickly and learned the hard way.

The next morning, we started the engine with trepidation and knew right away that the prop was damaged. We shut off the engine and sailed slowly down river using the current for a boost. After anchoring again at Ayamonte, we replaced our lost anchor and stern anchor line at a fisherman's supply store (for about half the price of what one would cost in the States). We considered ourselves lucky at that since we knew any prop repair would be costly. In the calmer, clearer waters at Ayamonte, we both went overboard at slack water and looked at the prop underwater. The prop shaft was bent. A check in the engine room showed the torque had damaged the engine motor mounts and what else we didn't know. We needed a haul-out facility with a repair shop.

After looking over the charts, the Spanish port of Chipiona, at the mouth of the Rio Guadalquivir, seemed a good bet since it had a marina, boat yard, and lift. Luckily, the winds were perfect for sailing on to Chipiona since we couldn't motor at all. When we reached the dog-legged harbor mouth, we radioed the harbor master who came out in a small motor boat and towed *Sanctuary* into a slip. We started arrangements for a haul-out, dreading the price we would have to pay for our stupidity. There we were set to repair our boat in an exotic location again. *Sanctuary* was hauled out on a large travel lift the next day. The damage was more than we imagined:

1. The prop shaft was grooved and bent and needed to be replaced. 2. The cutlass bearing bracket was bent and needed to be re-

placed. 3. The old packing gland wouldn't work on a new shaft; it would also have to be replaced. 4. The engine motor mounts had pulled out and would have to be replaced. 5. The engine would have to be realigned. 6. The rudder "play" had caused a slight cracking near the entry point on the stern and would need to be reinforced. 7. The rudder would have to be removed, and the bearings at the boot/foot and the top would have to be replaced. 8. A rubber packing gland on the rudder needed to be replaced. 9. Once the rudder was repaired it would need to be refiberglassed and repainted.

All the work added up to a large fool's tax. We lucked out in two ways: the yard manager spoke fairly good English, and we'd met our dock neighbors, an English couple named Pat and Dave Jerwood, on holiday aboard their sailboat *Chetwynds*. Aside from being an absolutely delightful couple, they owned and operated a marina and boat shop in Avon, England. Dave knew a wealth of information about how to go about the repairs and donated a lot of his time to Jim, going over the damage, the options, and in general helping us "sort it all out," as he said.

Work started right away, but we knew the repair process would take at least a month, maybe more, so we resigned ourselves to life on "the hard," determined to make the best of the unexpected costly situation. The yard manager was the only one who spoke English, so I got out my Spanish dictionary and started learning boat-repair words.

The marina did not have a washing machine, and I soon found out that there was not a public washing machine anywhere in the entire city of Chipiona (population 17,000). In desperation after a day of walking all over town carrying my dirty laundry and looking for a Laundromat, I limped into the only open hotel I could find and begged them to do my laundry. Even begging and offers of money didn't work.

All the way around the world I washed small articles of clothing by hand in buckets. I always found a machine sooner or later for the heavy items like sweatshirts, jeans, and sheets. I could not imagine doing all the laundry all the time by hand all winter long, especially when it started raining every day. I was discouraged.

I lugged the dirty laundry back to the boatyard and climbed up the rickety ladder to get aboard, winching the laundry basket up and wrestling it over the safety lines. Thinking about climbing up and down the ladder to get aboard every day for months wore me out. My mind boggled at the idea of washing laundry by hand as well. For the time being I stuffed the dirty clothes into the "V" berth (out of sight, out of mind), gathered up Jim, Dave, and Pat, and the four of us went to town for a nice steak dinner.

The next day Jim rigged up a hose leading from the galley sink drain out into the harbor. That way I could wash dishes in the sink as usual using water from our tanks. We set up a pail with a lid to use as a nighttime slop bucket. During the day we'd climb the ladder and hike over to the bathroom (way on the other side of the boatyard). At least there was a shower there, too. (Maybe I could do the laundry in the shower?) Thank goodness for small favors.

Parts were ordered, and the repair work progressed slowly. We assisted as we could or sat and waited, getting on with daily life in our new home. The warm climate in Chipiona was similar to southern California's with bougainvilleas and other flowers still blooming in October. Lamps made of bubble glass blown into wrought-iron frames lit the walkways. Red tile roofs accented stucco or adobe-walled houses with 12-foot tall oak doorways and windowed balconies. Hand-painted tiles set into the white walls added bursts of color. Hardly any people were on the streets. Where was everyone? The marina manager told us that tourism had replaced fishing as the main industry in Chipiona, but by October 1996, when we hauled out, the season was over. The tourists had gone home and the town was buttoned up tight for the winter. Stores along the *paseo* (walking street) opened only Monday through Friday from 10:00 a.m. until 2:00 p.m. if they opened at all.

As we wandered around town, Jim and I stood out like red capes to a bull. After a few days, the locals at the vegetable store, the bread shop, the pharmacy, the newspaper stand, and the butcher shop all recognized us and knew who we were and where we were staying. "You live on a boat?" "Yes, we live on a boat, a sailboat." "You sailed the boat from America?" "Yes, across the Atlantic." "Oh, you're the ones on that boat hauled out in the yard." "Yes, that's us."

The Castilian Spanish spoken in Chipiona was quite different from the Spanish we had learned in Mexico, but people listened patiently as we struggled with pronunciation and the more formal grammar. I continued to ask everyone about washing machines. Everyone gave me the same answer: No Laundromat.

Then one sunny day a fellow wearing shorts which showed off a long tiger tattoo that flowed up his left leg rode up on a bicycle and called to us in English through the boatyard fence: "Hey, are you from the States? Did you sail here from the America?" "Yes," we replied, and after a chat we learned Henry was a Mexican-American, retired from the U.S. Navy and living in Chipiona with his Spanish wife and their daughter. He wanted to get a sailboat and sail across the Atlantic to America. From then on Henry rode his bicycle to the boatyard just about every day, to bring us an English language newspaper, to talk about the boat repairs, our boat, and ocean sailing. One day, to my great delight, Henry and his wife invited us over to their apartment for lunch and to use their washing machine. This kindness meant so much to me and our yellowing hand-washed clothing!

Between shopping and working on the boat, we rode the bus about 80 km to Seville, the fourth-largest city in Spain. An inscription on the Jerez Gate in one of Seville's large parks says of the city: "Hercules built me, Caesar surrounded me with walls and towers, the King Saint took me." Buildings and museums from all three eras cried out to be toured. Mostly we enjoyed looking at them from the outside since boat repairs had eaten up so much of our money. A group of cruisers were wintering in a marina on the river in the heart of town. We reconnected with some friends, and the marina manager cooked us all a huge paella dinner. Seville was exciting, but we gladly retreated to the relative calm of Chipiona.

As winter progressed, everything aboard *Sanctuary* was no longer calm. The winds howled, and daily rains pelted the hatches. One especially windy night the mast vibrated and the rigging sang. Unfamiliar noises—a vibration under the waterline and a clanging on the port side—woke us. Jim climbed out of the dry cabin to find the cause of the noises. I cringed as he went out in the dark to scale the ladder tied to *Sanctuary*'s side. He climbed back up to reenter the cabin a few minutes later, and after drying off said, "Good thing I checked. I retied a loose, vibrating jack stand, and resecured the banging ladder, too." Would this haul-out never end?

Sanctuary was relaunched on New Year's Eve, after 65 days on the hard. We had paid our stupidity price in full. High winds created a nasty swell in the harbor. *Sanctuary* heeled so much at the dock that visiting Spanish friends became seasick. We were afloat and in motion again!

I forgot the bucket-carrying and the awkward climbs by ladder to the ground. We put the sails back on, and in spite of the heavy rain, we sailed on New Year's Day to Puerto Sherry, the site of a more secure marina in which to complete our winter layover. I gave it gold stars for its Laundromat, indoor swimming pool, and no sea chop in the harbor. The two-mile walk into the nearby town of El Puerto de Santa Maria for groceries was a healthy one, but I didn't care because the Laundromat was right at the end of our dock! Hard times were over.

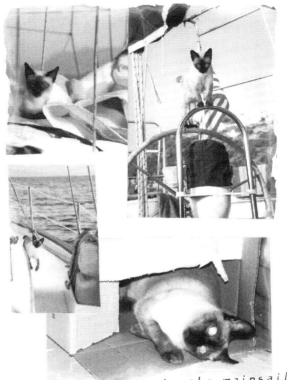

Chica on the sidedeck, the mainsail, the wheel/binnacle & in a box.

One of our favorite markets in El Puerto was near a pet store. A blue-eyed, scruffy, stubby-tailed half-Manx and half-Siamese kitten cried each time we passed her cage. "Poor scrawny thing," I said, "no one wants the runt of the litter and with no tail to boot." One day as I let her out of the cage she purred and licked my face. A week later she was still in the pet store cage. The week after that we took her home to *Sanctuary*. "Chiquita Banana" adjusted easily to life aboard. (Later she sniffed the wind and rode in the belly of the mainsail when we were underway.)

From January to April we refinished *Sanctuary*'s entire interior teak while picking kitten hairs out of the varnish. Jim completed other maintenance. Between projects we rode the bus or train and toured Spain some more. The Prado Museum in Madrid, with paintings by Goya, was our favorite tourist site. We attended *Semana Santa* (Easter week celebration), Carnival, and *Feria*. A high-stepping horse-drawn carriage carried us to the four-day flamenco-filled celebration. Our stamina was sufficient for one evening only. On *Feria's* high note, we left El Puerto and headed across the Strait of Gibraltar to Africa.

Morocco: Which One Would It Be?

May 1997

"Trust in Allah, but tie your camel."

—Arabian Proverb

We slipped into the harbor of Tangier, Morocco on May 10, 1997. There was no room to anchor as we had planned, so while Jim eased *Sanctuary* into position, I readied our dock lines in order to side-tie to a fishing boat at the crowded dock. As Jim jockeyed *Sanctuary* alongside, I draped fenders and scurried to secure the bow line first. I felt *Sanctuary* rock and looked up in surprise as three rough-looking men, with guns strapped bandolier-style across their chests, abruptly stepped aboard.

There was no "Howdy do." I got the bow and stern dock lines tied in spite of the men in my way, and we ferreted out, in a jumble of French, English, and Spanish, that the three represented Immigration, The Military Police, and Customs (or possibly they represented Bribery, Fear Control, and Extortion). During the "Checking In" process, they made away with two packs of cigarettes (since we don't smoke, these were packed deep in a locker, stockpiled for our anticipated Suez Canal transit), two cassette tapes they "discovered" in another locker, tried to take our wine (I didn't let them by asking, "Are Muslims allowed to drink?" as I removed the bottles from their hands), all of our ship's papers, and our passports. They pawed through my clothing in a most disgusting manner, peered through my prescription sunglasses, sneered at our sailing magazines, and left no locker untouched. Since we assumed the guns were loaded (extra rounds of bullets lined their belts) we didn't protest anything too intensely and made no reply when the Customs Official said clearly, in English, "*Sanctuary* is a very strange name for a boat."

Meanwhile, Chica, our new kitten, climbed up on the head of the Immigration Officer and began chewing his hat. He clawed her off, otherwise ignoring her, maybe because he assumed she was one of the five or six wild cats from ashore which by then prowled around on our decks.

The three officials abruptly quit searching and "suggested" that we hire Azzi to be our guide. "Just who is Azzi?" I inquired. At that point the three stepped off *Sanctuary* and on stepped a fellow in a long white robe. We had noticed him on shore earlier, squatting in his voluminous robe and imperturbably watching the check-in process.

We were exhausted from our passage across the Strait of Gibraltar. I was very uncomfortable in the presence of Muslim males while still wearing my sailing shorts, so just to get Azzi off the boat, we agreed to let him come back in about two hours and "guide" us to dinner. I shooed the wild cats off with Azzi, clamped all the portholes closed even though it was hot, and we hunkered below wondering what we were doing in Morocco anyway.

As the sun went down and people disappeared from the boat harbor, we ventured out into the cockpit and took in the view of fishing vessels, ferries, and freighters. Trains passed close by on shore, and the white buildings of the city glowed ghostlike in the twilight. Off our stern, high on a steep bluff in the *medina*, the 100-year-old Hotel Continental looked down on us. From a distance, the city of Tangier and the old hotel with its blue tiles, wrought iron balconies, and fringe of palm trees, evoked romantic flashes of the Humphrey Bogart movie "Casablanca." The city of Tangier, we discovered, however, was more similar to "The Treasure of the Sierra Madre"—only in Arabic.

We read that 90% of the adult males of Morocco were unemployed and realized our guide's purpose was not to show us around. His job was to keep all the other would-be "guides" at bay. When Azzi returned at 7:00 p.m., he paid another man a few *dirhams* and a pack of cigarettes to shoo the wild dock cats away from baby Chiquita while we were off the boat. He warned us about pickpockets, told us to stick close to him, waved some other "guides" aside, and we set off for dinner.

Azzi offered to take us to a belly-dancing show. We were so tired we could hardly walk much less watch belly dancing. We only wanted to sit down and said, "No, thank you. Just take us to a quiet restaurant, please." Azzi obliged, and I ordered lamb couscous which was served in a lovely earthenware bowl towering with steamed vegetables and lamb topped with onion and raisin sauce. It was delicious. Maybe this was why we were in Morocco; I had been waiting for a taste treat like that for ages. Jim enjoyed shish-kebab with tomato sauce and a beer called "Flag." I stuck to tea served from an ornate hammered teapot and poured into a tiny glass etched with stars. By 9:00 p.m. we were ready to return to *Sanctuary*. Azzi was horrified that we ended the night so early, so we hired him for a proper tour of the city in the morning.

Azzi arrived the next day at 10:00 a.m., and off we went again. In an attempt to blend in with the locals, we dressed in our most conservative clothing. We therefore spent the better part of four hot days in Tangier modestly attired but dripping wet. Most of the Muslim women wore *djeballahs* (floor-length caftan-type robes) on top of other clothing. In addition to the hooded robe, they wore head scarves tied under their chins. Some wore a veil as well. When combined with all the other gear, only their eyes and hands were visible. Mysteriously, they appeared cool and calm, or were their looks ones of resignation? Many men wore the djeballahs as well, topped by a tall fez or small skull cap.

High-pitched wails pierced the harbor, bus, motorcycle, train, radio, and people noises. The five daily calls to prayer, broadcast over loudspeakers from mosques throughout the city, demanded action. Men obeyed the wails, pulling out small rugs from within folds of fabric, kneeling, and touching their foreheads to the ground. The women keep walking. So did we, sticking to Azzi like gum on a hot sidewalk.

Azzi hustled us through the *medina*, a maze of *souks* filled with junk and treasure, pointing out things we might buy. We settled on a kilo of perfect strawberries for only 60 cents and a round of fresh goat cheese on a palm leaf for 75 cents and bargained with a trinket salesman for some beads. We passed burlap bags of spices including henna for the hands and kohl for the eyes. At the Berber market, women wearing conical hats with black tassels, their red and white striped skirt pockets bulging with mint leaves, sold handmade brooms and brushes. Drums, their ceramic bases stretched with goat skins, tilted in towering stacks. Levi jeans (or imitations) sat piled next to *djeballahs*. Silk fabric, silk thread, and embroidered backless silk shoes rested under glass. Carpets covered walls, ceilings, floors, hung out of windows, leaned against buildings, and every shopkeeper spoke enough English to call, "You Engleesh? Come een, come een. Een Morocco we bargain, don't be shy."

Azzi, wanting to sell us as much as possible in as little time as possible, hurriedly swept us through the most interesting parts of the city by taxi—which had no handles to roll down the back windows. When we asked to stop at a restaurant for lunch and a bit of a rest, he called the taxi to a halt and proceeded to lead us, sweating, thirsty, and exhausted uphill on foot back through the *casbah*.

At last Azzi pointed toward a cool cavern where we were greeted by a friendly gentleman with a pointed beard dressed in the traditional *djeballah*, fez, and curled-toe slippers without heels or backs. As we entered, the stranger clapped his hands, and several humps of cloth came to life, turning on the lights, arranging cushions, and bringing out tables. The man exchanged hugs, kisses on cheeks, several nods, and handshakes with our guide who then introduced us in a smear of sounds that we couldn't imagine meant anything. A second man, dark, wrinkled, and looking 150 years old, slipped off Jim's backpack as another hooded robe removed my hat and took our packages. As our things disappeared, our guide said, "Don't worry, they are safe." We had just entered the den of Ali Baba and the seven thieves.

Ali Baba clapped his hands again, and looking at us, ordered "Tea." I said, "No, thanks. We don't want tea. Water will do." Azzi, our guide, said, "Never drink the water in Tangier." There was another babble of soft sounds undecipherable to us. Azzi said, "Do you want your tea sweet or very sweet?" I said, "We would like to go to a restaurant." Azzi replied, "You will insult the man if you come to his home and do not drink his tea." We ordered sweet. A woman dressed in all black with a veil over her face brought two glasses stuffed with mint leaves covered with hot, sweet water.

One sip was all we dared take of the sickly sweet concoction, and we again asked Azzi to take us to a restaurant. He explained that our host wanted to show us his collection of genuine Berber handmade Kilim carpets. I said, "What would we do with a carpet on board a boat? We live on our boat and don't own a house." Azzi said, "He just wants you to see them—a show." Another clap of hands brought more men in hooded robes who started unrolling carpets.

The carpets were incredibly beautiful, from lush, thick, wool piles with deep, dark, rich colors to worn-thin silk of faded earthen colors yet finely made into fantastic patterns. Each carpet was a masterpiece. Soon Jim and I were discussing with each other which ones we liked best. We wondered and imagined what they must cost. I had to ask, "How much is this one?" The answer: "Just pick out five most favorite ones, we will remove the rest and then I can make you a crazy price." I said, "We are only curious about the price, and besides, we live on a boat and don't have a house for a carpet anyway." The answer: "Don't worry about price; just pick your favorite three from the five you have chosen." My response: "We are only curious. We don't want one."

Ali Baba gave us a price on the three we had chosen as our favorites, and we immediately repeated that we were just curious and couldn't afford any of them. The salesman then told us, "Think of it as an investment. You can always sell it for much more than they cost when you get home."

"But we don't have a house—and we're not going home."

"Don't worry about a house, who needs a house? You are buying a work of art."

"We don't need a work of art."

"It will be part of your inheritance to your children." The next thing we knew, we were negotiating the price on "The one most favorite that if we did like just one which one would it be?" The more we resisted, the lower the price came until the amount was just a fraction of the original. We would have been fools not to buy one at the ridiculously low bargaining price. Finally Ali Baba said, "Take at that price—then I go shoot myself with gun." We felt so bad about getting the fellow down so low on his price that we felt obligated to make the purchase. Where were we going to get the money to live on for the next month?

He wrote up a ticket. Since we could not use our credit card, we'd return the next day with a check. The seller agreed to send the treasure by air freight, insured, and guaranteed to arrive in the States as soon as the check cleared the bank.

"Which one would it be?"
carpet, Tangier

We finally retrieved our packs and packages, got out of the carpet store, and asked again for a restaurant. Azzi again reminded us to watch our wallets, backpacks, cameras, sunglasses, hats, anything in our pockets, or anything else of value. Basically, we were to watch anything not permanently attached to our bodies. He said very seriously, "There are people here that will cut your throat for the shirt off your back." In a lighter tone he added, "Of course they would not stab you because it would cut the shirt." No one touched me, but Jim nudged me saying he had felt several hands slip in and out of his empty pockets.

I didn't know that Jim, as a joke, had taken a wallet-sized pad of notebook paper and drawn sketches in it intended to spook a thief such as scary cartoons of skull and crossbones, or thieves getting their hands cut off by Allah, or pigs with cloven-hoofed hands holding the Koran. After folding it up as if it were a wallet full of money, he had put it into the outside pocket of his backpack. As we finally sat down at lunch, he examined his backpack and then told me and Azzi what he had done and that the little cartoon "wallet" was gone. Azzi yelled at him saying, "You could have your throat cut for such blasphemy."

We ate and rolled our tongues around lamb with onions, squash, chick peas, garlic, coriander, lemon, cinnamon, oranges, and olives over couscous with almond cookies for dessert. Sweet, hot, mint tea arrived in tall etched glasses. Out we went from the restaurant back to the *souks* with the smells of rotting fish, mint, dates, olives, sweat, and diesel fumes, and with all the noises: the chicken squawking, dog barking, wailing, yelling, motor grinding, curb jumping, nerve stretching din. No wonder the locals went

Morocco: Jim & guide

often to the quiet mosques (which non-Muslim, "Great Satan" heathens, could only look into but not enter).

In the heart of the *casbah* we toured Dar-el-Makhzen, the Sultan's palace turned museum, which sat on a hill overlooking the sea toward Gibraltar. We appreciated the Sultan's garden choked though it was with weeds. The high walls muffled the city noises, and as we sat in the shade under the tangerine trees, we noticed the colors—sun-bleached green, pink, yellow, purple, rust-streaked white, and gray—colors and scenes that had inspired Matisse. Old tiled fountains with stagnant water enticed the only birds we had heard or seen since arriving on Moroccan soil. Recuperated, we plunged on through the *casbah,* passing intriguing, expensive, yet derelict-looking whitewashed villas. We drank coffee at the Cafe de Paris and sweet mint tea at the Hotel Continental.

That evening back aboard *Sanctuary,* I read for the first time the tourist warnings issued by the U.S. government, various tourist guides, and the Moroccan Consulate. The Consular information sheet stated: "Morocco has a moderately high crime rate in urban areas. Criminals have targeted tourists for assaults, muggings, thefts, pickpockets, and scams of all types. Commonly reported crimes include shipping inferior rugs as a substitute for the rugs purchased by the traveler." Oh, dear!

What should we do? Was the carpet sale a scam? Did we pay too much? How did we know we got the deal of the century? No wonder Ali Baba came so low on his price. The shop would switch rugs on us or just never send one. He seemed such a nice man. How would we get out of this one? We looked at the receipt I had signed, and printed in several places was "No Cancellations" and "We reserve our right to refuse cancellations." We had been "slam-dunked."

We comforted each other saying, "That's all right. We haven't given up any money or the check. We'll simply never go back. Let's leave on the next high tide or slip out in the middle of the night." All we had to do was get our passports back from the Immigration Officer and our ship's papers from the Port Captain and be cursed by Allah at the worst.

The next morning, before we got moving, Azzi appeared. He wanted to take the check to Ali Baba himself for our convenience (more likely to get his commission). We told Azzi we weren't going back to buy the rug. His nostrils flared and his lips drew tight as he told us it was impossible to cancel the deal. The seller would simply put a hold on our passports and the port captain would stop us from leaving. "It is Moroccan law. You can go to jail."

Remembering all too well how Azzi had been "suggested" by the three gun-toting officials who were in possession of our passports, we switched to plan number two: write a check with an irregular signature that would never clear the bank. Therefore, Ali Baba wouldn't send the rug (or inferior rug) and we would be long gone before anyone got wise to our scheme. We prepared a check payable to the rug dealer that Jim signed with his left hand. His signature was so bad it could have said "Ima Phoney" and no one would have noticed.

We gave Azzi the check to deliver. He disappeared in a taxi, but returned shortly saying, "You must go to the bank to cash the check. Otherwise, the carpet seller will file a complaint. You won't be able to leave Morocco until the check clears and he gets his money."

Plan number three: It really was a lovely rug. If we were stuck buying a rug we didn't want, didn't need, and might go to jail over, then we might as well get the right one and take it with us. At least it was "The most favorite, if we did like one, which one would it be."

So we cashed the check at a bank, went back to the carpet store, had them unroll the carpet to make sure it was the one we had chosen the day before, gave them the money, took our carpet, went back to the harbor and retrieved our passports and ship's documents from the Port Captain. With guns strapped to his chest as usual, he followed us to the dock and commanded, "Captain, start your engines."

We left.

Across the Mediterranean

May 1997—October 1997

> "The traveler sees what he sees; the tourist sees what he has come to see."
>
> — G.K. Chesterton, Essayist, Novelist (1874-1936)

After leaving Tangier, we sailed on to little-known Ceuta, a small Spanish enclave of about 10 square miles tucked away on the Moroccan coast of Africa. Check-in was a breeze. After helping us with our dock lines, the Port Captain simply handed us a form to fill out saying, "Bring this over to the office when you can. Welcome to Spain."

At the squeaky clean marina, clear water flowed from a tap (we filled our tanks without worry of amoebas or worse), the electrical outlets worked (we plugged in to shore power and charged our batteries), and the telephone system worked (we called our families). In the easy-to- navigate town, supplies were inexpensive (rum was only $2.22 a bottle), boat fuel was even more reasonable (diesel was 67 cents a gallon!), there was a laundry service only two blocks from the marina—and there were no touts on the streets. Tangier squatted a scant 25 miles to the west along the African coast, but Ceuta lay light years away in atmosphere. We breathed easily.

As soon as we secured *Sanctuary* to the quay wall, our American flag and blue-eyed tailless cat began to attract attention. Many of the locals strolling along the docks stopped at *Sanctuary* to ask us about our journey and blue-eyed Chica who quickly became a star. She had adapted to life aboard with great aplomb. Ceuta did not have any wild cats around the marina, so while in port Chica lounged atop the furled mainsail on the boom or on the life sling on the stern surveying her kingdom. In spite of not having a tail, she balanced easily on the stainless steel rails along *Sanctuary*'s stern and jumped across the water to shore without a problem.

A day or two after we arrived I chipped a tooth, and when I went to a dentist for a repair he greeted me with, "Oh, you're from the American boat in the harbor with the cat aboard—I'll be glad to fix your tooth."

We decided to give Morocco a second chance, so with Chica and *Sanctuary* snug and safe at the dock in Spain, we rode a bus the short distance to the border. Many Moroccan women on their way home loaded down with full shopping bags crowded in the aisles. We got off the bus to walk across the border alongside hundreds of other people carrying bags, boxes, or sacks, or pushing carts. The border itself, guarded by both the Spanish and the Moroccans, was grimy, dirty, and smelled like a river of piss.

To enter Morocco, we filled out numerous forms, and then, along with a few other English-speaking foreigners, we were escorted to a small room to wait, presumably while our passports were checked in some fashion. Neither taxis nor buses were allowed across the border, and all passengers in private cars were questioned. We watched as several of the cars were thoroughly searched. A parking lot on the Moroccan side was packed with confiscated cars, their owners having been arrested for trying to smuggle cigarettes and liquor into Morocco. Finally, our passports were returned and we were cleared to enter.

After discovering that the nearest bus on the Moroccan side was three kilometers away, we hired a taxi to drive us to Tetouan. During the drive along the coast, we passed sand dunes, hills, eucalyptus trees, roadside pottery stands, a Hyatt Hotel, a Club Med, and a river of people, some walking with burros, going to and from the border to the bus stop. Moroccan policemen scattered along the route randomly checked cars. Our taxi was stopped; we were inspected with hard stares and waved on.

The city of Tetouan was somewhat similar to Tangier with ruins from Phoenician and Roman eras, a *medina* with s*ouks*, and wonderful food, but there was no pressure of guides or tourist traps. We walked around freely, shopping or not as we wanted, and returned to Ceuta in the evening. We crossed over again a few days later, investigating more of Morocco and its Mediterranean coast, but didn't stray too close to Algeria. We were quickly sated by the taste of our first Muslim country.

After two weeks, we left the coast of Africa and set sail back to mainland Spain, harbor-hopping from Motril to Alicante and squandering a few days here and there. While Jim read or spliced ropes, I swam or spent lazy days writing or painting watercolors of the hillsides and castles that overlooked our anchorages. Morocco crushed us. Spain renewed us.

It seemed that we should show more interest in Roman and European history, the route of Ulysses, the Christians, and the Moors and the whatever. We guiltily read guidebooks but just couldn't summon the energy to venture inland to rent a car, or ride a train, or catch a bus, or walk around another castle. We took most of our history lessons as we found them—accidentally. Discovery bumped into us as we talked with the locals who sold us vegetables or fresh fish or met fellow cruisers with whom we shared anchorages. As we gunk holed along the SE coast of Spain, we crossed paths with sailors from Holland, England, France, Sweden, Germany, Canada, and the United States. Friendships were easily born out of the common labor all of us shared in sailing our boats hundreds, and sometimes thousands, of miles to converge in any given anchorage. Conversations shared over potlucks, a gallimaufry of dishes, rang out over the water in a raucous medley of languages.

The Spanish islands of the Baleares serve as Europe's Hawaii. After a 24-hour sail from Torrevieja on the mainland, we set our hook in a lovely bay at the Balearic Island of Formentera with the cleanest waters we had floated on since Scotland. We skipped along all of the islands of the chain, sometimes anchoring in isolation but most often swinging on our hook among charter vessels. Jim and I sat in our cockpit enjoying the show of the mostly German and British bums and breasts. Hotels, cafes, and beachfront bars lined most of the shores, and tourists splayed on beach towels roasting like chickens on Spanish spits. Technically we were tourists, too, but we mentally separated ourselves from the masses since we traveled turtle-like; our home was always with us.

On June 22, 1997, we abandoned Spain and enjoyed an uneventful (how we loved "uneventful") three-day passage back to Africa. We watched dolphins and birds and listened to the seas, the light winds, and our radio, hearing only, "All cheeps, all cheeps, all cheeps, sécurité, sécurité, sécurité, for weather information go to channel 25, 82, 10 and up." The weather forecasts were for mild winds until on the third day a gale forecast surfaced. We arrived safely at port in Bizerte, Tunisia, before it struck.

After setting our hook in a protected spot in a lovely, wide harbor, we idly wondered why no other boats were anchored. Soon a young man wearing a military-type uniform powered a small inflatable boat over to *Sanctuary*'s side and demanded that we move to the scruffy-looking dock. "We'll be glad to check in; we'll ride our dinghy over right away. Is there a reason we cannot remained anchored?" This resulted in a loud barrage from the young man who turned out to be a "National Policeman." We surrendered, upped anchor, and "docked."

Jim and I had vowed from the beginning to learn the basics of the main language of every country we visited. Therefore, we carried dictionaries and interactive tapes or CD language lessons aboard *Sanctuary* for Spanish, French, German, Russian, Portuguese, Italian, Greek, Turkish, Arabic, Thai, Malay, Japanese, and more. We both spoke Spanish fairly well. During our layover in England in 1996, we took French lessons, reasoning that if we could not speak the first language of a country (such as Arabic) then French would be a good second language to know.

Arabic proved a stumbling block. Before we arrived in Morocco we studied Arabic, yet once we got there we let the guide Azzi, who spoke English, translate. Well, Bizerte would be our chance to try, if not Arabic, then at least the French we'd learned a year earlier. We had spoken it rarely, but after noticing the signs in Bizerte written in both Arabic and French, I thought I could use my pocket dictionary and squeak by. My French did squeak by at the first shop, where I bought a lovely hand-painted plate and a small basket. At the bread and the vegetable vendors, I also managed the purchases and counted out in French the *dinars*, the Tunisian currency.

By the time we got to the last shop on our route, a small, dark stall crowded with nuts and spices, I was tired. Waist-high burlap bags overflowed with both shelled and unshelled nuts of all types. Spices spilled out of smaller cloth bags stacked atop big barrels. The prices were written in French and Arabic on pieces of cardboard mounted on sticks stuck haphazardly into the piles of products. The potpourri of smells overpowered me. I wedged myself between the bags and barrels, and women wearing headscarves squeezed past me as they choose spices. Jim was the only man in view except for the burly, fast-talking shopkeeper. I understood enough words to know that the shopkeeper and all the women were talking about us.

I wanted to buy just a little bit of *harissa*, a type of very hot and spicy red chili paste. I asked, in French, for the amount I thought would fit into a baby-food jar. After I asked, the shopkeeper, clapping his hands, stopped everything; a small boy materialized from behind a burlap bag and ran to the stall next door. "Jim," I asked, "What's happening?" He shrugged. Back came the boy with two large gallon jars. As the shopkeeper dug deep into the *harissa* and began to fill one of the jars, I realized he was packing them for me. In the babble I heard what translated to the equivalent of "$52 American dollars, please."

"No, no," I said (in my obviously awful French), "There is a mistake; I just wanted a little amount. We can't pay $52. I'm sorry."

The shopkeeper began to yell. At this point I wasn't sure whether he spoke Arabic or French, but I knew a curse when I heard one. I burst into tears, lurched out of the shop, and plastered myself to the stucco wall, sobbing uncontrollably. The watchful women backed away as if I were contagious, but the shopkeeper turned into a lamb, came out, and began patting my shoulder as if I were a child, apologizing, and handing me a small handful of candy. While I dried my eyes, Jim completed the resulting six-dollar purchase of a small jar of *harissa* and some almonds.

Carthage (where the Christians were fed to the lions) was a hot walk around a dusty site. The King's palace lay immediately next door, its garden wall guarded by very young boys brandishing sub-machine guns. They instructed us not to take pictures of Carthage with the camera aimed toward the palace. Okay, Sir, whatever you say.

We left Carthage to visit Sidi Bou Said, a traditionally whitewashed blue and white city. It had cheerfully painted doors, interesting crafts, no boys with weapons, and more tasty lamb and couscous. In Muslim Tunisia, the majority of women were not shrouded in *djeballahs* like the females in Morocco, but men and women both stared at my short, gray, uncovered hair. Together Jim and I were as much a curiosity to the Tunisians as they were to us.

As we moved from harbor to harbor in Tunisia, polite, but extremely firm, port officials kept us in check. Anchoring (which we preferred) was not allowed, and we were required to moor in marginally habitable "marinas." The five-times-daily singsong voices wailing from mosque loudspeakers that called the faithful to prayer, the circumspect demeanor of the women, the unsmiling faces, even the oppressive, stifling heat constantly reminded us of how very distant we were from freedom of speech, dress, and religion. An abridged tour of Tunisia's edges was sufficient.

Sailing on fair winds, *Sanctuary* flew to Malta from Tunisia at an average of seven knots with only a reefed main and staysail. The Maltese officials did not want our cat ashore, and therefore required us to anchor (contrary to the Tunisians, who required us to be at a dock at all times yet cared not a whit about the cat—there were no rules for her). So, in Malta, thanks to Chica, we swung alone on the hook smack dab in the middle of Valletta Harbor. All the sailors we met, who were crowded together and "med moored" (beam to beam, bow or stern to the wall) asked us, "How come you get to anchor?" "All because of our cat," we answered.

We hauled containers of water back to our boat since *Sanctuary* was not even allowed to pull over to the dock lest our cat contaminate the rabies-free shores. Oh, the vagaries of beliefs, governments, and politics. We did enjoy the English-language newspapers, chandlers, and quality British products sold in the many stores.

Letters from friends and the cruising grapevine had told us that some of the cruisers we'd met in 1990 and 1991 in California and Mexico had continued west about the world. Thus, old friends traveling at our slow pace had subsequently sailed "up" the Red Sea and were in the Mediterranean. *Sanctuary*'s east-about route would cross their west-about route somewhere, and we enjoyed the first unexpected reunion in Malta with *Wirraway*. We reminisced about the Sea of Cortez and then swapped some of our charts of England and Spain for some of theirs of Turkey and Israel.

Next stop: Greece. The Bay of Navarino, Pylos (on the southwestern portion of the Peloponnese Peninsula), was a lovely anchorage where we swam and relaxed on the beach. With friends Glynn and Lynn Stevens from *Bats*, we set off on a long hike looking for Nestor's Palace. The sketch map we had proved wrong, and the entire day was a hot, dusty, long, wild goose chase. Instead of Nestor's Palace, we found a beautiful beach, lots of olive groves, lemon trees, and a small village where we ate lunch surrounded by grapevines. Local men sat next to us under the shade trees drinking ouzo. Around 3:00 p.m. we wearily rounded the last sand dune that led to our dinghy, looked out to the bay, and were shocked to see *Sanctuary* missing from the anchorage. She was gone, and a boat flying a French flag was anchored in her spot!

Scanning the bay anxiously, we thankfully spotted *Sanctuary*'s hull and mast about two miles from where she should have been. We ran to launch the dinghy. In a panic Jim lifted the heavy dinghy by himself, jerking in shock as his back shot through with pain. We vowed to tend to his back shortly but first had to recover our boat. As we sped across the bay and drew closer to her, we saw that *Sanctuary* was tied to timbers of a floating fish farm. A young woman emerged from a cabin attached to the farm and, speaking perfect English, told us what had happened: "I'm from the United States and here in Greece visiting my father who owns this fish farm. We noticed your sailboat when you anchored a few days ago. This morning another sailboat came in and raised and lowered their anchor several times. Later, we saw your boat drifting slowly away. The French boat must have dislodged your anchor. We knew you were not aboard, and my father took his motorboat over, got a line on her, and towed *Sanctuary* over here."

The father and daughter refused any offers of monetary acknowledgement for the rescue, accepting only our heartfelt thanks. We wearily got Jim aboard without more damage to his back, put him below, and re-anchored in a new position closer to *Bats*. Lynn, a nurse practitioner, gave Jim a professional exam. She determined he had pulled the muscle badly but had not ruptured a disc. So we treated Jim with Tylenol/codeine, ibuprofen, rubs, anti-inflammatory meds, and rest, rest, rest.

I took over as nurse. The weather became iffy, so with help from Glynn and Lynn I med-moored *Sanctuary* to a dock about five miles from our anchorage. The spot became our enforced home for the long, dusty, hot weeks that Jim lay below decks flat on his back. He gingerly moved a bit more each day. I walked into Pylos, practicing halting Greek to buy beautiful fresh vegetables, yogurt, feta, and other cheeses. Salvos, a local baker, spoke English and supplied me with encouragement regarding Jim's recovery as well as bread and cookies. Salvos also offered his address as a mail drop which allowed us to receive a shipment of medications. With rest and pain meds, Jim's back healed. After three weeks, he was able to climb the companionway stairs again. He'd crab over our stern ladder and lower himself into the cool salty water of the bay. The daily saltwater soakings spurred him back to health, and we tenderly winged on to other areas of Greece.

We quickly discovered a preference for Greece's smaller anchorages and villages. At harbors near famous sites, we anchored behind cruise ships coughing out crowds of sunburned tourists of all nationalities. Shouting taxi drivers, grasping touts, and curb-jumping motor-cyclists added to the din. Joining the herd, we "saw" what must be seen. We climbed to the top of many hot, dusty hillsides. (Surely there must have been trees when the buildings were first constructed?) Among all the temples, castles, churches, frescoes, mosaics, dusty statues, and over-photographed vistas, we did visit a few places that stood out in our memories of summer.

The first of these was Monemvasia, a 1,000-year-old medieval city. Much of the unique walled city still stands and has been renovated. People enter the thick walls through tunnels, and cars and motorbikes are prohibited (oh, blessed relief). The ancient rock houses, their tiled roofs shaded by grapevines and fig trees, have been converted into hotels, restaurants, and summer homes. We wandered narrow stone pathways, passing houses and churches, and paused on a hillside overlooking the Aegean. I enjoyed the view. Jim did too since several very well-endowed female tourists were sunbathing topless on the beach below us.

Squeezing *Sanctuary* past cruise ships, we joined the hordes on some islands or avoided the crowds on others still secret. Wending our way north, we anchored in Pireaus Bay so we could visit Athens and the Acropolis. After touring the famous ruins, we appreciated a different day with some local Greeks. Natives John and Maria Lirintzis, (cousins of Jim's so distant the details evade me) took us in hand and showed us "their" Athens. They lovingly introduced us to wonderful Greek seafood and specialties we would have missed without them and drove us into the countryside for a breath of fresh air. Back in the city, we continued touring by visiting The National Museum of Archaeology. We lingered over the modern-looking Minoan and Mycenaean jewelry created in 2000 BC. Returning to our anchored home, we recuperated from the millions of people in Athens (half of whom seemed to be taxi drivers).

Further north, later in the summer, we shared a car with friends Bill and Marti Tatum from *Capers* and traveled into central Thessaly to visit Meteora. Our tourist brochure described the monasteries as "unworldly hermitages composing one of the most breathtaking sites on earth." Huge, gray rocks jutted from a flat plain as if they were stalagmites placed by a giant. The strange, stark beauty of the rocks in contrast to the plain had us stopping the car to gape—unable to drive and crane our necks simultaneously.

In the ninth century, persecuted monks lived as hermits in the rock's faces. To escape continued attack, they climbed spider-like, higher and higher, until they could go no farther, building their monasteries on the points of the rocky needles. (Some possibly ascended all the way to heaven since in the climbing and building they fell hundreds of feet to their deaths.) All monks, supplies, and building materials were hoisted to the top of the formations in rope-basket slings or on rope ladders. The persistent monks lugged and tugged and carved and painted, creating dwellings and churches that even on flat land would impress, but perched on pinnacles, stunned. Visiting the remaining intact monasteries (accessible now by paved roads, paths, steps, and bridges) called for fortitude and stamina. The trek was breathtaking in many ways.

After visiting Meteora and reading about the Greek Orthodox

Church and its history, we learned of Mt. Athos, a monastic area in a region southeast of Thessaloniki. We planned to sail to the supposedly beautiful and remote area but then discovered that women were not allowed to set foot in the area. Even visits by men were limited to 10 non-orthodox men per day with written permission obtained in advance. Boats couldn't approach the shores closer than 500 meters. *Sanctuary* would have to obtain a permit just to "sail by" the coastline. We scrapped the idea.

Meanwhile, artifacts more than 12 centuries old were being removed from Mt. Athos for the first time and assembled in Thessalonica for a once-in-a-lifetime exhibit. If we couldn't visit the area, we could at least visit some of the relics. Along with our traveling buddies, we drove to Thessalonica to view the "Treasures of Mt. Athos." (My girlfriend Marti and I were among the first women to see the relics. Did our female eyes damage them?)

The treasures included dishes and implements used and created by the monks: prayer beads, silver chalices, handwritten Bibles, other illuminated manuscripts, cassocks, frescoes, mosaics, and altars. All the artifacts were returned to the Mt. Athos region at the end of 1997. The exhibited photographs showed unspoiled shores we had not sullied with our female presence, boat, or anchor. The area did look beautiful. Impressed with the show, and curiosity satisfied, we sailed on to other areas of Greece more eager for the female tourist dollar.

When we bought our boat in 1990, she was named *Skiathos*. Sailors have a strong superstition against changing a boat's name but, even though we hesitated, we decided, for several reasons, to take the risk. First of all, what did *Skiathos* mean? We had no idea and neither did anyone else. (We later discovered that the previous owner's wife had named her after a beautiful Greek island she wanted to visit.) Second, we felt *Skiathos* would be difficult to spell or for people to understand over a ship's radio. Third, how was it pronounced: Skee-thos? Sky-ath-oos? Ski-at-us? Key-a-toes?

The new name was easy pickings. By 1990, Jim and I had been business partners for 15 years and married for 13. We were together constantly and, after a long day at work, we often hashed over business problems during dinner or late at night. A few years into the partnership, we realized that we needed to separate our personal lives from our business lives and vowed not to discuss business after 5:00 p.m. on workdays, or at all on our rare days off. It was a great idea when we remembered. We kept catching ourselves saying to each other, "Please, no business at home." Finally, we hit on a code word—"sanctuary." If one of us forgot the no-business rule, the other need not entertain a long discussion—just offer up "sanctuary" and enough said. When we left it all behind, our boat became, of course, *Sanctuary*, and of course, we had to sail to Skiathos, the Greek island whose name we had scraped off her hull seven years earlier.

Skiathos was indeed beautiful. The locals ashore said that in ancient Greek, the name *skiathos* meant "shade" or "shelter." Maybe we hadn't changed *Sanctuary's* name after all.

The Turkish Spay and the Exiled Camel

October 1997—August 1998

"Many things in Turkey are NQR (not quite right)."
—Sheila Nelson, fellow cruiser, *Cusar*

After dawdling along through the Greek islands of the northern Aegean, we entered Turkish waters and tucked into the marina in Kuşadasi for the winter. We had barely checked in with the Port Captain and the Harbor Manager when we were invited out to dinner with a group of friends already berthed in the marina. That evening we met Rick (Colonel, United States Army, Retired) and Sheila (Physical Therapist, Retired) Nelson who had been living in Turkey aboard their sailboat *Cusar* for 13 years. They were officially retired but certainly not retiring. Meeting Rick and Sheila made all the difference in Turkey.

We hit the ground running. The next day we joined Sheila (who was fluent in Turkish) and Fatma (Sheila's longtime Turkish friend) on a private cruisers' group tour of Ephesus, site of an ancient Greek and later a major Roman, city. The intricate carvings and columns of the Roman marble ruins stood out against surrounding vineyards, cotton fields, and olive and orange groves. On the way to the site, we passed Turkish women whose heads were covered with patterned scarves, wearing *shalvars* (huge, baggy trousers) topped by layered, loose blouses, vests, and sweaters. As they bent over their hoes working in the orchards and fields, they could have been mistaken for citizens of ancient Rome. In contrast, at Ephesus, fashionably dressed vendors hawked souvenirs in any of five languages.

A few weeks after our visit to Ephesus, Sheila organized another tour. During the winter months, when farm work halted, many rural Turkish families wove carpets or produced other products such as copper pots or ceramics. We set off to a village north of Izmir to see the handwoven rugs. En route, we passed fields of sheep, cows, cotton, melons, and tobacco. Sheaves of sesame stood waiting to be dried. Ilker, a Turkish carpet dealer and friend of Sheila's, accompanied us, and the village weavers had been alerted that potential buyers were on the way. As we drew near the village, carpets sprouted across the hoods of farm trucks or hung off walls, balconies, or out of windows.

Turkish carpet sketch

Unlike the aggressive carpet dealers in Morocco, the Turkish families and weavers were polite, almost reticent. Children shyly came out of hiding and followed us as we walked around the village, welcome to look or buy, as we wanted. A carpet in view meant "Our house is open, come in" so we ventured into the homes in which they were woven. Carpets in progress were warped on tapestry-style looms, their frames running vertically from floor to ceiling. At one home, a mother and her two daughters sat side by side on a low bench facing the loom, fingers and shuttles flying as the three worked simultaneously on each row of weft.

The patterns of the Yağcibedir-style carpets woven by the villagers in Karakaya were memorized and handed down from family to family for generations. The area vegetation determined the dominant colors of dark indigo and rich wine red sometimes accented with cream or soft brown. Traditions have changed (most carpets in Turkey are mass- produced and chemically dyed), but in the village of Karakaya, the weavers raised the sheep, spun the wool, and created the dyes from local plants. As we walked from house to house shopping, we passed groups of women outside stirring the skeins of wool stewing in the dye baths, which simmered in huge kettles balanced over open fires. The kettles were blackened from years of use. Many cruisers who accompanied Sheila and Ilker on the tour bought small Yağcibedir carpets for their cabin soles. No pressure to purchase was necessary since the quality and beauty of the workmanship sold itself. Cruisers and villagers were satisfied at the end of the day, and *"Gule, gule"* (a Turkish goodbye meaning "Go smiling") rang out as we left to return to our boats.

Many stray cats roamed around the docks near the dumpsters in the marina where *Sanctuary* was berthed. Chica was 10 months old and due for her first heat. We did not want kittens, and we searched around Kuşadasi for a veterinarian to spay her.

Dr. Mutlu Yuvez advertised "English Spoken," so we made an appointment but took Turkish-speaking Sheila with us for insurance. The stairway to the office smelled like urine, and smoke hung heavily in the air of the office. We cautiously pulled Chica from her carrier and said we wanted her spayed. The smiling veterinarian replied, "She is a beautiful cat. Don't you want her to have kittens?" We said, "No, we live on a sailboat. We don't want a litter of kittens in our small space."

He seemed to understand and said, "Yes, of course I can spay your cat." We asked, "What will the price be?"

In Turkey, as in many countries of the world, the price of almost everything—unless prepriced or put into writing—is negotiated in advance. The theory seems to be: if you're fool enough not to ask and negotiate the price first then you are probably foolish enough to pay whatever is charged. Furthermore, as we discovered, some unscrupulous merchants loved a good fight and changed a verbal deal after it was done. It was "my word against yours." After several previously unexpected and unpleasant "price versus word" confrontations, we learned to negotiate, dicker, haggle, argue, bargain, and, upon reaching an agreement, to demand a settlement in writing while smiling in the face of anger and frustration. Fortunately, few negotiations were adversarial. Thus, how much would it cost to spay our cat in Turkey?

Negotiations started with tea. During "tea" we made idle conversation with Dr. Yuvez about our marriage, our children, his marriage, his children, our boat, his house, America, and Turkey until such time as he seemed to have sized up our worth and decided how much he thought we would pay. After much chit chat we asked Dr. Yuvez for the second time, "How much will the spay cost?" He finally said, "It won't be much."

We countered: "How much will not much be?"

He said, "Approximately $150.00"

We parried: "Spaying a cat in the USA only costs $80 or less in some pet clinics. In Spain, if Chica had been old enough, the spay would have only been $25.00." Sheila, who had not been needed to translate, spoke up and said, "There is another vet in Kuşadasi; we can try there."

Dr. Yuvez quickly came back with, "Of course, for our friends from another country there would be a discount of—oh, say—$50."

We said, "This is still too much," picked up Chica and started to leave. Dr. Yuvez asked, "What do you want to pay?" We began negotiating again and finally settled on a price of $75—half his asking price. Only after he wrote the negotiated price down on the back of his business card did we agree to come back later for the operation.

The next morning we brought Chica back to the office/surgery of Dr. Mutlu Yuvez. It was crowded with noisy men smoking smelly Turkish tobacco and drinking tea. When Dr. Yuvez noticed our entry, he clapped his hands and about half of the men left. He moved old newspapers and boxes off a table and wiped it with a dirty rag.

He asked us to pay first which we hesitantly did. (If Chica died on the table, he would already have been paid, and we doubted that he would refund our money.) He carefully counted the American dollars and stuffed them into his pocket. From a pile of cardboard boxes, the vet dug out an old box containing his surgical tools and came up with a pair of electric hair clippers. He proudly held them up and said, "Very good clippers—made in USA."

Next, the animal surgeon unrolled a filthy rag that had blood splatters on it from previous operations. The instruments were strange-looking devices that we supposed he planned to use on our Chica. He grinned asking, "Do you want to watch?" and waited to see if we were repulsed by the idea. We were, and he chuckled as he translated to the men in the office who then looked at us and chuckled in unison. He sobered himself up for a second, made a straight face, and said, "Come back after three this afternoon." As we left the office and walked down the dirty stairway, we heard muffled sounds of laughter and Turkish banter.

When we returned at 3:00 p.m., the office was again full of Turks smoking and drinking tea. A hush fell over the room as they noticed our entry and awaited our reaction. Our kitty lay lifelessly on blood-splattered newspaper. An inordinate amount of fur had been shaved off her left side, and an incision about three inches long had been crudely stitched. It didn't look right to us, and we asked, "Why is she spayed on the side instead of lower abdomen, and why is the incision so large?"

Dr. Yuvez, inspecting the incision as though he had just noticed it himself, replied with a grin of accomplishment, "This is the way we do it in my country." We got Chica back to *Sanctuary* where she barely survived a festering infection obviously obtained from the unsanitary conditions of Dr. Yuvez's surgery.

Three months later, a wild-eyed Chica began behaving very strangely: crying, moaning, restlessly pacing, begging to get out of the boat, and raising her rump in the air and kneading. If she had not just been spayed, we would have thought she was in heat. After 24 hours we gave up thinking it was impossible and accepted the obvious. Chica was in heat! Dr. Yuvez must have done nothing but shave, cut, and stitch our cat. Did he think we would be long gone from "his country" when our cat came into heat? Little did he know we had sat out the Mediterranean winter in his town's port.

Back we went to his office, which was filled as usual with tea drinkers. The doctor looked surprised to see us, then scolded the crowd and quieted the noisy banter. He managed a false smile and said, "Come in, come in, have a seat. Can I get you some tea?" Chasing two old men out of a couple of chairs, he directed us to sit in them and said, "Please, please have a seat."

We said, "Chica is in heat!"

Dr. Yuvez indignantly exclaimed, "Impossible! How can that be?"

We shot back, "She's been driving us crazy moaning, crying, yowling, spraying, kneading, and trying to get out of the boat. We know how a cat in heat acts. She has not been spayed!" We declined the little cups of tea, and Dr. Yuvez broke his smile, waving the tea boy away. Turning back to us he smiled widely again and admitted that he had intentionally left one ovary in the cat "for strong bones and good growth." Disgusted with Dr. Yuvez, we looked at each other and got up to leave. Dr. Yuvez, still trying to save face, said, "Bring your cat to me. I will give her a hormone shot and that will be that. It won't cost much." As we made for the door, he yelled, "Okay, for free. I will give her a hormone shot for free."

"No thanks."

We walked across town and found the other veterinarian, Dr. Nevzat Yildizli. Dr. Yildizli honestly admitted he did not know how to spay a cat. He offered to take Chica to the School of Veterinary Medicine located in a larger town about two hours inland. He surmised that the previous vet had only taken one ovary out along with the uterus. Without a uterus the hormones from the remaining ovary would cause her to go into a state of perpetual heat that would eventually kill her. Chica needed to have the other ovary removed. We negotiated a price for his part of the deal and had him write it on his business card.

The next morning Dr. Yildizli drove to the marina to pick up Chica and us. There was room for only one more person in the car, so I went along. Two women sat in the back, and I was to sit in the front. Dr. Yildizli opened the trunk from which emanated a horrible yowling. Inside a small cage lay a severely mangled cat with festering wounds and covered with crusted blood and crawling insects. I almost gagged, snatched Chica back, and said, "I'll carry her in the carrier on my lap."

The doctor blithely said, "Fine," shut the trunk and casually told me, "Oh, I picked that injured cat up off the road. Students at the school can practice on it." I paled and sat quietly for most of the bumpy ride.

We finally arrived at the veterinary school, and carrying Chica in her carrier, I followed Dr. Yildizli into the entry hall with its vaulted ceiling and stairway going up to the second and third floors. I stopped before a very large, complete animal skeleton that crowded the lobby with neck and head bones reaching up to the second level. The barking of dogs shook me out of my contemplation as it finally dawned on me that the skeleton I saw was that of a camel and that Turkish vets knew nothing about house cats. Cats were animals that lived outside in the garbage cans and dumpsters and were tolerated only because they kept the rat and mice populations down. Turkey was a country of horses, cows—and camels.

Dr. Yildizli motioned me past the barking dogs chained to a rail attached to the wall. Students seemed to be learning how to give them injections. I held Chica's cage high. Just about that time a door in the hallway opened, and a fellow smoking a cigarette and wearing a blood-stained apron emerged. In the room behind him, on a stainless steel table, lay a comatose dog. The man was introduced to me as the "Head of the Veterinary School." My cat and I were then led to the cafeteria to wait until the dog surgery was completed.

As I waited, I thought about my choices. I could bolt with my cat and get back to the marina on my own, but Chica would surely die from the unabated hormone-induced "heat." If I did not bolt, but politely declined the surgery and waited for a ride back, the result would be the same. The only remaining option was to go ahead and let the vet operate and hope our poor Chica, whom we loved, would survive.

The surgery was smoky with smelly Turkish tobacco. Dirty tea cups littered the counters and the sink. As I brought Chica into the room, the teacher and a few students wearing blood-spattered aprons greeted me kindly in Turkish and English. They listened intently to Dr. Yildizli's description of the problem, nodding in understanding. They lit cigarettes, and while I held Chica, they gave her a shot. I mimicked hand washing and table wiping hoping they would get the idea. Their response was to offer me an apron. I said, "No, thank you," in Turkish, left the room, and went outside for some fresh air.

About an hour later, Dr. Yildizli summoned me from the steps outside. As I returned to the smoky operating room, the surgeon, with a cigarette hanging from his lips, proudly held up a bloodied organ. It looked like a kidney to me, and I could only hope it was the offending ovary.

Dr. Yildizli drove me and my poor lifeless-looking cat back to the marina. He handed me a slip of paper saying, "Here is my telephone number at home. Call me before I leave my house at 10:00 a.m., and I will come by and check on Chica."

I said, "We aren't going anywhere, there is no need to call, just stop by on your way into town."

He responded, "The marina is out of my way, and I don't want to come by unnecessarily. Please call me." In other words, "If your cat is alive in the morning, I'll come by to check up on her. Otherwise, I won't come out of my way."

Sheila organized more tours, and we toured on our own in Istanbul. By March, 1998, I spoke enough Turkish to ride the bus to nearby Izmir for excursions by myself or with girlfriends from other boats. As usual, among other activities, Jim and I worked on *Sanctuary,* repairing and maintaining her in another exotic location. A year had passed since our

Spanish haul-out, so out *Sanctuary* came for her annual bottom-painting.

Sheila, a very experienced Physical Therapist, paid particular attention to Jim and his Parkinson's disease symptoms. His arms and legs were locking and freezing more and more often, and the constant strain on his posture led to back pain. She prescribed some specific exercises for him. These and the tri-weekly aerobics classes she led helped. Time and the PD symptoms marched on, so while we put *Sanctuary* through her annual repair and maintenance, we put ourselves through our annual conversation: "Are we going to continue?" "Is Jim well enough?" "If we continue, what is our route going to be?"

If we continued sailing around the world, our route led southeasterly down the Red Sea and across the Arabian Sea to India. A spot in the Arabian Sea would mark our "halfway 'round" point. There was no easy way "back" once we entered the Red Sea. If we decided to quit, Turkey, or perhaps Spain, were the last good places to sell the boat for a long, long time and distance.

After a lot of soul searching, we decided to continue. For the first time, we had to hire or ask other people to do work Jim had previously been able to do. The hiring of help didn't bother us per se, but depending on people other than ourselves added to the risks of our voyage.

For example, prior to every departure we routinely inspected all of our running and standing rigging. Inspections were critical because something as simple as a missing cotter pin on a shroud fitting could cause the rigging or mast to fail. The wind, salt water, and sun all wore and worked and weaseled their way into, over, and about portions of our sailing gear day after day, and like the links in our anchor chain, each link of our wind-machine gear depended on every other link for strength. Our small diesel engine was fine for getting *Sanctuary* in and out of port, but only her sails could carry us across oceans. Sailing depended on proper, secure, and strong rigging.

The majority of the inspections could be made at deck level, but the fittings at the top of the mast and at the spreaders required going aloft. Jim ordinarily sat in a bosun's chair and hauled himself up the mast using a block and tackle rig (similar to one used by mountain climbers) attached to the main halyard. For safety, I tethered and tailed him on a second halyard, the staysail. If any fitting on the chair, the main halyard, or the climbing rig parted, the second halyard would save him.

Once aloft he and I both cleated off, and he used his legs to keep from swaying away from the mast or whatever else he worked on. His hands, arms, and legs no longer worked properly nor did they have grip or strength enough for him to haul himself up in the old hand-over-hand method. I could winch him up, but that would not allow for a second halyard for safety. Even if I could haul him up, his hands could no longer perform the tedious maneuvers required for repairs.

I could go aloft but was not strong enough to lift myself hand-over-hand. Jim might be able to winch me, but again, his arms were undependable even for winching. Neither could he manage a second tether for safety. We solved the problem before leaving Kuşadasi by hiring a rigger to check all our fittings and rigging aloft. This marked the beginning of what became a new routine: finding someone in every port before every offshore portion of the journey to check our rigging. This also began a new era of vulnerability: if something went wrong aloft while at sea, we could no longer take care of ourselves.

In May of 1998, with our rigging inspected, our cat recovered from her spay, a new coat of bottom paint on *Sanctuary*'s hull, and all of her other systems inspected, maintained, or repaired, we filled our water tanks with 150 gallons of fresh spring water, restocked the food lockers, and said goodbye to friends we had made in Kuşadasi over the last seven months. We were bound for Egypt and the Red Sea.

True to our slow-cruising fashion, it took us another five months to get to our destination. Checking out, and then checking in again, we bounced from Turkey to Greece and back, ambling slowing south. Rhodes, Greece, was a cauldron of hydrofoils, cruise liners, tourists, buses, motorcycles, and souvenir shops. We squeezed *Sanctuary* onto the wall just under the Knights of St. John's castle and enjoyed this crossroads of the Mediterranean in spite of the crowds. After living in the thick of Rhodes City for a week, we nipped back to Turkey for a quiet anchorage. Since Turkey was building marinas and tourist hotels along its eastern shores as fast as trucks could haul bricks and cement, we rarely knew in advance what lay round the bend: a pod of dolphins, a herd of goats, a treasury of ancient ruins, or a rabble of construction workers.

We touched into Ciftlik, Ekincik, Kisilkuyruk Koyu, Yasillkoy, and Bucak Deniz—places often as exotic as the names sounded or sometimes as commonplace as an American strip mall. Fethiye, with its protected anchorage, was a mixture of both. We based there to visit a bit of "old" Turkey away from the coast. We saw Lycean tombs, Roman and Greek theatres, and spectacular canyons, and we bathed in the mud of the Dylan River. The carpets for sale were beautiful, but we bought antique beads with our souvenir money. After good times with other cruising friends, we unstuck and continued on to Kale Koy, Ucagiz, Gokkaya, Cineviz Limani, and Antalya.

In late July we slipped into Polemus Bay, a quiet cove on the southeast coast of Turkey. The peninsula that formed the cove was virtually inaccessible by land since the terrain was hilly, rocky, scrub brush. Only goat trails wound through the brush across a small isthmus to civilization 50 miles away. The rare visitor arrived by boat. The anchorage was well protected from prevailing winds. Our cruising guide informed us that across the headland of Polemus Bay's northern shore, another cove (also inaccessible) was littered with the sunken ruins of a Byzantine city. We planned to hike across the headland to snorkel over the sunken city. And, of special interest to me, the guide mentioned that the lone Turkish family living in Polemus Bay owned a camel!

In the Turkey I imagined, camels roamed, and tribesmen, Lawrence-of-Arabia-style, galloped over Turkish hills astride them. The Turkey I discovered, however, was plagued by stray cats, dotted with goats, and stuffed with toy camels for sale in the *souks*. No tribesman had ridden a camel over any hill in my sight. I had examined the camel skeleton at the veterinary school but had seen few live ones other than those that stood dejectedly outside markets and carpet shops. Outfitted in costumes with glittery trim, the camels indignantly endured the efforts of their owners to solicit tourists to climb up into their saddles for photographs. These were not the camels I envisioned, and I avoided them.

Jim and I both looked forward to quiet Polemus Bay and I to its camel. As we sailed into the bay and set the anchor, I scanned the surrounding desert hillsides covered with low scrub. A herd of goats negotiated a rocky path led by the whistles of a turbaned herdsman. The clear, turquoise waters of the bay lapped rocky shores broken by the porch and dock of a single, small house. Flags decorated the porch of the house, indicating that the Turkish family living there hosted a small restaurant. Chickens foraged around the house, and a small fishing skiff lay at the dock. The only people visible, other than the goat herder, were sailors aboard two boats already in the anchorage. We breathed a sigh of relief. Our quiet bay really was quiet, and we settled in, planning to relax for three or four days.

The next morning, preparing to hike across the peninsula to the sunken Byzantine city, we gathered our snorkeling gear and rowed ashore. As we approached the small dock at the Turkish house, a man appeared and took our lines. With his limited English and our limited Turkish, we determined that the path to the sunken city began behind his house. He said his cafe served beer and soft drinks and offered a dinner of fresh chicken or fish. If we wanted to eat, we must order now for the 7:00 p.m. dinner. We immediately placed our dinner order and then headed to the path behind the house. The man, Mohammed, went off toward a goat pen.

As we rounded the house, I saw a large camel on the path! I was excited. Here was the real thing just a few feet away. I walked up to the camel, stopping short only when Jim said, "Lyn, maybe this camel isn't friendly."

Just as the words were out of Jim's mouth, Mohammed waved his arms frantically and yelled from the goat pen, *"Hayir, hayir"* (No, no)!

Not really understanding why he yelled, "No, no," I nonetheless assumed it had to do with the camel. I looked into the camel's heavily eyelashed, sweet-looking eyes, the camel looked into mine, we both stood still, I backed away, and the camel went back to chewing cud. After some non-intelligible discussion with Mohammed in his goat pen, we continued on our way to the bay across the peninsula.

Along our walk across the desert, we passed an ancient well still providing fresh water. Several abandoned old stone houses nestled under scrub trees. We passed crumbling Byzantine city walls and fields. The main part of the ancient city, complete with sarcophagi and small theater, tumbled down the hillside into a bay. Because of the huge marble ruins, the bay was not navigable, and we and our sailing companions enjoyed a lovely snorkel over the sunken, carved pillars and seaweed-surrounded mosaics. After our swim we hiked back to the Turkish house. The goats, bells ringing, followed us along, but there was no sign of the camel.

At the dockside café, we drank beers served by Mohammed's daughter. His wife showed us her kitchen where she baked flat Turkish bread using a wok-type pan over a charcoal fire on the floor. She also had a wood-burning oven, and our evening meal would be cooked in this oven or on a small grill.

Back aboard *Sanctuary*, we relaxed for the afternoon, and as the sun went down, we again rowed ashore to share dinner with six other cruisers. As we sat drinking our beers and sodas, the goats meandered home and some wandered into the restaurant. A big face on a long neck snaked around the corner of the house, and a head leaned over toward our table—the camel was back! The daughter shooed the camel away, then got a bucket filled with corn mash and proceeded to feed him. Here was my chance. I asked her if I could feed the camel. The daughter looked dubious but let me offer him some balls of mash.

He ate the mash out of my hand, Jim took some photographs, and it made my day. I fed a camel! The camel, satisfied, wandered away, and we tucked into our own dinner.

As we dined, a small motorboat approached the dock; a Turkish couple embarked and ordered dinner. We welcomed them to our shared table, erroneously assuming they didn't speak English. I continued my excited chatter about the camel. The Turkish couple, speaking English, broke into the conversation saying, "You fed that camel?"

"Yes," I replied, "Why are you surprised?"

"Well," they said, "Don't you know the history of this family, this restaurant, and that camel?

"No."

"Well, here is the story of that camel:

Lyn feeding the exiled camel, Polemus Bay

"About 15 years ago, Mohammed, the older of two brothers, lived in his native village of U---, about 50 miles away from Polemus Bay along the Turkish coast. As the elder, he married first. At the time of the story, Mohammed and his wife had one child, a small baby girl. Mohammed's younger brother, Ibrahim, finally got married, and in typical Turkish fashion a three-day wedding celebration was held. At the final wedding party, it came to light that Mohammed had betrayed his wife and child and was in love with Fatma, the bride-to-be of his younger brother, Ibrahim. At the wedding feast, to the horror of the entire village, a jealous fight ensued between the two brothers during which Mohammed bit off the ear of his brother, Ibrahim, and ate the ear! The families and villagers were outraged, and a village council was held to decide Mohammed's fate. Mohammed was banned from the village never to return. Exiled."

"Mohammed left in disgrace. He wandered from village to village, but his disgrace proceeded him and he was not welcome anywhere. Time passed, and he at last sent word back to his wife (and daughter) that he had found an abandoned Byzantine city and had created a home of sorts in a ruined stone building. The long-suffering wife took her young daughter and walked days over the desert to join him. More years passed, and little by little the disgraced husband and his family built a small house on the edge of Polemus Bay. They acquired some goats, some chickens, added a dock, fished, and gradually created a life of their own away from the old village and their previous lives. Mohammed and his forgiving family survived in exile."

"Meanwhile, back in the old village, the one-eared brother, Ibrahim, had married Fatma anyway. The bride had come to the marriage with a full dowry including a camel. Fatma did not have a good reputation. She was also known to cruelly beat and mistreat her camel. Camels are reputed to never leave an old argument unsettled, and one day the beleaguered camel took his vengeance, crushing Fatma with his weight. He pestled (*havanda dövmek*) her to death with his knees and the pad on his mighty chest."

"After burying Fatma, the village elders again held a council, this time about the camel. The elders, using two rocks, mashed and destroyed the camel's testicles. They then banished the castrated camel from the village like Mohammed before him. Exiled. The camel wandered, survived, and at last appeared at the house of Mohammed in Polemus Bay. There he stopped, unbidden, unfettered, and unconstrained. There he remains."

There are no roads to Mohammed's house—simply foot paths through the desert. Only sailors and memories of Fatma visit Mohammed, his family, and the camel in exile.

From Mersin to the Suez

August 1998—October 1998

> "Cruising is the art of repairing your boat in exotic locations."
> —Jim Marco, cruiser, *Intention*

By August, the daily temperatures along Turkey's southern coast topped 100 degrees. Getting in the hot seawater offered no relief, going ashore was excruciating (to prevent burns we layered towels between our bodies and the hot rubber pontoons of our dinghy), even getting dressed left us dripping from the effort. We lay under our sun awning in the cockpit spraying each other with water in hopes of cooling down. Usually a bit of a breeze started up as the sun went down, so we sailed slowly and lazily along our route by night. There was little boat traffic at night, it was a lot cooler, and we had no worry about sunburn. We anchored by 8:30 a.m., swam around the boat before the water heated up, and then hugged the shade again until the sun went down.

Mersin was our last official port in Turkey. We thought we'd completed most of our yearly boat work in the spring before we left Kuşadasi. But when we arrived in Mersin in August, we discovered, to our dismay, that a good bit of the work done in Kuşadasi was "NQR" (Not Quite Right). Therefore, in the stifling heat, we were once again repairing the boat and keeping up with maintenance. August's list of things we worked on was typical:

1. Mailed a package to our insurance company hoping to obtain coverage for the Red Sea.
2. Greased the prop shaft.
3. Replaced the belt pulley on the Yanmar generator (a redo from NQR in Kuşadasi).
4. Removed, rebuilt, and replaced exhaust manifold (a redo from NQR in Kuşadasi).

5. Washed two buckets of clothes by hand (no Laundromat in town).
6. Walked to the market and bought vegetables.
7. Looked for kerosene—no luck finding any.
8. Repacked the stern lazarette (which had been unpacked in order to reach the Yanmar pulley repair).
9. Decanted 18 liters of oil into smaller, sturdier containers which would ride in the lazarette without rubbing through and leaking.
10. Serviced and greased the anchor windlass.
11. Rewrapped half hitches on the rungs of our swim ladder with three-strand Dacron cord (to provide a better grip for our hands and feet–bare stainless steel was slippery).
12. Filled nail holes on the teak rub rail that had lost their packing.
13. Made a new scratching screen for Chica's dirtless cat box.

While Jim and I were in the post office mailing the insurance package, the fellow behind us in line started talking to us in English. He introduced himself as Mr. L., telling us he worked three jobs as a shipping agent, a tour guide, and an English teacher. He invited us for an afternoon get-together at his house with his five English students saying, "They have never been able to speak to native English speakers before."

A few days later, we arrived at the appointed time at his address. As soon as the door opened, we could tell his wife was not happy. Even though the apartment was spotless, she seemed to have dressed sloppily on purpose, moved in a brusque manner, and scowled at us as we greeted her in Turkish. The students had already arrived, and everyone began chatting in a combination of English and Turkish except the wife. In the course of the conversation, Mr. L. brought out the couple's wedding pictures, telling us that the marriage had been "arranged." (Maybe that was why no one in the pictures was smiling.) In the photos the bride wore a fancy western-style white gown and full western-style makeup and hairdo (head uncovered). In several of the photos, she also wore a red sash which Mr. L. told us meant that she was a virgin. Mr. L. confessed that the arranged marriage was not going well. They had no children, and his parents blamed her. In fact, he told us that the "no children" problem was his and that he'd recently undergone surgery which he hoped would correct the childless situation.

Meanwhile, the atmosphere around Mrs. L. thickened, yet she dutifully served home-baked cookies, banana cake, and Turkish tea. Mr. L. talked breezily in front of his students, pointedly ignoring his wife. We stayed an agonizing three hours and at last tore away. Our Turkish *Teşekkür ederim* (Thank you) to the wife fell on deaf ears.

After about 10 days at the dock in Mersin, working on *Sanctuary* in the 90° to 100° heat, we were anxious to leave. I suffered a bout of dysentery which left me with a feeling of distaste for the city. When we'd first arrived, we'd had easy use of fresh water. Then the Port Captain decided (after he got the water bill for the month before) that too much water was being used.

There was one water spigot for the entire dock of four cruising boats, twenty-seven *gulets*, three power boats and occasional strays. The fishing fleet of more than 40 small boats had broken their water tap, so they came over from their dock across the way to the large boat dock to get water also, so approximately 65 boats used one tap with one hose. (All and all only about 20 of the 65 boats were occupied daily.) Local Turkish families walking by to and from the "Luna Park," a carnival-type spot near the marina, also used the water, stopping to fill up water bottles or taking dock showers in their swimsuits. The hose itself had no shut-off nozzle, so whenever the spigot was on, water ran freely. Many Turks never turned it off.

In any event, the Port Captain put a lock on the box. Anyone wanting water had to walk about half a mile in the hot sun to the Port Captain's office to get the key, and then, when finished, walk back and return the key, so Jim and I quit using water. The Turks quickly caught on to their own solution. They got the key and returned the key but left the padlock on the box so it only appeared to be locked. That worked for a while until the Port Captain came out of his office, down to the dock, and found out.

Then the Port Captain gave the key to "The Man with the Blue Hat," who had to unlock the spigot box for each user and then relock it. That didn't work at all, as "The Man with the Blue Hat" could only occasionally be found, and when he was, he would unlock the water and then disappear. People lined up contacts and made deals such as, "If you get water, when you finish don't turn it off, just send someone to get me and keep it on for me, Okay?" More water got used when it was locked than when it wasn't! As for *Sanctuary*, we filled our water tanks, buckets, dock shower, deck sprayer—everything we could fill—and left, since the nicest thing about Mersin, the H_2O, was gone!

View from Turkish anchorage

Larnaca, in Greek Cyprus, had what we needed to complete our preparations for our Suez Canal transit and the Red Sea passage. We picked up our list from Mersin and carried on:

    1. Mailed souvenirs we'd bought in Turkey back to Jim's mother to store in her garage. (By the time we completed our circumnavigation, her garage shelves were lined with 18 boxes we had mailed from different spots around the world.)

    2. Got shots for yellow fever.

    3. Purchased malaria pills for me. (Jim couldn't take them because of conflicts with his PD meds.)

4. Called the Indian Embassy. They said we did not need advance visas for India; they would be issued at our first port of call.
5. Got $1,000 cash in U.S. $20 bills for Egypt, which required all Suez Canal Transit payments in cash, U.S. bills only.
6. Repaired our Single Sideband Radio.
7. Took apart all our hatches, redid water seals, and re-varnished the frames.
8. Touched up all the interior varnish.
9. Ordered and received a three-month supply of PD meds.
10. Recharged our fire extinguishers.
11. Started a Single Side Band net with the three boats going "down" the Red Sea. The name, "Wrong Way Net," was an inside joke since everyone said we were going "the wrong way."
12. Paid our medical and insurance bills in advance since we had no idea when we could mail anything next.
13. Went over our provision list again and bought 90% of all the staple provisions we expected to use in the next six months.
14. Rechecked and ordered extra engine spares. We had no idea when we could find those again either and bought four to six each of all filters, o-rings, pulleys, fan belts, injectors, seals, impellers, gaskets, etc.
15. Got out, raised, checked, and rigged the spinnaker.
16. Got out, raised, checked, and rigged the genoa.
17. Cleaned port cockpit lazarette and repacked it.
18. Put new covers I had sewn on all our fenders.
19. Organized, checked, and repacked all our dock lines.
20. Repaired our anchor locker. While we repaired our anchor locker and the chain was out, we checked all the links for the entire 300 feet and turned the chain end-for-end, repainting and re-wrapping all of the color-coded markers every 50 feet.
21. Went over all our notes from other cruisers and the SSCA bulletins for any information we could find about the countries along the route.
22. Replaced the engine thermostat.
23. Bought back-up fan belts, grease-zert fittings and other spares for the generator and alternator.
24. Hooked our laptop to a phone at the marina office and searched the internet for information regarding diseases and State Department warnings for all the countries along our route from

Israel to India.

25. Looked over our charts from Cyprus to Singapore. Discovered a few gaps and listed four charts we needed.
26. Read all the information I could find on Israel and Egypt, the next two countries on our route.
27. Faxed the U.S. Consulate in Eritrea for safety information.
28. Faxed a marina in Indonesia for a cruising permit.
29. Washed the laundry.
30. Labeled all our photos—originals, diskettes, and negatives.
31. Reprioritized our "To Do" lists.
32. Went over our budget—we were spending too much money.
33. Made a batch of "make do" spice for salad dressings, etc.
34. Serviced the winches.
35. Sewed courtesy flags for Jordan, Israel, Egypt, Sudan, Eritrea, Yemen, Oman, India, and Sri Lanka.
36. Got typhoid fever shots.
37. Bought liquor and decanted it into heavy, plastic containers.
38. Repackaged all other liquids not in sturdy containers.
39. Repacked all cereals, flour, beans, pastas, and other staples sold in paper or cardboard packages into special, sturdy, square, plastic containers.
40. Visited a dentist who checked our teeth and repaired one of Jim's fillings.
41. Photocopied our medical receipts and prescriptions, matching each medication with the proof that it was a legal drug to have on-board.
42. Researched the new weather fax frequencies to use for Red Sea weather information and made a log of times and stations.
43. Repaired our American flag.
44. Found two of the four charts we needed and bought them.
45. Cleaned the stern locker and checked the autopilot arm while the locker was empty.
46. Completed coloring in all the black and white charts for the next 500 miles.
47. Refilled our propane tanks.
48. Re-bolted and reseated both water tanks (another NQR job done in Kuşadası).
49. Re-glassed, repainted, or re-varnished all the shelving and cabinetry we had taken out to get at the water tanks.

We were, as our British friends said, "knackered." To top it off, Cyprus was in the midst of a four-year drought. The showers were turned on only from 5:00 p.m. to 7:00 p.m., and water for the docks was available only three days of the week. As *Sanctuary* sat in the harbor collecting dust blown onto her from the dry, sandy shores, I cleaned her decks by washing them with saltwater and then rinsed the rigging by hand using fresh water from our converted bug sprayer.

At the end of each work day, we collapsed with the crews from two sailboats also preparing to tackle the Red Sea. We shared "Happy Hours" and potluck dinners, comparing notes on our strategies for the assault. (One crew changed their minds and decided to wait a year.)

September 26, 1998: *Underway to Ashkelon: Light NW winds, a lovely sail.*

September 28, 1998: As we sailed slowly toward Ashkelon and lay about 50 miles off the coast, an Israeli reconnaissance jet scared us by buzzing *Sanctuary* at a very low range. A short while later, an Israeli naval gunboat sped into view, slowed to our speed when about 500 feet off our stern, and then hailed us on the radio. We answered the call, and a naval officer closely questioned us about who we were and where we were headed, then ordered us to change course to 220°, which put us parallel to the coast and added a dogleg to our destination.

I replied, "Israeli Navy, this is sailing vessel *Sanctuary*. Why do we need to change course, sir? We are on a proper heading for Ashkelon."

"Sailing vessel *Sanctuary*, this is the Israeli Navy. You must keep your vessel out of the "Prohibited Zone." We will stand by while you alter your course to 220°. This is the Israeli Navy, over and back to Channel 16."

The course they demanded was the "long way 'round," but we obeyed: "Sailing vessel *Sanctuary* altering course to 220°. *Sanctuary* clear and back to Channel 16."

Around 11:00 p.m., while Jim was off watch and sleeping, an unidentified power boat tagged and circled us for about an hour, standing off at about a mile. I assumed it was a naval vessel but did not know for certain, as there was no reply to my calls on the radio. Suddenly, the power boat sped right up on our stern and aimed a powerful searchlight directly into our cockpit, blinding my night vision. I didn't care who they were, I was very irritated.

I hailed them: "Unidentified motor vessel on my stern, Unidentified motor vessel on my stern, this is the sailing vessel *Sanctuary*. Identify yourselves and switch to channel 13. *Sanctuary* standing by Channel 16 for a reply."

"Sailing vessel *Sanctuary*, Sailing vessel *Sanctuary*, this is the Israeli Naval vessel X, switching to Channel 13."

"Israeli Naval vessel X, do you copy *Sanctuary* on Channel 16?"

"*Sanctuary*, this is Israeli Naval vessel X, we copy you, go ahead."

"Israeli Navy, this is *Sanctuary*. Your light is blinding my night vision. I repeat, your light is blinding my night vision. I need it to sail our vessel. Turn off your light and tell me your intentions. *Sanctuary* over."

The Israeli Navy must have taken me for a complete fool for confronting them and realized we posed no threat. Without another word they turned off their powerful searchlight and backed away. Not far, however, as the Navy vessel maintained a steady four-mile range, following us all the way into the port of Ashkelon and escorting *Sanctuary* directly to an arrival dock. As we tied off, military forces demanded that Jim and I disembark. A low rock sculpture embedded into the sidewalk on the dock was carved with a pair of lips and the words Terra Santa (The Holy Land). We quietly contemplated the sculpture while armed guards loomed over us and security forces and their dogs boarded *Sanctuary* to check for bombs.

Sanctuary was declared "Bomb Free" and we moved to a berth in one of the last marinas we would see for thousands of miles. We happened to arrive on the eve of Yom Kippur, the Jewish "Day of Atonement." For 25 hours, there would be no shops open, no public transport and nothing happening. I was thrilled, as we would enjoy an enforced day of vacation! Welcome to Israel.

A few days later, we rented a car to visit the Negev Desert and the Dead Sea. The sea looked beautiful from a distance, but when we got into the water it was oily with salt and required repeated showers to wash off. While driving through the countryside, we passed many hitchhiking soldiers. The four who rode with us (including one female) were not talkative. We did learn that military service was required for all Israelis, male or female, upon reaching the age of 18.

The Jewish holiday of "Sukkoth," also celebrated during our stay, included palm tents erected to remind the Jews of life in the wilderness after the exodus. The day we visited the divided city of Jerusalem, multitudes of Jewish worshipers and other tourists milled around including many Hasidic men who wore hats that looked like fuzzy, black flying saucers. Many Jews proclaimed their faith at the "Wailing Wall," banging their heads against it and crying aloud. Because of "The Problem" (as people called the war with the Palestinians) tensions were high, so we watched and listened to the wailing, praying crowd at the wall from a distance. The Israelis, not wanting any disturbances for their holiday, had closed the Muslim mosques and other sites. The Israeli forces (teenagers wearing riot gear and carrying automatic weapons and clubs) were visible in great numbers, along with strategically-parked ambulances and police riot vehicles.

As we (and many other people) were continually searched and subjected to metal detectors at checkpoints and entrance gates, we felt intimidated by the Israeli show of weapons. Against the stern warnings of the Israeli guards, we crossed into the Palestinian (Arab) and Christian sections of the old city. All was peaceful in Palestine; we saw no weapons and no military. We shopped in a few stores, looking for antique beads. In one I found some interesting old prayer beads inlaid with silver, which I bought. As we made our purchase, we chatted with the shopkeeper who said to us as we left: "When you see Bill Clinton, tell him not to give the Israelis so much money."

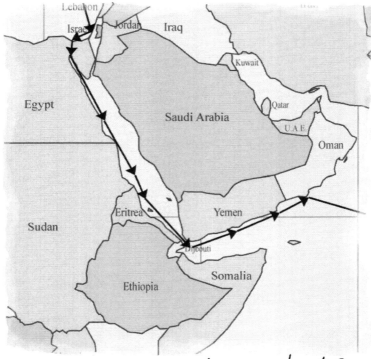

Route from Israel to Oman

The Egyptian Pilots

October 1998

> "Don't bother stopping in Egypt—just buy the video."
> —A cruiser we met in Israël

October 9, 1998: *0945 hours: Underway to Port Said, North winds, 15-20 knots.* A brisk, overnight sail from Israel carried us to the entrance of the Suez Canal and the small-boat staging area at Port Faoud, Egypt. A stiff crosswind and a lively chop in the mooring basin conspired against us as we set our bow anchor and backed *Sanctuary*'s stern up to med-moor to the crowded dock. An audience of men lounging on the shore under the shade of some tall palms watched our every move as Jim jockeyed the boat into position and I frantically ran first to the bow to lower the anchor then back to the cockpit to climb over the stern rails and jump ashore with two stern lines. As *Sanctuary* heaved and pitched in the wind and chop, Jim and I struggled to adjust our lines quickly to keep our boat from surging into the concrete wall on our stern or onto the catamaran on our port side. We had barely tied off the lines properly when two of the shore watchers got up and approached us.

One of the men who approached represented the agency we had hired. (We'd arranged in advance for assistance with the voluminous paperwork and formalities necessary for our transit of the Suez Canal.) The other man was an Egyptian Customs Agent. We gathered our passports, and our ship's, medical, and cat's documents and climbed over *Sanctuary*'s stern to follow the two to the shade of the palms to begin the first of the required paperwork. The Customs Official was loathe to make the stretch from the concrete dock to the heaving deck of *Sanctuary*, so he stared at her intently from the safety of the shore, waved his hands, clapped, and declared us cleared for Customs.

As the sun set, the transit paperwork had barely begun. The small boat harbor lay on the port side of the canal entrance at Port Faoud while the offices of the agency and the Canal Authority sat on the opposite

Port Faoud anchorage
Egypt

shore in Port Said. Since our transit was scheduled for early the next morning, one of us needed to cross the canal by ferry that evening, visit the agency office, complete the paperwork, and pay the fees.

Seven years of progressing Parkinson's disease had given Jim a very soft voice, so soft that people often asked him to repeat things several times, sometimes yelling at him in frustration, "Speak up!" not realizing he was unable to "speak up." The disease also affected his handwriting—it was worse than the average doctor's script, and he could not fill out carbon copies. Also, by 5:00 p.m., after a long night and day of sailing, Jim was exhausted and unable to walk very well. Therefore, he was not a good candidate for answering questions and filling out multiple copies of papers. Someone had to visit the agency, and someone needed to stay on board. So, even though Jim was the Captain and I was dubious about going to Port Said at night without him, I was elected. The agency employee agreed to pick me up and drive me over on the ferry and back.

I changed from my sailing clothes into long pants and a long sleeved blouse, stuck a scarf in my bag in case I wanted to attempt to blend in with the Muslim women, gathered our documents into my waterproof briefcase, and after hiding $550 in U.S. $20 bills in a secret pocket of my pants, went ashore to meet the agent. Port Said was shrouded in darkness as I squinted through the dirty window of the agent's car trying to see where I was being taken. The agent drove into an underground parking lot in what looked like a half-completed building. I got out, and the agent escorted me to an elevator illuminated by a single feeble light ominously blinking off and on.

The elevator ground upward, and I breathed a sigh of relief as the doors opened to the agency's suite of rooms. Black leather Deco-style furniture gleamed in the reflection of huge mirrors. The agencies head, Mr. Nagib L., sat behind an impressive desk complete with four telephones, a notebook computer, and red leather desk accessories. A golden "Eye of God" hung on the glass balcony door behind him. He waved me into one of the leather chairs; I sat and handed him our papers.

Several women hovered. As one of the women (dressed in a long, slinky pantsuit, three-inch stiletto heels, lots of gold jewelry, heavy makeup, and a hairdo worthy of the TV series *Dallas*) carefully moved my document bag off of the stainless steel end table, I realized the table was in fact a refrigerator. I declined an offer of a beer, so she produced some lemons, then made and served me fresh lemonade.

Meanwhile, as Nagib stamped, photocopied, printed, and flourished several papers, he delivered a non-stop running commentary on pilot problems, canal problems, and political problems with Israel and the United States which included a comment about Clinton and "his stupidity with the Jewess Monica Lewinsky." (Jim and I had been subjected to tirades or snickers about President Clinton since mid-1998.) Finally, after an hour listening, filling out forms, and waiting, I fished the fee of $455 in U.S. currency out of its hiding place in my pants, handed it over, and got back our documents. I checked them over and noticed that our passports had not been returned.

"Ah," said Nagib, "as an Egyptian, I am allowed to buy only

Egyptian beer. Since you Americans are allowed a case of beer per passport, I will use them to buy two cases of better beer." In spite of feeling trapped, I managed to strike a deal of one case for Nagib, one case for my husband, and waited while assistants went out into the night to buy beer. They returned after a nerve-wrenchingly long time. The beer taken care of, Nagib handed back our passports saying, "Remember my warnings about the pilots, and have *Sanctuary* ready to transit by 0830 tomorrow morning."

We had been warned. While in Turkey, Cyprus, and Israel, all the ocean voyagers we met who had sailed into the Mediterranean via the Red Sea, the Gulf of Suez, and the Suez Canal had given us information and tips. All had a story to tell about the pilots put aboard their boats. The stories were good and bad. Most, however, were horror stories and warnings.

Unlike the Panama Canal, the Suez did not have "locks" or significant changes in water level. Basically a wide, deep ditch, the Suez was controlled and regimented by Egyptian military officials at regular stations along its entire 90-mile length. Two onboard pilots were assigned for slow-moving sailing vessels such as ours which required two days to transit the long canal. One pilot would board the first day then disembark in the evening while we anchored overnight in Lake Timsah, halfway through the canal. The next morning a new pilot would board for the second part of the canal transit. The pilots were ferried to the transiting vessels and retrieved by Canal Authority launches.

Nagib had said, "Have two packs of Marlboro cigarettes in flip-top boxes and five U.S. dollars as a tip for each of the pilots. Don't give the pilot his *baksheesh* (tip or bribe) until he is stepping off your boat," he continued. "The pilots are paid a very good salary, so don't be persuaded to give them anything more. You are not obligated to give money and cigarettes to the checkpoint policemen or the skippers and line handlers of the launches. They are all paid employees." He further cautioned, "Thievery is common. Don't let a pilot go below deck unattended for any reason."

Cruisers had many stories about theft. A pair of expensive prescription sunglasses (an item useless to the pilot but difficult for the sailor to replace) were stolen from one sailboat. We heard reports of stolen money, cassette tapes, pocketknives, binoculars, and hand-held radios—anything a pilot could get his hands on. The list continued.

If lucky, we wouldn't get the "farting, spitting, motion-sick, throwing up, or pissing-over-the-rail pilot." Another cruiser described a pilot with a bad case of gas and diarrhea who used the shotgun method by standing on the toilet seat. He cautioned, "Give your pilot a bucket and show him the side rail."

A dive-boat skipper who transited the Suez Canal on a regular basis advised, "Give the pilot a handheld VHF radio to use and show him where to sit. Give him magazines to look at but no girlie magazines. Don't let him take the helm because if he does any damage to your boat or the canal, you, not he, are responsible. Never, under any circumstances, give your pilot alcoholic beverages to drink!"

The female cruisers had warned me to dress conservatively and to cover my arms and legs. If the pilot grabbed or tried to touch me (a common experience) they advised, "Reprimand him immediately, severely, and in no uncertain terms."

The next morning we got up early to prepare *Sanctuary*. I draped towels over our TV set, VHS player, and tapes. We stowed all small gear such as extra binoculars, glasses, flashlights, and hand-held compass out of sight. I hid our wallets and the good Nikon camera, leaving out only an Instamatic for canal shots.

Then I got ready. Even though it was already about 80° at 8:00 a.m., I put on the ankle-length and extremely baggy *shalvar* pants I had bought in Turkey and then squeezed into a very stiff sports bra that flattened my breasts to pancakes. Over the bra I wore a tee shirt and then a loose, long blouse that came up to my neck, down to my wrists, and flowed over my already-swathed hips. My hands, bare feet, and face were visible. I was miserable, but by Allah, certainly not tempting.

We anxiously awaited the arrival of our first pilot. Two hours after we had been told to expect him, a nasty-looking launch with big black tires as fenders approached *Sanctuary*'s starboard side. The launch's line handler helped the pilot, Asid, off the launch, and Jim and I welcomed him aboard. The line handler hung on to our rigging as the launch skipper stuck his head out of the pilothouse window and asked, "You have cigarettes for us?"

Jim said, "No, sorry, no cigarettes."

The line handler then demanded, "Then you have beer for us."

"No beer!"

"You have something for us, captain?"

Jim, sensing they were not going away easily, asked me to get two cigars which he handed to the line handler. As the line handler slipped both cigars in his pocket, he said, "You have some for the skipper?"

Jim replied, "One of those is for the skipper."

The skipper stuck his head out and demanded, "What about mine?"

"He has yours," Jim repeated. A short argument ensued, and as we turned away we heard and felt the skipper intentionally grind the big black launch tire into *Sanctuary*'s clean, white fiberglass topside. The line handler gave it one last try, "How about a *Playboy*?"

Jim yelled, "No!" The skipper, gunning the launch, sped away, rocking us with a malicious wake.

The pilot, Asid, sat quietly on *Sanctuary*'s port side picking his nose and occasionally leaning over the safety line to spit into the wind. I held my breath so I wouldn't inhale his mist. A swarm of flies circled his bare feet. (I had asked him to remove his hard, black-soled shoes when he came aboard.) He did not come below, did not finger any of our gear, ate the lunch I prepared for him, and thanked me for it. At appropriate times he rolled out his small prayer carpet in the cockpit, looked at the compass, found east, knelt, touched his head to the carpet, and sang his prayers, *"Ashadu an lā 'ilāha 'illa-llāha, wa 'ashadu anna Muḥammadar rasūlu (A)llāh."* (I bear witness that there is no God but Allah, I bear witness that Muhammad is the messenger of Allah.)

Asid was a gentleman until the end. After all-day motoring, we finally approached the launch station at Lake Timsah (Ismailaya) in the middle of the canal where *Sanctuary* would anchor for the night. Jim handed Asid 10 U.S. dollars rubber-banded to two packs of Marlboro cigarettes in flip- top boxes and thanked him for a fine job he never had to do. Asid stared at the cigarettes and money for a few seconds, his eyes sad as if in disbelief. Then he looked up and said, "Ten? Only ten? Make it twenty please."

I said, "Our agent told us to give each pilot only five U.S. dollars. We gave you five extra as a bonus already."

He then turned to Jim and pleaded, "You can make it twenty dollars, captain, please?"

I said, "No! Ten is more than enough. We are not giving any more."

Jim decided not to wait for the launch to pick him up. "I'm taking you to the dock, okay?"

"Okay, but can you help me captain? You can do it—twenty dollars—only—please, Captain. Can you afford another five dollars, Captain? Please."

I could tell Jim felt embarrassed as he said, "Give me another five dollars, Lyn."

"But Jim—well okay, if that will satisfy him—fine." I gave Jim another five dollars.

As Jim handed it over, Asid said, "and a cigar."

Breathing a sigh of relief as he stepped off *Sanctuary* and onto the dock, we gave him a cigar, and that brought a smile back to his pleading face.

As the launch arrived the next morning, our new pilot bounded aboard and scampered below deck before we could stop him. I went below and found him in the main salon lifting up the covering towels. His free hand was full of cassette tapes he had pulled out. "Oh, Madame, just looking, Madame," he said.

I herded him up to the cockpit, asking him several times before he finally removed his hard-soled street shoes which left black heal marks on the fiberglass deck. Meanwhile, Jim was talking to the second launch crew, who were asking for cigarettes and *Playboy* magazines. This crew, however, took a couple of cigars appreciatively. When Jim returned to the cockpit, the incredibly smelly pilot put one arm around me, his other arm around Jim, and said, "We are one family and we work together, okay?" I squirmed out from under his arm and gave Jim a look that telegraphed "trouble."

"My name is Mohammed. What are your names?"

"I'm Jim and this is Lyn."

As he called Jim, "Captain," and me, "Madame," he lit up a cigarette. I said, "No smoking, please." Smoking was not allowed aboard *Sanctuary*, and he was not to be an exception.

Mohammed, determined to smoke, responded, "Mohammed be very careful. Do you have tray for ashes?"

Jim and I exchanged "Oh, well" glances. I had no ashtrays, so I got a can for him to use. (The next day we found ground-out cigarette butts and ashes on the deck and in the cockpit well, a burn hole in the fiberglass, and another hole in a good towel I had brought on deck when I served him lunch.)

We got underway, heading for the entrance to the canal and the second half of our journey. Before we turned into the canal, Mohammed started working on his *baksheesh*. He wanted to know what *baksheesh* we gave the other pilot and requested cigarettes for himself. I lied and said we gave the first pilot five U.S. dollars and two packs of cigarettes. He continued to cry poor and work on us for a bigger *baksheesh* during the entire transit.

As we turned into the canal, Mohammed asked to take the wheel. Jim said, "I've got it just fine, thank you." The pilot professed, "Mohammed very good pilot. You'll see. Rest, Captain, Mohammed steer."

Jim figured he couldn't do any harm and it would keep him occupied. Earlier Mohammed had explained that we would meet a northbound convoy of ships and that *Sanctuary* needed to stay on the right side of the channel. After Mohammed almost hit several large channel markers, Jim took back the wheel and manned the autopilot.

We should have let him continue steering. With his hands free he was destined to cause trouble. Jim turned away to set up the autopilot and didn't notice that as I walked past Mohammed, he reached over and patted me on the hips. (How he found my hips I'm not sure, as I was dressed in the same ironclad, lumpy outfit as the day before.) A few minutes later he grabbed me under my arms on the sides of my breasts and squeezed. I threw his arms down, jumped forward, and without even thinking, balled up my fist, pointed my other hand in his face, and spat out angrily, "Don't you dare touch me again."

He thought I was going to hit him. He backed away and with a mock apology said, "I'm very sorry Madame, Mohammed just wants to be like family."

I replied with a growl, "Just keep your hands off me." In spite of the fierce reprimand and his apology, I had to avoid him all day. He never quit trying to touch me.

Several miles later I offered Jim and the pilot coffee or tea. Mohammed wanted sugar with his tea, so I gave Jim his coffee and Mohammed a cup of tea with some packets of sugar and a spoon. He looked at the sugar, read the label, and threw the packets back at me.

"Don't you want the sugar?" I asked.

Pointing at the packets as though they were poison, he sneered, "It's from Israel."

I put away the sugar packets with the Hebrew label and found some other sugar for him. From then on, Mohammed scrutinized everything we gave him to eat or drink to make sure it was not "Israeli poison." It dawned on us that the pilot the day before had asked for a cola with his lunch but didn't touch it. We had purchased the colas in Israel and they too had Hebrew labels.

Mohammed showed us photographs of his family. He told us his daughter was deaf and needed special learning equipment. His son wanted to go to college, but he couldn't afford to send him. His wife had diabetes and needed weekly doctor appointments. He himself had a bad back and needed periodic therapy. To make his point, he slapped his out stretched palm with the top of his other hand saying, "All the doctor wants is money, money, money every week! You know how much money the doctor makes?" Slapping his hand in his palm harder he said louder, "Money, money, money is all they want." I asked him if the canal authorities provided any kind of medical care for him or his family. He responded with a sneer and then a growl, "They provide nothing, not even a decent wage." (Nagib, our agent, had told me earlier that the Suez Canal pilots are well-paid employees of the Egyptian government.)

I asked Jim and Mohammed if they wanted anything more to drink. Mohammed said he would like a beer. Remembering the dive-boat skipper's warning I asked, "How about a cola or iced tea?"

"No tea! You have beer for Mohammed?"

Jim wanted a beer and said "I'll have one." Jim and I had a small tiff because I knew Jim couldn't drink a beer and not give Mohammed one, and we had been warned, "Don't give the pilots alcohol." Jim won though, and I got each of them one beer.

Mohammed drank only one beer, but one was enough to loosen him up. He was on a roll. He wanted to hear music: "Michael Jackson or Spice Girls." I explained that we didn't have Michael Jackson or the Spice Girls. I also did not want him fingering through all of our tapes. "Sorry Mohammed, no music."

Mohammed wanted cookies, candy, peanuts, snacks, and more beer. "No more beer, Mohammed."

"Then you have Coca-Cola for me? No Diet Coke." I went below and poured a cola into a cup for him so he wouldn't see the Hebrew label. Getting bored, he asked Jim if he had any magazines. Jim said, "Sure, you want to see a sailing magazine?"

Mohammed said, "I like ladies. Ladies magazines. You have ladies magazines?"

"No we don't have ladies magazines." He quickly glanced through a sailing magazine and threw it aside.

At 4:30 p.m., Mohammed made a call on the VHF radio. He said his conversation was with the upcoming (second to last) checkpoint station. They wanted us to stop there for the night because small craft are not allowed to navigate in the canal after 4:00 p.m. We would continue in the morning with Mohammed spending the night aboard *Sanctuary*.

Oh, no! No way.

He explained that he wouldn't be paid for this service but would expect big *baksheesh*. The only alternative was to pay the policeman at the upcoming way station a small *baksheesh* to let us continue. The last way-station officer would also want *baksheesh* to let us go through after hours. We agreed to pay five U.S. dollars, plus a pack of Marlboro cigarettes, to each of the way station policemen so we could continue to the end of the canal and Port Suez. Mohammed said, "Get the cigarettes and money ready to throw ashore to the officials." As we passed the way stations, no one came out. Slipping the cigarettes and money into his bag, Mohammed said, "I will pay the policemen their *baksheesh* tomorrow."

We belatedly figured out that the entire "Late in the canal—little *baksheesh* payment" was a hoax.

As we finally approached Port Suez and the end of the transit, Mohammed said, "You give Mohammed his *baksheesh* now."

Suez Canal Pilot

Jim asked me to get out the *baksheesh*. I said, "Okay, but we still have a half hour to go. Don't give it to him until he is leaving." I tried to secretly pass the two packs of Marlboros with money rubber-banded to them over to Jim, but Mohammed saw us. He had to know, "How much *baksheesh* you give Mohammed?" Jim said, "I'll give it to you when we get there."

His response was, "Mohammed needs money for doctor bills, for school, for children." Jim replied, "We are giving you what we gave the first pilot and that is all we will give."

He asked, "How about collectible money?" We didn't know what he meant. "What is collectible money?" He explained, "Money you can no longer use like Cyprus money or Israel money, any kind of money, Mohammed take it. Do you have gift for me like T-shirt or hat or something? Mohammed need shirt." Noting to myself that he wasn't averse to touching Israeli money, I only said, "We don't have any Israeli money." I succumbed and gave him a new *Sanctuary* polo-type shirt. Then he wanted pants. He showed us a poorly-repaired seam in the waistband of his trousers saying, "I need pants!" "No, Mohammed, our pants wouldn't fit you." He grabbed me and gave me a kiss on both cheeks and did the same to Jim. He asked for his *baksheesh* again, so Jim gave it to him. He looked at it and said with a sneer, "You are a rich man and all you can give Mohammed is five dollars? Was Mohammed not a good pilot?" Then he hung his head and looked down and sadly said, "Mohammed was family. Can you give me more than five dollars?" He saw Jim caving in, perked up, and said, "Make it twenty more."

 "No way, Mohammed. I'll give you five more and that is all, and I'm not a rich man."

"Okay, Mohammed take fifteen more dollars and be happy."

Jim asked me to dig out another five U.S. dollars, handed it to Mohammed, and said, "This is all, Mohammed. No more."

Mohammed had to get something more to win the negotiation. "And a cigar."

"Okay, Mohammed, and a cigar."

The launch to pick up the pilot stood alongside *Sanctuary,* and as Mohammed stepped aboard he said something in Arabic to the crew with a tone of derision. They reacted with sneers, dirty looks, and laughter. The launch skipper ground a big, black tire into *Sanctuary's* white port side and sped away.

The next day we met the Port Captain, who asked, "How did the transit go?"

Jim said "The canal transit was fine, but our second pilot was not good."

He responded, "Oh. Did he do something wrong?"

Jim thought for a second, "No, he didn't do anything wrong."

"Did he break your boat or steal something?"

"No, he didn't steal anything."

"Then what was the problem?"

Jim replied, "He was obnoxious."

The Port Captain leaned back in his chair, folded his hands, and resting them on his big potbelly, said, "I can send a report to the canal authorities, but there is no crime in being obnoxious." He paused for thought and then continued, "Just the same, they should know you weren't happy with his behavior."

Jim felt he was causing the Port Captain unnecessary paper work and said, "If it's not too much trouble."

The Port Captain leaned forward on his elbows and said, "Of course, there will be *baksheesh* for me, oh say, five U.S. dollars and two packs of Marlboro. Oh, and I'll take one of those cigars in your pocket."

The Gate of Tears

October 1998—December 1998

"The Bab-el-Mandeb (The Gate of Tears) is a strait located between Yemen, on the Arabian Peninsula and Djibouti and Eritrea, north of Somalia, on the Horn of Africa, that connects the Red Sea to the Gulf of Aden.
The strait derives its name from the dangers attending its navigation, or, according to an Arab legend, from the numbers who were drowned by the earthquake which separated Asia and Africa."
—Wikipedia, 2010

With *Sanctuary* on a mooring at Port Suez, we hired car and driver for a tour of Cairo about three hours' drive inland from the canal. The famous sites, including King Tut's treasures in the Egyptian Museum, the Sphinx, and the pyramids, brood in Cairo among millions of people, cars, goats, donkeys, and camels. A one-day whirlwind tour was enough for us, with the fast pace blowing off most of the flies, dirt, and dust. We topped *Sanctuary*'s tanks with fuel and water, bought some fresh vegetables, and prepared to continue south from the Gulf of Suez to the Red Sea.

We set the sails, and with the wind at our backs enjoyed a fast run from Port Suez to Damaran Abu Mieish, our first anchorage in six weeks! The coast, with low-lying desert dunes, offered no real protection from the insidious wind. Even though the anchorage was rolling, we stayed for an extra day, as I had caught "Mummies' Revenge" (probably from the food I ate in Cairo) and needed rest and soda crackers. We didn't swim due to sharks in the water but sat in the cockpit listening to the wind and staring at the coastline as *Sanctuary* swung on her hook.

The next day we upped anchor at 5:30 a.m. and with steady NW winds enjoyed another fast downwind run. We were tempted to keep going without stopping overnight but suspected the winds would increase to 30 knots or higher as the sun rose, so we anchored at 11:30 a.m. after only 35 miles. The winds did increase. It was too windy to launch the dinghy and go ashore, so we sat again in the cockpit, staring at the dunes and red hillsides.

Navigating the Suez at night didn't really appeal to us with its reef-strewn shoreline to starboard and shipping traffic to port. Therefore, we clung to a battle plan of setting sail at dawn, running fast in the 20 to 25 knots of wind and then setting the hook early in the day before the relentless afternoon winds of 30 to 35 knots swooped upon us. As we sledded farther and farther south away from the activity and shipping of the canal, fishing boats became our only company.

Camels and goats grazed on the shores of our *marsa* (small bay) anchorages. Occasionally, we sat off villages composed of squat, mudbrick houses gathered around a singular moon-topped mosque, men in *djeballahs* and white turbans, and women shrouded in black kicking up dust as they walked the village paths. We appreciated this Egypt, the one south of the canal. The few people we met (mostly fishermen) were friendly and courteous, not the grasping touts of pyramid land demanding *baksheesh* at every turn. Birds were plentiful, and we spotted ibises, herons, flamingos, kingfishers, and hoopoes. Jim caught fish again: tuna, wahoo, and mahimahi.

The waters of the Gulf of Suez, as they flow into the Red Sea, are deflected by the land masses at the tip of the Sinai Peninsula to the east and the mainland of Egypt to the west. The Strait of Gubal, where the two bodies of water meet, is burdened by a group of islands of great interest to divers but treacherous to transiting vessels since they are fringed by reefs. Furthermore, additional water ebbs and floods into the Gubal Strait from the Gulf of Aqaba (between the Sinai and Saudi Arabia). *Sanctuary* was about to enter a washing machine.

Rather than hit the churning waters head on, we decided to crab across, so as we approached the Strait we crossed the Gulf of Suez over to the Sinai Peninsula. We edged *Sanctuary* along the Sinai and then positioned ourselves at the last tenable anchorage on the peninsula's western shore.

We got lucky. We left our anchorage at El Qad at 6:00 a.m., and after negotiating past Shag Rock, turned to starboard and barreled across the Strait on a beam reach in 25 knots of wind, making seven and a half knots under reefed main and jib. The three-meter seas were lumpy and confused, but we met no big ships in the channel, and we lurched into the lee of Gubal Island breathing a sigh of relief at having safely made it across a very worrisome body of water.

Our afternoon anchorage at Endeavour Harbour on Tawila Island was idyllic, and we took a great tension-releasing swim. We were also lucky we hadn't done any motoring except to set the anchor, as while we swam we noticed *Sanctuary*'s propeller and shaft were completely fouled with a big wad of net. Welcome to the Red Sea.

After a bit more harbor-hopping, we anchored off Safaga, Egypt, and traveled inland to Luxor to visit the temples and tombs of the ancient kings and queens. As usual, Jim and I enjoyed the unexpected more than the "must see" places of the guidebooks, and the beauty of the Nile was unexpected. Remove the few telephone poles, ignore the cars and tourist buses, and the banks of the Nile looked as they must have in the times of the pharaohs, with mud-brick houses and donkeys bearing mounds of grain and sorghum urged on by running children swishing palm branches. The women tilled the fields as men in long, white robes and turbans fished along the Nile's banks. Papyrus waved at the edges of the green river, and herons and ibises bolted into flight, disturbed in their hunt for insects by laden camels elegantly walking the shoreside paths. The tomb-riddled hills in the distance and the desert colors in the foreground were punctuated by the sharp red of a shawl or the faded blue of a fisherman's boat. As we walked along the shores, we hired a father and son to give us a twilight sail in their *felucca*, the *Nile Moon*. We'll remember our sail on the Nile long after we've forgotten the temples and pyramids.

The Nile Moon

The Red Sea lived up to its name. Hot winds blew at gale force across the red mountains of Egypt's eastern desert, and the very air was stained red with the dust. The winds churned the waters, mixed them with the sand, and whipped *Sanctuary*'s decks with a sticky, red icing. I covered everything below with sheets, trying this time to hide our possessions from the red fingers of the desert. We continued inching south hoping to find an anchorage that would shelter us from the defeating elements. We settled on Marsa Umbeila. Marked on the most recent (1945) U.S. Defense Mapping Agency chart as "Wreck," the old rusted hull of a freighter, one of the many casualties of the reef, was still evident after 53 years. Like a troll, it defined the outside parameter of the main reef. We paid our respects and slowly picked and poked our way through the dangerous reefs searching for the simple, black post markers which were difficult to spot against the brown edges of the reef. Holding our breaths, we cautiously navigated a shallow, narrow passage to enter a mile-wide lagoon. We sighed with relief when we finally dropped the anchor in the well-protected north corner of pristine Marsa Umbeila.

Marsa Umbeila was uniquely beautiful. After we turned our engine off, we reveled in the silence and then heard a dull "clink—clunking." With binoculars we puzzled out the source of the "clunk": handmade goat bells. We strained to see a Bedouin hidden amongst the scenery prodding his goats south through the low, dry chaparral bushes. Shore birds chirped and fiddler crabs "popped" as they skittered along the sand. Then we noticed something else. Camouflaged in a dun-brown hooded robe, we'd mistaken a camel herder sitting in a hump for a pile of sand—until he moved. His small herd of camels foraged on the leaves of the desert savanna trees in the distance. Swinging our binoculars back to the herder, we watched the back of his hooded robe as he followed his camels over the rolling hills to the north. To the west and beyond the savanna trees and the sparse vegetation that grew in a quarter-of-a-mile-wide band around the *marsa*, an alluvial plain of desert sand stretched and sloped to the foot of distant mountains. The barren, lifeless red mountains, scrubbed by wind and sand, towered above the desert as weathered monuments to an inhospitable terrain.

Braving the possibility of sharks, we swam anyway in the *marsa's* refreshingly cool, calm, and clear waters. As we dried off after a fresh water rinse, we noticed a cloud of dust on the horizon. Grabbing our binoculars for a better look, Jim said, "Something is coming down the road, possibly cars." "It can't be cars," I said. "There aren't any roads here–only Bedouin tracks. We are hundreds of miles from any roads." Something raised that trail of dust. Squinting into our binoculars, we looked again.

Talking on top of each other, we said, "Who would be—? Wait a minute, wait a minute, it's camels with people walking beside them!" Sure enough, although distorted by heat waves coming off the hot desert floor, we made out the shape of three camels with three figures. As they came closer, Jim reported, "They look like soldiers, and they are coming this way." The men wore military fatigues and scarves that wrapped around their heads covering all but their eyes. Two of the men had automatic rifles slung on their backs. Leaving their camels to graze, the three walked to the edge of the water near where *Sanctuary* gently rocked at anchor.

We decided to take the diplomatic approach and waved in greeting. Jim hollered, "Hello." The soldier obviously in charge removed something from his shirt pocket and read from a well-used, wrinkled piece of paper, calling: "You come here." Jim responded, "Give us a few minutes."

The soldier repeated, "You come here." Jim said, "Okay! Okay! No problem." Jim held up one, then two fingers, as he said, "One or two minutes. No problem." Jim motioned to our inflatable and mimicked launching it to come ashore.

The soldier yelled again, "You come here." We quickly lowered the dinghy to the water as the soldier repeated, like a script to follow over and over until he got the intended result, "You come here."

I yelled to them, "Do you need to see our passports?" He responded, "You come here."

Jim told me nervously, "Hurry up. Bring the damn passports. Get out three cold colas, three packs of cigarettes, and anything else you think they might want. I don't like this. Come on! Let's get going before these kids get itchy fingers."

All smiles and grins, we quickly paddled ashore. The soldiers had removed the scarves from their faces but left them hanging from their heads with one scarf tail down the back and the other side wrapped around the throat and neck. The commander in charge looked about 20 years old and wore a handgun strapped in a side arm leather case. He removed his scarf completely and pulled out a folded brown beret from inside his shirt. He unfolded the beret and removed a pair of sunglasses. He then put on the Ray Bans and the brown beret which had an official-looking emblem on its side. The other two soldiers looked not more than 16 or 17 years old at best. They had moved their automatic rifles to their chests as if they were ready to use them.

They greeted us with stern faces that did not turn into friendly smiles even as Jim placed a cold cola in each hand. The commander said something, and the three of them put the colas on the sand in a little pile and resumed the stern looks. We could see them eying the three packs of cigarettes Jim held in his hand. They knew we were waiting for a favorable outcome before distributing the cigarettes.

The soldier in charge took our passports and opened Jim's to look at his photograph. He hiked his sunglasses up and squinted at the photo then opened his eyes wide to focus on Jim. He did this several times, then repeated the process with me. He handed Jim his passport, randomly opened a page, and asked, "Come from?" Jim found the page with the Egyptian stamp and indicated by pointing at the date that we were legally checked into Egyptian waters. Then Jim pointed at the ground and said, "We, okay."

The soldier then pointed south and asked with a high tone in his voice as though incredulous, "Go?" I joined in, pointing south, responded, "Yes, south." Jim chimed in, swallowed hard, pointed south, and said, "We go."

We were nervous for good reason. Sailors in Cyprus and Israel had warned us to watch out for the notoriously impatient shore patrols. Most sailing traffic enters the Red Sea via the Arabian Gulf and proceeding north, approaches the Egyptian coast after having left the Sudan and Eritrea to the south. All vessels, however, whether going north or south, were required to check in at the first port of entry they reached, before stopping. The first Egyptian port of entry coming from the south was Safaga, well to the north of the southern border. Therefore, if we had been sailing north, our stop at Marsa Umbeila would have been illegal. Jim as captain would be subject to arrest, and *Sanctuary* could have been impounded until an exorbitant fine was paid.

We crossed paths with a northbound cruising couple while both of our boats were anchored at the southern entrance to the Suez Canal, Port Suez. As they sailed north along waters of the southern Egyptian shoreline, heading to an entry port, their steering cable broke. Disabled and drifting dangerously near a reef, they called via VHF radio for help from any vessel. The Egyptian Navy responded and towed their disabled vessel into one of the southern ports. The couple were then arrested for not having a visa and fined $6,000 U.S. dollars.

Sanctuary, on the other hand, had entered Egyptian waters from the north, and we had obtained our visas and all necessary boat documents long before Umbeila. As understanding dawned, and the soldiers realized they wouldn't have to arrest us, they sighed in relief. The soldier in charge broke into a big smile and said, "Welcome." After a round of handshaking and smiling with Jim, they merely bowed toward me. The two younger soldiers repeated, "Well—come, USA. Verdy well—come."

With hand signals they suggested coming aboard *Sanctuary*. I made a pillow out of my hands, indicating that we were going to sleep and they could not come aboard. Jim noticed their disappointment and tried to explain with a wild charade: For three days and three nights we had fought the wind and waves. Putting up and taking down sails. Reefing sails and raising sails. He picked up a stick and drew in the sand the coastline and the reefs. He tried to demonstrate that coming in through the reefs was very difficult, and that we were tired and needed sleep. They watched him with wide eyes and open mouths as if he were a crazy man, then looked at each other and shook their heads. They no longer wanted to come aboard *Sanctuary*.

The soldiers held a momentary conference and then picked up the sodas from the beach. Each took a pack of cigarettes from Jim, furiously shaking his hand again. I automatically put my hand out for a shake, belatedly realizing my error—of course they would not shake this hand, attached as it was to a woman with uncovered arms and face. The officer neatly folded his sunglasses, put them in his beret, folded the beret, and slid it into his shirt. All three rewrapped the scarves around their heads and faces for protection. They waved goodbye and started walking. After a few steps, the commander turned and gave us a classic Arabic farewell by touching the tips of his fingers to his forehead then touched his heart saying, *"In'shalla"* (Go with God). They entered the trail among the low chaparral, gathered their camels, and mounted them as the trail turned to desert. We returned to *Sanctuary*. As we reboarded we turned toward shore and saw three figures distorted by the waves of heat. A cloud of dust drifted out into the desert and faded away.

A day or two later we rolled on south with the winds still behind us. We decided not to visit Sudan, so we bypassed Port Sudan and Sawakin. After two days and nights of tedious tacking through a reef-strewn area, we were again exhausted. Neither of us had slept due to constant sail changes and constant navigational challenges. A cove near Sudan's southern border looked inviting. The chart showed the anchorage free of hazards, the shores uninhabited, and it was far distant from any port likely to have officials. The fact that we were not checked into the country was a risk we decided to take.

We battled our way into Khor Nawarat, Sudan, anchoring with relief. We scanned the horizon 360 degrees. The chart was right, the shores were uninhabited. The only signs of life were birds and sharks, their fins slicing the calm turquoise water as they swam lazily to and fro. The wind howled outside the lagoon, but *Sanctuary* stood protected. By late afternoon, thunder and lightning accompanied the winds, and we watched as the clouds burst over the mountains in the distance. It only drizzled in our anchorage, so we settled in to wait out the weather, content that our peace would not be disturbed.

The next morning produced more of the same: stiff winds, dark clouds, rain over the mountains, and a drizzle on us. In the afternoon the sky cleared, and we sat in the cockpit gazing toward the horizon. We were too afraid of the sharks to swim. A disturbance on the water near the entrance to the cove drew our attention. We both lifted our binoculars exclaiming, "A boat is coming this way—fast." As I hurried below to put on more clothing than the skimpy shorts and tank top I was wearing, Jim called out progress reports: "It looks like four men—they may be military—it's not a fishing boat—uh, oh, oh, no, they have a gun; there's a big machine gun mounted in the middle of the boat; they are coming right for us—what should we do?" By that time I was back in the cockpit, and we concurred: there was nothing to do but wait and see what they wanted. We vowed to remain calm, gave each other a big hug, and sat down to meet our fate.

The boat slowed to a crawl as it approached us, and we could see the crew clearly. The four wore one military uniform between them. One wore the dun-colored beret with military insignia on the side; the second a sturdy pair of military boots; the third a pair of military camouflage pants; and the fourth wore the matching camouflage shirt. The three without boots were barefoot. The three without camouflage pants wore shorts or sarong-type lower garments. The winner of the boots wore a tee shirt over his shorts; the other two were barechested.

We might have relaxed at the ragtag sight but for the fifty-caliber machine gun. We'll never know if it was loaded, but the fact that one of the four had his finger on the trigger was enough to keep us silent until they spoke to us. Surprisingly, the man on the prow gently fended their boat off *Sanctuary*'s tender, fiberglass hull. The fellow with the hat seemed to be the leader, and he greeted us in fairly good English, identifying the group as a Sudanese Military Patrol. He then politely asked where we were going, took a look at our passports, shook hands with Jim, and welcomed us to Sudan.

As we chatted, Chica, our blue-eyed Siamese-mix cat, wandered out into the cockpit and began sniffing the two men who had come aboard. They quieted as she walked up to them, finally breaking their silence to ask, "Can she see?"

"Yes, why?"

"Because her eyes are so pale." (My intense blue eyes were hidden behind sunglasses.)

After assuring them that we would up anchor in the morning and either come straight to Suakin to check into Sudan or continue on to Eritrea (as we planned), the four accepted a gift of sodas and packs of cigarettes, bid us goodbye, and left without rocking our boat.

Early the next morning, we pressed still farther south on what were to be the last of our favorable Red Sea winds and sailed into Massawa, Eritrea.

It was wintertime in Eritrea, and the temperature was only 88 degrees instead of 110. It might rain inland, but the desert coast of the Red Sea continued to be hot, dry, and dusty even in winter. *Sanctuary*, coated with red dust and salt, was anchored near the old bombed-out palace of Haile Selassie. We began Thanksgiving Day 1998 in the cockpit drinking our coffee as the singsong early morning call to prayer wafted over the water from the mosques. Chica spent her day chasing and catching flies. Later, we ate a combination of the local produce: chard, tomatoes, potatoes, onions, carrots, and cabbage. No turkey was available here; even a chicken was hard to come by.

Massawa, Eritrea

Eritrea, listed as the African country with the lowest GNP, was definitely poor. A fight for independence with Ethiopia was apparently won at a high price. Much of what we saw ashore was bombed out rubble. But if the people we met were any indication of the entire country, we believed the Eritreans would recover and thrive. The citizens were a mix of Christian and Muslim. In spite of lack of money and modern methods, there was basic cleanliness, evident industry, and a certain pride. We were met with exceptional friendliness everywhere, and there were no demands for *baksheesh*. We helped the economy as much as we could by eating meals ashore and by purchasing some of the beautifully made handicrafts.

An overnight visit inland to the mountain capital of Assawa was worth it just for the bus ride. Goats, chickens, vegetables, bags of salt and flour, building materials, and two tourists (us) all jostled for space among robed and turbaned men, black *chador*-cloaked women with veiled faces and others with face tattoos, nose rings, and gold earrings. There were also men in suits and ties and modern-looking Eritrean women dressed in short skirts and high heels.

There was no schedule, as buses did not depart until full, and they meant *full*. The one-and-a-half hour wait on the bus as the process unfolded was a lesson in ingeniousness and patience. Finally, the bus, packed tight as a pickle jar, began a winding journey over and through the mountains, stopping at every village, hut, crossroads, or bend in the road. We stopped for goats, boys on bicycles, women and children walking on the curves, approaching vehicles, camels (wild and in herds), military men, arm wavers, donkeys, and even a tribe of baboons! Finally, at Giftan, about midway to our destination, we stopped for a rest.

Jim and I were the subject of much curiosity and lots of smiles. Three young men with shining eyes, who looked about 20, wore the typical head scarf and long white robes layered with colorful vests. They sat near us, and we chatted cheerfully with them, each not having a clue what the other was saying. Finally, I asked if I could take their picture, and they laughingly agreed. Then the three, as if in a skit from Groucho, Harpo, and Chico Marx, performed a "let's exchange headscarves" routine. I snapped photos as they unwrapped, exchanged, and rewrapped each other's turbans, laughing and smiling, hands and elbows flashing.

Our "day or two" in Massawa turned into two weeks when a DHL shipment of medicines scheduled for "next-day air" took an extra week. Jim suffered from a bout of food poisoning or something that produced chills, fever, aches, and diarrhea. We dragged our feet leaving Massawa, since we knew the winds would shift soon and that our "downwind Red Sea sailing" days were over. We also were in the midst of another "should we or shouldn't we" conversation.

My journal entry from November 30, 1998, says it all: *Anchored, Umm Es Sahrig, Eritrea, 15° 36.72' N, 39° 27.78' E, Winds, SE 15 knots; Jim just told me he wants to quit cruising in Oman, that he doesn't feel safe anymore. We've been worried about his strength and balance for a while, and he is increasingly stressed about boat handling. So, we are talking about shipping Sanctuary back to the USA from Salalah. That should be an adventure in itself! So we need to continue and get Sanctuary from here in the Red Sea to Oman, about another 600 miles I guess—haven't figured it out. His arm strength has disintegrated lately, along with balance, and he has dizziness problems. Whatever infection he got here in Eritrea has really hit him hard, too. So, sell Sanctuary and decide what we are going to do next.*

Feels incomplete to not finish our circumnavigation, but Jim's safety and health is the most important thing, and I don't want to go alone or with anyone else.

At the moment I feel sad, stymied, upset, and afraid. Even though things are bad, I still am more afraid of quitting than of continuing. Still, I worry about Jim almost all the time and am never at ease anymore, constantly worried about him falling and/or staying on board, or just plain illness. He looks "haunted" much of the time, strained. So much is a struggle for him because of PD. He seems to be feeling defeated. Acknowledging the limitations PD creates must be awful for him. I know, yet really don't know, what it is like for him; it is difficult for me to tell reality from fearful upset.

In the middle of nowhere, as it were, we could only continue, so that we did, reinitiating our "sail at night, rest during the day" formula. The winds shifted, and for the most part were dead on our nose (for the direction we wanted to go) so that forward progress on a pounding close haul demanded frequent short tacking. We slogged along with seas building and winds roaring. Sailing 70 miles took 24 hours. During one passage I went into the galley to cook dinner, opened the port food locker to get a canned ham, and found a bag of flour (triple bagged!) burst open. The flour had sifted over the other locker contents, and as I began cleaning it up, I discovered it had also been full of bugs, which crawled throughout the whole locker.

So, as *Sanctuary* lurched and rolled in the middle of a terrible, lumpy sea I emptied the locker, threw out five pounds of flour, cleaned, sprayed and de-bugged the locker, repacked the food I had unpacked, and then cooked dinner! I baked all of the bread we ate (unless we were in port), so throwing out five pounds left me low on flour and unhappy. After dinner I inspected all the foodstuffs we had recently purchased in Eritrea and discovered more bug-infested flour, bug-infested Tang, and a suspect jar of mayonnaise. Oh well, at least the Danish canned ham we had stowed since England was still good.

A much-needed "lay day" at Wadi Edi, Eritrea, cheered us up, and we puttered around cleaning the boat. With no evidence of sharks, I got in the water and scraped barnacles off the hull. Jim relaxed and seemed much calmer after acknowledging some of his upset and fears. Meanwhile, I reread the warnings on a new medicine his doctor had prescribed which he had begun taking in Cyprus. Side effects could include: dizziness, trouble sleeping, unusual weakness, stomach upset, and hallucinations—just what we didn't need. Maybe that medicine caused some of his problems. (Weeks later I was able to call the doctor, and we discontinued that prescription.)

While we were anchored at Wadi Edi, four fishermen came over asking if we wanted to trade sodas or cigarettes for a fish. We were down to the last six packs of cigarettes we had bought for trading, but since we were almost out of the Red Sea we said, "Yes." They also needed oil, so we gave them two liters of 30-weight oil, communicating in a mixture of English, Farsi, Italian, and sign language. Oil was universal in the language of outboard engines—no problem there. They smiled, we smiled, and the delicious but unidentified fish lasted us two days.

Saturday, December 5, 1998: 0230: Raised anchor and left Wadi Edi with a distance to go of 37 nm to the next secure anchorage. In good conditions, we could sail that distance in six to seven hours. Well, it wasn't good conditions, and the journey took us 12 hours. Most of it was a windward slog. The weather really deteriorated in the final two hours. The SE wind picked up to 25 knots and gusted to 30. The seas white-capped, and we could not fall off or tack due to rocks on the starboard and reefs to the port. Turning on our 36 HP engine helped us stay our course, and *Sanctuary* clawed her way into an anchorage off Dannabah Island, Eritrea.

The chop in the anchorage was too rough for swimming. The closer we got to the Bab-el-Mandeb, the "Gate of Tears," the worse the winds got. We had a lovely night's sleep, even with a roll from the east. The surrounding islands and mainland were all volcanic lava terrain, red and black cinder cones—in other words, "heat sinks." The bleached shore showed little vegetation. One fishing boat cruised through the anchorage; otherwise, we didn't see any local people. In 1996, a British cruising couple had been arrested in this bay presumably for stopping without clearance papers. We, however, had visas, and an additional document from the Port Captain in Massawa gave us permission to anchor along the coast of Eritrea.

The torture continued the next day. We left Dannabah at 1:30 a.m. hoping to be up before the winds. The winds never slept, and again it was a slog in 20, then 25, then 30 knots on the nose. For 13 hours, we short-tacked back and forth across our path only to find the wind had shifted just enough to make the new tack unsuitable. Hard on the wind with reefed main and staysail, our forward progress made good was a miserable one and a half knots.

During the slog we heard a loud "thump," and as the staysail fluttered erratically, we realized the staysail stay had broken. The pounding of the bow sent up a steady spray, so I stripped off all my clothes, put my safety harness on, clipped onto our safety line, and crawled out to the foredeck. The "T" bracket had broken out of the quick-release fitting on the deck and was completely sheared off—metal fatigue much like our own mental fatigue.

All we could do at the moment was lower the sail and tie off all the bits and pieces of the turnbuckle. Wind conditions were too much for the jib, so we turned on the engine for a boost and ploughed through short, steep seas that increased as the water shallowed. By noon, when we finally anchored at Ras Terma, the winds howled at 35 knots and were still steady at 20 knots at 5:00 p.m.

Were the winds caused by the hot air rolling down off the volcanic mountains, or were they produced by the squeezing of air, currents, and seas through the narrow 17-mile-wide Strait of Bab-el-Mandeb (Gate of Tears)? We weren't sure, but felt the Strait was aptly named. We were still more than 70 miles from the Gate and were almost in tears already. Each sailing day took a recovery day. Our "recovery day" at Ras Terma was spent jerry rigging the forestay system. After taking apart the "quick-release" fitting, we rigged up a shackle affair so that we could fly our very important staysail. After close examination, we discovered that the toggle bolt "T" had broken due to a poor weld in the manufacture. It was amazing that it lasted as long as it had.

Just about the time we packed our tools and spare shackles, a boatful of "Navy Men" approached. They didn't have uniforms but did have an AK 47. Jim and I looked at each other and silently mouthed to each other, "Badges?! We don't got to show you no stinking badges!"

After examining our papers, the navy men told us we were in a military zone and ordered us to leave as soon as the wind died. Our reply: "Gladly." We would be thrilled to get out of the Red Sea and away from Africa, a rough, difficult experience.

I'm not sure why we left our last anchorage in the Red Sea, Fatuma Deset, Eritrea, at 9:00 a.m. It seems rather late in the morning. Perhaps we waited to see what the winds were doing. The passage was so rough I made very few log entries. I was either too busy navigating or too tired to write.

I do have the entry I made the next day, December 12, 1998: *We are out of the Red Sea!!! I feel let out of purgatory into heaven. The last 24 hours were definitely the "Gates of Tears or Sorrows." When we left Fatuma Deset, all was okay. At three to three and a half knots until Perim Island (a Yemeni island on the east side of the strait). We then had short, blocky sea, an opposing current, winds on the nose, and the very busy shipping lanes. No sea room, tacking took us backward, and any course seemed to be dangerous because of the elbow of the traffic lanes. Plus, by the time we actually needed to turn left, to port, it was 11:00 p.m., dark, and the moon not up. Altogether a very long, very tiring 24 hours.*

Once we popped out and turned east towards Yemen and Oman, we were in the light winds and steady seas of the North East Monsoon. The sea is deep, and the swell is long and regular. What a difference! Plus, the water is not as salty, so even the air is nicer, and at last we are not being sandblasted.

We spent all morning cleaning the red sand off the lower rigging and decks. The salt crystals are like rock salt, and the entire exterior is encrusted with red, sandy, salty mud. Have as much of it off as we can reach, but all the lines and sheets are filthy red. Oh, someday we'll have some fresh water to wash the boat. We feel better already and as if we have the strength to go on.

Halfway 'Round

December 1998—January 1999

"Hell hath no fury like a bureaucrat scorned."
—Milton Friedman, American Economist 1912

Our first day out of the Red Sea was a magical "four-star" day, the day armchair sailors visualize when dreaming about sailing around the world. In our voyage the reality rarely met the dream, and therefore, it was a day to remark upon with beautiful sailing under perfect quartering winds over deep, azure water, flat seas, no traffic, and no hazards. To celebrate our release from the Red Sea, we broke our rule of "no alcohol underway," drank a cocktail at sunset, and then made love in the cockpit (also something we rarely did underway) popping our heads up every 15 minutes to check the horizon.

We sailed blissfully along overnight en route for the port of Al Mukalla, Yemen. The next morning, however, when Lee, aboard *Quest* in Ashkelon, relayed us the weather forecast for the Arabian Sea, we changed our plans. A cyclone was forecast to hit the coast, centered at Salalah, Oman. Cyclonic winds were due to blow at up to 60 knots, and 25 knots were expected in Aden which we had passed to port miles earlier. The safe harbor of Al Mukalla lay at least 42 hours ahead. We'd be caught out if we continued, so we turned back toward Aden.

We did not like to give up miles we'd gained, and we did not look forward to another dirty harbor and grimy city either. We retraced our steps reluctantly, arrived at Aden, and checked in to a frenzy of activity. As soon as we stepped ashore, two ship's agents, Omer and Mohammed, attached themselves to us like limpets. Both spoke English, Mohammed owned a taxi, and together they announced that they were: "Ready at the

Calm seas after the Gate of Tears

harbor for any service or other boat friends by your influence 'til you leave Aden." Between the two of them, our "Nannies" (as we nicknamed them) did certainly provide "any service."

After the ubiquitous paperwork with the Harbor Officials was completed, Omer and Mohammed marshaled us through the dusty, pockmarked streets of Aden to the best market we had experienced since Turkey. From open-air stalls with dusty aisles tumbled produce I hadn't seen in months, including that most outstanding of vegetables, the one that signified "civilization" to us, fresh, perfect, lettuce! Omer helped us pack our bounty into Mohammed's taxi, and together with the Nannies, we bounced along Aden's potholed streets to an air-conditioned supermarket. It was small by American terms but large in the eyes of two weary sailors who had not seen a clean, plucked, and sectioned chicken in more than three months. Exclaiming over tinned butter (a difficult-to-come-by staple for an ocean voyage) tinned cheeses, flour without bugs, and other foodstuffs we needed for our upcoming crossing of the Arabian Sea, we bought many bags full, taxied back to the harbor, and ferried them on board. I spent our second evening in Aden washing vegetables in a sanitizing bleach solution, repackaging goods sold in cardboard into sturdy, waterproof plastic, and logging everything into our food lists.

The whirlwind continued the next day. We upped anchor and moved over to a nasty fuel dock. Its slippery, rusty deck was puddled with spilled diesel. Fenders were not enough protection against the constant wake in the busy harbor, and as we filled our 90-gallon tank, *Sanctuary* surged hard against the rusty dock, adding battle scars to her fiberglass hull. Next we jockeyed *Sanctuary* to a different dock to buy some precious fresh water. While at the water dock, I hosed down our rigging (still red and salty from our months in the Red Sea) and filled all six of our onboard buckets with water so I could wash our halyards and sheets (not bed sheets—the ropes used to trim our sails).

After almost all day on deck in the hot sun taking on fuel and water, we wearily motored *Sanctuary* back to the anchorage area to reset our hook. As soon as the hook was set and we plopped into the cockpit, Omer appeared onshore, hailed us, and yelled through cupped hands, "I found internet hookup for you."

Internet hookup was not commonplace during our journey, and we hadn't been able to send e-mails since Port Suez, so we looked at each other for agreement, and then called back to Omer, "Just a minute while we change clothes and pack up our laptop."

E-mailing our families was far easier and more satisfactory than calling. World time differences often meant that when we were ashore during the day and could find a telephone, it was night for our family and friends back in the United States, and they were asleep. So we e-mailed, and sometimes while doing so we caught a family night owl at the computer. Chatting via "instant message" was fun, and my mother especially found reading about where we were easier than straining to understand the unfamiliar place names over bad phone connections from halfway around the world. (Cell phones were not commonplace during the years of our journey. The worldwide satellite phones available at the time cost thousands of dollars, and charges started at 90 cents per minute, fees we could not afford.)

While ashore we asked the Nannies to arrange a tour of Yemen including the ancient city of Sana'a. The Nannies, however, advised us not to leave Aden, since in recent months two Belgian tourists had been kidnapped by tribesmen near Sana'a, the German embassy had been bombed, and another bombing had occurred in Sana'a.

Furthermore, the Nannies did not think it safe for us even to venture into Aden without them. We took them at their word, and when we left the harbor area, at least one of them accompanied us and walked closely behind us in the markets. Nothing really untoward happened, but while in the market on the first day, several men stopped dead in their tracks in front of me blocking my way and staring at me intently. Many of the men were attired in western-style clothing, however, the three who stopped me wore the more traditional dress of turbans and long white robes, belted at the waist with *jambias* (large curved knives). I wasn't frightened: it seemed the men were mostly curious about me. Then again, perhaps I was fodder for a stoning, having dressed (according to their beliefs) shamelessly.

Almost all the Yemeni women we saw in Aden looked like sandal-footed ghosts who'd tumbled into a coal bin. Long, black, voluminous robes draped from neck to ankles and to wrists, covered them in full. Long, black scarves encased their heads, black fabric veiled their faces, and the entire headscarf contraption fell to waist length, adding a second or third layer of heavy cloth to the burden. A few women shot furtive glances at us, their dark eyes barely visible in the narrow slits of their veils. I could only guess at the demeanor of the majority of the black-shrouded women though, since many of them were completely masked and faceless without even slits in the veils for their eyes. So, I, a female with short, gray hair wearing long khaki pants, a bright blue long-sleeved blouse, and sporting a white face open and beaming beneath a large- brimmed sun hat, must have seemed a cool peacock to them. The temperature was in the high 90°s, and I was actually miserable and sweating. Although, in view of the wretchedness around me, misery was a relative term.

In any event, we did not tour the interior of Yemen and after three fast-paced days in Aden, we departed the harbor on Thursday, December 17, 1998. As we crept along the coast, sailing toward Oman at a slow four knots, we listened to a BBC radio broadcast and learned that the U.S. and Britain had bombed Baghdad the day before due to noncompliance of the weapons inspections. The BBC reported that the Arab world was especially upset since Ramadan, an important Muslim holiday, would start the following weekend. An American House Judiciary Committee had recently alleged that President Clinton had lied to the Grand Jury regarding Paula Jones, his relationship with Monica Lewinsky, and furthermore, had obstructed justice. In reporting that information, the BBC intimated that the bombing might have been a ploy by President Clinton to avoid impeachment. After seven years of sailing abroad, we felt so far removed from the politics of the United States that our reaction was basically one of worry regarding anti-American sentiment. How would we be treated or received in Oman, another Muslim nation?

Our more immediate concern was for the weather which we hoped would not deteriorate. Light winds prevailed, and as we slowly sailed along, Jim threw our "meat hook" overboard in hopes of catching a fish. He hooked a red meat sierra, a fish we didn't care for but Chica loved, so we kept it, and Jim filleted it for her. She gobbled a lot of it up right away, but we cut her off and put the rest into our freezer. We'd give her little "kitty fishcicles" as needed. (She'd worry them around until they melted, then eat every last bit.)

I baked two loaves of bread, caught up on writing letters to our families, wrote an article about the Red Sea for a sailing magazine, and composed some e-mails, saving them to a disk so we could send them when we reached a port and found an internet connection. Meanwhile, I received weather faxes twice a day via our SSB radio.

We also spent part of the easy six-day sail from Yemen to Oman looking for the source of a saltwater leak we had discovered a month before. *Sanctuary*'s bilge was normally dry. If it was wet, something was wrong. Any time our automatic bilge pump turned on, we looked immediately to see what caused it. In spite of the fact that the bilge was less than perfectly clean, it was necessary to dip a finger into any water found there and take a small taste, since we first needed to know whether the water was fresh or salt.

The leak in question was saltwater, and we had not been able to pinpoint its source. Our first suspect was the anchor windlass. Affixed to the bow, it had a hawse hole through which the anchor chain fed into a bow locker. The bow chain locker drained via a pipe directly into the bilge sump. Small amounts of water that dripped off the anchor chain after we brought it aboard were thus pumped out of the boat from the sump. We had raised the anchor hours earlier, and that bit of water was long gone. Maybe water was coming aboard from the hawse hole itself? We plugged the hawse hole when underway. Perhaps we had lost the plug, and saltwater splashing on the bow was running into the boat via the anchor windlass. No, the plug was in place, and the saltwater wasn't coming from the anchor windlass.

Perhaps our emergency bilge pump was backed up? No, we checked the entire system; that wasn't it. The cockpit lockers, if flooded and not properly sealed, would drain into the engine room and then into the bilge. Maybe the cockpit port-side locker had taken on water due to a hit with a beam sea? No, we had resealed all three cockpit lockers, and they were watertight. Besides, on our easy point of sail toward Oman, we didn't take on any beam seas. Could the packing gland around the prop shaft be leaking? No, we plugged up the first section of the bilge which caught the small drip from the gland. It wasn't that. Was the toilet in the head leaking due to a loose fitting or hose clamp? No, we unpacked all the head lockers and followed the pipes to their watertight conclusions.

After cleaning the bilge again and wiping it bone dry, I lay on the cabin sole with all the bilge boards out and watched, and waited, and pounced on the trickle that slowly appeared. Eureka! The culprit was a bad connection from Turkey—Not Quite Right—on the heat exchanger which had rusted from not being galvanized. At last we knew the cause of the leak and added the repair to the ever present "To Do" list. Sweaty and dirty from searching for the leak, we finished cleaning *Sanctuary* inside and out, then took a hot sun shower out in the cockpit.

Northerly winds continued to blow lightly but steadily, so the slow six-day sail to Port Raysut, Salalah, Oman, was peaceful. Even though Jim's arms frequently "froze" and his balance was iffy, he was much calmer since we'd escaped the Red Sea. The lighter winds and easier sailing conditions allowed both of us to sleep during our off watches, and we arrived in Salalah three days before Christmas 1998 well rested and ready to greet a new country.

Jim & Customs Officers Salalah, Oman

After anchoring, we waited patiently for the port officials to come aboard and check us in. As we sat in the cockpit, we looked around at the clean, well-built harbor and nice-looking buildings on the shore. The difference between the standard of living in The Royal Sultanate of Oman and the countries of Red Sea Africa and the Middle East that we had previously visited was dramatic and very apparent even before going ashore. When the officials came aboard they were polite, and their long white robes were shining and spotless, their beards groomed and trimmed, and their colorful turbans were wrapped just so. The check-in process proceeded smoothly, and it was really a pleasure to be greeted graciously, without sneers, weaponry, or demands for bribery.

Later, we got a ride into the town of Salalah, the cleanest and neatest city we had visited since leaving England! The Sultan obviously had plowed oil wealth back into Oman, providing modern roads, communications systems, schools, goods, and other first-world services. We were pleasantly surprised that the diversity of products available included cranberry sauce and frozen turkeys, so while the Muslims celebrated Ramadan, we and our British friends Beth and Bone Bushnell from *Splinters Apprentice* celebrated our escape from the Red Sea with a full Christmas dinner.

Jim strung lights on *Sanctuary*'s mast; I decorated a tiny artificial tree for the main salon; and we cooked vegetables, baked bread, cut up fresh fruit and coconut for ambrosia, and even baked a pumpkin pie (which came out a little lopsided due to the wake from passing fishing boats). Beth and Bone roasted a turkey and made dressing and homemade cranberry sauce, then brought it over to *Sanctuary*. We toasted the great food and company with wine, stuffed ourselves in the traditional way, rested a bit, and then made room for dessert of fresh whipped cream-topped pie with a nightcap of sherry (from Spain).

The four of us went ashore to call our families; otherwise, we took off Christmas Day and the day after, Boxing Day. Too soon, we were back to work. Beth and Bone had to repair a leaking fuel tank in their sailboat, and since we were preparing for a 14- or 15-day ocean crossing, all our rigging needed to be checked. Checking the rigging was one of the things we had worried about when we left Turkey. How could we take care of our boat since Jim couldn't get up the mast anymore, nor could he hoist me?

Bone came to the rescue. He climbed the mast with a special rig he had, cleaned our tricolor light, and replaced some reflective tape which had come undone, repaired our jib roller furling foil, and checked our rigging out to both spreaders and all the way down to the deck. In exchange for all that help, we assisted *Splinters Apprentice* with taking their forestay down and putting it back up and gave them as much assistance with their fuel-tank repair as we could. Both boats' crews practiced the art of repairing your boat in exotic locations.

Even though we hadn't shared many anchorages, we had been in almost daily radio contact with Beth and Bone since we'd departed from Cyprus four months earlier. Our routes would diverge when we left Salalah. *Splinters Apprentice* would head to the Maldives; *Sanctuary* was bound for India. We didn't know when, or whether, we would meet again. We'd enjoyed their company, but the cruising saga of forming instant friendships, then soon having to say goodbye to those friends, unfortunately continued. After seven years of life afloat, we'd become accustomed to the process, but that didn't make it any easier.

Tuesday, January 5, 1999: *0600 hours, Winds NNE 15-20 knots, Range: Port Raysut, Salalah, Oman to Steamer Point, Cochin, India, 1,363 nautical miles.*

It took us almost five hours to break free of the "washing machine" effect caused by the Jabal Samhan headland of Oman. The wind shifted and spit at us as it surged and swooped from sea to land, and my hands soon blistered from so many sail changes. As we crabbed away from Oman, the sea floor deepened, the effects of being near land lessened, *Sanctuary* burst out of the churn, and we settled into our course for a close reach across the Arabian Sea.

I braced myself in the navigation station and checked my calculations one more time: from San Francisco in 1991 to Oman in 1998, we had sailed an easterly wandering path of 23,000 miles—only about 2,000 nautical miles shy of the Earth's circumference at the equator! In spite of all the thousands of miles we'd accumulated in our nautical wanderings, we'd yet to reach our "Halfway Around the World" point, and it lay just ahead of us in the Arabian Sea. We were set to reach the mark on January 7, 1999. In anticipation of the occasion, I plugged in our laptop and printed a small sign we planned to hold as we photographed ourselves crossing the line.

January 7th, "Halfway Day," started okay but deteriorated. The wind died to almost nothing, so we decided to spend a little fuel, charge the batteries, and motor awhile. We turned on the engine and just got it going when the fan belt broke. Okay, we didn't need the engine anyway. The spinnaker was far from my favorite sail; it usually took so much work (especially from me since I had to go out on the foredeck to set it). We dug it out of the locker anyway, and I wrestled it out to the foredeck. In spite of the fluky winds, we got it set and drawing nicely, so I went below to the nav station to see how close we were to our halfway goal. I had just calculated that we were only five miles from the mark when I heard a loud "snap."

Jim called from on deck, "Oh, shit! The spinnaker's down and in the water!" I bolted up the companionway stairs and out on the deck to discover the spinnaker pennant broken, the halyard stuck at the top of the mast, the spinnaker itself dragging in the water, and *Sanctuary* idling in light winds. Two hours were lost turning circles while we rescued the wet, salty, heavy spinnaker, dragged it back aboard, and stuffed it under the dinghy which we carried on our foredeck. Meanwhile, we'd forgotten the fishing line we had been towing, and it snagged around the rudder. So we had to untangle that snare. We sorted it all out, showered, the wind came up, we set the jib, and at 2030 hours, on January 7, 1999, we crossed the halfway mark at Latitude 15° 45' North, Longitude 57° 19' East.

Sanctuary Halfway Around the World in the Arabian Sea

We took a picture with the new digital camera we'd bought in Oman, and that was about it for celebrating. In spite of the sailing gloves I wore most of the time to keep the salt blisters down, my hands were blistered, I had an ugly bruise on my right shin, a tear on my left thumb, and a bruise on my right elbow. My hands were so cramped I could hardly write in the log or my journal. I ached all over from all the winching and sail hauling. I did write after making the mark: *"If only we could keep on as it is now—creaming along at four knots, no seas, light winds. Keep it up, Zeus and Neptune, please!"*

The opposing current of the NE monsoon slowed us down a bit, but with steady northeasterly winds and very little shipping traffic to worry about, we settled into a nice passage routine jogging along at about four and a half to five knots close hauled. The heel of the boat made cooking a dicey affair, but I braced into the galley and got on with the job. Jim snagged a rainbow tuna with his "meat hook," and Chica caught the smaller flying fish that landed in our scuppers, so all three of us were fish happy. Days slid by. Jim tweaked the sails, always aiming for the fastest point of sail balanced by a nod to the comfort of the cook. I wrote articles for sailing magazines or tuned in weather reports and kept a daily radio schedule with *Splinters Apprentice*, who was racing along downwind to the Maldives.

I loved the new digital camera we had purchased in Salalah and began constantly taking photos of Jim and his rainbow tuna, Chica with her flying fish, the fresh bread I baked, the set of the sails, and the spray from the bow wake as we creamed along toward our goal. By January 16th, we were only 292 miles from India. I read about our anticipated landfall of Cochin and wrote in my journal: *"Sailing along in perfect conditions. No swell: main, jib, and staysail flying on a lovely beam reach. I baked two loaves of French bread, we gave each other haircuts, took long showers, and I sat down to read for a while. Ah, if all passages could be like this."*

The last night before reaching India was the worst of the passage because of the fishing fleet. About 60 miles off the coast we began passing many fishing vessels, dhows, small open boats with two or three men in them, and larger 60- to 80-foot vessels with outriggers and/or long lines. Tracking their movements during the day was challenging, and sailing through the maze at night was tedious. Many of the vessels showed improper running lights; others had no lights at all, simply lighting what appeared to be kerosene lanterns as we approached. Radar did not pick up the smaller vessels, and during our watches we were often startled when a light appeared suddenly off our bow where none had been before.

We had a horrendous scare at 0330 when a vessel we had been tracking for two hours or so turned and came straight at us doing 15 knots. (We could plot this rate of speed using our radar.) We were not sure whether or not the fast approach was on purpose, but it surely seemed so. The vessel had been trolling for fish at a steady slow pace, and as he barreled toward us we were helpless. Falling off our point of sail would have put us directly to him, and in any other direction we would have stalled. As Jim struggled to remove the brake from our engine prop so that we could start the engine, I turned on our deck lights (our running lights were already on), got out our powerful search light, and shone it directly on our sails. At the last possible minute he turned off, and we escaped a ramming. What happened? Did he do it on purpose to scare us? Did he not see us? We knew our running lights were visible from at least five miles, and they were working fine. We'll never know, and we worried over the incident for a long time.

The next afternoon, 14 days after leaving Salalah, we sailed into the entrance to Cochin harbor past dhows and the strange counter-weighted butterfly nets of the shore-based fishing fleet. The green coastline of India beckoned invitingly, and we planned to leave *Sanctuary* anchored in the protected harbor three or four weeks while we toured the country. Around 1300 hours on Tuesday, January 19th, 1999, we dropped the hook at the designated anchorage in front of the Customs and Port Control building off Steamer Point near the Taj Malabar Hotel.

Butterfly shore-based fishing nets

Sanctuary was quickly boarded by a Port Control Officer. Since it was the last day of Ramadan, he said we'd file some papers aboard and come ashore the next day to finish the check-in procedure. So we filled out two copies of one paper for Port Control. Just as we finished that, the Customs Officer came aboard. He required four copies each (we provided the carbons) of five different forms. I pressed hard, but had to re-copy page four of several of the forms. Each had to be signed by the "Master" (Jim) and stamped with our ship's stamp. All the form-filling and stamping took two and a half hours! The check-in procedure exhausted us more than the passage had, and we were thrilled to be told to stay aboard. Punish me by not allowing me ashore! Welcome to India.

The next morning the check-in procedure continued. We visited the customs office to obtain permission to move our boat to a more suitable anchorage, filed a declaration that we had no "arms or bonded stores," gave up our ship's documents and got receipts for them, and then paid 200 *rupees* (about $5) for Port Clearance. Finally, after three hours with Customs and Port Clearance, we were directed to the last hurdle, Port Immigration, three kilometers down the road.

Customarily a Port Immigration Office simply issued us, as visiting sailors or seamen, shore passes good for travel outside the port. So far in our journey, we had checked into 29 countries or territories, and obtaining a visa or shore pass had generally been (if time consuming) easy. Some countries required a visa for inland travel, and officials issued it to us on the spot. It was typically valid for three to six months. Others checked our passports and issued nothing at all.

In other ports, upon departure, we returned the shore pass to Immigration and retrieved our passports which were sometimes stamped with an exit stamp. Upon getting port clearance from Port Control, we took our clearance papers to Customs. After paying duties, excises, and taxes if necessary, our ship's papers were returned. We, and our vessel, were then cleared by Customs and the Port Police to leave the port.

Ports of Entry we had encountered were geared for large merchant vessels laden with cargo and large crews. For merchant vessels, the described procedure was handled by a hired "Shipping Agent" and not the ships' officers. In many places, we, as visiting seamen aboard a small sailing craft, seemed to be tolerated as a formality and a pain in the port officials' backsides.

Advance information we had about entry into India was conflicting. One cruiser had said we needed visas issued in advance of arrival. Others had reported that no visas were necessary. Therefore, we spoke with an Indian official at the Indian Embassy in Cyprus who informed us that, as sailors, we did not need visas. We took his word and did not acquire tourist visas in advance for India.

In eight years of checking in and checking out, we had encountered a few grumpy Port Captains, disgruntled Customs Officers, and "It's Monday morning and I haven't had my coffee yet" Immigration Officers. We'd mostly been greeted warmly, although we had sometimes been asked for bribes. We'd walked miles from office to office in the hot sun and sat for ages waiting for one more rubber stamp to be thunked down. We had waited aboard tensely while strange men wearing guns pawed through our belongings "inspecting" them. *Sanctuary* had been searched stem to stern, potatoes had been "confiscated," bottles of wine had passed hands, and the cat had been either ignored or looked at under her tongue. Never had we been denied entrance into a country.

Therefore, in Cochin, India, we expected Immigration to issue a shore pass as usual. Not finding a *tuk-tuk* or taxi, we trudged three hot, dusty kilometers to present our passports and entry papers to an Immigration Officer in the small, four-room Immigration building to which we had been sent. We requested a three-week shore pass. The official took our passports and ship's entry papers, then left us sitting in a dirty, dusty room along with stacks and stacks of forgotten paperwork. As we waited restlessly, wondering what was happening, I surreptitiously took photos of our surroundings with our small digital camera.

Stacks of forgotten paperwork in the Immigration Office

After almost two hours of enforced waiting, the Chief Officer in charge of Port Cochin Immigration sent a liaison who moved us into another office. The liaison demanded a tourist visa (which we did not have) and immediately said we could not be in India without one. (Strangely, instead of speaking to us directly, the Chief Officer communicated via his obedient liaison by telephoning from the room next door.) The liaison relayed the message: "Go back to America and get Tourist's Visas and then return to India." The more we tried to reason with him, saying that we were on a sailboat and couldn't return to America, the more stubborn he became. The liaison became hostile.

Puzzled by the turn of events, we were at last directed to beg by writing a note explaining our need for a shore pass. I wrote that we required fuel, water, and food after 14 days at sea. Also, we needed to make boat repairs (our wayward spinnaker, for one thing, the leaking heat exchanger for another) and purchase necessary items for the boat. The liaison took our note to the Chief Officer in the other room and returned after a long while saying, "It is being considered. Wait here for a decision."

Finally, the curt liaison officer returned saying, "You have been granted 48 hours to get what you need. Return after 48 hours with your shore passes, get your passports, and leave Cochin by 1300 hours on Thursday the 21st, or you will be arrested, taken off your boat to jail, and criminally prosecuted. Do you understand?"

As we handed over our passports in exchange for the 48-hour shore passes we replied, "Yes, we understand."

The Immigration Officer had started the 48 hours from the time we dropped the hook, so we actually had only about 24 hours remaining on our shore passes. We rushed back to the dock and hired Ali and Najib, two locals working from their rowboats, to help us re-provision. Ali rowed us across the river to the fruit and vegetable markets. Nearby were some historical sites and an interesting-looking antique section of town. We blazed through the tourist section, purchased some old silver beads, got fruits and veggies, took some photos, jumped into a three-wheeled motorized rickshaw, visited Ali's home to meet his two lazy sons, had a quick but terrific meal of Indian cuisine at Ali's favorite restaurant, and Ali rowed us back to *Sanctuary*. We were exhausted, but two hours later Ali rowed across the river with 50 gallons of dirty diesel fuel which we carefully filtered into the tank. Two hours after the fueling, at 2200 hours, Ali and another fellow again rowed across the river with 150 gallons of beautiful, fresh water which we siphoned into our thirsty water tanks.

Wednesday night we stewed over the shore-pass snafu and just knew something wasn't right. We decided to contact an Indian Customs Officer we knew by way of an international sailing club we belonged to, the Ocean Cruising Club. We had been corresponding with our Customs Officer friend from Goa for more than a year and thought maybe he could help us obtain a three- or four-week pass. So, bright and early Thursday we called our Customs Officer friend and learned that he would be visiting Cochin on Friday. He assured us that, as sailors, we did not need a visa, said the local Immigration Officer was misinformed, and advised us to turn in the shore passes, get our passports back, and he would see us Friday. If there was a problem, he'd straighten it out. In any event, we could leave Cochin and sail north to Goa where we would be allowed to stay.

We needed our passports anyway in order to get money to pay for the fuel and the water, so back we went to Immigration, turned in our shore passes, got our passports, and went on our way. There were no ATMs, and obtaining funds required visits to five banks and took most of the morning. We were beginning to not even want to visit India. We did like the fabulous food and stopped for another great buffet lunch. We really didn't want to risk being arrested, so we decided to check out completely and head for Goa immediately. We'd leave a message for our friend about our decision.

When we arrived at the Port Control building at a little after noon, just before the 1:00 p.m. witching hour (1300 hours) set for our departure, it was closed for the day! We couldn't leave without checking out of the port. There was nothing to do but return the next morning to clear out with Port Control. We'd start the process early and leave, hopefully without attracting the attention of the Immigration Officials. We returned to *Sanctuary* to plan our early morning escape.

At 1500 hours, two hours past the time Immigration wanted us and *Sanctuary* out of India, a Port Police motor launch with four police officers came alongside led by "Mr. Liaison," the go-between Immigration Officer. They tied the launch alongside *Sanctuary* and the Port Police Captain read from an official-looking document. "Are you James V. Foley and Carolyn H. Foley?" Mr. Go-Between pointed at us and said, "That's them." We responded, "Yes, that's us."

The Police Captain informed us that we were under arrest for violating the Immigration Code and were in India illegally. By order of the Immigration Department, we must come with them to be criminally prosecuted.

We were shocked, Mr. Go-Between was grinning, and the Police Captain knew he had the dirty job of arresting two unfortunate people.

They came aboard *Sanctuary* at our request and followed us below. Jim asked them to sit down and offered them coffee, tea, or a soft drink. They refused. We explained about the closed Port Control office, how we could not get our papers, and our dilemma. We told him we really wanted to say in India longer and visit the country. The Port Police Captain seemed to understand. Mr. Go-Between sat smugly silent. I showed the Police Captain pictures from our trip and some articles I had written about other places we had been. The Police Captain was enrolled, but Mr. Go-Between squirmed in his seat.

The Port Police Captain was interested in us and our life as cruisers. He asked about *Sanctuary* and sailing a boat so far across the ocean. He questioned us about our previous lives and life in America. He became determined to help us. Mr. Go-Between was not happy. The Police Captain scolded Mr. Go-Between, and they carried on a heated debate in Hindi. We could tell the Police Captain was fighting for our side.

Switching to English, the Police Captain said, "I don't want to arrest you, but the Immigration Chief has ordered me to do so, and I must obey. There is nothing I can do except (and here he lowered his voice) I'll leave you for the evening so you can prepare *Sanctuary*. I'll be back tomorrow at 0900 hours to take you for prosecution."

Mr. Go-Between reluctantly succumbed. The Port Police Captain, turning back to us before leaving *Sanctuary*, said, "Why don't you write a formal letter to the Immigration Chief. He has the power and authority to grant you a shore pass. Explain who you are, why you came to India, and why you need a pass. Ask him for 10 days instead of three weeks. Let him know why you need the time. Before I take you to jail tomorrow, I'll stop by the Immigration office to ask him again not to arrest you." We thanked him, and after the two left, sat down and wrote a pleading letter.

Friday morning the Port Police Captain arrived at *Sanctuary*, took us to shore aboard the Police launch, and drove us in his police car to the Immigration Office. The Immigration Officer angrily tossed aside the letter without looking at it.

Even though the Port Police Captain went to bat for us, he was only able to get us 24 hours more, which was just long enough to retrieve our ship's papers that afternoon and leave the next morning. We left Immigration disgusted with the bureaucracy and headed for the Port Control Office again. It had not opened as scheduled and was still closed.

This time we jumped into a rickshaw, went directly to the Police Captain, told him about the closed office, asking, "What can we do now?" He put us in his jeep and angrily took off for the Immigration Office. He told us to wait in the jeep and he went in by himself. We heard shouting and arguing in Hindi coming from inside the little immigration building. The Port Police Captain returned, grinned, and said, "It's your lucky day. You have until Monday at 1300 hours, go enjoy yourselves." did. For the next three days we crammed in as much as we could. We gave up on finding the boat parts and made only essential repairs. We ate Indian food and drank Indian beer. From dawn river canoe trips until late evenings at the Kathakali Dance Theater, we quickly enjoyed what we could of India.

Kathakali dancer

Monday morning we made our final trip to the Immigration Office in Cochin, turned in our shore passes, and waited for our passports to be given back to us. Finally, the officer we had never seen but only heard from the other room, came out and, in the fashion of a martinet, tossed our passports toward us. Throwing our previous letter on the desk, he leaned toward me, and spittle flying, hissed, "You are a liar!"

Bristling and gritting my teeth to remain outwardly calm, I said, "We are not liars." As I stared at his angry face I noticed a pin of the Communist Party on his uniform lapel. Silence reigned. The Immigration Officer directed a policeman to "accompany" us until all the rest of our clearance papers were obtained. The policeman wearily ferried us around town for this chore which took almost four hours! He watched from the shore as we rowed back to *Sanctuary*.

We had not had lunch, so while Jim began preparing *Sanctuary* for departure, I began cooking pasta, intending to make a salad we could eat before we left. Just as I removed the boiling hot pasta from the stove to drain it, *Sanctuary* begin rocking. The anchorage was calm, so what was going on? I looked out the porthole and saw a 50-foot Navy launch circling alongside with officials waving papers and calling, "James Foley, Carolyn Foley, raise your anchor. Leave now. Raise your anchor. Leave India now." As we hastily raised the anchor, the launch hovered nearby and then followed us as we motored out of the harbor. The pasta draining in the sink lay forgotten.

Our Customs Officer friend had suggested that if we went to Goa, we could check in with no Immigration problems. The Immigration officials in Cochin, who had met our friend when he tried to intercede on our behalf, had threatened us: "Do not go try to go to Goa; we will have you arrested for sure. Your friend the Customs Officer will not be able to help." Exhausted from the tension of dealing with a brick-wall bureaucracy, we turned to port out of the harbor and set sail for Galle, Sri Lanka, instead.

A Banshee, Some Elephants and Monkeys

January 1999—August 1999

"Some days you just want to run over the dog."
—Goring, Sri Lankan Driver

Five stressful days in India left us exhausted, tense, and feeling incomplete. Night fell all too quickly after we were "escorted" out of Cochin Harbor, and we settled uneasily into our passage routine. I rescued the limp, congealed pasta from the sink and made a salad of sorts for us to eat. We determined to put the dictatorial Immigration Officer to the back of our minds and focus instead on the good things about our short stay in India. The night passed tediously, but smoothly, and my ruffled feathers began to lie down. The next day I unexpectedly got my dander up again.

We were quite used to encountering assorted types of vessels at sea. They fell, roughly, into these categories:

1. Large (over 100 feet) freighters, tankers, cruise ships, military vessels, ferries, and large fishing vessels. This type of vessel was easy to see, easy to track, and generally speaking, showed their colors during the day and had proper running lights on at night.

2. Vessels between our size of 40 feet and less than 100 feet: This size vessel included smaller fishing boats such as lobster boats, fishing dhows, smaller passenger ferries, medium to large sailboats, good-sized powerboats, trawlers, and motor yachts. Again, vessels in this category generally flew identifying colors, followed the rules of navigation, and had regulation running lights on at night or in foul weather. A few, such as the fishing vessel who aimed right at *Sanctuary* as we sailed toward India, scared us, but most of the time it was safe to watch midsized vessels closely once first sighted, figure out their course and speed, then check periodically on their progress and ours as we each continued along our

routes.

    3. The last category of vessel—small fishing vessels, sailboats, and power boats under 40 feet—gave us the most headaches. On spotting smaller vessels we often asked, "What are they doing?" Usually the vessel posed no threat but simply required that close attention be paid to their possible actions. Whether day or night, small vessels were also more difficult to see in the first place, and furthermore, many of the smaller vessels we encountered around the world seemed not to know the rules of navigation, chose to ignore the rules of navigation, had no running lights, didn't display running lights, or overall just didn't care.

    We had grown used to these small boats. We were also quite used to what a small fishing boat looked like, especially the ones we had seen plying the Red Sea, the Arabian Sea, and most recently the small fishing boats along the coast of India. The open fishing boats of about 20 feet usually contained one or two men sometimes with a makeshift awning amidships, sometimes powered by a small 20-horsepower outboard and always with visible fishing gear. Of course, most often the men were actually fishing and either trolling lines, or laying out nets, or reeling them in.

    When not fishing, and on their way to a new spot or back to shore, they went about their business and didn't shift course erratically or proceed at breakneck speed. Sometimes they approached us at a steady pace, waved, held up fish miming, "You want to buy?" or some such and went on their way depending on our response. All over the world, we had made many a nice trade or deal with fishermen.

    So, as we sailed slowly about 12 miles off India's coastline and spotted a fast powerboat in the distance speeding directly toward us, our sensory antenna pricked up. Through our binoculars, we scrutinized three rough-looking men in a boat about 20 feet long. No fishing gear was evident, they were not dressed like fishermen, and their boat sported a very large, new-looking 45-horsepower outboard. They looked like trouble.

    Since we were sailing, there was nothing to do but continue on our course. (Even if we turned on our small 36-horsepower engine, we couldn't outrun them.) The powerboat came up fast and almost ramming *Sanctuary*'s hull, gave our boat a nasty bang with their bow. One of the men grabbed our cap rail, and the three began harshly demanding water. I tossed them some bottles of water even though I could see plastic gallon containers of what looked like water in the bottom of their open powerboat. The roughest-looking one put his hand on a stanchion, moved a foot toward our toe rail, and started to board *Sanctuary*.

I'd had enough of being pushed around by strange men. I didn't know what they wanted, but I knew these men were not innocent fishermen, and they were not coming aboard. Without thinking, I grabbed our boat hook, ran along the side deck toward the intruder, brandished the boat hook, and shouted, "NO!!" at the top of my lungs. I jabbed the boat hook at the man trying to board and stomped toward his fingers. He moved his hand. I punched the brass-tipped boat hook out wildly again and screamed some more, "NO—NO—NO-O-O! Get away!" The man trying to board hesitated. I took my moment and jabbed the boat hook onto their boat, pushing it off as far as I could and still screaming, "NO—NO—NO-O-O!"

My sheer manic energy won out, and they stood off, buzzing around us like an angry hornet, waving their fists in the air, and shouting who knew what at us. At last, they powered off, leaving a rooster tail of water in their malicious wake. In case they came back, Jim went below and got the only thing we had aboard that could be considered a weapon, a machete. We'd bought it in Central America for cracking coconuts. It hadn't seen the light of day in ages, was badly rusted, and not of much use.

"Oh, well," Jim said, "Your banshee-like screams will keep them away. They've probably never seen a woman like that and think you a witch for sure."

My adrenaline settled down, and we sailed into the second night of our passage to Galle. Most of the night and the next day we had the horizon to ourselves. A smooth beam reach calmed me further, and both of us slept soundly on our off watches. About 100 miles from Galle, we saw a 70- or 80-foot fishing boat idling about five miles distant. The captain, Sunny, hailed us and asked a lot of questions such as, "Who are you? Where are you going? How many people are aboard?"

The questions Captain Sunny asked were normal ones. Ships passing at sea often wondered where the other was bound. During offshore passages I almost always hailed the infrequent vessels we encountered. Thanks to the three thugs of the day before, I was wary. As Jim did not speak much on the radio due to his PD-soft voice, I was doubly wary of Captain Sunny's questions. Women at sea were scarce, and I felt vulnerable discussing, "How many people are aboard?" I reluctantly swallowed my fear and replied honestly. Captain Sunny said his vessel, *The*

Rising Sun, hailed from Madras, India, and that he and his crew had been out fishing for lobster for two months. Their hold was almost full, and they would soon head in to port to sell their catch.

    I hung up the radio microphone, sat down in the cockpit, looked astern, and was surprised to see the *Rising Sun* make an abrupt turn, plowing straight toward us! Oh, no, what now?

    My fears evaporated as Captain Sunny called and said he was heading over to give us lobster. As we continued to sail along, the Captain gently nosed the bow of the looming *Rising Sun* up to our stern. His crew threw us a monkey fist with a line attached and then slid a five-pound bag full of lobster and red snapper down the line. They took pictures of us (and Chica with her nose in the fish bag), we took pictures of them, and Captain Sunny's random act of kindness renewed our faith in the essential goodness of humanity.

Sri Lanka, in January 1999, was a country enmeshed in civil war. The Tamils in the north fought with the Sinhalese in the south over power to own and rule part of NE Sri Lanka. The continuing skirmishes included bombings in 1998. Special measures were taken to protect the seaports including Galle Harbor, the only anchorage allowed to visiting yachts.

    Entry into the inner harbor of Galle was only permitted after the Navy searched *Sanctuary* and dove underwater on her hull looking for limpet mines. We were then sequestered in the inner harbor, where a net was drawn across the entrance from dusk to dawn to keep out the "Tamil Tigers." We were protected yet slept only sporadically during our month-long stay since random depth charges set off by the Navy to stun any potential underwater attackers reverberated and boomed nightly off our hull, stunning us in the process.

    The harbor at Galle was a crossroads. *Sanctuary* was the only boat heading east and one of the very few to have come "down" the Red Sea in 1998, so we were besieged with questions from the crews of the 15 to 20 sailboats staging in Galle for their assault on that daunting body of water. Most crews planned to skip India and would sail directly from Sri Lanka to Oman, then Yemen, and into the Red Sea. Therefore, we easily traded or sold all our charts and guides for the Red Sea and the Mediterranean. In exchange we received information and almost all of the charts we needed for Malaysia, Indonesia, and Thailand.

    All of us were making boat repairs. In our case, repairs included hiring a young crewmember from another boat to rescue the spinnaker halyard which had been stuck at the top of the mast since early in our Arabian Sea crossing. We also took it easy for a change. We hadn't really relaxed since leaving Oman, and both our birthdays, my 54th, Jim's 51st, had passed in late January and early February almost without comment and certainly without celebration.

We cleaned *Sanctuary* stem to stern with fresh water, enjoyed long hot showers, and then just sat in the cockpit for sundowners, watching life on shore idle by. On the evening of February 6, 1999, it began raining and continued to rain off and on for 24 hours. We sat in wonder, soaking it up. I checked my journals and the Captain's Log and realized it was the first rain to fall on *Sanctuary* since April of 1998, when we had been in Turkey! I got out the still-salty spinnaker and spread it on deck to wash it off, and both of us played in the rain like kids in the springtime. The decks and rigging were finally clean of the Red Sea, and I felt clean of that part of the world too and ready for Southeast Asia.

First, we wanted to enjoy Sri Lanka. We arranged for Chutta, a young Sri Lankan fellow, to watch *Sanctuary* and feed Chica. We hired Goring, a driver with his own van, for a four-day interlude into the interior. With Goring at the wheel, the jungles and villages of the southern coast fell behind as we edged into lowlands filled first with palm trees, then banana plants, mango, and papaya trees, then rice and wheat fields as we drove higher. The ascent northward brought us into cool mountains. The hillsides were carpeted with vegetables, acres of tea plantations, and stair-stepping rice paddies. We passed oxen, water buffalo, cattle, and the two main modes of human transportation, the bicycle or the *tuk-tuk*. The higher we got, the more beautiful were the surroundings, with large terraced plots of cabbages, beets, beans, carrots, onions, radishes, and more rice.

We toured intricate Hindu shrines and temples with golden Buddhas surrounded by monks, monkeys, and lotus blossoms. At the Horton Plains, we rode past elk and wildflowers for a hike to "The End of the World," a site so high that we never actually saw the top of the cloud-shrouded mountain.

Goring took us to an "elephant retirement home" where a few old elephants that could no longer work were cared for and served as a tourist attraction. We had seen working elephants during our travels. The retirement home offered the chance for a close encounter. A 65-year-old "old lady," as they called her, loafed in the river, and the trainer encouraged me to wade in and help bathe her. Of course I got a trunk full of water sprayed on me, too. Riding her was grand, until she sidled over to a wall of concrete steps in order to let me disembark. My leg scraped the wall, I screamed, and in the nick of time the trainer prodded the old lady who had innocently almost crushed my leg between her body and the concrete wall. Jim passed on the elephant ride and later opted for a healing ayurvedic massage instead.

The Sri Lankan countryside we saw was beautiful, but the ill-repaired roads and villages were a maze of people, children, dogs, bicyclists, trucks, buses, monkeys, cows, and goats. Drivers even had to watch for wandering water buffalo and evade elephants. Every town, village, crossroads, and turn in the road seemed to have a scrawny-looking dog lounging nonchalantly smack dab in the middle of the roadway. For the four days of our tour, Goring constantly had to make sudden stops to avoid animals. We lurched, we swerved, he honked, and we drove around them. One day, after a lot of near-misses, Goring said plaintively, "Some days you just want to run over the dog."

Lyn riding an elephant in Sri Lanka

Back on board we brushed away Chica's shedding hair, aired out our stuffy boat, and searched several Post Offices in Galle looking for the package of Jim's medicines that should have been waiting for us. The mail wasn't in Galle; maybe it was waylaid at the Main Post Office in Colombo? Trying to describe our package over the telephone using a mishmash of two languages was too difficult, so we rode the train to Colombo to search the mysteries of the "Foreign Mail Center Exchange" at the main Post Office in person. We presented a gift of rubber stamps, stamp pads, pens, pencils, and writing paper to the head mailman, and he led us into a cavernous backroom piled high with "undeliverable" packages to search for ourselves. Bingo, package discovered. Maybe the gift helped our package appear.

After a month of nights punctuated by the booms of depth charges, we surrendered and quit Galle bound for—Thailand? Indonesia? Malaysia? The winds would decide.

Our hull needed cleaning after sitting so long in dirty water. The waters of the inner harbor were far too nasty to swim in, so after checking out of Sri Lanka, we snuck over to a clean, but forbidden, anchorage. (Visiting vessels were only allowed to anchor in Galle Harbor, period.)

After dropping the hook, we dove overboard with our tools to scrape the barnacles off *Sanctuary*'s bottom. Both of us were out of shape after a month in the harbor but succeeded in removing most of the growth off the hull, and we loved having a swim. We showered and were sitting in the cockpit resting and admiring the beautiful, calm anchorage when a naval vessel came by and the officials demanded that we leave. Ah, goodbye, Sri Lanka.

We were off, with 1,100 miles to go. Hoping for steady northeasterly winds, we got little wind at all. The passage across the Bay of Bengal was a frustrating exercise in sail changing when there was wind and motoring in flat, hot seas when there wasn't. We rationed our precious fuel, and sailing as much as we could, squeezed every knot out of the rain squalls that marched across our course. The *Peanuts* cartoon character Pigpen existed under a cloud of flies; we lived under a rain cloud. For three days my log entries contained drawings of *Sanctuary* directly under a rain cloud. The block of ice we packed into our broken refrigerator melted all too rapidly in the sweltering humidity between the rain squalls.

On the fourth day out, we encountered east-northeast winds, and with three sails flying, we slowly beat our way toward Indonesia. Still fighting rain squalls and a countercurrent, *Sanctuary* moved at a snail's pace. Complaining did no good, so we made a game out of "how many times in a day can we reef the main, unreef the main, roll out the jib, roll in the jib, tack, put up the staysail, take down the staysail, then start all over again?"

I wrote several letters, and thanks to the rain the entire boat was squeaky clean and our water tanks were full. I baked bread. By day nine almost all the ice was melted, so I cooked every dish I could think of with our ground beef: meat loaf, spaghetti, hamburgers, scrambled hamburger, tacos, and mini pizzas with hamburger instead of salami. Why had we bought so much meat when our freezer was broken? Out flew our main, our jib, and our staysail, and still our progress was agonizingly slow. As we drew near the northern Indonesian island of Weh, we stopped. The four-day breather at Port Sabang provided a taste of Indonesia. We enjoyed watching the locals in their colorful batik sarongs (worn by both men and women), the markets were good, the harbor was quiet, and the food was spicy and different from the Indian/Sri Lankan fare. Planning to sail to other parts of Indonesia later in the year, we continued to Malaysia.

We arrived in Malaysia March 17, 1999, our 22nd wedding anniversary. A quiet anchorage provided a lovely spot to celebrate both the anniversary and our safe arrival in Southeast Asia. Another downpour refilled our water tanks, and the next morning at sunrise the singing and chattering of the parrots woke us. As we sat in the cockpit with our coffee, monkeys gamboled down from the jungle-covered hillsides surrounding the anchorage, then ran out into the tidal flats, hunkered on the rocks, and hand-fished for crabs. Buteos, kingfishers, sea eagles, and hornbills flew past our mast. Until we ran out of fresh food, we moved *Sanctuary* from anchorage to anchorage as the spirit called us, luxuriating in the beauty and quiet of the unpopulated outer islands. We didn't go ashore but technically needed to check into Malaysia, so we headed to Kuah Town, Langkawi Island, to "enter" the country and fill out the paperwork.

Sanctuary hadn't been in a marina since Ashkelon, Israel, six months earlier. The rocking docks at Langkawi were poorly anchored, and there was a fender-crushing swell every time a ferry sped by; even so, we paid for a berth and enjoyed the luxury of simply stepping off the boat to walk ashore. The marina had a swimming pool and gave us easy access to grocery stores, markets, internet cafes, and restaurants. Using the marina address, we sent for our mail. As usual, we also needed to make repairs, and we started on our list: first, fix the refrigeration that had been broken since early February. (After two attempts with local repairmen in Sri Lanka, we had resolved to fix it ourselves.) During the passage, we had figured out what was wrong with it, and now that we were ashore sent a fax to the USA and ordered parts.

Our awning (which had been made for *Sanctuary* way back in 1990) had disintegrated beyond repair. It was an important piece of equipment protecting us from the sun and its heat or when it rained allowing us to leave the portholes open for air circulation. After scouting around town for someone who could remake the awning, I finally decided to sew it myself using the old one as a pattern. When at anchor, we ran the generator if I needed to use my electric sewing machine. In a marina and plugged into shore power, I could sew without noise. I bought 24 yards of Sunbrella™ (a special awning fabric resistant to ultra-violet sun rays and also waterproof), set to work, and finished a three-part full boat awning four days later—just in time to test it in a deluge. The new awning worked perfectly; as we sat in the dry cockpit, the rain-protected foredeck hatch stood open and drawing air! Success!

Other projects moved slowly along. Our refrigeration parts arrived. Jim took the system apart and installed the new parts. After two months of using block ice, our freezer worked again. Ice cubes! We could catch and freeze fish again! Cold sodas! No more wilting vegetables. Ah, the little comforts of iced tea and ice in my cocktail.

We cleaned the galley, reinventoried our food lockers, rebuilt the toilet, changed the engine oil, inventoried our engine supplies, bought new filters, worked on our rigging, and started a mainsail repair. We took Chica ashore to a vet for rabies, distemper, flu, and leukemia shots, and both Jim and I visited a dentist for checkups and teeth cleaning. Little by little our chores got done, and our reward at the end of every day was a lovely swim in the marina pool.

The port of Langkawi was another crossroads. Sailboats from Australia, New Zealand, France, England, America, Hong Kong, Canada, and Germany mixed company. We met many of the cruisers and usually enjoyed "Happy Hour" or dinner ashore with some of the group. *Sanctuary* was the only boat going "the other way." All of our extra charts had been traded away in Sri Lanka, but we still had information to trade. Our ears perked up when we heard "Japan."

We hadn't officially decided on our route. The grapevine news about Indonesia was not good. We had heard reports of killing, looting, and burning by Indonesian soldiers throughout East Timor and other areas. Some of the cruisers we met had fled Indonesia and made for Malaysia for safety. We decided to skip Indonesia and continue along the coasts of Malaysia, Singapore, Borneo, the Philippines, and then hop to the islands of Japan, and cross the Pacific from there.

We had little or no information about Japan until we met Jan and Nick Wooller, an Australian couple from sailboat *Yawarra*. They had sailed to Japan three times and shared a lot of information with us. As I did for every country we visited, I started a three-ring binder with tips about harbors, anchorages, check-in procedures, radio nets, weather information, and a beginner's language dictionary.

We walked into town almost daily, shopping either for repair parts or food. We learned a little Malay and a little Chinese; however, so many of the Malay and the Chinese spoke English to each other and to us that our language skills didn't progress very much. The people were friendly, the food was excellent, and the cost of living in Malaysia was very low. We understood why some cruisers never left the area; we were becoming attached to the dock ourselves!

Our marina visit approached the two-month mark. In a flurry of activity before leaving our berth, we repaired the dinghy motor, cleaned the rust off the stern anchor, remarked our stern anchor line, repaired the staysail bag, washed the boat, filled up with diesel (filtering all the fuel as it came aboard) wrote an article for a sailing magazine, sent and answered e-mails, had the hull cleaned and bottom scraped, organized our Japan and Philippines information, wrote out a "charts needed" list, researched airline prices, purchased tickets to fly to the USA for a visit, taught another cruiser how to use a laptop, got our mail (including Jim's medicines) and shopped for and restocked all of our staples lockers!

Life in the marina had been enticing. We loved having easy access to a swimming pool, but were ready for something new and needed to get moving again. We paid our bill, untied the dock lines, and moved *Sanctuary* over to an anchorage. Later the next day we sailed down to Penang Island about 55 nautical miles away. We anchored off Georgetown in the "junk" anchorage, not sure if it was so named because of the junk in the harbor or because Chinese junks used to anchor there. We had smelled the busy town, the odor a combination of diesel oil, engine soot, and Chinese cooking, for miles at sea before we spotted it. In spite of the tall buildings and the look of a large city, the next morning we heard bird sounds before any other noises.

We whistled for a sampan which ferried us to a rickety jetty, home to a Chinese house village on stilts over the water. The walk to actual "shore" took us past the open doors of the villagers. Temple shrines sat in the front rooms of all the homes, fish dried on porches, people squatted on the floor to eat, and cats roamed amongst the children playing in the spaces between the houses. Arriving at the city streets, we saw old Dutch, English, and Chinese buildings rubbing shoulders with Buddhist temples, mosques, and Hindu temples. Big, shiny glass skyscrapers, housing "Looking Good" and "Komtar" shopping malls, presided over everything.

We rode a bus to a computer fair in one of the big skyscrapers, where we bought a new Toshiba laptop. (I traded my old computer to a fellow who had come aboard to repair our refrigerator. Yes, it needed repairing, again, since the repair we made was NQR.) After the computer fair, we visited "The Chemical Man."

We wanted oxalic acid (to use in cleaning our waterline) and chloroform. (I soaked cotton balls in the chloroform to put in our flour and rice to kill weevils.) The reputation of "The Chemical Man" had preceded him. We had heard of him in Turkey more than a year earlier. Cruisers who'd already sailed through Malaysia said, "You can get any chemical you need from him. Just be careful where you step."

As we approached the chemical man's shop in the heart of Penang, we saw reasons for the warning. It was scary. Drums of chemicals stood on the crowded sidewalk surrounded by parking automobiles and jockeying motorcycles. Walking single file up to the door, we could barely squeeze inside because the aisle was so narrow. (In the USA similar places are called "path houses.") Chemicals in all types of containers, assorted cardboard and wooden boxes, and yellowing papers were everywhere stacked floor to ceiling on rickety shelves. Bottles with Chinese writing on them balanced precariously, edging over some of the shelves. Items were piled so deeply that most of the walls were not visible. A major disaster crouched like a tiger ready to spring.

The cheerful owner, a slight Chinese man about 70 years old, spoke very good English and was eager to help us with our chemical needs and any questions about Penang. His ancient body, however, evidenced his life's work: his fingernails were dark brown, chemical burns spotted and etched his scarred hands and arms, his neck was fused in place, and his skin exhibited a strange off-color.

We stood stone-still as he scuttled away to find what we wanted. He returned from the shadowed depths of the shop, and we paid for our purchases. I gripped Jim tightly to prevent any misstep, and we slowly, carefully, and intently backed out into the hodgepodge of the city. Once outside we gulped instinctively—a dreadful mistake. The mix of bicycle rickshaws, motorcycle rickshaws, buses, and jerking cars, all stirring dust and coughing heavy exhaust (no emission control) made breathing deeply in the streets of Penang fairly dangerous as well.

In early June we sailed back to the islands off Langkawi and anchored *Sanctuary* in a jungle cove again. The calm waters were murky due to a recent rain. Our hull was dirty and scummy with oil and diesel stains from days anchored in the "junk" anchorage off Penang. To clean the waterline, I sometimes sat in the dinghy, tied it to *Sanctuary*, dangled my feet in the water, and leaned over to scrub the boat. This time, in spite of the murky water, I jumped overboard to work my way around the hull from in the water.

Jim stayed onboard. As I cleaned, he managed the spray bottle of the newly-purchased diluted oxalic acid and followed me around the boat tendering a line I could grab. Hanging onto the line with one hand, kicking to stay afloat, and scrubbing with the other hand was tedious, tiring work, and cleaning the waterline and most of the upper hull took two hours. I wearily climbed up the stern swim ladder and sat in the cockpit to shower with the nice fresh hot water Jim had prepared for me. Then I noticed something in the water off *Sanctuary*'s stern. I gulped and called out, "Jim, what is that snake? Oh my God, it's a boa constrictor!" I had gotten out of the water just in time to avoid the eight-foot-long danger.

Back at the moorings off Langkawi, we prepared *Sanctuary* and ourselves for a trip back to the States. The owner of the moorings, Roger, and his Thai girlfriend, Ta, would boat-sit *Sanctuary* and Chica. We cleaned out our refrigerator and packed gifts for our families. I went over the charts we'd need for the rest of our journey and listed ones to order while we were at home. Jim did the same with his PD medicines, and we faxed his neurologist for an appointment.

Our six weeks in the United States in 1999 were bittersweet. We enjoyed visiting with our families and our friends in California and Texas but missed our boat and cat and life afloat. Parkinson's had changed us both. On the boat we adjusted our schedule to whether Jim was "on" or "off" his medications. If he couldn't walk far ashore, we simply sat down, gave him a break, and waited until he recovered. If he couldn't lift something, or some other symptom bothered him, I realized why and waited for his shaking or other symptom to pass. Much as they loved us, friends and family often didn't understand why Jim couldn't drive to see them, or why they couldn't understand his speech, or why I would say, "We need to sit down now; we'll catch up with you later." The tensions of air travel, freeway travel, and the fast pace of the life we had left behind wore on both of us, but Jim especially.

Vegetarians and a King

September 1999—January 2000

> "The world is so full of a number of things, I'm sure we should all be as happy as kings."
> —Robert Louis Stevenson

Our return trip from the States, with an eight-hour flight, layover in the Detroit airport, and a twelve-hour layover in Osaka, Japan, gobbled up three days. The last leg involved a ferry ride from Penang to Langkawi and then a final dinghy ride from the ferry dock out to *Sanctuary*. We drifted through much of August on waves of exhaustion, slowly puttering through the ubiquitous repairs or necessary grocery shopping ashore.

By September we'd recovered and arranged for a boat-sitter for *Sanctuary* and Chica for the second time. Leaving *Sanctuary* bobbing on a mooring in Malaysia, we took a ferry to Thailand and then boarded the "express sleeper" night train. The train clacked past the green countryside of southern Thailand from Hat Yai to the bustling city of Bangkok, where we disembarked. The taxi to our hotel, in the heart of Bangkok's infamous Chinatown, crept through the gridlocked streets—we could have walked faster.

Constant noise, filth, and air pollution epitomized life in Bangkok, a city of six million people. The next morning our noses began to run and our eyes burn as we bravely stepped into the population and traffic malady. Our throats hacking from air pollution, we kept a fistful of tissues in hand as we walked around discovering Bangkok. Street kitchens and street merchants, lining every thoroughfare and sidewalk, sold anything imaginable. From gold and gem dealers with fabulous rows of wares to the silk merchant's colorful stalls stacked high with textiles (some of them fluttering like flags in the breezes created by passing cars), the goods and services offered overwhelmed us. Streams of people surged and flowed.

Abruptly, the crowd parted like a wave meeting a rock. People were carefully stepping over and around a man's body lying on the street. His head was heavily indented by a car bumper or a mugger's club, and blood coagulated near one closed eye. No one who passed seemed concerned. No one stopped to check or help the man. Everyone simply stepped over or around him and hurried along. The man's body partially blocked a jewelry store and the employees inside seemed unconcerned.

Frantic and confused, we stuck our heads in the door of the gold shop and asked, "Does anyone speak English? There's a man hurt and lying on the sidewalk. Has an ambulance been called?" The English- speaking merchant replied, "They are very busy in the morning (picking up bodies). They will come." He had his own life to worry about and his own struggle for survival in an unforgiving environment. In the depths of degradation, life was cheap.

Gold Buddha in Bangkok

The next day we fought off con men and small time hustlers posing as guides and gatekeepers to the shrines. We haggled with the *tuk-tuk* drivers about where we weren't going and how much we weren't going to pay. The "legal" metered taxis took circuitous routes, and fares often jumped in price erratically and exorbitantly. Mirrored, gold-encrusted, tree-shaded shrines and temples honoring the predominant Buddha resided amidst all the hustle and bustle. We saw Buddha standing up, Buddha sitting down,

Buddha lying down, a solid jade Buddha, a solid gold Buddha, a silver Buddha, a six-stories-high Buddha, but mostly Buddha sitting lotus style mediating for resolve. With our hands in prayer position in front of our faces, we mimicked the locals and bowed respectfully. We placed lotus flowers in homage on altars and lit incense. We noticed one dilapidated, almost forgotten, shrine with a fresh, perfect bunch of bananas sitting on the altar as an offering. Jim was tempted to take one and asked me, "Who eats these offerings besides the ants, flies, cockroaches, and rats?" "I don't know," I replied. "Maybe the Buddha does. Look how fat he is."

Desperate for a clean, quiet haven, we choose a seafood restaurant solely on the basis of its sign advertising air conditioning. Inside, all the walls were rimmed with huge, bubbling saltwater aquariums stocked with live seafood. The prawns for our meal were jerked out of one of them and cooked perfectly. As we ate, a local patron seated near us chose a live eel for his dinner. The waiter snagged the swimming eel out of a tank with a hook, hung it on a rack on a portable table, wheeled the wiggling eel over, skinned it alive, cut it into bite-sized portions, and served the pulsating, raw creature to the customer who calmly proceeded to eat the wiggling chunks of eel flesh. Even though my prawns were cooked, I promptly pushed them aside and stuck to the rice.

One morning, with an official guide, we visited the Royal Palace. We learned a great deal about Thailand's picturesque past including some history of the Royal Family. Our timely tour coincided with the Premier of China's patronizing visit to Thailand's King. Bangkok lined the major thoroughfares with banners and flags marking the meeting of the two heads of state. We sat in a privileged visitor's stand on the edge of the Chao Phraya River (which runs through the middle of Bangkok) to watch a special royal boat procession.

Later, after the river reopened for traffic, following a phalanx of orange-clad Buddhist monks, we boarded one of the crowded river ferries (used as city buses), and ploughed up and down the river as far as the ferry went. On Saturday, we shopped almost all day at the huge Chatuchak Market, purchasing arts, crafts, jewelry, beads, and gifts. "How are we going to get all this stuff back to the boat?" Jim quietly bought another strong shopping bag. Seven days later, we repacked our overstuffed backpacks and moving on, rode an evening train to the ancient city of Chiang Mai.

Chiang Mai, 600 kilometers north of Bangkok, serves as a gateway to the hill country and Thailand's Hill Tribes. We hired Jin (who spoke nine languages and several dialects) as a guide for a trek through the rolling hills of northern Thailand. He led us to the villages of the "Lisu" (who fearfully hid from us), the "Karen" (who kept pigs tethered under their huts while they worked in nearby rice paddies), the "Akha" (who aggressively pursued us through their village offering to sell us silver and woven goods), the "Lahu" (with beautiful weavings which they gently offered for sale), and the "Plong" (very shy and very newly-arrived to Thailand from Burma and Tibet).

All of the tribes lived simply in bamboo huts, eking out a living farming small land holdings. Some sold their crafts to the backpackers and hill visitors. We purchased several textiles woven using back-strap looms and a few pieces of hand-wrought jewelry. Back in Chiang Mai, we shopped for other crafts: hand chased and repousse' silver bowls and jewelry, hand constructed and decorated fans and papers umbrellas, lacquer ware, silk sarongs, etc. Our budget, and the size of our backpacks, limited our purchases.

We enrolled at the Chiang Mai Thai Cookery School for a highly recommended cooking class. School began at the local market where our teacher, Perm, taught us to identify and purchase the main ingredients for Thai cooking including hot peppers, lemon grass, and frog legs. A minibus carried us to his home just outside the city. Under a large, covered patio equipped with a cooking station for each student, we listened to Perm as he manned his central cooking island.

Perm demonstrated how to use a wok for stir frying, how to make and reduce a cooking stock, and how to put together the ingredients for a cold, yet hot and spicy, Thai salad. His instructions included a warning about the intensity of the Thai peppers and the roughness of the indestructible lemon grass. Both are used in many Thai dishes. He said, "Be careful not to use too much pepper, and remove the seeds if you don't want your Thai dishes too hot. Be cautious not to touch your eyes with pepper juice on your fingers. Wash your hands before you use the bathroom as well. If you forget, your sensitive parts will remind you."

He continued with his remedy to cool down: "If you eat a hot pepper and can't handle it, don't drink liquids—that won't help. Eat the sticky rice." Sticky rice, we learned, was special Thai white rice that absorbs the fiery pepper oil and is better than splashing down water. Lemon grass, popular in Thai dishes because of its delicate sweet lemon taste, is also known for its fibrous toughness, its sharp edges, and its ability to pass through the intestines unscathed.

"Only one problem with the sticky rice and lemon grass," Perm said. "Don't eat so much of them together or you will get a Thai Fire Ball."

A student asked, "What is a Thai Fire Ball?"

Perm replied, "You'll know when you have one."

All the students gathered at a large table and proceeded to feast on a banquet of food we had cooked ourselves. During the feast, Jim chomped on a Thai pepper. A pretty British girl sitting next to him noticed his Thai salad loaded with the infamous red Thai peppers and lemon grass. In proper British tones and lilt she asked Jim, "Are you going to eat those?"

Bragging, Jim said, "We have been to Mexico where the hottest peppers on earth grow. These can't be any hotter than a Mexican jalapeño, and I just love this lemon grass."

She wished him good luck as though he was going to need it. Much to his embarrassment, he found that he should have heeded the warnings. I watched from across the table as he chewed up and swallowed a large pepper he described later as "the hottest pepper I ever imagined possible." He gasped, and choking for air, started to hiccup uncontrollably. He automatically reached for the water glass.

I noticed his face get red but didn't pay too much attention to him. I went on with my meal and enjoyed dessert during which we learned to identify and prepare Thai fruits that we had seen but hadn't realized were edible. Jim seemed unusually quiet, and later on he told me the rest of what had happened: "My lips burned, my throat was on fire, and my esophagus felt like I had just inhaled a liter of hydrochloric acid. I was about to cry for help when somebody pushed the bowl of sticky rice toward me and said, 'Eat some rice. That should help.' The rice did help, and I lost count of how many bowls I ate trying to put out the fire. I slumped down in my chair and tried to silence my hiccups and cover up my embarrassment."

Two or three days later, Jim complained to me and continued the pepper story: "I know things aren't right. For two days my esophagus has been burning, and I've been burping and choking up hot acid from the Thai pepper experience. Today I've had sharp cramps in my lower abdomen. Oh, Lord, it's awful. I've been sitting on the can trying to pass whatever is burning its way through my lower intestine."

I didn't want to hear it and said, "Stop—this is more information than I need." He insisted on continuing. "Finally, stretching, tearing, abrading, and burning its way through, I gave birth to a "Thai Fire Ball" about the size of a tennis ball. It was followed by an avalanche of hot burning and bloody diarrhea."

He was inflamed for a week and couldn't sit comfortably in any position. I was glad to hear the end of the pepper story, and since then Jim carefully pulls out all the Thai peppers and lemon grass before eating any Thai food.

We left Chiang Mai and returned to Bangkok. I didn't mind the two-day wait for a night train south to Malaysia since we had, as I told Jim, "Two more days of shopping." We reboarded *Sanctuary* in Langkawi, and after a few days waiting for a package of Jim's medicines to arrive, we checked out of Malaysia so we could head for the western island of Phuket, Thailand, for a more mundane excursion, a boat haul-out. Before we departed, I spent a day attempting to scrub all the barnacles off our hull in preparation for sailing again. The current was strong, and I gave out about halfway through the job.

Even with the remaining barnacles slowing us, we thought we could arrive at our first anchorage in daylight since it lay only 35 nautical miles away. We set out to enjoy our first sail in quite a while. About midday, as we reached gently along under jib and mainsail, we heard a loud "thunk" on the hull. Nothing was visible in the water; there were no rocks on the chart, no nets or buoys and nothing to our stern. Seeing nothing unusual, we continued sailing.

We anchored around 3:30 p.m., and I immediately went overboard to finish scrubbing the barnacles off the hull. On my first dive I saw a big mess of line wrapped on the propeller. Ah, source of "thunk" solved. I struggled for at least an hour diving and rediving with my tethered knife to cut the shaggy old net away.

We continued harbor-hopping along the anchorages in the Butang Group and along the western coast of mainland Thailand, skipping over to the islands off to the east of Phuket peninsula and dilly-dallying as long as we could.

At Ao Chalong, the southern sailboat anchorage for Phuket, we checked in with the Harbor Police and waited for the "Immigration Man" to arrive. Official office hours posted were 0800—1400. The officer arrived at 1100 hours looking barely awake and sleepily checked us in to Thailand. After completing the paperwork, we, with friends Beth and Bone, our pals off *Splinters Apprentice*, rented a jeep for the following day. All four of us wanted to look at boatyards, inspect their equipment, price a haul-out, and do some provisioning.

With both crews ready to tackle the chores, we piled into our rented jeep early the next morning. First, we drove to Robinson's, a grocery store selling staples for reasonable prices. We especially wanted olive oil, since we'd used all 10 liters of homemade oil we had bought in Turkey.

Our second stop was a shoe store for Bone whose large English feet were much bigger than those of the average small Southeast Asian. In Phuket, a town catering to tourists, he finally found shoes in larger sizes. Next on the list was Singa Battery, where we learned that gel cell batteries could not be bought in Thailand.

All the cruisers raved about our fourth stop, G.C. Huat Hardware, and we did find hose fittings. Huat Hardware was one of those dark, messy, hot, railroad shops we had become used to with every inch not walked on covered with dusty, dirty-looking merchandise. Fan belts and other odd bits hung from the ceiling. One filthy desk centered it all, surrounded by four Chinese merchants and employees. When the phone rang, several items had to be moved before anyone could answer it.

Each time we asked for a boat item on our list, a rapid conversation took place in Chinese. We settled as far out of the way as we could and watched an employee disappear into the dark bowels of the store. Rustling was heard. Toes were stepped on. Sometimes a measurement was rechecked. If a local customer came in, all progress toward our requested item was postponed. Otherwise, assuming that our request (aided by a sample in hand, or a drawing of the intended item) had been understood, the required item sooner or later appeared and "Finished" was sung out. We, the *farangs*, then walked away at least partially satisfied since it was "Take what is, choices no got." Versions of this process had been repeated in many a shop, beginning with Egypt where the shopkeepers were not Chinese, but the process was almost identical.

That day Jim and I got lucky and walked away with most of what we had come for as did Beth and Bone. Fifth stop: Phuket-Thai International Hospital where, after much to-do, handing over of stool samples, and a return five days later, it was determined that Jim and I both had the amoebas we had suspected. Subsequently, we began treatment with flagyl. This process had also been repeated around the world, beginning with Mexico. We drank only bottled water in restaurants, we treated the water we took on board, and we watched where we ate and what we ate, but since we enjoyed eating local foods in most of the places we landed, we unfortunately paid the price from time to time during our journey.

After the hospital, we ate a late lunch and then continued to two different boatyards. We liked the looks of one of them. The price was right, so we paid a deposit and confirmed a time and date for our haul-out at the Ratanachai Shipyard. At our next stop, the "Clean Imported Meat Market," the meat at least looked clean, so we bought some ground round and several heads of impressive organic, hydroponically grown lettuces and cabbages. Our day of shopping left us just enough time to drive back to our dinghies on the beach at Ao Chalong before the tide changed. We quickly unloaded the jeep, piled our purchases into our dinghies, powered out to our boats, unloaded the supplies, put the meats away, and then turned around and powered back to shore racing the low tide.

With low tide behind us, the four of us now had six more hours ashore with the use of the rented jeep, so we drove around the island, poked around a secondhand store with books in English, and ate dinner at a restaurant. Afterward, we returned the rented jeep and then, before the next low tide, rode our dinghies back to our boats. Worn out from a jam-packed day, we fell asleep as soon as we hit our berth.

Frantic noises at 3:00 a.m. woke Jim and me all too soon. Chica had caught a swift and brought the frantic bird below as a "gift." When I tried to take the bird away from her, she growled at me. The poor bird died, and I never did figure out how Chica caught the bird from the deck of an anchored boat. Since I was up early and wide awake, I started to work logging all the boat supplies and food stuffs we had bought into our inventory. A few days later we slipped into the boatyard on a rising tide.

With *Sanctuary* hauled out onto a cradle, our field of view included fishing boats in various stages of repair. The boatyard shrine lay to our stern. The shrine, with spirit house and altar for blessings, occupied a six-foot-square oasis of trees and flowers among the noise and debris of the busy Ratanachai shipyard. We needed all blessings available, since more work was required for *Sanctuary* than we had anticipated. Ratanachai became our home "on the hard" for 18 long days.

The yard was swept each evening by workers who then changed into clean white clothes for a ceremonial offering of incense and fruits at the shrine near *Sanctuary*. The work went along steadily, if slowly, but in spite of the clean yard we nicknamed our home "Camp Fish Breath" because of the fish-processing plant next door. Was it worse to suffer from the heat and keep the boat closed up, or to have a breeze below and suffer from the awful smell?

Up and down the ladder we climbed while a crew sanded our hull down to the gel coat. Jim was not doing well. All the climbing was very difficult for him. Things he used to do with ease, Parkinson's made almost impossible. His left elbow locked and froze so often that it remained inflamed and painful.

Lyn on board Sanctuary in the boatyard with shrine at the left

Meanwhile, I sewed new wind scoops, completed a new canvas bucket, and recovered our cockpit cushions. Once the sanding was complete, we waited for the hull to dry. In the rainy climate, drying the hull was a problem, so the yard rigged a tent over our entire boat. Slowly the hull dried, and the filler and then the first coat of epoxy went on. I continued sewing while work progressed on the hull. Like the yard workers, we enjoyed the end of every workday when the fish plant closed, work in the yard was complete, and all the sounds of hammering, scraping, sanding, and sawing were stilled. We took to climbing down the ladder to sit in the oasis of the shrine after the daily blessings were over. Blessed be peace and quiet for the crew of *Sanctuary*.

A "Vegetarian Festival" was scheduled in Phuket Town with street stands and booths selling vegetarian Thai food. A brochure stated: "The Vegetarian Festival is a religious event originating from China. The mendicants abstain from eating meat and perform religious rites for nine days and nights in order to purify their bodies and minds and to get rid of evil. Perilous acts are performed by mediums who are in hypnosis."

"Perilous acts, hmm, wonder what they are? Maybe they'll walk on coals," I said. "I don't know either," Jim replied, "Doesn't matter— let's go get some vegetarian Thai food." Looking forward to the food stands, we went into town and saw that the streets were very crowded with people dressed all in white. A parade seemed to be in progress. As a man at the beginning of the parade took off his shirt and began flailing himself with sharp swords, I cringed. "What's happening?" Someone in the crowd who spoke English told me that believers were engaging in self mutilation and body piercing to show that god protected them.

As more and more people joined the parade, the body mutilation and piercing went from bad to worse to grotesque to sickening. The "believers" pierced their mouths, cheeks, arms, or other body parts with skewers, knives, trees, roots, car parts, umbrellas, poles, model boats, large broken mirrors, chains, flags, hacksaws, axes, swords, hammers, and even live snakes. Most had attendants to keep the crowd from bumping into the ends of the objects protruding from their bodies and to balance the weight of the large, heavy items used for the torture. Some flayed themselves with axes and swords. Several sawed on their tongues, yet overall there was little blood supposedly because of their beliefs. They grunted like dogs and their eyes were wild.

We were caught in a nightmare with hundreds of marching, pierced, and mutilated people with wild animal eyes. (Most were men, but some were young girls and women.) At times the pierced hysterics veered off the parade route to wave flags over incense and food offerings set up on shrines by the roadside. Locals all dressed in white bowed the *wai* bow. Firecrackers exploded continuously, so we stuffed our ears with tissue.

I felt nauseous at the sight and was afraid one of the crazed "believers" would swing an axe on the crowd. The pierced people did not look hypnotized or in a trance, they looked mad, insane—inhuman. We frantically looked for a way out of the pressing crowd and finally elbowed our way to a tiny restaurant set back from the street somewhat away from the melee. Holding my head in my hands, I sat down in the restaurant where the female owner laughed at me.

We forgot about Thai food of any type, and Jim (who was also disgusted) held me tight and steered us as far away from the procession as he could. After what seemed like hours, we were able to circle around the circus of madmen and make our way back to the boatyard and *Sanctuary*.

Later Jim broke into semi-hysterical laughter about the "one-upmanship" of the pierced maniacs. The next time we went to town, all the photo shop windows were plastered with photographs of the hysterics.

We bought a few to use as proof of our reliability; otherwise, we were sure telling the tale would brand us hysterical liars!

Sanctuary, with a spray of orchids woven on her bow and firecrackers popping from her inner forestay, relaunched in mid-October, 1999. Thai fishermen believe that evil land spirits settle on the boats while ashore and that firecracker noise will scare those spirits back onto the land where they belong. The fresh flowers adorned the bow in thanks to the good spirits for the safe haul-out. We complied with the tradition. The yard manager gave us a string of firecrackers, and I lit them just as our keel touched the ocean again. A *farang* sailor who relaunched his boat an hour ahead of us refused the flowers and firecrackers. Subsequent to launching, his boat's motor would not start and a rehaul was required for further work. Hmm…Tricky land spirits at work?

With our vessel satisfactorily repaired and blessed, we sailed among other islands near Phuket, returning later to Malaysia to share Thanksgiving with crews from three other American boats.

In December we ventured south along the Straits of Malacca, visited Pinang again, and then stopped at Lemut as Christmas neared. Moslem Malaysians observe Ramadan. The manager of the tiny yacht club in Lemut, however, graciously provided a full Christmas dinner for the crews of the boats from Europe and the United States. Afterward, a local group sang carols. The cruisers really appreciated the acknowledgement.

After Christmas we ventured on to Port Dickson and danced our way into the New Year at a sixties "Rock Around the Clock" party with a disc jockey who switched his patter from Malay, to Chinese, to English, and back again with ease. Many locals attended along with the few people from boats berthed in the marina. The end of the millennium, dubbed Y2K (year 2000) blasted into Port Dickson, Malaysia, to the tune of Bill Haley and the Comets, and the only computer problems were aboard *Sanctuary*.

A glut of e-mails from the United States had issued warnings saying that computers running on old operating systems would crash at midnight on December 31, 2000, due to Y2K and a Microsoft programming glitch. Strangely, on New Year's Day I discovered that our floppy diskettes were infected, not with a computer virus, but with a live fungus growing on our media! A local computer guru advised me to clean every diskette and every drive carefully with Q-tips and rubbing alcohol, or disk cleaner, which I did. In spite of the careful cleaning, both the floppy drive and the hard drive on our laptop computer crashed, and I feared for all the media, data, and music I had stored on the drives.

I spent January 1, 2000, and a few days after, working on the recovery process. I finally killed the fungus, fixed the computer, and recovered most of the data. Vowing not to go through that chore again, I bought a CD write drive for our laptop and switched to fungus-proof CDs for music, movies, and computer backups. We sailed a few days later for Singapore.

The Point of No Return

January 2000—May, 2000

"There is a point at which everything becomes simple and there is no longer any question of choice because all you have staked will be lost if you look back. Life's point of no return."

—Dag Hammarskjold, 1905-1961

Before tackling Singapore, we bedded down in an anchorage just five nautical miles shy of the busy port to plan our attack. Horror stories abounded about Singapore's ship-infested traffic lanes, so we raised anchor at 0730 on the morning of January 14, 2000, in order to have a full eight hours of light and good visibility for whatever lay ahead. The planning served us well, because navigating in Singapore waters did indeed test our joint skills. The amount of traffic in the myriad lanes was astounding—even more than during our scary nighttime crossing of the mouth of the Thames River four years earlier.

With both of us on watch, we wove *Sanctuary* through a minefield of oil tankers, cargo ships, dhows, fishing boats, cruise ships, tug boats, garbage scows, patrol boats, and other watercraft. So much traffic clogged the waters that the six-mile range on our radar was useless. The screen glowed almost solid green from the "returns." Packed like gumballs in a jar, each ship's rebound was indistinguishable from another's.

After eight hours of dodging disaster, we edged over to the "Small Craft Anchorage," a rolling spot on the SE side of Singapore Island. We wearily lowered our anchor and sank into the cockpit in exhaustion. As *Sanctuary* pitched and rocked in the unpleasant swell, we looked at a map of Singapore City and realized that not only was the "Small Craft Anchorage" uncomfortable, but the shore access/beach landing was dicey. The landing offered no safe place to leave our dinghy and was miles from the heart of the city. We revised our plans and decided to move to Malaysian waters for easier access to Singapore. The next morning, after an uncomfortable night at anchor, we hauled the hook up and sailed around the island to the north of Singapore to the Straits of Johor (a moat-like body of water between Singapore and Malaysia). A causeway dams and spans the strait, and we followed our noses to a spot on the chart near the Malay city of Johor Baharu with Singapore to the south.

Our hunch proved out, and we anchored in a nice, safe bit of water just off the Malaysian Police Dock. *Sanctuary* lay protected from weather from all directions and sat in flat calm even as a late-afternoon squall blew over us. Ah, a good home.

In various anchorages around the world, we awoke to the noise of birds or dogs or monkeys or fishing boats or calls to Muslim prayer or generators or howling winds or thunder or occasionally curious children peering in the portholes or church bells or depth charges (Sri Lanka) or, most frequently, a call on our VHF radio. Bolting awake in the Straits of Johor took the prize when the sound of hundreds of car horns blasted us out of our berth at 5:00 the next morning.

We'd been so proud of our safe anchorage spot that the significance of the causeway just off *Sanctuary*'s stern did not register. Our berth was a stone's throw from the main highway into Singapore where four lanes of traffic abruptly narrowed into one. Each workday morning hundreds of drivers horned, bulldozed, and racketed their way toward the officials in the Immigration booths who slowly processed the papers necessary for exit from Malaysia and entrance into Singapore.

Jim on the cuaseway- Johor Baharu, Malaysia to Singapore with a sea of motorcyclists

Grinning and bearing it, we set about making semi-final plans and purchases for crossing the Pacific Ocean. Our intended route from Singapore would lead to Borneo with stops in Brunei and Sabah, Malaysia; then we'd skirt through the Philippines, hop to the southern islands of Japan, and gunk hole on to Hokkaido, Japan, then set off to cross the Pacific to Alaska. Since leaving Oman, we had stockpiled the necessary charts and had begun studying and watching the weather patterns along the route.

Once and for all we needed to decide: "Are we going to complete our circumnavigation?" Singapore marked the "point of no return." From beginning our journey in 1991, we'd said, "We'll continue as long as it's fun, as long as the money lasts, and as long as Parkinson's will let us." All the way around the world, after arrival at every major port, we reassessed our situation. The answers to the fun and money part had been "Yes, we are having fun, and the money is lasting."

The question of whether Parkinson's disease would let us carry on was more difficult to answer. Parkinson's had continued a nine-year, slow, yet relentless, march into our lives. It began with a tremor, annoying, but somewhat controllable. It progressed to head shaking, arm locking, leg giving away, no good grip, loss of strength, balance losing, and falling down danger. Medicines no longer worked all the time, and Jim was frequently "off," with long periods of time when the medicines did not work. The biggest problem was that "off" arrived unexpectedly– it couldn't be predicted. "Off" created uncomfortable, sometimes dangerous, effects, and required daily, sometimes hourly, adjustments to what we were doing. An annoyance had become a serious consideration.

We almost gave up our journey in Turkey. Sailing down the Red Sea had been a major hurdle. In Oman if we had found a viable way to ship *Sanctuary* back to the USA we would have. We didn't, so we more or less tiptoed across the Arabian Sea and then crossed the Bay of Bengal holding our breaths against a major physical disaster. We'd made it, and lollygagging around Malaysia had given Jim (and me) a nice rest. Nonetheless, Parkinson's symptoms had taken a toll on Jim (and me). By the time we arrived in Singapore, Jim was really out of steam.

All of his symptoms had worsened: more tremors, more stiffness, more freezing, more difficulty walking, more difficulty talking, and more difficulty sleeping. Just functioning on a daily basis wore him out. Since his grip was not reliable, I had to double-check everything I handed him by saying, "Have you got it?" His balance was so poor that he stumbled and fell and bumped and lurched both on land and on the boat. When underway he was always tethered to the boat by special systems we rigged up. Still, the danger of his falling overboard was all too real. In order to compensate for his unresponsive body, he rested more often and took things more slowly. I shouldered more and more of the physical necessities (especially the deck work) of sailing. He functioned without much danger in the cockpit and down below, so we adjusted.

The compensations we made worked well enough to get by on shore, at anchor, and on short harbor-hopping passages, but the big question we needed to ask, and answer truthfully, was: "Should or could Jim safely make the ocean passage from Japan to the United States?" If he couldn't, or shouldn't, what would we do?

Would I sail alone? Would we hire a crewmember or a delivery captain? Would Jim fly back to the United States? Would we both fly back and hire a delivery crew for *Sanctuary*? Would we put *Sanctuary* on a freighter and ship her back to the States? Should we give up and sell *Sanctuary* in Singapore?

We'd tossed the questions around for months and kept coming up with the same answer: we didn't want to give up no matter what. Jim said, "I'll quit only if you think it will endanger you. I don't want to give up. If I quit now and don't make it around the world I'll be incomplete the rest of my life. I have to die sometime, and I'd rather die at sea attempting to complete the circumnavigation than in an armchair at home wishing I had tried."

Not that I wanted anyone to die at sea—I didn't—but I agreed with Jim for different reasons. Having another crewmember onboard would cost me more energy than I would gain in benefits. I'd have to cook for one more, clean for one more, and give all that extra psychic energy to one more person. Just thinking about it wore me out. Even if, in the worst case scenario, Jim couldn't do anything, I could manage the boat myself. It wouldn't be fun; I'd be strained; I wasn't nearly as good as Jim at sailing, but I knew I could do it.

On the other hand, if I were incapacitated, could Jim care for me and physically manage the boat, too? Maybe, maybe not, but after weighing the risks we might subject each other to, we decided that giving up was not an option. After deciding, a weight lifted, and we set about preparing *Sanctuary* and ourselves with everything we felt we needed to learn or to bring aboard in order to make our final ocean crossing as safe and as easy as we could. Even though the date was months and many nautical miles away, Singapore, the modern heart of Asia, was the spot to start our preparations. So, we attacked that great city, with all it offered for our passage, with resolve.

After fixing a water pump, getting the rest of the charts we needed, sending for Jim's medicines via DHL, setting up a weather info/ham net schedule, checking the condition of all our sails, installing new engine batteries, purchasing new bifocals for me, upgrading our laptop, and topping our fuel, water, and provisions, we checked *Sanctuary* out of Malaysia. (Only Jim and I had crossed the border into and out of Singapore–*Sanctuary* lay anchored in Malay waters.) On February 5, 2000, we set sail for the port of Muara, Brunei, on Borneo about 600 miles away.

The first day underway tested our Singapore resolve, as we sailed in winds of 25 knots with a nine-foot swell and lumpy seas. Our staysail hadn't been used in a long time, and when I went out on deck to rig it, I discovered that the hanks were frozen shut with salt. We hadn't checked our sails well enough after all. I unstuck the hanks by spraying them with fresh water, then set the sail and reefed the main. We lumped along. (Lesson learned: we checked the storm staysail right away. Its hanks were also salt-water-frozen shut, and we cleaned them immediately.)

We settled uneasily into our passage routine, later using the storm staysail as the winds picked up even more. Of course the forecast had been for 10 to 15 knots, but we experienced 25 knots and more. We continued along speedily, if bumpily, passing Pulau Subi-besar, part of a group of Indonesian Islands. Chica had lost her sea legs as well. Generally on a passage she joined us in the cockpit and even roamed the deck chasing flying fish. Not this passage! She stayed below wedged into a spot on a shelf by the nav station or sandwiched into the sleeping bag with the off watch person, licking our heads or stuffed next to us like a sardine.

Four days of high winds and lumpy seas exhausted us. Finally, after several very large seas broke over *Sanctuary*, we hove to for the night of February 9th. Heaving to dampened the conditions for us, but even then *Sanctuary* rolled with the seas, and we were unnerved as the winds howled and the waves growled under our hull. In spite of little to no shipping traffic, we kept an anchor watch.

After some sleep on my off watch, I got up the next morning and cleaned up the mess from the day before. I was salt-encrusted from all the foredeck sail changes, and one of the large waves had pooped the companionway as well. A bit of a clean made us all feel better. The wind died down, we shook out the sails, and Chica ventured out into the cockpit. When the sailing became gentler, Jim threw out the meat hook and caught a mackerel. Chica loved mackerel, so the fish would provide her with food for days to come. As usual, she couldn't wait, jumped in the middle of the melee, and proceeded to eat herself sick before Jim even finished cleaning the fish.

Our lumpy reach across the South China Sea reminded us that reefing early worked for us as did heaving to when we needed a rest. We lost a lot of time by heaving to for eight hours, but then again, speed was not our primary goal: arriving safely was. A big part of arriving safely included conserving our energy. Jim functioned as long as he could rest well in between watches, so we repeated one of our ongoing mantras: "Comfort and safety first, speed second."

Our destination, Brunei, was a small country not quite as large as the state of Rhode Island, yet it ranked 26th in the world for GNP. In simple terms, it was a very rich country especially for its size. As we drew closer to The Royal Sultanate's domain, we began to understand one of the reasons for the country's wealth: oil. The wells lining Brunei's short but rich shore stood in vast fields about five miles off the coast and looked like cities.

I stared at the fields for four hours during my sundown watch. Light after light came alive, illuminating the horizon and glittering like jewels in the Sultan's crown. We changed shifts; I slept for four hours then got up in the dead of night to their full blaze and glory again. The wells on the horizon looked the same as the ones I had stared at four hours earlier. I asked Jim, "What happened, did the wind die and are we dead in the water?" "No," he said, "The oil wells all look alike, and the fields just go on and on and on, that's all."

We approached the Port of Muara and motored up the channel to the small-boat anchorage. In the distance we spotted a sleek, 200-plus-foot white motor yacht which reminded us of one we had seen in Greece that belonged to Onassis. What rich mogul would be vacationing in tiny Brunei? A gold insignia on the yacht's side looked like a child's drawing of a seagull, a very curvy spread out "w," but with dots in the center of each valley. From a distance some more curvy letters above the "w" looked like Arabic. We gave up trying to decipher the vessel's name using binoculars. As we drew close alongside, all became clear. The curvy letters spelled the vessel's name, *Tits*, and the gold symbol represented a pair of very generous breasts. (The dots were the nipples.) The Sultan's brother, Prince Jefri, owned the yacht. (The media dubbed him "The Playboy Prince.") Jefri's billionaire lifestyle was rumored to be financed with funds swindled from Brunei's treasury. (A lawsuit between the two brothers about the funds was later dropped.)

Our stop in Brunei didn't last long, and we harbor-hopped up the coast of Borneo to Kota Kinabulu, Sabah, Malaysia. Instead of anchoring near the modern busy city, we opted instead for a beautiful, secluded cove on Gaya Island. We rented a mooring for eight U.S. dollars a day, used their clubhouse, and rode the daily ferry to the mainland.

We needed a minimum of six months of staples aboard to carry us from April until August, when we expected to arrive in Alaska. Shopping in the modern city of Kota Kinabulu would be easy and inexpensive. The town had net cafes, big supermarkets, hardware stores, chandleries, a large, wonderful "fresh" market, lots of good restaurants, and the buses were well organized and easy to use. We had struggled in Singapore to haul supplies to the boat. Kota Kinabulu was a manageable size, and the ferry ride to our anchorage was easy and relaxing.

I provisioned in earnest for our ocean crossing, riding the ferry back and forth to town to buy cheeses, dried fruits, boxed juices, long-life milk, canned hams, beans, rice, flour, pasta, and more. We didn't plan to stop long in the Philippines or expect to find much in the way of provi-

Lyn packing can goods & staples for the Pacific crossing

sions there. Japan was reported to have high prices, so I cleared clothing out of two additional lockers and filled them with food as well. I spent a good part of the 45 days we were anchored off the resort near Kota Kinabulu shopping. After every available locker was stuffed with foodstuffs and all logged into our inventory system, I declared the job done.

Meanwhile, Jim repaired the generator fan belt, rewired the engine starter and alarm, repaired a leak in the anchor chain windlass hawsehole, and supervised a young sailor who checked all the standing rigging. All of Jim's work was hampered by a cracked and abscessed tooth. The first dentist we found didn't fix the problem, and Jim suffered through weeks of pain until we gave up on the first dentist and found a different one who did a good tooth-repair job. Jim suffered too long because of the first dentist, but we were lucky the problem was found and corrected while we were at anchor and that the abscess had not developed in the middle of an ocean passage!

Sanctuary was down on her water line with all the extra food stores and full diesel and water tanks. Jim and I felt a little down, too, since we'd be leaving old cruising friends behind when we sailed on toward Japan. We said our goodbyes over the ham net, reminiscing with friends about the good times we'd had since sailing into Langkawi, Malaysia, a year earlier.

We checked out of Malaysia on April 9, 2000, to set off for Palawan, one of the larger islands of the Philippines. As we watched the weather carefully and picked our route, the last words of the Malaysian Port Control Officer rang in our ears: "There are pirates in the South China Seas. Advise someone in every port of your route and stay away from The Balabac Strait and the Sulu Sea area, too."

As we beat past a shoal water spot during our first night out, we had a tense encounter. The lights of two or three small fishing boats (too small to show up on radar) suddenly appeared out of nowhere. It was unnerving, and we wondered if they were actually fishermen. The "pirate warning" had given us the jitters, but we calmed down, rationalizing that the fishermen probably only lit their lamps when they saw us.

The winds picked up to 15 knots, and *Sanctuary* made a quick beat across the Balabac Strait the next day. We reached the Palawan Passage and were more or less in the lee of Palawan Island with a large uncharted area to our port. Our chart read: "Palawan Trough, Uncharted, Dangerous Ground." We were certainly happy to stay as far away from the dangerous area as we could, and after tacking to port on a close reach, we came about much sooner than we probably needed to, just in case.

Three days later we anchored at "Fish Bay," a lovely small bay with a few houses ashore. I swam over the anchor which was well set in sand in 28 feet of water. Secure in our tiny protected harbor, we ate an early dinner, and both of us turned in for a full night's sleep together. The next morning we took a "lay day," and instead of pressing on, we puttered around *Sanctuary* doing chores. I researched anchorages and colored in some of our black and white photocopied charts while Jim changed the engine oil and oil filters. When it rained I went out and scrubbed the decks clean, a playtime more than a chore. While snorkeling in the afternoon, we swam with a sea turtle and hovered over neon tetras as they darted around large vase sponges. As we surfaced from snorkeling, we saw several *bancas* (a type of sailing/fishing boat with double outriggers and bright sails) skimming the water in the distance like dragonflies.

Philippine "bancas" at anchor

The next day held no wind, so we motor-sailed to a new anchorage charging our batteries in the process. We anchored early at an uninhabited hole in the wall. It was completely spotless and beautiful, with the bottom clear at 50 feet below. It was tempting to linger, but the next morning the wind was up, and so were we. Our next anchorage, a "make do," didn't even have a name on the chart. We dubbed it "Bay Rock Bay" since, when we went snorkeling, we discovered a very large uncharted rock. A *banca,* with a chicken on the rail and a rooster crowing, sailed by to a house on shore where the man aboard unloaded his fowl.

Our long-range plan didn't allow much time for the Philippines, so we continued on to Coroncorong Bay on El Nido Island. A fellow in a *banca* approached us offering to supply us with fuel and water. We didn't really need either one, but here was an easy opportunity to top off our tanks, so we hired him and his two children to fill our diesel and water cans. I dragged out all my laundry buckets, and he filled them with fresh water, too, so I washed six "loads" of our clothes.

Washing day on *Sanctuary* was similar to stomping grapes. I filled one bucket with fresh, hot water (heated by the sun) added soap and then the clothes, which I left soaking for at least 30 minutes. After a good soaking, I dumped half of the dirty, wet clothes and water into another bucket, and hanging onto the shrouds, stepped into the first bucket and proceeded to stomp. (Dumping half the clothes out allowed room for the agitation.) After a good stomping, I picked up each individual item of clothing, scrubbed the tough spots, and checked for cleanliness. Using a shroud as a wringer, I wrapped each item halfway around and rung out the soapy water with a twist. I then put the washed, soapy item into a bucket of clean fresh water. More stomping. After the agitating rinse in clean water, I rung each item out again and put it aside for the line. As the rinse water became soapy, I used it for wash water. I continued the cycle until all the clothes were washed. Washing a week's worth of our clothes used about 15 gallons of water, so having extra buckets of fresh water that we hadn't hauled aboard was a godsend.

After the clothes were washed, I rigged a clothesline from the shroud on the port side over to the staysail stay and back to the shroud on the starboard side. The clothing hung above the deck of the boat and flapped freely in the breeze which facilitated drying. Sometimes if the day were very hot, I simply pinned the wash to the safety lines. The clothes couldn't flap on the safety lines, and big items like sheets and towels always needed the "high lines." The sun acted as dryer and bleach, and since I washed in the cool of the morning, most everything was easily dry by mid-afternoon or sooner. None of the precious water was wasted. I used the last rinse water to clean *Sanctuary's* decks.

Our taste of beautiful spots in the Philippines left us wondering if we should change our plans and linger for another season. Our goal of "Alaska in July" demanded traveling at a steady pace, so in spite of the temptation to stop longer, we pressed on and arrived in Bolinao, Luzon

Island, the Philippines, by the last week of April.

Jim manned the helm, *Sanctuary* was still moving, and I stood at the bow waiting to drop our anchor (which was still in the chock and hadn't begun its descent to the water yet) when the first of two locals motored over to meet us. As we proceeded to set the hook, watch our drift and swing, and set the snubber, the first local, Bill (an old, retired British captain from Hong Kong who lived in Bolinao full time), hovered in his boat offering anchoring advice and information about the lack of supplies ashore. We continued with other "putting the boat to bed" chores as he obliviously chatted on and on.

About the time Bill left and Jim and I sat down to catch our breaths from our four-day passage, Rick (American, retired Navy, married to a Filipino wife) popped over. He said, "I'm here to stay in the Philippines, never going back. I've gone native." Even though a Navy man, obviously he, too, did not realize how tired we were after a four-day passage in a small boat, since he stayed chatting for over two hours. Nonetheless, he provided a wealth of information since he had lived in Bolinao for over 20 years.

After our welcome committee departed, we took a breather, and later we started making lists. In 12 days, we had consumed a lot of our Malaysian supplies. We'd have to go shopping to top up our food—again! (The cycle didn't end until we waved goodbye to Japan.) Off we went, puzzling the shopkeepers in tiny Bolinao who couldn't understand why we returned to the market two and three times a day. They happily ferried us and all of our purchases from town to the dock and back again in one of the colorful "tricycles." The veggies from the wet market were overripe and only lasted a day at most, but the beer (34 cents a bottle), the really good rum (77 cents a liter!), and the beef and chickens (which we cut up and froze) were all a real bargain.

Before we left, we topped our water from a freshwater spring. Our first time at the spring we dinghied over around 2:00 p.m. and hauled 10 gallons of water from the source upstream and back to Sanctuary. Before loading our cans of water, we soaked in the downstream "bathing" area, enjoying the breeze and the cool water which we shared with the local fishermen, the housewives, their children, and a water buffalo! We'd learned our lesson, and the next day we went to the spring at 6:30 p.m. instead. It was practically deserted at that hour, which made loading our water containers much easier without having to watch out for the children and water buffaloes.

Every Filipino we talked to had a typhoon tale to tell. Typhoon tales were exactly why we had passed through the area at a rapid pace. We wanted no tales of our own, and the season for avoiding those powerful storms was very short. So, once again, instead of enjoying one more beautiful anchorage, we breathed deeply, looked hard at the weather forecasts (no typhoons in sight), and at the end of April 2000, plunged north, bound for Ishigaki, Japan.

Land of the Rising Sun

April 2000—August 2000

"You can't 'out-gift' the Japanese."
—Cruisers from *Yawarra*, who sailed to Japan three times.

As *Sanctuary* approached the Bashi Channel north of the Batanes Islands of the Philippines and south of the tip of Taiwan, she unwittingly sailed into a washing machine. Tide and wind against the fierce Kuroshiro current thrashed *Sanctuary* around like a load of hapless laundry. Jim and I hung on to whatever was at hand and set the sails as best we could to minimize the beating but basically bore the pain and discomfort until the tide changed. Inevitably the tide changed, but the wind didn't, and battling wind against current, we continued the agonizingly slow forward progress of only three knots even with three sails flying.

As we inched onward, we dug our sweat pants and shirts out of a deep locker, the first time we had needed or seen them since Turkey. The Bashi Channel spit us out, and we reached peacefully past Taiwan to Ishigaki, one of Japan's southernmost islands, in the Ryukyu Chain. After six days at sea, we skirted into Ishigaki's small-boat harbor, impressed by the two clean, well-constructed, and precisely-engineered outer harbors and their massive typhoon-proof breakwaters.

We tied to our first dock since New Year's and were greeted by a small army of two customs officials, three immigration officers, two coast guardsmen, one health administrator, and one port official. Paperwork was filled out, a precursory search for contraband and firearms was made, and the bowing officials, in their white gloves and spit-shined black shoes, backed their way up the companion way and off *Sanctuary*.

The sailors we had met who had been to Japan told us: "Japanese hospitality is overwhelming. They are generous to a fault and go way out of their way to make you feel welcome. Don't try to out-gift them because you will lose."

The generosity began immediately.

Several people had been standing quietly on the dock. As soon as the army of officials left our yacht, the people stepped up and began introducing themselves in a mixture of English and Japanese. They had noticed *Sanctuary* and her American flag as we entered the harbor and had come to welcome us to Japan offering to take us shopping, take us to dinner, or show us the island–whatever we wanted or needed. As politely as we could, we requested a night of rest, but made a date for the next morning.

The whirlwind began the next morning at 9:00: Fumiko and Kazume took us for an island tour which included a visit to their sailboat, *Hamiko*. We visited the 200-year-old house of a Japanese king, a Zen temple, and the top of the highest mountain on Ishigaki; we viewed Ishigaki from our guides' two-story house which was under construction (they were living on their sailboat in the meanwhile), then had lunch at a *soba* (noodles) restaurant. In the afternoon we were treated to a visit with some of their friends, retired musicians who had previously played cello and viola with the Basel Orchestra. All of this happened on the first day!

On the second day, other new Japanese friends continued the overwhelming hospitality by taking us to different parts of the island, treating us to another fabulous, beautifully-presented lunch at a Japanese noodle restaurant, and delighting us with a tempura shrimp and vegetable dinner brought to *Sanctuary*. Still another couple served homemade ice cream and dessert as we visited with them in their lovely house overlooking the Pacific Ocean. (Before we sailed from Ishigaki, they presented us with homemade bread, cake, and vegetables from their garden.) Another Japanese sailor brought us a six pack of local Ishigaki beer. He was proud of the beer and tickled that Jim enjoyed it, even though we knew it had cost him $3600 Yen ($35 dollars).

We'd only been in Japan two days and were already overwhelmed. How could we reciprocate? All of our offers to contribute in any way were declined. I created gift bags of fresh-baked peanut butter cookies, some other American items, and a tee shirt with *Sanctuary's* name and photo on them. At least we had something on hand to offer in thanks and return for the effusive generosity showered on us.

Meanwhile, most of our new friends returned to work during the days, so we poked around Ishigaki on our own and found the local library. Using it challenged the little bit of Japanese we knew, but we sent e-mails and photocopied some charts we had borrowed.

We shopped for groceries, and yes, Japan was expensive. We didn't buy much beer, but some of the fresh, beautifully-presented fruits, vegetables, and beef were reasonable. With careful comparison shopping, watching out for sale items, and doing without $15 watermelons, we stocked *Sanctuary* with fresh food. We were glad, however, for all the staples we had purchased back in Malaysia and the Philippines. We invited our new friends over and cooked an American classic meal of hamburgers and potato salad. It was a big hit.

Kusa, one of our guests, was a weaver for a small shop that created one-of-a-kind custom silk kimonos. Her husband, Furi, picked us up the next day and took us to the shop. Each kimono took three months to make, starting with the pattern, thread counting, dying of the thread, and then the ikat weaving. Kusa and her fellow worker, Tomo, were hand finishing a kimono, and Tomo showed us her beautiful, softly colored, award-winning obi.

After 11 slightly stupefying days, we left Ishigaki, waving goodbye to a host of new friends and armed with lists of names and addresses of their relatives to meet throughout the rest of Japan. We stopped at Nagowan and then continued toward Amami Ōshima. The weather changed, so we ducked into the quiet harbor at Unten, on Okinawa Island, to sit out a passing typhoon which skirted our protected anchorage dumping rain and winds on us. After the typhoon passed, we went ashore to the tiny village which had only a few houses, a few fishing boats, and one shop serving noodles. We walked over hillsides to the larger town of Nakasone, passing many tiled-roofed homes with lovely gardens along the way. Rows of carrots, cabbages, beans, tomatoes, peppers, and squash colored the hillsides, with fields of sugar cane and aloe in the background. After two hours we reached the town, shopped for vegetables, and then looked for a bus back to the anchorage. The next one would not arrive for three hours. What to do? We had hoped for a *sento* (Japanese bath house), but there wasn't one. Tired as we were, rather than waiting for the bus, we began walking slowly back to the harbor and *Sanctuary*.

As we dragged our feet toward our anchorage, two young girls, walking home from school and playing with "Slime" along the way, joined us. Laughing uncontrollably, they threw the sticky, icky toy on each other, peeled it off, and threw it again. Giggling, they practiced their English on us and learned about our sailboat in the distant harbor. They said "So far," and we said "Goodbye." About 15 minutes later, we were surprised as a car stopped for us. The girls and their mother had driven out to take us back to *Sanctuary*! As they dropped us off at the harbor we invited them aboard, but they were afraid to cross the water in our tiny inflatable.

Similar weather and similar encounters continued to be our Japanese saga. We'd head out, then duck, anchor, sit, wait for high winds to pass, enjoy a spot while waiting, and then continue northward as far as possible. As we proceeded, the other half of the saga, that of the always-friendly, always-hospitable Japanese, also repeated itself. At every turn we were invited into homes, chauffeured to the store, cleansed at *sentos*, escorted to the sights, soothed with sake, fed home-cooked meals, presented with fans, tea sets, calendars, cards, fruits, cakes, or cups of tea. One day as we shopped in a small market, a stall keeper called us over and surprised us with a hot vegetable sit-down lunch served impeccably at a tiny table in the back of her booth. There was no charge, and she seemed almost insulted when we inquired. Why? Just because we were guests from very far away and just because, because, because… that's the Japanese way.

Someone in Naze mentioned a marina in Miyazaki. We followed a sketched-out chart into the described harbor, carefully watching our depth sounder and looking for masts, the telltale sign of sailboats. We spotted one small, lone sailboat. Just one sailboat? That didn't seem right, but we tied to the harbor wall anyway. An even smaller sailboat came in and side-tied to us, as there was no other room. All of our maneuvering with the other boat was done in sign language. Masa Nagai, who spoke English, came over and said the marina for yachts was 20 minutes farther along the coast. He sketched out a much better small chart and then arranged to meet us the next morning at the marina to take us shopping, use the internet, and photocopy some "real" charts for us. Whew!

We got up at 5:00 a.m. There was rain but no wind, so we pulled on our leaking rain gear and motored in the rain to the bigger marina. Fortunately two Japanese sailors were on the dock and helped with our lines since, as we began to tie up, the wind started blowing with a vengeance. We dried off and were eating breakfast when Masa arrived to take us shopping. As we poured him a cup of coffee, his friend, Tatsuyuki, materialized.

All four of us squeezed into Masa's small car and drove in the pouring rain to a giant, warehouse-style wholesale market. It was impeccable. The fish market (the cleanest we had ever seen), was packed with buyers bidding on the fish as they were unloaded. We'd caught enough fish of our own, so we moved on to buy some gorgeous and affordable vegetables. After vegetable shopping, the two took us to the meat and chicken section. We stuffed our purchases into the tiny trunk of Masa's car, and they drove us back to *Sanctuary*.

We pulled out the *bento* boxes (the Japanese version of a prepared deli plate with sushi, sashimi, and other Japanese delicacies) we had bought for lunch for the four of us. Luckily, we had purchased the large size since one by one other members of the Miyazaki Yacht Club showed up to meet "The American Sailors." Lunch turned into a party and a training session since Masa had with him a copy of the complete pilot book of the eastern coastline of the Japanese islands from Kyushu to Hokkaido. One of the sailors was a delivery captain, so between their English and our limited Japanese (and our reference dictionaries), the group gave us excellent information on the ports, any hazards, good shopping stops, and where to check in and out. We had only the most rudimentary of charts aboard, so the afternoon of navigational information about Japan was a godsend. By 6:00 p.m. we were exhausted. The shopping, the boat full of people, and the constant effort required in multi-lingual conversing had worn us out.

The last of the sailors stepped off *Sanctuary*, and we sat down but almost immediately heard the dock lines creak and felt the boat rock as a foot landed on the deck. Masa, along with two friends, was back again! Between the time he had left, and his return, he and his friends had purchased (and drunk most of) a bottle of sake. We must, they said, go out to a noodle house for dinner. How could we refuse? So, off we went to dinner, then a bar, then a *sento,* and finally, finally, they drove us back to the marina. It was past 11:00 p.m. and the gates were locked. We couldn't rouse anyone, so we climbed over the fence.

Surely the locked gate would give us a good night's sleep. We were exhausted at 6:00 p.m. and were positively staggering at 11:00 p.m. My head hit the pillow and I sighed with relief. Then we heard a loud knock on the hull. I whispered to Jim frantically, "Don't answer!" Just about then we felt the telltale rock of the boat and weight of a person on the deck. Jim jumped up, snatched on his underwear, and sprang into the cockpit to beg off one more invite to drink another bottle of sake with yet another generous sailor. Our friends had warned, "Japanese hospitality is overwhelming." We thought it was an understatement.

Masa (a retired fisherman who years earlier had lost one of his boats in high winds in the dangerous Bashi channel) devoted a full week of his life taking care of us. He drove us and our Japanese-brand life raft miles to the factory for inspection and repacking. He caught octopus for us and prepared it Japanese-style, bringing all the essential utensils and ingredients over to *Sanctuary* for a special feast. He and others escorted us to shops, to famous sites, to bars, restaurants, baths, and homes. We reciprocated as best we could but stood helpless in the flood of attention, able at last to only "go with the flow."

Encroaching weather systems pressured us to keep moving. Typhoons cropped up frequently on the weather fax. Most of them headed for the Philippines. Their usual routes would alter northward as the season progressed. Planning to start across the Pacific by the first of July, we hoped to avoid typhoons as their paths advanced. Osaka would be our last major stop with a short visit inland to Kyoto. It was mid-June, and we were running out of time.

Masa with octopus he caught & cooked for our dinner

The day we left Miyazaki, we said "Goodbye! Thank you!" to Masa and all the other club members we could find. Then we sailed only 25 miles. We simply needed to anchor somewhere and recuperate. A night without company was blissful. The next morning we began harbor- hopping toward Osaka, the next place in Japan that we planned to stop for a while. Harbor-hopping—the process of making as much way as we could during daylight, then anchoring at night and starting the forward progress over again the next day—allowed both of us to sleep all night, and we avoided the stress of navigating the heavily-trafficked shipping and fishing lanes in the dark.

We'd been invited to the Osaka Hokko Yacht Club, a perfect spot to berth while touring inland. After tying up at the club and checking in with the officials, the welcome and sake parties and touring began again. Jim, due to his bad balance, slipped on the dock and bruised his tailbone. I strained my shoulder trying to lift him, so both of us went back to *Sanctuary*, took pain pills, and hunkered below to recuperate. More of the club members in Osaka seemed to work, so the touring rush was not quite as frantic, and after Jim's tailbone recovered, we snuck out on our own and rode the bullet train to Kyoto. The ultra-modern 16-story Kyoto railway station (one entire floor a bookstore) impressed us almost as much as the ancient Golden Palace, the Nijō Castle, and other historic sites. Kyoto is a traditional Japanese arts center, and I was in craft shopper's paradise purchasing handmade paper and fans.

Golden Palace, Kyoto, Japan

Another day while poking around Osaka we found a flea market with old kimonos, lacquer boxes, fans, and all sorts of food vendors. We splurged on lunch at a sushi bar. Jim loved the raw fish (I didn't) but I enjoyed how it looked and wished I'd painted a watercolor of it instead of eating it. The next day I left Jim working in the engine room and wandered around the kimono shops, pachinko parlors, 100 yen shops, calligraphy shops, and kitchen stores. My Japanese was sufficient to buy lacquer ware tea cups, and a bright red *uchiwa* (handheld fan) with a good-luck cat painted on it.

Again we were a curiosity, and many of the yacht club members took us shopping, invited us to dinner, or took us touring. In particular, a yacht broker named Noby Kobayashi, and his wife, Hiro, were exceptionally good to us. Both of them spoke excellent English, which made our time together more relaxing for me, anyway, since I usually spent a large part of everyday translating—or trying to.

  We carried around two dictionaries, one with English and Japanese *kanji* translations (based on the old Chinese characters) and another with *romaji*, a translation of Japanese based on Roman letters. Many of the Japanese we met spoke some English, some spoke a lot, and some spoke none. We spoke only a little Japanese but could read or recognize several pertinent *kanji* symbols such as the one for "harbor." Each day we ventured out caught us paused on street corners in bus or train stations, or in markets, craning our necks, struggling to read the signs or timetables. Purchasing anything or asking questions was challenging. Many times a small crowd materialized, gathered around, and together poured over our maps and dictionaries, babbling to us and to each other until realization finally dawned: "Ah, so!"

  On June 29, 2000, we were up early. I baked a loaf of banana bread for Mr. Okuda, the Yacht Club Harbor Master. After I delivered the "thank you" bread, we moved *Sanctuary* over to the fuel dock for diesel. The process took most of the morning, yet we didn't mind, as it was the first refueling encounter we ever enjoyed.

  Refueling usually included tying *Sanctuary* to a precarious rocking and rolling dock with jagged, rusty parts exposed along the edge facing our hull. The docks were invariably dangerous with slippery puddles of diesel mixed with salt water and oil. Most pump handlers watched with either disinterest or disdain as Jim maneuvered *Sanctuary* gingerly toward the dock and I ran back and forth adjusting fenders and attempting to protect our hull from the unsavory screws, bolts, and broken bits dangling from the dock's edges. After the fenders were secure I gathered the dock lines (fore and aft) into my hand, hung on the shroud while balancing on the rub rail, and scrutinized the dock for the safest place to land as I jumped ashore.

  Rarely a fuel-dock employee would accept the toss of the stern line so that I could man the bow line without having to juggle both. I considered myself lucky to land without skidding on dirty, slick diesel. We'd tie the boat up, adjust the fenders against the surge, and then give the attendant an estimate of the amount of fuel we needed. He'd turn on the pump, and Jim and I would wrestle the gigantic fuel line over to *Sanc-*

tuary. Generally, since fuel docks were intended for vessels much larger than our tiny sailboat, the large nozzles of the fuel line would not fit into the entry hole for our diesel tank. Therefore, we carried a dedicated diesel funnel. Jim sat on the side of the cockpit holding the funnel in place while I manhandled the large, heavy fuel line over the safety lines and aimed it at the funnel. We juggled the nozzle together, hoping to keep the flow of the fuel slow enough not to spill over but fast enough that we could fuel in about 30 or 40 minutes. Of course, every time another vessel passed, or approached the fuel dock, *Sanctuary* rocked. The motion spilled diesel onto our side decks. Once I got Jim balanced with the funnel and the nozzle, and the fuel flowing, I monitored the wakes as best I could so he could shut off the nozzle before disaster. We'd learned from years of refueling to have an entire roll of paper towels, rags, and a spritzer of cleanser ready for the mop-up process. I hated fuel days, since even with all our precautions we invariably had a mess in the scuppers afterward and a scum on our water line from diesel we and others before us had spilled.

    The fuel dock at the Osaka Club was a pleasant surprise. It was clean with no snaggy, rusty bits and no diesel on the decks! Two dock workers, dressed neatly in clean uniforms and wearing white gloves, casually and competently took our dock lines and then proceeded to do the work. They unscrewed our gas cap, dragged over the gas line, and one held the nozzle for the fuel while the other managed the funnel. After delicately starting the diesel flow, they stopped fueling every 20 liters to wipe up any small spills using clean rags they had at the ready. Jim and I watched bug-eyed at the immaculate service. I was so amazed I felt like kissing them but refrained, and when they finished I took their photos as they put their white gloved hands together and bowed.

    We moved *Sanctuary* back to a berth. Even though there was no spilled diesel, I washed the decks with fresh water anyway for the first time since New Year's in Port Dickson more than six months earlier. During the afternoon we relaxed on board for a while and then I baked more cookies to use as thank-you gifts for our upcoming goodbyes. With the cookies in the oven, I arranged and labeled charts of Alaska in anticipated order of use. After plotting the Great Circle Route from south of Tokyo to Dutch Harbor, Alaska, I entered coordinates along our anticipated route into our GPS. Even though we'd purchased most provisions in Malaysia, we'd bought a few packs of noodles and rice to replenish what we'd used in Japan. I packed them away and then began stowing the loose items we wouldn't need on the passage.

Jim unplugged the electrical cord (used to charge our batteries) from the dock, and after filling our water tanks, stowed the cords and the water hoses deep in the stern lazarette. The next morning we checked out with the officials. The hard part was left, that of saying goodbye to all the friends we had made at the Osaka Hokko Yacht Club. So many people had been kind to us in Japan; our two-month visit seemed short. We would have loved to linger longer but needed to keep our date with the Pacific Ocean. We said goodbyes, untied our dock lines, and headed out early on the morning of July 1, 2000, making our way down Osaka Bay and out to a jumping-off point on Japan's Pacific coast.

Crossing the Pacific

July 2000—August 2000

"Life is either a daring adventure or nothing. To keep our faces toward change and behave like free spirits in the presence of fate is strength undefeatable."

—Helen Keller

Shingu Ko, a large, natural bay, is protected on one side by land, two sides by rocks, and on the fourth side by an extensive Japanese breakwater that guards the entrance. Our first night we anchored in the outer harbor, just inside the breakwater, with two freighters for company. The next morning we lowered our dinghy and investigated the inner small-boat harbor. After tootling around in the dinghy, we decided Shingu was the perfect spot from which to stage our departure, so we went back to *Sanctuary*, raised the anchor, and moved into the inner harbor, where we side-tied to a wall. Afterward, we checked in with the Harbor Master and the Customs Officer, telling them of our plan to depart from Shingu to sail across the Pacific Ocean.

Upon hearing about our upcoming passage, the officers offered us daily weather information since they routinely received Japanese weather faxes four times a day. Meanwhile, they said we couldn't leave Japan until an immigration officer checked us out, and no officer was available until three days later. That suited us. A three-day delay would give us time to shop for fresh food for the crossing, set up a ham radio schedule, send some last-minute e-mails, and take a few more deep breaths before the 2,990-mile passage to the Aleutian Islands of Alaska.

While we waited, we met a Japanese couple, Noboru and Masako, who lived on their sailboat, *Rah II* (which was also tied to the harbor wall). They had a car, and the day before our planned departure, they took us shopping for three weeks' worth of fresh fruits, vegetables, and eggs for our journey. After shopping, we drove to a lovely, natural Japanese bath where hot sulphur waters gurgled out of a rocky spring that overlooked the edge of the ocean. We sat in the springs and soaked as the waves of the Pacific crashed onto the rocks below us. I gazed out to sea trying to gather my strength and mental fortitude for the days before us.

On the anticipated day of departure, we were up early and received a weather fax over our SSB radio. The fax had shown clear mild weather the day before, so I was shocked to see a typhoon heading for Japan! It wouldn't be safe to leave port with a typhoon barreling toward us. We climbed off *Sanctuary* and walked over to the Customs Office to meet with the officials as previously planned. They were all atwitter about the typhoon, as were we.

A typhoon is a storm system with sustained winds greater than 64 knots. The winds of the system can extend for 100 miles, 200 miles, even 300 miles from the center. The storms usually have an area of calm called an "eye." The low criterion is 64 knots of wind—but typhoon winds can top 125 knots. We had barely survived a similar Force 10 storm when crossing the Atlantic. That storm broke our wind indicator, pegging it out at 70 knots, the end of its scale. Until it was repaired, every time we looked at it, the stuck wind arrow mournfully reminded us of just how strong winds could get.

Shrine gates frame Sanctuary as she lays tied to the wall at Shingu

Memories of our 1995 storm experience stuck like that arrow in our minds: winds so strong they blew me up the mast track along with the mainsail as I struggled to lower it; winds so strong I could not stand upright on the foredeck and was forced to crawl inch by inch out to the bow to set the parachute sea anchor; winds so strong we could not hear each other speak and yelled face to face just to be understood.

We remembered the waves. As *Sanctuary* slid down their steep sides we looked up, and up again, watching as they foamed and crashed at a height higher than our spreaders. We remembered the motion. After losing the sea anchor, poor *Sanctuary* lay ahull, rolling first to port and then lurching back to starboard. We lay below on the cabin sole, wrapped together around the base of our keel stepped mast, hanging on to each other and the mast for dear life as the spreaders grazed the foam with each roll. Only the weight of *Sanctuary's* lead keel brought us upright before capsize. We remembered those hours all too well. No, we would not leave port in a typhoon.

Typhoons can occur in all months in the North Pacific Ocean. We had already carefully waited in order to make our track from Japan to Alaska during July, the month with the least recorded incident of typhoons and high winds. So we would wait a little longer, sit out the typhoon, and set sail after it passed.

Since the Harbor Master, Immigration, and Customs Officers were already gathered in the Harbor Master's office, they decided to go ahead and check us out of Japan, but advised us not to leave. After an animated conversation in Japanese, the three switched to English, telling us they all agreed that Shingu was no place for a small sailboat to weather a typhoon—the holding was bad and the harbor too shallow. The Harbor Master got out a detailed local chart pointing out a perfect small but deep typhoon hole five miles away. He then ushered us to his car and drove us over to the tiny harbor.

The little "hole" technically belonged to a fishing cooperative, and pleasure craft were not allowed. But all the shallow-draft fishing boats were heading upriver for even more storm protection. *Sanctuary* couldn't go upriver because of our deep keel, and her tall mast couldn't pass under the river's low bridges. Therefore, we were given permission to anchor in the center of the tiny harbor to weather the storm. The Harbor Master made arrangements with the cooperative and then drove us back to Shingu.

We boarded *Sanctuary*, untied from the harbor wall, and armed with the chart and instructions the Harbor Master had provided, motored the five miles south to the hidey-hole of Ugui Ko. We tiptoed past a maze of large rocks that guarded the entrance and into the harbor, assessed the best spot for protection, and dug in the anchor. I put on my swimsuit and snorkel gear and swam over the anchor to make sure it was set well. It was. Back onboard we discussed setting a second anchor but decided against it since we were well protected from surge and could swing 360° as the winds shifted. We were alone in the harbor except for one very small sailboat tucked way over by the outer breakwater. By the time we anchored and cleared *Sanctuary's* decks in anticipation of high winds, it was 2000 hours. We were tired, but the night had just begun.

To make sure we weren't dragging, we set up some sights: a line on the entrance light, a line on the light at the fish cannery, and a line on another point ashore. We'd keep an anchor watch, four hours on, four off, for each of us. We also set up a radio schedule for frequent updates of the typhoon's progress and track. After eating a very late dinner, satisfied that we had done what we could, we sat down to wait.

By 0600 the next morning, July 7th, the barometer had dropped from 1012 to 1005, and winds gusted to 25 knots. We plotted Typhoon Kirogi on our chart as it swept toward Tokyo at eight knots, carrying winds of 125 knots and raising the seas to heights of 24 feet. We swung on our anchor rode, occasionally snubbing up hard with a strong gust. Rain stung our decks, and when we stuck our heads out into the cockpit to check our points ashore, we could see explosions of saltwater as huge seas crashed against the breakwater. Inside the harbor, as the wind whipped the waters, small rollers crested and foamed, but because of the protection, they amounted to nothing.

All day we continued our anchor watch, checking our points on shore, checking the rising wind speeds, and monitoring our barometer as the pressure dropped to 998. By 1630 in the afternoon, the barometer raised a notch, and we knew we'd gotten lucky. Typhoon Kirogi, like a dog with a bone, had tugged our anchor rode, swung us around in circles, and shaken our rigging with 50-knot winds, but dropping the bone, had veered off leaving us unscathed.

The next morning, July 8th, broke clear and bright, and at 0600 the seas in the harbor were flat and the wind dead calm. I baked banana bread, and we relaxed with our coffee in the cockpit, chatting about what to do. We decided that, even though the typhoon had passed, we wouldn't leave yet. It was calm inside Ugui Ko, but we knew it would take time for the rolling seas outside to die down. Also, thanks to anchor watches and nervousness, we hadn't really slept in two nights, which was no way to start a passage. We had eaten several of our precious passage tomatoes, so later in the morning we went ashore in search of replacements and there met a last, but memorable, taste of Japanese hospitality.

As we walked into small Ugui, we passed a beautiful vegetable garden. Along the roadside, a box was stacked with peppers, tomatoes, onions, squash, and other vegetables. We couldn't read the sign, but the vegetables appeared to be for sale on the honor system. Unable to determine what to pay, we looked around and saw a man nearby working in his garage. We hailed him. He spoke little English, but we understood, yes, the vegetables were for sale and the price. As we bought the entire box full, he asked, "Where are you from? Why are you buying vegetables?" (Buying vegetables was not a "normal" tourist activity.)

I got out my translation dictionary and after much cross-referencing and sign language, Mr. Muramoto understood our replies. Mr. Muramoto, dropping his work tools, said, "Wait a minute. I'm going to call my brother." In a few minutes, his older brother rode up on a motorcycle, bringing us the green tomatoes we needed, more peppers, cucumbers, and other vegetables picked from his garden. Both refused any payment for the bounty. They drove us to the grocery store where we spent our last yen on staples for the passage. Mr. Muramoto's wife served us tea and ice cream after which the brothers visited aboard *Sanctuary*. (The wife was too nervous to get into our dinghy.) The brother, Hirofumi, had served in the Second World War, and as he put it, "killed two round eyes."

Early in our voyage, Jim and I had determined to avoid politics and religion as topics of discussion with people we met along our route. Hirofumi, however, seemed to want to talk about his experiences. As we thumbed our dictionary and struggled to keep up with the discussion as it flowed, we realized by the end of the visit that nothing had been lost in translation after all. History had happened and lives had been lost, but neither the two brothers nor the crew of *Sanctuary* were to blame for the past. We mutually accepted each other with the hand of friendship. Later ashore we took photos, and then we returned to *Sanctuary* to raise our dinghy aboard and again prepare for departure. The Muramoto family had armed us with fresh food for the trip. More than that, they'd given us a taste of human kindness to savor along the way.

Ugui Ko, Honshu, Japan. Sunday, July 9, 2000: 0700: As we cautiously motored *Sanctuary* out toward the Pacific Ocean, I braced stiff-legged on the cockpit combing. Raising my binoculars, I searched anxiously for signs of the dangerous rocks we knew rimmed the doglegged channel of the tiny harbor. Suddenly, Jim tugged at my sleeve and said, "Don't worry. I'm steering and watching for the rocks. Look back over your shoulder." I turned, and ringing the ships bell as loudly as I could, shouted *"Sayonara!"*

In my anxiety I hadn't seen the small group of Japanese well-wishers standing on the quay waving goodbye to us as we left to cross an ocean. The Shingu Harbormaster, Noboru and Masako from the sailboat *Rah*, Higashi Muramoto, his wife, his brother Hirofumi (who had given us the vegetables), some fishermen, and the fishing cooperative president had all gotten up at first light to gather on the quay and cheer us on. What an honor! We took turns looking back to wave goodbye as we jogged *Sanctuary* past the entrance rocks that had aided in protecting us from Typhoon Kirogi.

Once past the entrance quay we set the sails and by 1600 hours had settled into our passage routine. The winds were steady from the south, and with the aid of the Kuroshiro current, *Sanctuary* reached on her beam at six knots, rising and falling only a little in a slight swell left over from the typhoon. We crossed a main shipping route that led toward Tokyo, and most of the traffic fell behind.

The next day gave us our last glimpse of land as we sailed between the outlying islands of Miyake Shima and Mikura Shima. A volcano had erupted two weeks earlier on Miyake, and people had been evacuated from the island. We couldn't spot the volcano and could barely see the island lights from five miles away due to a layer of fog. Light winds followed the fog, and we ghosted along at barely two knots.

After *Sanctuary* entered the Kuroshiro current, we flew along for hours in light winds on a beautiful beam reach at nine knots. As the sky filled with mare's tails, the barometer dropped, the winds picked up to 25 knots, and the swell increased. We knew a change was coming. Jim had not adapted as quickly to a passage routine as I, and his sleep patterns were still erratic. We opted to follow our "Safety and Comfort First" rule and shortened sail. By 2130 the winds were steady at 35 knots gusting to 40; we were glad we had reefed early. We hove to for a while so Jim could rest, but the howling wind kept him awake, so I raised the storm staysail, and we got on with sailing through the early morning and most of the next day with the one lone sail.

We followed our heaving to routine for the fifth night with heightened and breaking seas. As the winds steadied, we began to sail again, finally raising the jib as the winds settled into 15 knots from the SSW. A few gannets and stormy petrels followed us awhile. Otherwise, we had no company but the winds and the clouds and the seas.

We continued rolling uphill. With waves rushing down behind

and under our hull, we surfed ever northeast. *Sanctuary* sounded like a fat washerwoman returning from the well with her sloshing, clanking buckets, thighs rubbing together, skirts, apron, and apron strings slapping in the breeze, releasing a steady whistling moan, heaving, and struggling with the weight of her burden.

Navigating while underway across the Pacific

And we were loaded, too much so, probably. *Sanctuary's* tanks were full; she carried 150 gallons of water and 90 gallons of diesel. On deck were 10 additional gallons of water, 30 additional gallons of diesel, and six gallons of gasoline for our Nissan outboard. Every food locker (six dedicated, plus the galley and the "garage") was crammed to the brim. Everything we anticipated for three meals a day for 48 days (our estimated passage length, doubled) was aboard. The refrigerator was packed, the freezer was full of eight kilos of meat, and there were two slings full of fruits and vegetables.

For the first week, we ate mostly fresh foods along with some pasta. I'd made a lot of salads and on the fifth day out, baked a loaf of bread. We'd burned some diesel on the first day; otherwise, we used diesel only to run our generator to charge the batteries. The weather was still warm, and we wore shorts in the daytime and some of the night, putting on sweat pants in the early morning hours.

The miles inched by with periods of steady sailing and periods of heaving to in gale-force winds. On July 16th, day seven, 0300, I logged: *Hove to, again! 40 knots of winds, breaking seas. Where are these winds coming from? Not on any weather fax, supposedly we are in the middle of a 1017 high. We are not happy with these high winds and seas.*

7/16/2000: 1200: Still hove to. Seas still breaking with growlers. They are at least 12 feet, maybe higher. The winds have lessened a bit to 30 knots, but we are leery of setting sail again just yet because of the growlers. It has been a slow day for us with only 89 nm made good. But not too bad since we were hove to for nine out of 24 hours. Oh, well. We think we came too far north (37°) too soon. When we do set sail, we are going to forget the great circle route and head almost due east until we get to 160°, then we will see about northing.

Jim is having an anxiety attack and is sure that Sanctuary is falling apart at the seams, that the keel is going to fall off, a complete litany of horror worries. I have a difficult time calming him, and finally I slip into anger. We said awful things to each other, and I don't like it. Seems like on every passage Jim goes into a downward cycle.

I mentally put Jim's anxiety on a shelf and just said, "Hmm, is that right?" whenever he said the keel was falling off. At last I fell into a deep sleep on my off watch but woke up feeling as if I hadn't slept at all.

7/17/2000:1900: *My watch. Quiet evening. The wind is so light; we are ghosting along downwind at 3 knots under a sometimes flogging jib. Hard to believe this is the same sea we were on this time yesterday in full gale, raging winds, breaking seas with foam, and spray blowing off tops. At least we are moving in the right direction, and sailing.*

Three good signs we saw today: a turtle, a school of dolphins, and a whale! First sightings of marine life in so long, now all three in the same day. Took showers this afternoon—otherwise not much doing after baking bread. One third of the way(distance) there! Celebrated with chocolate candy bars. Although, since we are going so slowly, I am worried about how long it is really going to take us.

7/18/2000: 1445: *Receiving 24-hour weather fax. Having a lovely sail, winds ten knots, moving along at five knots, calm seas, and bit of swell, warm.*

Jim and I existing in uneasy truce. Sanctuary doing beautifully. She loves to sail and gallops along. A few mare's tails to the east, but barometer steady at 1016. Looks like an afternoon wind to me. Fax shows tropical depression passing well to the west of us. I hope we have had the worst of it and that the rest of the passage is smooth sailing.

Cleaned and polished two brass cabin lights, cleaned some old creeping crack cure out in the cockpit, discovered the chain plates are leaking slightly, cleaned around the damp spots, and rearranged some of the gear to prevent any saltwater damage. Neatened up the boat in general, maintaining a low profile with Jim.

7/19/2000: 0930: *Lovely night last night. Winds steady at 18-20 knots. Some gusts and lumpy seas, so we reefed the main and used the staysail. Sailed a bit slower at five and a half knots, but that's okay. We sacrifice speed for comfort. Now this a.m. winds lighter, all three sails flying high. Heading for waypoint number five at about 160° E, 45° N. The high is well-established, so we are sailing along the outside and inside millibars. I keep trying the ham e-mail system (Airmail) and the system tells me my messages are sent, but have not had a reply for over a month.*

Working on cleaning the brass cabin lights: two down, four to go, plus the clock and the lantern. Sanctuary has accumulated a lot of dust, which, at this point, is rather sticky due to the salt in the air. Early in the a.m. everything feels especially damp.

1850: *Jim going below, my watch. Reefed main for the night. Jib and staysail flying. Beam reach in about 15 knots. We probably didn't need to reef, but it keeps us from interrupting the off watch since we always have the second person come out. Tonight, for first time in a while, deep fog, visibility about one mile, so using radar. We haven't seen any ships in three days. According to the weather fax, we are just inside the fog line and won't have it for long. Soon we will be riding the second millibar of the 1032 Pacific High. No fog and if weather holds true about 15 k SW all the rest of the way to the Aleutians.*

We actually sailed 130 miles yesterday, but because we were heading more easterly to stay out of the storm path, only 114 of the miles were toward our goal.

Distance Made Good as of 1900 hours on 7/19/2000: 375 miles short of half-way! It will be lovely to be halfway since it will all be downhill from then on!

July 20, 2000: 0130: *My second night watch: fog! Even though it is not raining, everything outside is so wet it is dripping, and a pool of water has collected in the cockpit. If we could capture it clean somehow, we could get gallons of drinking water. At this point Sanctuary is too salt-encrusted to collect this water. I need to go out and clean, and then, perhaps, we could catch some. Otherwise, moving along on a steady beam reach, no traffic at all.*

Jim still having anxiety. Feels the keel is falling off. I inspect the bilge to show him all the bolts are fine and then refuse to discuss it any longer. I am sure it is just his fear and effects of medicine, seasickness, talking.

July 20, 2000: 1900: *My evening watch. I like this watch after dinner. I can sit and catch my breath (usually, if the weather is okay) and rest between watching before going to sleep.*

Very busy today. After dinner the fog set in, winds picked up, and because of an occluded front on the weather fax, we put up the storm staysail. Perhaps too soon (as usual) and not needed, but it is so dark and so wet in the fog tonight we thought better now than if it gets messy later. This is like washing the car, this way we won't need it. There is a tropical storm on the fax we are watching, too. It is 600 nm SW of us and don't believe it will be a problem, but we are watching it carefully just the same.

Polished the clock, we both took showers; I worked on a "Pacific sweater" I am crocheting. I tried the ham "Airmail" again. I found out we have a message but for some reason wasn't able to receive it.

July 21, 2000: Day 12: 0930: *Winds steady SW all last night. Fog also* steady. Now, in the light of day, we can see about a quarter mile. We seem to be in a gray bowl. If it weren't for electronics, we wouldn't know the world was still there. We keep watch by radar.

Tried "Airmail" again—still can't get our message. Jib now flying, too, doing six knots. Still working on my brass-cleaning project and crocheting a sweater. Restocked the galley from the hard to get to food lockers. Nine tomatoes left, and they are holding. (These are the ones that came directly from the two brothers' gardens.)

Fog, rain, and now no wind. We decided to motor to charge our batteries. We are watching our diesel carefully. The current is with us, so at 1500 rpm we are doing seven knots. We don't like the noise.

July 21, 2000: 2300: *Heaving to in 35 knots of wind. Heavy rain. Can't write.*

July 22, 2000: Day 13: 0400: *Still hove to. The heavy rains have passed, the winds are starting to moderate. Seas confused. Barometer at 1012. Cold, too. Think we have been hit by the occluded cold front. Shame we had to heave to and spoil a great progress day.*

Talked with one ship in the night, a Chinese bulk carrier, headed for Los Angeles then Peru. Our first contact other than with each other for 12 days.

1600: *Another rain squall, but fog has partially cleared, and we can see blue skies ahead for the first time in three days. Yahaha hoowie, sun! We are sailing, slowly, in fluky winds.*

Foul weather gear is now hanging all over the aft cabin, and wet clothes hanging in the engine room too. Can-lid cut on my left thumb. Ouch! I now realize how much I use that thumb! We are wearing sweat pants, long-sleeved shirts, and socks all the time now. We were lucky to have been warm and wear shorts for so long.

July 23, 2000: Day 14: 0145: *Motoring again. There is no wind, and I am worried. We tried sailing, but all we did was drift backward. There is not any current here to help us. We are using diesel and banking on the sun heating the air up tomorrow and giving us a breeze. We are not in fog anymore, and it has quit raining. Cold and gray. We can probably see about four miles, but there is no way to judge as there are no landmarks.*

1845: *Wind came back from the SE! A light breeze, just enough to keep us going at five knots. Lovely! No swell. May we be blessed and these good winds continue.*

Afternoon celebration for being halfway across the Pacific to Alaska: hot tea with honey and rum! Yum!

2100: *Some little birds are following Sanctuary, and every time I open the companionway (closed now all the time because it is cold out) I can hear them chirping. It is so dark out I can't see them. Shining a flashlight into the darkness just absorbs* the light. Looking toward the bow, I can make out a horizon line, that's all. We are sailing in our own circle of light cast by the tricolor and the navigation station light glowing from below.

The wind is so light tonight I can't hear it. All the sounds are muted. Just gentle slap of water against the hull, a bubble sound of trail we leave, a slight flap of the jib, barely kept full by the light winds, and the back and forth whir of the wheel turned by the autopilot. The loudest noise by far is the refrigeration fan which could probably be turned off. We also ate a chocolate bar in celebration of being halfway across the Pacific. I got just a few chocolates while we were in Malaysia and have hoarded them for this passage and this occasion since April.

As of yesterday the last lettuce, last fresh peppers, most of the spring onions, and cucumbers are all gone. What's left fresh: tomatoes, carrots, white onions, potatoes, one orange, 10 eggs, a few green onions, one cabbage, and five apples. Not bad I suppose after 15 days. I would have bought more but didn't have room. The refrigerator and all of swinging baskets and forward fresh food baskets were full when we left Japan.

July 24, 2000: Day 15: 1200: *Degenerated into a windward slog. Intended course is 45°, exactly where the wind is coming from. By pinching it we are doing 10° to 13° only. Just got the fax which forecasts more of the same NE 15 knots. Who knows, the fax could be wrong. For now, it's sunny! The booby prize.*

July 25, 2000: Day 16: 0800: *Hove to since 2000 last night, 12 hours. The NE 25 K winds increased as did the seas, and the barometer dropped to 1010. It is difficult to accept the idea of "losing" a day, but it makes sense for us to sit out this low pressure. Even if we wanted to torture ourselves and the boat by trying to sail in this, we would only go in the wrong direction as we did yesterday, tacking back and forth all day and getting nowhere.*

After a miserable three hours and several sail changes, we only made one nautical mile good toward Dutch Harbor. We were exhausted and disheartened. So, we gave up and hove to in hopes the low will pass.

Jim and I both are getting some much-needed sleep. I slept straight from 0400-0700 for the first time in three days. Jim told me Chica licked my face and climbed all over me, and I didn't even know it.

The person on watch checks radar every 15 minutes and looks out to check the wind, seas, deck, etc. Otherwise, I read, write in my journal, or crochet. Sometimes I get out the computer, but even hove to the motion is usually too much to sit easily at the computer. With the journal I can wedge in somewhere.

We have the Espar (diesel forced-air heater) on now. Jim figures it uses about one and a quarter gallons of diesel every 24 hours. I keep track of that, and the generator diesel use, and if we motor.

I did a plot and a fix; in spite of bashing to weather all day yesterday, we only made good 15 nautical miles. An embarrassment. Today, heaving to: zero progress. At least we are not going backward. I feel myself wanting to fall asleep even as I write. Wake me when it's over.

The weather fax shows us on the western edge of a 100-millibar low. We seem trapped because it is heading just where we want to go. Nothing to do but sit and wait. The roll of the heave to is just enough to make doing much difficult. I did, however, make tuna fish pasta salad for lunch.

2000: Still hove to after 24 hours. At night it is more difficult because we can't see the seas, and the howling of the wind sounds so ominous.

July 26, 2000: Day 17: 1045: We have been hove to for 38 hours now and have drifted SW about 25 miles. The winds are now starting to shift to the ENE. The seas are still quite large, more than 12 feet, but the tops have quit blowing off, and they are starting to smooth out and not grumble and crumble. Also, there are some faint lulls in the howling winds. The sun is coming out at times, and it is much warmer. The barometer is at 1004, but it feels like the bulk of the low has passed to the west, and we are now getting the winds on the backside. We will have to wait a while for the seas to die down, but an amazing thing is that once the howling wind fan is turned off the seas lie down very quickly.

I went on deck to retie the halyards that had come loose and to get the bag out of the mainsail. The worst part was the bitter cold from the wind—not the wind itself. If we had encountered these same winds in the tropics it wouldn't be as debilitating as the cold. We have had a couple of "slappers" on the bow, but generally we are hove to very well and can see our slick. We have also tested the slick with floating paper towels which go out abeam of us.

Yesterday, to our surprise, we were visited by an Alaskan fur seal! He seemed to be alone, not with a pod, but looked quite healthy and happy. Swam around and looked at us, lolled in our slick, and then went off. Had a chocolate face, dark flippers, dark tail flippers, a light cream belly, and brownish back. We also saw a pod of dolphins the day before and some whales.

The sun is out—hooray! The high can't be far behind.

July 27, 2000: Day 18: 0130: Wrong! The sun was out, but the high seems to be hiding. The winds and seas came back with a vengeance. We have been hove to now for about 54 hours and are very tired of the relentlessly rolling seas and ever-howling wind. I just want to tear my hair out and scream back at the wind. It seems like a living thing, a siren's voice, or the howl of a madman or sometimes the whisper of a hundred ghosts or the p-s-s-t of a man calling around the corner, or the wh—o who—whoo of a forest full of trees and owls or the high-pitched whistle of off-tune dog walkers on a dark night.

Speaking of dark nights, they make me dread the sun going down. Somehow, when we can see the waves, it's easier. Even if they are big, we can see if they will grumble and break, or if the wave train is regular, they'll roll on by. But on a night like tonight, with no moon or stars, we can't see anything, and when we hear the hiss of an approaching wave, we can't tell the size or condition. Nerve-wracking, wondering what or when one is going to hit us.

0630: Underway again after almost 60 hours hove to. We are bashing to weather again in seas of 10 feet, winds 20-25 knots, NNE. Making good so far on a course of about 15°-20°. We actually want 50°, so that isn't as bad as it could be; at least we are heading more or less toward our goal. Best of all is getting out of the clutches of the low-pressure system. Possibly we will be out of the worst of the seas and winds in six to eight hours with us going NE at five knots and the low, according to the weather fax, heading west at 5 knots. If not too happy about the sailing conditions, glad at least to be moving. It is not as bitterly cold as it has been.

2015: Going to windward but not bashing too badly. Sailing with storm staysail and triple reefed main. Winds NNE 20 to 25, seas still up and high, but we can tell the low is passing at last. I'm very tired. The noise and the motion from such high winds for so long a time is so wearing and the cold is, too. Jim feels the same, but maybe got a bit more rest than I did.

We change sails up and down, up and down. First the staysail, then the storm staysail, then shake a reef out of the main, then put it back in. I'm in and out of foul weather gear all day long. I feel like a fireman and should leave my pants around my boots. Rained most of the day today, too.

July 28, 2000: Day 19: 1400: *A busy day with leftover sloppy seas in the a.m., rain, and I can hardly remember what all. I know, jib in and out several times. I set the staysail in*

Jim in foulweather gear, mid-Pacific

the pouring rain. But around 1000 the seas lay down, the winds calmed, and the sun came out. We set all three sails and have had smooth sailing, knock wood, ever since.

We took showers, I made peanut butter cookies. Chica even came out into the cockpit, and it was warm enough to sit outside and eat. I hung out all our wet clothes to dry.

July 29, 2000: Day 20: Range: 1,183 NM: 0200: *Foggy, cold, but sailing, if slowly. I need to suit up, bring in the staysail, and set the jib. This takes a major effort, and I'm working up to it.*

0930: Hours later and many sail changes later. Still cold, still foggy, but winds shifted to southerly, and we are running almost downwind with staysail and reefed main. Last hour, seven knots. I cleaned the interior and got out a complement of canned goods from a deep locker and moved them to the galley.

2125: Have sailed along downwind all day. Slowed down a bit in the evening, and the roll of the swell a bit uncomfortable, and when the sail deflates, and bangs, it is unnerving. But, still and all, it could be worse, so I'm not complaining. We are hoping we've gotten lucky and will have fair winds and calm seas the rest of the way to Dutch Harbor. If we keep up our pace, we could be there in nine days.

July 30, 2000: Day 21: Range: 997 miles: 1900: *Much up and down with the sails. Trying to eke out something from little or no wind. Awful rock and roll and sail bang. Finally, because of the sail bang, after trying every sail combo we could think of, we now have staysail alone and doing about four knots. Not enough wind to keep even that full, only the current helps us.*

Between all of the sail changes I made: Oatmeal for breakfast, scrambled hamburger and coleslaw for lunch, and tomato, cheese, and ham sandwiches on homemade bread for dinner. I baked the bread in between repairing a torn seam on the mainsail. That was not exactly fun on the rolling deck. But now, when we raise the main, that seam should at least last until Dutch Harbor.

Three weeks at sea is wearing very thin. Weather fax shows two low-pressure systems behind us. Neither very low, I'm glad to say. With a little luck, we will stay ahead of them. The high looks so close on the fax, and 997 miles to go doesn't sound far at all on paper, but for our little boat it is still a long, long way.

The fog lifted a little during the day, and we got some feeling of sunshine or daylight, but mostly we exist as a pea pod in a bowl of gray soup. Both of us are tense from bracing for the roll. We can't set anything down inside unless it is wedged or has a non-skid bottom. Cooking is a delicate ballet. It is excruciating to listen to the thump of the rigging as we fall off a wave. Sanctuary shakes when the wind catches the sail on the other side. Oh, well, at least we are moving forward, inch by painful inch, on the chart.

Jim has a tooth with a receding gum, possibly gingivitis or peritonitis. I'm feeding him extra vitamins and lots of water and juice, and he is gargling with hydrogen peroxide. We'll get him to a dentist as soon as we hit shore.

July 31, 2000: Day 22: 0840: *Motor sailing. Just enough wind to sail two knots with awful sail bang. We are 940 miles from Dutch Harbor and have enough diesel to motor a little, so we are using some of it today. Hoping the winds pick up with the rising sun shining today for the first time in a long time. Even some blue skies and white clouds. Barometer is dropping though, so we feel like a low-pressure system is on the way. If so, there is nothing we can do. Mended Jim's Helly Hansen pants which were falling apart at the inseams.*

Motoring all day in no wind. We tried to sail several times but only drifted backward in the one-knot current. Booby prize: sunny and warm.

Low pressure shown on the weather fax for the last several days totally disappeared and was not on the 1740 fax at all. What happens to these systems? If we are in the high, where are the southerly 15 knot winds shown on the fax? Sometimes it seems we are on a liquid treadmill, and someone is projecting photos of weather on a screen like a movie backdrop and that all our movement is an illusion. The cold is all far too real though, and the fog is wet and drippy.

Distance to go to Dutch Harbor: 889 miles. If we could sail five knots, we could be there in seven days! If is a big if! A little over four knots yesterday, so I can't hold my breath. Now with no wind we are worried about getting becalmed. The wind is feast or famine. I took to polishing the seven brass light fixtures we had aboard plus a brass kerosene lantern. Polishing is an endless loop but with no wind to speak of, I might as well do something. Since we had no wind in the mainsail, I also lowered it and hand-repaired a broken batten trace.

August 1, 2000, Day 23: 12:30: *Made good just 95 miles yesterday, a lot of it motoring. Sailing along since midnight at barely three knots, but we don't dare motor any more. We must conserve our fuel for charging the batteries and running our diesel heater.*

Took showers in the head since we had hot water from motoring yesterday.

Barometer at 992, which usually means a lot of wind, but we have almost none and are only making good three knots. We are wondering if we are going to be hammered with high winds due to the low millibars, but there is no swell and no indication of any winds to come. Drizzling now and foggy.

1900: *Sitting at the nav station as usual for beginning of my evening watch. Jib rolled in as the wind is getting up. Jim in his sleeping bag. I have only the small light on so he won't be disturbed. Heavy fog and bitterly cold out. Pitch black, so I check radar every 15 minutes and poke my head out every 30 minutes to look at the sails, feel wind on my face, etc.—more often than that if I hear the wind shift or change. The low seems to be passing over us especially since we have NW-W winds,* which would be on the backside, and the barometer has risen two clicks in last two hours.

I'm thankful we did not get hit by the low and seem to have only the effects of the lower, southern edge of it.

2445: I spoke too soon. Hove to, again. Barometer dropped to 994, low hit us with a vengeance. Winds steadily increased, shortened sail to triple reefed main,

View towards the bow
Underway - Pacific - FOG!

then it got too much with side slappers, so now hove to. Maybe we'll sail in the daylight, just too difficult now, especially in cold, cold wind and so pitch dark we can't see anything. We had to turn on the mast lights for every sail change.

August 2, 2000: Day 24: 0418: Winds still howling, huge seas, still rolling under our heave to slick. The barometer is up to 997, so I calculate the worst of it should be gone by 1400 hours. Jim thinks we can sail soon. 1300: Gale got worse at 0630. We decided to set the parachute sea anchor which took at least an hour. We had never used this gear before, and it was all overkill and too hard for me to handle. The rode too big, and too heavy, the same with the bridle and the snatch block. Once we got it overboard, the parachute was beautiful, but the bridle didn't work and jammed up by the hawse pipe. Since we couldn't get it all set right, and the sea anchor line was chafing on the hawsehole, we decided to bring it in which took an hour of excruciating winching. Dragging it aboard the bow was extremely dangerous, too. I finally got it all back aboard, and put away. Another hour. Meanwhile, we went back to normal heaving to.

We are both still recovering from the entire episode and have learned how NOT to deploy a sea anchor. It is stuffed in its bag, a tangled mess now. Meanwhile, the millibars have gone from 990 to 1003. The wind is still howling but has shifted to the WNW. We can sail on it soon. Jim desperately needs some rest. I got soaked out on the bow, and it is very cold, 64° or less. Plus add in the wind.

The noise is excruciating. The relentless howling, screeching wind and all the boat noises we can't stop, the rigging, cans in lockers, water tanks sloshing, and the rush of the water under the hull, the occasional bow slapper. Add in the motion and give me an aspirin. The roll—left, right, then head up, bow falls off, level for a split second, then left, right, left, right, left, right, heel, heel, lurch, fall off, hesitate, start over again.

My arm muscles are burning, and I've lost my sense of stability. I feel like crying or yelling or both but will do neither. Jim is on the edge and not doing well. The cold is so hard on him, and it slows down his already slow, suffering body even further. I wish we had never started this passage, but that's a useless thought, as here we are, and this is what we've got.

Let the seas calm. Let the winds calm, let us be safe, and finish this passage to Dutch Harbor safely.

1500: *Underway with WNW winds. Reefed main and staysail.*

2000: *So sore, especially my arms, from all the winching and hanging on. I'm moving like an old lady, in pain while doing almost anything. We shook the reef out of the main, and I could hardly move. Today took a lot out of both of us.*

August 3, 2000: Thursday, Day 25: 0540: *Days are going by in a blur except for the gales. Today is memorable: the sun is shining brightly, and we are sailing along on a fairly comfortable beam reach. Seas are still 12 feet or more, leftover from the gale I suppose, but regular and not breaking. I'm so tired I'm ditzy and nodding off.*

1900: *It has been a very nice day. The sun was out all day, and the winds stayed steady at 15 knots. We seem to be just inside a high-pressure system. The low that smacked us has gone up to the Aleutians and north.*

Baked bread and a pizza round for homemade pizza dinner.

An easy beam reach, quietly sailing, cooking was a pleasure. Jim sat in the cockpit most of the day. Not too cold. Only changed sails twice. We're still recovering from the gale/sea anchor day. I'm a bit sore but feeling much better after two uninterrupted off watches with three straight hours' sleep each time. Plus, we both had naps today during the day and treated ourselves to hot rum toddies this afternoon. Oh, we are longing to get there: range to Dutch Harbor is 657 NM. Slowly inching our way.

August 4, 2000: Day 26: 0330: *Raining, cold 58° even inside. Something is wrong with the heater thermostat, and the heater doesn't come on right and doesn't* cycle correctly. Probably needs cleaning.

Nice beam reach. Flat seas, steady 15 k winds. Lovely, if wet, cold and foggy. So, we just use the radar for watch with only one blip in the last 24 hours.

Wearing thermal long johns with sweat pants over one pair of cotton socks with one pair of wool socks over, leather indoor scuff shoes over, one heavy tee shirt, one long-sleeved polar shirt, and one Irish wool sweater over. Wrapped also in blanket as I write and still cold. Hope Jim can fix the heater when he wakes.

1830: We worked on the heater from 0400 to 1300 and it is still not fixed. Replaced the glow plug, took it out, inspected the fuel lines, cleaned the fuel filter, checked the ducts, checked all three fuses, inspected the air vent, and cleaned all the electrical connections. It starts but fuel does not ignite. We think the problem is a sealed unit called "universal control switch." We do not have one and no way to repair it until Alaska where there are several dealers. Meanwhile, I got scared of really being cold and then calmed down, rested a bit and baked peanut butter cookies as much to heat up the cabin as anything. It is 66° inside the cabin and feels really cold, especially on the feet. I'll put on another pair of socks.

Jim just went down off watch. Beam reach, light rain, dark as pitch, fog but barometer up (1015). I am wearing Jim's fleece teddy bear suit. He has added a second fisherman's wool sweater. We got lucky and didn't have to change the sail set today. May the calm winds and calm seas continue.

August 5, 2000: Saturday, Day 27: *Range: 517 NM:* 0247: My morning watch, cold inside (63°) with no heat. Outside, SW 12 K, sailing with three flying, fog, and wet from fog, but a blessing. No high winds, fairly calm seas. Weather fax shows a low dogging us, and a tropical depression about 350 miles south, heading NNW. Both are worrisome to look at on the chart. Both could either hit us or dissipate within the next six hours. We call the faxes "Terror Fax."

We are both starting to smell, but it is too cold to get undressed and shower especially now

Cold - Before Jim fixed the heater

without a cabin heater. Since we haven't had the engine on at all in a few days, we have no hot water for an interior shower. Even though we could heat water to fill the sun shower, it is too awkward to use inside and the cockpit is out of the question due to wind, rain, and cold. So, we will have to stink.

1940: *I just suddenly realized that we are only 60 nm from the nearest Aleutian Island, Kanaga! We are 435 nm from Dutch Harbor, but if we wanted to harbor-hop through the Aleutians, we could! Hard to believe, and it gave me a shock to plot our position on a small-scale chart. But we will not stop. We are anxious for inhabited land, short on fresh food, and having a broken heater makes life aboard very uncomfortable. Also, the low-pressure system is still dogging us, and we don't want to get stuck in an outback anchorage in bad winds. So, we are sailing slowly tonight, tacking off course to keep on going.*

Fresh food remaining after 27 days: two apples, two eggs, three onions, one tomato. Used the last of the cabbage, carrots, and potatoes tonight. Plenty of other stuff like cheese, but that's it on veggies.

August 6, 2000: Sunday, Day 28: 1830: *Haven't had much energy for anything today. Really in a blue funk but kept my spirits up as best I could for Jim. Did only 89 nm yesterday, bucking a NE headwind and tacking. Finally motored some just to make headway. I put on extra clothes to stay warm, adding one more wool shirt and one more pair of wool socks. The problems are peeing and getting on my boots. I have to take off clothes for both. A long process, so I have to plan early for both events.*

Sent an "Airmail" e-mail via ham radio to Mary (my sister) and Dennis (Jim's brother). No messages for us. Barometer up to 1020, temperature around 63°. Hot soup helped keep us warm. 350 nm to Dutch Harbor. These last few miles seem so slow, but when I look at our chart of the Pacific and see how far we have come, I'm amazed. The passage has become a way of life.

I'm imagining land and trying to picture Dutch Harbor from looking at the sketch chart. I got out Encarta and another CD atlas and tried to find the population. One map said 250 people. I know that is not right but have no other information. There are two supermarkets, an airport, a big crab-fishing fleet, and a ferry service to the peninsula.

We are both really stinky. It's been six days since we had a shower. Still too cold even to use the cockpit. If the sun comes out tomorrow, we'll see. At least we might have hot water for indoors if we run the engine. First, we have to add more diesel to the fuel tank from the deck jerry cans.

August 7, 2000; Monday, Day 29: Monday: 1130: <u>*A red letter day! Jim fixed the heater!*</u> *He persevered and opened one of the "sealed" parts. He found a melted insulator which he took off, cleaned the contacts, put back and—working!*

We'll replace that "box" when we get to Dutch Harbor. Meanwhile, I feel human again instead of like a polar bear.

I defrosted the freezer and cleaned the refrigerator. In the process I found two beers which Jim drank in celebration of the above. Took showers earlier by heating water on stove, put the water into the sun shower, and tied it to the towel rack in the head. By awkwardly crouching down in the head, we were just able to wash and spray water on ourselves, contained by the usual use of the shower curtain. This was before *the heater was fixed, so we huddled by the lit oven to keep warm while drying off.*

Lyn grinning because we sighted land

Put 20 gallons of diesel from the deck into the main tank. That leaves 10 on the deck.

Sailing slowly at not quite three knots. Even with diesel in the tank, we must save it for battery charging. So little wind we creep along. At least we are moving in the right direction, and we are warm!

August 8, 2000: Day 30: 0100: *My nerves are wearing thin. We have just enough wind and swell to sail at three knots with a* lot *of mainsail bang. Completely nerve-wracking. I didn't sleep at all during my off watch. One half of an onion left; otherwise, no more fresh food.*

1900: *Busy again today: retyped and printed "To Do" lists. Lots of work to do on Sanctuary before we leave Dutch Harbor. Calculating and refiguring how much diesel remains. Took long watches so Jim could rest. He has a cold or sniffles or something. Went over food lockers, counted and consolidated food. Retyped and printed food list. Learned how to use "Excel" better to print out "To Do." Cleaned the "V" berth, the "catch all" spot.*

After recalculating our diesel, we decided to motor awhile. Now we are sailing. Desperately need a haircut—Jim says I look like a silver-backed gorilla. What a thing to say. Gray and shades of gray. Passed Amukta Island, passing Yunaska now, and heading for Samalga Pass just south of the "Islands of the Four Moun-

tains." Umnak Island will be to our starboard.

As we neared the end of our North Pacific crossing, *Sanctuary* slipped into Samalga Pass with the Islands of the Four Mountains to port and Umnak Island to starboard. The islands, totally obscured in fog, were visible only on our radar screen. As we nosed into the Bering Sea, heading east toward our landfall destination of Dutch Harbor (a fishing port tucked in on the north side of the island of Unalaska) the fog lifted, exposing something we had not seen for thirty days—land! I shouted, "There's Umnak Island, and there's snow on the mountains!" The last two days of our passage proved fantastic. After days of bleak fog, the sun shone blindingly, brilliantly. Light winds blew perfectly for a slow broad reach, and Umnak Island slid quietly past on our starboard as if it were moving and *Sanctuary* was still. Huge volcanic peaks of black basalt rose from startlingly green tundra punctuated by waterfalls that stood out like bright, undulating ribbons. The orange beaks and black- and-white coloring of flocks of puffins added an artistic counterpoint to the giant scenery. We sat in the cockpit scanning the island with binoculars. It was breathtaking, especially after a month of seeing only ocean and sky.

Dutch Harbor, our destination, drew slowly closer—only 100 nautical miles to go. I was on watch, Jim asleep below, when two fishing trawlers appeared on the horizon. Our VHF radio began to crackle, and I heard a call: "Sailing vessel, sailing vessel, this is the *Arctic Dawn*. Who are you? Where did you come from, and where are you going? How come you are out here in the Bering Sea?" Jim woke up as the trawlers drew closer, circling us. The captain of the *Aleutian I* chimed in, calling and repeating the questions.

We replied, saying we had sailed 30 days from Japan and were headed for landfall in Dutch Harbor. With that the crews of 10 hearty seamen on each boat came "All Hands on Deck" to see the spectacle of *Sanctuary*. They cheered, "Welcome to Alaska!" One fellow yelled several times, "You're crazy!"

Called crazy by Alaskan fishermen? The fishermen might really have called us fools had they known we'd left San Francisco and sailed around the world, dealing all the while with Jim's Parkinson's disease and all its manifestations.

Safe in Dutch Harbor's small-boat harbor, we sidled up to another visiting sail boat and side-tied to her. The harbor was crowded, filled with

Alaskan fishing vessels under 50 feet in length, and we tucked *Sanctuary* in tight. As soon as we tied up, I climbed over our neighboring boat, ran down the dock and up the ramp, knelt, and kissed the ground screaming, "Ya Hoo! We made it—we're back in America!" Fishermen standing around the dock chuckled, asking Jim, "Why is she doing that?"

We were home, back in the United States of America! We expected to sail the 2,900 miles from Shingu to Dutch Harbor in about 25 days—it took 32 instead. Five gales blew, including one which kept us hove to for 72 long hours. Sailing slowly, day after lonely day, engulfed in fog, and often pelted with cold rain, we persevered, refused to surrender to Parkinson's disease, and were safely home at long last. It was great to be back in America—even though Alaska felt like a country of its own.

Tying the Knot

September 2000—June 2001

> "Everything good come from Amerika. Now and Forever"
> —Logo on a tee shirt sold in Thailand, 2000

As we sat in Dutch Harbor, winds blew—winds so strong they picked up gravel from the parking lot and pelted the decks of *Sanctuary* and other boats in the harbor. Our lines creaked and our fenders flattened almost to bursting as *Sanctuary* lurched like a wild stallion on her mooring lines. Glad enough to be in port and not at sea in the ferocious winds, we hunkered below listening to our lines creak and the winds howl. After eight hours the winds decreased. A few days later the accompanying pea soup fog lifted long enough for a short take-off-and-landing airplane to arrive, bringing with it more than a month's worth of our mail and Jim's medications.

Russian Orthodox church, Unalaska Island, Alaska

With the wind calmed and our packages aboard, we untied our dock lines and left Dutch Harbor, making our way to Paul Island, an outer island off the Alaska Peninsula. After a calm and starry night at anchor in Kupreanof Harbor, we woke to a beautiful morning with a clear, crisp sky. A mere whisper of air ruffled the water. The weather forecast called for less than 25 knots of wind for the next 24 hours, so we plotted a course to a sheltering harbor 50 nautical miles away anticipating a perfect day's sail at a speed of about five knots.

We raised anchor, I tied it into its chock, and we headed *Sanctuary* cheerfully, and unknowingly, toward the worst weather we would experience in 10 years of ocean voyaging.

That afternoon, as we sailed slowly toward our goal, the fine sunny weather and light winds changed for the worse. In spite of the forecast, a fast-dropping barometer and a building ocean swell revealed the truth—a blow was on the way. The winds picked up sharply and the sky and sea turned gray as the water began to churn. We shortened our sails as gale-force winds overtook us.

After adjusting the sails, I went below to check the chart, hoping to find a safe anchorage closer than the one we had planned to make. On the chart, Necessity Cove looked like a perfect spot to sit out the gale. A note in small print said "williwaws," but I didn't know what those were. Jim vaguely remembered fishermen in Dutch Harbor warning us to avoid bays and coves if williwaws were noted, so I pulled out the U.S. Sailing Directions for Alaska to look up the term. The directions stated:

> "These dangerous winds occur mainly along the Aleutian chain and Gulf of Alaska shores and are influenced by local topography. They are most frequent in winter and are usually the result of air damming up on the windward slopes of mountains. This air spills over in a strong gust on the lee side. That lasts as long as the dammed-up cold air lasts, which frequently is only a matter of minutes. However, such winds are violent, often reaching hurricane force, and their onset is sudden, often interrupting periods of near-calm conditions. Some locations sheltered from the normal winds of the area may be extremely vulnerable to williwaws."

I read farther and found another comment on the directions for Necessity Cove: "Although subject to strong williwaws, the cove affords good anchorage with winds from SW through W to N." We discussed our choices: stay out in worsening weather or risk a williwaw? We choose Necessity and nosed into the cove. It was calm and pristine. We breathed sighs of relief as we anchored *Sanctuary* in the flat waters of the small bay. I scanned the shore with binoculars. Waterfalls cascaded down the sides of Ship Mountain, its peak at 2,450 feet! I spotted wild berries lining the base of the mountain—maybe we'd go pick some. However, as the sunlight faded and the evening's weather forecast on the radio brought warnings for "gale force winds, and increasing" we shelved the idea of a shore excursion and settled down in the main salon for a quiet evening in our newly-discovered, well-protected cove.

Without warning, a very strong shaft of wind blasted straight down upon *Sanctuary*, knocked her over on her ear, and jerked her up sharply on the anchor chain. We were both thrown off the settees and tumbled to the floor shocked and scared. One warning shot was enough. We shouted to each other, "That was a williwaw; let's get out of here!" Picking ourselves up, we flung on our foul-weather gear and hurried up on deck. We upped anchor as quickly as we could and furiously exited the cove. An infamous williwaw had blown us over with a gust we estimated at upward of 50 knots. Such winds could sink *Sanctuary* or dash her to bits on the beach. Not wanting to experience another flattening, or worse, we aimed for the next safe harbor—Chignik Lagoon.

As we labored in the pitch dark toward Chignik, the barometer continued to drop. The falling numbers and a weather fax we received indicated that we were smack-dab on the leading edge of a low-pressure system with its full force heading straight for us. The system hadn't even been on the weather chart 24 hours earlier. It had materialized out of nowhere, and we were trapped in its claws.

Our wind indicator hovered at 50 knots. Its arrow jerked as gusts of 55 knots blasted us, screaming through our rigging. Confused and breaking 26-foot seas rolled and tossed *Sanctuary* as we tried to make Chignik, still 15 miles away to windward. Rocks and dangerous shoals surrounded us, and their proximity prevented short tacking. We turned on the engine to give us a boost but were losing the battle as *Sanctuary* made way only one-half to one knot per hour. At that rate Chignik lay 16 to 30 hours away—dangerous hours near treacherous shores in a steadily worsening storm. We remembered an old sailor's warning: "When in doubt—stay out." We gave up Chignik on and turned tail, heading *Sanctuary* south-east, away from the rocky shores, and out toward the safety of open water.

The winds and seas increased dramatically. *Sanctuary* ran before 30-foot walls of breaking seas and undulating ocean swells powered by steady 60 or more knots of wind. A violent Force 10 storm now held us in its clutches. As soon as we were well out to sea, we "hove to" positioning *Sanctuary* by using her reefed main to ride up and over the torrents of green water that crashed around us.

Exhausted by the night's battle, we slumped into the cockpit, watching *Sanctuary* to see that she hove to properly. Satisfied with the set of our sails, we went below and fell asleep on the cabin sole.

At first light Jim went on deck to check our triple-reefed mainsail and noticed daylight coming through a seam. The wind had increased so much that the sail was blowing apart. The tops of the waves sheeted off in such high volume that the rising sunlight shining through them created rainbows. Jim opened the companionway and yelled, "It's blowing rainbows out here—and the mainsail is struggling." I got up, climbed wearily into the cockpit, and shuddered as I saw the size of the waves and the valleys between the swells. *Sanctuary* climbed up and over mountainous walls of water, then plunged down and through walls of breaking foam. We needed to lower the struggling sail and set the parachute sea anchor.

As Jim was not safe out of the cockpit because of his imbalance, I was again in charge of the foredeck work. I struggled back into my foul-weather gear and boots, clipped on my safety harness, and dragged the sea anchor out of its locker. The winds were too strong for me to stand up, so I crawled out on deck to lead the sea anchor rode through a hawse hole on the bow. With fingers numb from the cold wind and salt spray, I slowly led the rode, talked my tired brain through the proper free and clear leads, and inched my way on my knees back to the cockpit with the swivel attachment for Jim to snug onto the sea anchor itself.

After throwing the parachute into the water and paying out approximately one wavelength of rode, I crawled forward again to add chafe protection to the line where it went through the hawse pipe. I lay on the bow, hanging on with white knuckles, blinded by the sheets of stinging water and with the wind screaming and deafening. Each time a wave rolled under us, the load on *Sanctuary* and the parachute sea anchor line temporarily slacked. I used the short slack time to adjust a three-foot length of old fire hose fashioned as chafe protection. Once I tied it into proper position around the line, I was going back to the cockpit and we could, relatively speaking, relax.

The parachute was our last line of defense in the storm. It would hold us about 45 degrees off the wave train and create a safety slick just as heaving to had done. I struggled with the gear at the hawse hole when the line suddenly whipped by me racing out of control and almost snagging my stiff, cold fingers. What was going on? Why had Jim let the line fly free? I realized something was dreadfully wrong, but I couldn't see Jim, couldn't even see the stern, blinded as I was by stinging sheets of water. I clawed and fought my way back to the cockpit, my heart pounding from the scare and exertion, yelling, "What are you doing?"

I stopped short when I got to the stern and saw Jim and the cockpit both spattered with blood. Jim was deathly pale, his fingers were bleeding, and his jacket had a dark black mark around the arm. I couldn't tell what had happened, but with the exception of his bloody fingers, he seemed to be in one piece.

He answered me slowly, "I thought one wrap of the parachute rode wasn't enough, so I tried to add another wrap on the winch. I uncleated the line to add a wrap, and *Sanctuary* lurched, and the parachute filled up with water and snapped up the line. Oh, Lord, that line pulled my right hand onto the drum before I knew it, trapping my hand between the line and the winch. My fingers burst open with blood from the pressure. All of *Sanctuary*'s 12 tons were on that line. Then she lurched again and threw me hard onto the drum, so my chest is all banged up too! I snatched my hand out when I could, but the line kept flying by—I couldn't stop it, I just couldn't stop it. I was frozen. *Sanctuary* rolled again and the whizzing line caught my left arm by the jacket sleeve. It pulled my left elbow to the winch, banging me again. It all happened so fast. My shoulder got pulled out of the socket."

"Oh, Lord," I cried, "Jim are you okay? You look okay except for the blood."

"Yeah, I think so. The line burned through my jacket sleeve, but I don't think it burned my arm. When the boat rolled a third time, the line slacked a bit and got tangled on that other winch, which stopped it long enough for me to snatch my left arm out. I had to shove my shoulder back into the socket. I think—I, I—it feels numb, but I think it's back okay." Jim hesitated and quit talking. I touched him asking, "What should I do—what can I do?" He whispered hoarsely, "I'm okay now. We can bandage my fingers and check my arm later."

Jim played down the incident for my sake, but as his explanation sunk in and I realized what had really happened, I burst into tears of upset, exhaustion, and relief. The line tangling on the second winch had saved him. Otherwise, the speeding rode would have burned through his jacket sleeve, wound his arm repetitively around the winch with unstoppable force, and twisted it off at the shoulder. He had narrowly missed losing his right hand—or his left arm.

The storm raged on, but at least we were relatively safe and mostly undamaged. The next morning, after the storm force winds shifted and calmed to a 35-knot gale, I struggled alone to haul the sea anchor back on board. Jim could barely move his left arm. (For the next five or six days, Jim was unable to use his left arm, and the fingers of his right hand were sore. It took about two weeks to heal.) After a mighty battle, I finally wrestled the water-soaked parachute onto the foredeck, packed it, and then stowed it in the sail locker. I hoisted the storm staysail, and we started running downwind to Lazy Bay, a well-protected anchorage on the southwestern side of Kodiak Island, where we anchored in calm bay waters. Both of us rested for twenty-four hours. The wind still howled in the rigging, but Lazy Bay lived up to its name.

Once rested, we got out on deck to hand stitch and repair the wind-torn seam in our mainsail. A fellow from a small cannery ashore came out in a skiff to see if we were alright. He said, "I heard on the radio that a sailing vessel was dismasted in the storm." Looking up at our complete, strong, one-piece mast, he continued, "I can see it's not you; do you know who it was?" We did not. (Four weeks later, while in the southeast coastal port of Yakutat, in the Gulf of Alaska, we learned the answer as we met and chatted with the five sailors aboard *Siberia*, a Russian sailing vessel. *Siberia* had been rolled 360° and lost both her masts in the same storm we had survived. After comparing logs, we discovered that *Siberia* and her crew had been rescued by the Alaskan Coast Guard just forty miles from where *Sanctuary* safely hove to.

Meanwhile, the storm blew past Lazy Bay, and we continued around the south side of Kodiak Island, through a mountainous fiord-like pass, and into St. Paul's Harbor. Together in a private bathroom at St. Paul's, we stripped off our layers of foul-weather gear and thermal underwear for a nice, long, hot shower. I cried again when I saw Jim's black and blue arm and chest for the first time. Jim hugged me and said, "Don't cry—I'm healing. We both survived, and we've sailed around the entire world! The ocean just slapped us to remind us how far we've come."

We'd come far, yes, yet we weren't quite done. We sat for a while licking our wounds in Saint Paul's Harbor, Kodiak Island. Even though *Sanctuary* had weathered the storm, she needed some tender, loving care, too. The autopilot was off by 30°, the mainsail had jumped its track, several battens needed more repairs than we could provide by hand, the engine mounts were loose, the steering cable needed replacing—the list went on for three pages.

In spite of the pending repairs, we felt antsy to keep moving south before winter winds truly set in. The storm had made us leery of leaving port without an excellent three-day forecast. Unlike a powerboat with an enclosed cabin for steering, *Sanctuary*'s wheel was exposed, and our cockpit dodger afforded little to no protection for us from high winds and bitter cold. Even though I wore full foul-weather gear, going out on deck to manage the sails was excruciating with high, cold winds, and the spray dousing from the crashing, breaking, cold, salt water numbed my hands and body. If either of us went overboard in Alaska's almost-freezing waters, we'd drown in minutes from hypothermia if nothing else. Just the thought gave me chills.

Jim couldn't help on deck at all anymore, and the weather was wearing my energy down fast. So we repeated our newly reinforced mantra, "Slow down, slow down, just slow down." Approaching our repair projects gingerly, we did nothing at all the first day except watch *The Spy Who Shagged Me* on DVD.

Two halibut fishermen we met in Dutch Harbor, Dave and his partner, another Dave, invited us over to Dave number one's house in Kodiak for a fish fry. A land visit with them and their families was such a pleasure, and the two Daves gave us even more tips and advice about Alaskan weather and anchorages.

We'd also made friends with Axel, an Alaska crab fisherman, and his girlfriend, Marlaine (also a fisherman). They lived together on their newly acquired sailboat, *Spirit,* and like us, were heading for a warmer winter berth. Axel and Marlaine contributed to our growing store of Alaskan information, and the four of us decided to stay in radio contact as both boats made their way south. Having friends on the water was good. We'd felt so absolutely alone while crossing the Pacific.

One weather system led to another, and *Sanctuary* and *Spirit* ended up in Seward at the same time, tied to the public docks, waiting out yet another blow. While we waited for a weather change, we hiked around Seward, then rented a car and drove over to Homer to visit some other friends, Bill and Peggy, a couple we'd met while vacationing in Mexico 17 years earlier. The interior of Alaska was in full autumnal glory, with brilliant yellow aspen and birch and rich green spruce set along the slopes of the two- to three- thousand-foot mountains with their snowcapped peaks barely visible in the clouds. Parked trucks lined the shoulders of the road that wound lazily along the azure Kenai River and assorted lakes and streams. The fishermen who owned the trucks lined the banks of the rushing streams, casting their rods, hoping to hook steelhead salmon.

September 29, 2000, Friday: 1100: After a day at the Seward Yacht Club gathering weather information off the NOAA internet site, we decided to head out to cross the Gulf of Alaska. We'd follow the tail of a low with a forecast high on the way. It was cold and clear, with winds steady at 15 knots when we untied the dock lines and headed down Resurrection Sound bound for Elfin Cove about three days' sail to the southeast.

On the morning of the 30th, we were well out into the Gulf of Alaska when Jim woke me from my off watch at 2:00 a.m. yelling, "Lyn, quick, you've got to see this!"

I awoke in a panic and jumped up into the cockpit in just my long johns not knowing what to expect. I thought I was hallucinating as I saw why Jim had called out—an Aurora Borealis! The sky pulsed, flashed, and danced with white, dazzling lights. The pulsing white morphed to subtle pinks, then flash-danced blues and yellows. It was a light symphony played against the dark of the infinite sky. I stayed in the cockpit, mesmerized, through my off watch.

The 4:00 a.m. weather report brought forecasts of gales. This time we were prepared. Before we left Seward, I had plotted not one, not two, but three routes to alternate anchorages. I fished one of the pre-plotted routes out of the chart table, and we easily altered course to Yakutat, the nearest one. By Sunday afternoon, October 1, 2000, the winds and seas had increased and were on the nose. At this point we didn't care about sailing; we simply wanted a safe port before a storm. We turned on the motor and bashed onward toward Yakutat. Hours later we slid into beautiful, large Yakutat Bay, fringed by tall glacier-faced mountains on one side and low, spruce-covered islands on the other. As we tucked *Sanctuary* into a slip in Shipyard Cove, it began sleeting. We breathed a sigh of relief to be safe in port.

The next day we walked into town, passing a few mobile homes surrounded by spruce forests with views of the glaciers in the distance. After eating a chiliburger for lunch at "Rets" ("Open All Winter"); we walked down the road to the post office and mailed post cards with aerial views of Yakutat; visited Monti's General Store across the road; walked a bit further to Tru-Value Hardware; passed a small park that surrounded an old train; looped back to Sitka Seafood; passed the home of the small Monti Bay Times; and did a bit of shopping at Mallott's General Store, where we bought four bags of food. We'd just walked about most of tiny (population 800, accessible only by air and sea) Yakutat by then, so we closed the loop back onboard *Sanctuary*, where we listened to the storm warnings on the radio—again. The rain started, the wind roared outside, but tucked into the snug harbor we could barely feel its effects.

The next day Jim hooked up our electricity; we'd have hot water for showers and not have to worry about charging the batteries. Settling down that evening to watch a movie on DVD, I felt cozy and safe for the first time in weeks. I hunkered down inside the boat and didn't go any-

Lyn & stuffed bear
Yakutat

where or do anything for two days. My energy was really depleted, and as I finally relaxed, I realized I had been hanging on by my teeth for far too long. The rest did me good, and on Friday Axel and Marlaine (who had come into Yakutat too) told us about a comedy act at the local bar, so the four of us went to the show.

We rigged our boat awning to keep the snow and rain out of the cockpit and snuggled down again as storm after storm surged across the Gulf of Alaska. Jim gave me a nice, short haircut, and I felt 100% better.

We both showered onboard with hot water, an easy luxury with *Sanctuary* hooked to shore power and shore water. The next day we walked back into town before the sleet started. We knew the route and traded books at Monti's General store, went to the bank, the hardware store, the grocery store, and the liquor store, all of which set us up for more days of bad weather. Yakutat was beginning to feel suspiciously like home.

Tuesday, October 10, 2000: *"Gales and storms forecast until at least Friday."* I wrote our quarterly newsletter which we mailed to about 60 people, then settled in with a book. Day after day slid by in the fog, sleet, and rain. Axel borrowed a car from the Harbor Master, and we drove around the peninsula, catching sight of a brown bear over by the town dump. About 30 miles farther along, we got out at Dangerous River, which connects to Lake Henrietta facing the Yakutat Glacier. We stood on a specially-built bridge with pointed steel girders designed to break up ice and watched bergy bits of glacier ice careening in the waters that rushed toward the sea.

Back in the car, we drove out to Yakutat Lodge with its view of the airport runway. I pulled on the moose-antler door handle to enter and was greeted by a stuffed brown bear standing on his hind legs. An old plane prop lay in one corner, and a chain saw stuck in a log sat on the other side next to a big piece of whale vertebrae used as a table holding outdated *Field and Stream* magazines. Some models of bush planes swung lazily from the ceiling collecting dust. In the dining room/bar, we sipped weak drinks, gazing idly out at the empty runway while dogs roamed underfoot, sniffing our crotches and begging for some of our French fries.

Low after low continued to blast through the Gulf of Alaska bringing high winds, high seas, rain, and sleet. I ordered a dehumidifier from Anchorage, but it would take days to arrive and, in the meantime, our lockers dripped two to three cups of condensation water a day. I removed all the books I could and shipped them to Jim's mother for storage in her garage. If we left them on the boat, they'd soon turn to mush in the constantly sweating lockers.

Everyone knew we hoped to sail farther south for the winter, and we quit laughing when the locals started asking, "Have you gotten a Post Office box yet?" We needed 36 hours of good weather to make it to the next safe port, and the forecast never varied: "SE Gale-force winds, 30 knots and higher, storm warnings for Cape Dixon, rain, seas 12 feet and higher."

Our dehumidifier arrived, so we plugged it in, tucking it under the main salon table and emptying its container at least once a day. If we stayed put, Jim would rig up a way for it to drain directly into the bilge. I wrote two articles for *Sail Magazine*, and we visited with some local shrimp fishermen and the Harbor Master and his wife.

On October 28th, we thought we'd found a break in the weather and left at 6:30 a.m. Distance to Elfin Cove, 142 nm, about 30 hours away if we averaged five knots. By noon, with a flood current against us, we'd only made good about 20 miles at a miserable average speed of just over three knots. Going that slowly was not acceptable, especially since the forecast shifted once again to gale-force winds and high seas. Tucking our tail between our legs, we turned back to Yakutat and immediately picked up speed to seven knots (thanks to the current) and slunk back into our previous berth. Axel and Marlaine (who'd sensibly stayed put) helped us retie the dock lines and politely said, "Oh well, prudent seamanship."

By November 1st we gave up on the idea of sailing farther south until spring and got a Post Office box. What a relief! I could finally quit worrying about the weather. We replaced our worn-out Espar heater in anticipation of an exciting, but cold, experience—winter in Yakutat, Alaska onboard *Sanctuary*. We rigged up our cockpit awning again, filled our propane tanks, and altered the dehumidifier so it drained directly into the bilge. A phone hookup was ordered, and the line snaked from the end of the road down the slippery docks to our boat. We hadn't used our telephone since winter in Turkey, so I dug it out of our deepest locker and then rigged up a computer cable, and we were "connected." Jim and Axel beefed up our electrical shore power to run the computer, heater, dehumidifier, TV, lights, and everything else all at once without worry.

One of the first calls we received on the phone was from Lin Pardey. What a surprise to hear her voice from halfway around the world, and a double surprise to hear the reason for her call. Jim and I had been awarded the Ocean Cruising Club Award of Merit (2000) for an "Outstanding Voyage." Technically, we were still about 1200 nm away from crossing our outbound path. Even so, the club considered our circumnavigation complete in terms of ocean passages.

We'd planned to formally complete our circumnavigation in the spring; now we felt simply bound to. After Lin hung up, we mulled over the conversation, and suddenly our achievement sank in. The goal Jim and I had created 26 years earlier—to sail around the world together aboard our own boat—was almost complete. We'd been voyaging for 10 years, sailing to 39 countries, and logging over 35,000 nautical miles with only about 1200 nautical miles left before reaching British Columbia to cross our outgoing track and officially tie the knot on our "east-about" circle. A circumnavigation of the world!

Most circumnavigators sail west to east ("west about") a predominantly downwind route. We sailed around the world from east to west which meant that the majority of our sailing had been the hard way, sailed to weather, or what some referred to as the "wrong way," or the "uphill route." We laughed wryly when Larry Pardey, in praise of sailing the route we'd chosen, said, "You did do it the hard way—after all, even a box can sail downwind." Plus, we managed the entire voyage with Parkinson's disease as an unwelcome, but constantly challenging, companion. We felt both humbled and acknowledged.

Axel and Marlaine, Sparky and Jody (the Harbormaster and his wife), and Jim and I planned a big potluck Thanksgiving dinner together. Sparky and Jody lived aboard their powerboat but during November would housesit for two weeks, so all six of us could use the house's "regular" kitchen, big table, and dishes for our meal. Together we cooked a traditional American feast with two turkeys, two types of stuffing and dressing, a ham, potatoes, corn, cranberry sauce, beans, bread, salad, and three pies. We lounged around cooking, visiting, and eating, then we watched two movies and afterward took a walk in the snow with Domino (Marlaine's dog) and Blackie (Sparky's dog). Since all three couples usually lived full time on board boats, we came back from our walk and took turns washing clothes and taking showers in the housesitting house. Ah, such things to do in a house, luxurious treats for people living aboard small boats. More friends arrived later in the evening, and as the lovely day stretched to an end, it began to snow again. We were truly thankful for good company, good food, a safe harbor, a lovely day—and nobody watched football!

The snow piled up, the temperatures dropped, and as winter settled into Yakutat, so did we. Shoveling snow off *Sanctuary*'s deck the first time was a fun novelty and then became a daily necessity. It was tempting to just hibernate below decks, but we set up a routine of walking to town and back each day just to give ourselves some exercise as much as anything. Getting dressed for the excursion took almost an hour since PD inhibited Jim's ability to put his arms through sleeves, pull on sweaters, zip zippers, and button buttons. As usual, Jim persevered and kept moving in spite of his disabilities.

There were very few boat projects we could do in the dead of winter, so I logged onto the internet and began searching for places we might like to live. We planned to complete our circumnavigation in the spring of 2001, sell *Sanctuary* as soon as possible, and move back ashore. Where would we live? We didn't know. Meanwhile, we flew to California on December 15th, visiting Jim's family and some of our long-time friends. After a quiet New Year's at home with Jim's mother and stepfather, we flew on to Texas to visit Jim's neurologist, my mother, sister, and other family in Texas.

Lyn shoveling snow off Sanctuary's deck

Leaving our families had been one of the difficult parts of deciding to sail around the world. My mother was 80 years old, Jim's 70 when we left. When we were ashore we kept in touch with both of them frequently. During passages we used ham radio or SSB radio or "WinLink" e-mail. No matter the contacts, during most of our voyage we were far away and missed many events in the ebbing years of their lives. We flew home about every 18 months, and each time we hugged them goodbye, we knew it could be the last for either of us or for either of them. Parting was never easy and sometimes agonizing.

As we neared the end of our journey, all the old questions resurfaced: Why had we sailed around the world? Jim's first neurologist had warned, "Don't do this foolish thing." Why had we gone anyway? We'd left behind elderly mothers, Jim's son, other family members, many friends, jobs, and a beautiful home—everything. What compelled us? For we *were* compelled. The simple answer: because the world was there, and we wanted to see it. More than that we were drawn onward by the challenge itself—an irresistible, driving desire to face fear and get through it, go beyond it, and stretch ourselves.

One day in 1994, after we'd crossed the Gulf of Mexico and sailed into Galveston, one of my nieces drove across Houston to our berth to visit us aboard *Sanctuary*. After arriving she said, "I really don't like driving on roads I've never been on before." Her comment pulled me up short. I realized that the life Jim and I had chosen was exactly the opposite; we almost always traveled on roads we'd never been on before. We rarely, if ever, returned to the port we'd just left, so every port was new. Almost every day we sailed a new route or went a new direction. Each time we raised the hook, we lowered it in a new spot on the planet. By its nature our journey required us to see each day anew.

Living aboard and the process of sailing required attention. Attention as in paying attention to *now*. What is the weather doing now? Where are we now? What are the winds doing now? What is on the horizon now? Be here in the moment, be here now.

Even anchored, or theoretically safe at a dock in port, we slept with part of our consciousness alert to *now*—to a shift in the wind, a change in the tide, a movement of light, a noise, or anything unusual. We were attuned and woke in a flash at even subtle changes in our environment. It was necessary to be attuned, our lives depended on it. A leaky hose connection in a house might be an irritant; a leaky hose connection on a boat could mean drowning. Sailing around the world kept us, by its nature, fully alive in a way we hadn't been before. That aliveness fed our dream and kept us going, even as the sensible, careful, reasonable, or fearful voices in our heads kept whispering, "Quit, give up, go home."

We returned to Yakutat and got Chica back from Axel and Marlaine (who had cared for her while we were gone and shoveled the snow off *Sanctuary*). Our ship-to-shore telephone line had cracked in the freezing weather, so Axel helped Jim rig a new one, a daunting chore on the slippery, ice-covered docks. Jim was walking better thanks to a new treatment and meds he'd received from his neurologist, and he was able to dress himself again as well. Winter whizzed by on a fast sled. We watched the Yakutat Eagles play basketball and enjoyed a lot of dinners ashore with friends we had made since October. Night after winter night, we again lay listening to the winds.

February 27, 2001: *High wind warnings, hurricane force winds, gusting to 70 knots, when walking ashore watch for flying debris.* We sat up all night, the winds howling and the dock lines creaking in protest. The next day dawned bright and clear, and Jim went crab fishing while I stayed aboard and worked on setting up a website for my newly revived bead jewelry business.

March 17, 2001: *Our 24th wedding anniversary. We still love each other, a miracle after all we have gone through and so many years aboard. We even held hands on the way home from town today.*

March 26, 2001: *I've lost track of the days, which alternate between sunny, clear, and cold to rainy, wet, snowy, cold and miserable. Jim hanging around doing a bit of crab fishing and a bit of boat repair. My website is still a work in progress. We listened to Raven Radio, the NPR (National Public Radio) station from Sitka. I've ordered spare boat parts, so when the weather does clear we can get to our projects.*

April 11, 2001: *Temperature up to 52°! We had sun for three days in a row and washed the decks and took photos of Sanctuary in preparation for listing her for sale. I worked on a magazine article and bought some daffodils at the grocery store. At least we know that spring exists somewhere! I made some more jewelry, and in the afternoon, we put the jib and staysail back on their halyards. Afterward, I cleaned the cockpit lockers, and we started talking about leaving Yakutat. The snow is melting, but there are still piles of it in the shade of the tall evergreens. The robins are singing, and the ravens are building nests.*

Tuesday, May 1, 2001: *We took Jody and Sparky to the airport. They are flying down to Missouri for their vacation, so we probably won't see them again unless we come back to Yakutat someday. Sad. They have been so good to us while we have been here. Afterward, we went to the NOAA office and looked at charts of the gulf and talked to Kimberly (the agent on duty) about lows and the possibility of sailing on Thursday.*

We filled our water and diesel tanks, bought groceries, and in general begin mentally preparing to leave Yakutat. Jim and Marilyn Marco were flying up from California to Sitka to sail a leg with us (very fitting since Jim M. taught us to sail and did the first leg with us in 1991). We didn't want to be late for our date with them (their vacation time) so, as usual for me, I began worrying about getting out of port.

Friday, May 4, 2001: *Gales, ice, sleet, rain, and hail off and on all day. Called NOAA. A high is forecast for Wednesday.*

Wednesday, May 9, 2001: *The temperature dropped, and our dock lines were frozen to the cleats, so I heated some water and poured it over them so we could get underway. The wind, of course, was on the nose, and we only made good three and a half knots—and this was the best weather window we had seen since last October! Chica threw up as soon as we got out of Yakutat Bay, and Jim looked green as well. By 1600 we were back in Yakutat. We gave up. It was miserably cold, raining, wind on the nose, and no hope of respite. We went into town later, and I picked up a copy of the Alaska Bush Shopper. A photo I had taken of the old Russian Orthodox Church in Unalaska was on the cover! I received $100 for my winning contest entry.*

Underway: Thursday, May 10, 2001: 0930: *Set out again to leave Yakutat. It's a beautiful day with full sun and light winds. Making good almost five knots in NW winds, motor sailing for an extra kick to make Sitka in 48 hours! Third time is a charm. Chica is riding on the dodger, no throw-ups.*

Sitka, Alaska: Wednesday, May 16, 2001: *Met Jim and Marilyn at the airport, they'll be aboard for two weeks while we head south through the "Inside Passage." We began a blizzard of shopping, talking, and eating and got underway around 1230, made a few miles, then anchored at Sukuoi Inlet for the night. With rain, and cold and narrow inlets and passes, we mostly motored on, through Serguis Narrows, into Hoonah Sound, onward to Saook Bay, then landing at Warm Springs Bay, Baranof Island where we tied to a small finger pier. The next day we hiked the well-beaten trail to a natural, warm spring on the side of a waterfall. The sun was shining, and it was the first time since October 2000 I hadn't had on a jacket when outside. We peeled off our clothes and soaked in the healing waters.*

Back onboard our ears perked up when we heard a familiar name on the VHF radio, *Jambo III*. That meant Jean, a sailing friend we'd met in Baja back in 1991 at the beginning of our cruise, was nearby. *Jambo III* and *Sanctuary* had parted ways in Costa Rica in 1993. It would be great to see Jean again, so we called her on VHF and planned a reunion in Chapin Harbor about 25 miles away.

The next day we sailed to Chapin Harbor, side-tied *Sanctuary* to *Jambo III*, and while all of us waited for the gale winds to subside, we reminisced for two days with Jean and her friend. A few weeks later we also crossed paths with Larry on board *Ocean Angel* and Al and Sandy on board *Jubilación*, other friends we'd last seen in Mexico. As our circle of the globe drew to a close, and we encountered friends we'd made early on, we acknowledged our accomplishment.

On we moseyed, with Jim and Marilyn still aboard, enjoying several more anchorages and small towns. Totem poles nestled under tall fir trees dotted the landscape. We searched for petroglyphs and at one point, sat on some bergy bits that had washed ashore from a nearby glacier. We also ate crab, halibut, and salmon. We'd paid a dear price for our fishing license and calculated at one point that the privilege of catching our own fish was costing us twice the going per-pound rate charged by the stores! Swift currents and tide changes in the narrow fjords forced us to carefully time our short day hops. I struggled with the calculations, but a new navigational software program helped me out with the complex formulas such that our 22-mile transit of the Wrangell Narrows coincided perfectly with the ebb and then the slack tides as they changed.

Jim Foley & Jim Marco - Alaska

Jim and Marilyn's vacation days flew by, so we quit lollygagging and motored swiftly onward so they wouldn't miss their ferry and subsequent plane flight home. Arriving in Ketchikan early gave us time to play tourist, so we visited museums, shopped for souvenirs, washed clothing, and took showers ashore. After the Marcos departed, we repaired a broken alternator and a leaking sink, then refilled our propane tanks and gave *Sanctuary* a spring cleaning.

The month of June blew into Alaska on the tail of another gale. We finished our repairs, I planned our route, and we took off again a bare 300 nautical miles away from our outbound track at Lund, British Columbia, the mark for the completion of our circumnavigation. We sailed into Prince Rupert and cleared into Canada with all the appropriate officials. Chomping at the bit now, both we and *Sanctuary* acted like horses heading for the barn. We wanted to get home to the USA, and unless the weather absolutely prevented a day's sail, we raised the anchor early each morning. On to Lawson Cove, Otter Shoal, Clothes Bay, and

Shearwater, where we sat out in the cockpit in the sun. Chica got off the boat and rolled on the dock, performing her version of sun worship.

Jim's brother Dennis, and his girlfriend would be sailing the last leg with us, so on we went via Codville Lagoon, Home Bay, and across the Queen Charlotte Strait to Vancouver Island toward Port Hardy to pick them up. As the miles ticked down toward completion, we took a two-day break at Walker Cove. As we sat in the cockpit gazing at the trees on the shore of the landlocked cove and discussing "What will we do next?" we realized how tired we were. We both had earaches, sore throats, and a feeling of general malaise. Perhaps we'd caught bugs due to civilization, or maybe our bodies were telling us something—a bit of sadness and regret as the journey drew to a close? Jim put old rock and roll on the CD player, and as we moped around nursing our colds and reminiscing over all the years and all the miles we'd sailed, the Grateful Dead blasted out, singing *Truckin'*, "Lately it occurs to me, what a long, strange trip it's been. Truckin', I'm a goin' home."

Epilogue: Swallowing the Hook

June 2001—December 2010

"Swallow the anchor: leave the sea and live ashore."
— *A Dictionary of Sailing*: Burgess

We crossed our outbound track in Lund, British Columbia, completing our circumnavigation. We retraced a few of our steps and sailed back to Seattle, Washington, where we sold our beloved *Sanctuary*. As I wrote in our last sailing letter, Newsletter 33, we completed our cruising life, created a new dream, and built a house in tiny Round Top, Texas.

I now make jewelry using glass beads I create by the ancient artistic method of lampworking. Information on my art and jewelry can be found on my web site: www.LynFoley.com.

Jim volunteers for experimental treatments for Parkinson's, and the positive results have allowed him to make jewelry again on a limited basis. He participates in our art shows, as best he can, as he battles the ongoing symptoms of PD. After 20 years, we remain committed to accommodating Parkinson's without surrender.

We are thankful for the assistance and understanding we received from our family and friends before, during, and after our journey.

Do we miss the sailing lifestyle and the boat? We do miss the friends we made and the camaraderie of the sailing community. We don't miss the worry about the weather, the storms at sea, and the constant boat repairs.

We are grateful for the freedom that allowed us to roam and to experience other cultures, other countries. We are grateful to the loving hearts that reached out to us both on sea and ashore. We are grateful to the strangers who, with a touch of their hands or a welcome into their homes or aboard their boats, surpassed politics, policies, and xenophobia to pass on kindness and goodwill. Their kindness allowed us to sail around the world.

We are left with love and fond memories of strangers who became friends. We are grateful that we were able to go anyway.

Glossary of Nautical and Foreign Terms

admeasurer One who admeasures. The person who calculated our boat's volume to determine the fees for the Panama Canal transit

aft Toward, at, or near the stern

aground The state of a vessel, part of which is touching the bottom. Not completely afloat. Held fast on the bottom

anchor watch The continuous vigil maintained when a vessel is anchored in rough weather. Special hands are retained on deck, take bearings, note if the ship drags, etc.

baksheesh A tip or bribe, supposedly to expedite service

banca Traditional Filipino boat, usually a simple dugout canoe, sometimes rigged with sails

bar The silting up of deposit or shallowing formed near the entrance to a harbor or inlet

bare poles A sailing vessel with no sails set is under "bare poles."

barometer A special instrument which measures the pressure of the atmosphere and indicates changes of the weather

battens Long, narrow strips of wood, metal, or plastic fitted into pockets on a sail to keep it taut

beam The breadth of a vessel at her widest part

beam reach Sailing with the wind on the beam

beat To beat to windward is to keep close-hauled on the wind.

before the wind Sailing with the wind aft; running

below "going below" is descending from the upper deck

berth (1) Any place in a harbor allotted for the accommodation of a vessel (2) A sleeping place or a specified cabin or place in a vessel

bilge (1) Rounded part of the hull where the side and bottom plates meet (2) The flattest part of a ship's bottom, internally, used for drainage purposes

bilge boards Removable boards built into our cabin sole that allowed us access to our bilge

binnacle The stand, or case, in which a ship's compass is housed

blow A noticeable increase in the force of the wind

board To get on or put a foot over the side of any vessel. "Boarding a vessel" signifies making an entry by any means, with or without force.

boathook A long stave with a hook affixed to one end used for fending off or holding a boat alongside or recovering anything, etc. (Our boathook had a permanent spot topsides, starboard.)

bollard A large, circular iron, concrete, or wood post fixed strongly in any required position to receive a ship's securing ropes

bone in her teeth The appearance of a boat sailing with exhilarating speed so as to create a prominent bow wave

boom A spar used to extend the foot of a sail

bo'sun's chair (or boatswain's chair) A device used to suspend a person from a rope to perform work aloft. (Ours included a more or less rigid seat.)

bottom The keel of a ship, often applied to that part of a ship below the waterline

broach In stormy seas with the wind aft, a boat may tend to slew around against her helm, thus putting the sails aback and endangering the mast, with the possibility of being turned broadside onto the sea with calamitous results.

cayuco A small boat used in the islands of the San Blas and Panama. Most often it was made from a dugout palm tree.

chain locker A space in the bow (below decks) where the inboard end of the anchor line was secured and the remainder stowed

chain plates Metal fittings secured to the sides of a boat to which the shrouds are set up

chock A wedge. To wedge so as to prevent movement

cleat A wood or metal fitting with two arms or horns to which a rope may be belayed

clew The after lower corner of a fore and aft sail, a metal loop attached to the lower corner of a sail

close-hauled Sailing as close to the wind as possible or within four to six points of it

Clyde Puffer A type of small steamboat which provided a vital supply link around the west coast and Hebrides islands of Scotland

coaming A raised wooden rail around a cockpit in small boats

cockpit The after well in sailboats where the helmsman sits

come about Fill in on a new tack

copra Dried coconut meat yielding coconut oil

cotter pin A split pin or metal fastener with two tines that are bent during installation; used to fasten metal together

course made good The course actually achieved on the chart after making allowances for wind direction and currents

course over the ground The direction of the track that a vessel has actually made, measured clockwise, from north through 360°; the direction the vessel is traveling in, using the compass

courtesy flag Flag of the host country flown in the starboard rigging of the visiting vessel after clearance has been issued. (Port officials have been known to take great offense if a courtesy flag is not flown.)

CQR™ anchor A "plow"-type of anchor whose flukes, when set, bury themselves in the bottom; known for its good holding power

cradle A frame used to support a boat when transporting her or hauling her up on a slipway, or resting her; to support a vessel during construction or work ashore

cruising To sail or travel about, as for pleasure or reconnaissance

cruising kitty A pool of money, allocated especially to support the lifestyle of living onboard a boat

current The horizontal movement of water; "setting" is its direction, "drift" is the rate at which it flows

cutlass bearing A type of stave bearing on the propeller shaft. It is designed to run immersed in water, allowing its use outboard of the stern gland or stuffing box.

dead reckoning A contraction of "deduced reckoning": The estimated position of a ship on a chart by calculations as distinct from plotting an observed position

dhow A lateen-rigged vessel common in the Indian Ocean seaboard. (We saw this type of vessel in the Red Sea and the Gulf of Arabia. We also saw modified dhows with no sails, outfitted with inboard engines.)

dinghy A small, open rowing boat having no conventional design or type, made of wood or molded bonded material, without cabin or ballast. Dinghies vary in length and are used for rowing, sailing, and all utility purposes. (We rowed our roll-up dinghy or used an eight horsepower outboard motor.)

dodger A screen of canvas or other material, fitted up as a shelter or protection. (*Sanctuary's* dodger was made of Sunbrella™ supported by a stainless steel frame. It provided some protection from salt water spray and/or sun.)

dorade A low vent fitted to the cabin top that permits the passage of air in and out of the cabin of a boat while keeping rain, spray, or sea wash out

EPIRB Emergency position-indicating radio beacons signal maritime distress. When manually activated, or automatically activated upon immersion, such beacons send out a distress signal. The signals are monitored worldwide, and the location of the distress is detected by non-geostationary satellites.

fair wind One that enables a boat to be sailed from one place to another without having to tack or gybe

farang General Thai word for Westerner

felucca Type of sailing vessel with a rudder at each end, common in Egypt

flood The flood tide is the rising or incoming tide; high water

forestay A wire rope fitted from the masthead to the bowsprit end supporting the mast

gel coat A material used to provide a high-quality finish on the fiberglass hull, designed to be durable, providing resistance to ultraviolet degradation and hydrolysis

Great Circle Route The shortest possible route between two points on the Earth's surface follows a great circle

gullet A traditional design of a two-masted wooden sailing vessel found all around the eastern Mediterranean. Today, this type of vessel is popular for tourist charters and diesel power is almost universally used, so many are not properly rigged for sailing.

Gulf Stream A warm current from the eastern seaboard of the USA which is deflected diagonally across the Atlantic to Great Britain

halyard Ropes or cables used for hoisting and lowering flags, sails, etc.

hank A metal clip-ring fitting for securing a sail to a halyard

haul out Move a boat from the water to a hard or slipway

hawsehole Large apertures cut in the bows through which cables or lines run

head A ship's latrine

heat exchanger A device to cool the engine using salt water to transfer heat

heave to Stop. Trim the sails so as to keep the vessel almost stationary. Used in the event of emergency or impending danger

Hoe Large, south-facing open space in the city of Plymouth, England

hold A special compartment or interior space used for stowing cargo

hove to Underway but not making way through the water

jib Foremost sail in a sailing vessel, triangular in shape

junk An ancient Chinese-design sailing vessel, still in use today, lateen rigged

kedge off To move a ship by laying out a small auxiliary anchor

knot A nautical measure of speed or nautical mile per hour (In reference to speed, the words "per hour" are not used as they are incorporated into the meaning of the word knot.)1 knot = 1.15 miles per hour

lay day In old usage, days allowed to unship cargo. In cruiser's usage, days at anchor not working on the boat or making any forward progress, true days off

lazarette A small storage compartment at the stern of a boat

lee cloths Canvas panels attached around the stern deck rails to offer protection from the wind and seas

lee shore The shore facing the lee side of a ship, being that onto which the wind would drive her if she were unable to make an offing

lie ahull A controversial method of weathering a storm by downing all sails, battening the hatches, and locking the tiller to leeward. Unlike in heaving to, a sea anchor is not used, allowing the boat to drift freely, completely at the mercy of the storm.

life sling A horseshoe-shaped man-overboard recovery system with a flotation collar and 150 feet of floating retrieval line, mounted on *Sanctuary's* stern rail

line A small rope capable of many specific functions, each with its descriptive prefix, e.g., heaving line, dock line, anchor line, etc.

log To enter or record in the log book all principal events connected with the ship and its working: the official journal of the voyage

main sheet Tackle by which a mainsail is trimmed when sailing

mainsail The large sail hoisted on a main mast

make and mend A half-day without work; not getting anywhere, ostensibly for the purpose of making and mending clothes

mano Spanish: hand

marsa Egyptian: anchorage, bay, or cove

meat hook A fishing line attached to a shock cord and then to the boat, trailed behind a sailboat to catch fish while underway

Med-moor A tricky method of docking in the crowded harbors of the Mediterranean, with the stern to the harbor wall, and the bow anchored, as opposed to the usual method of tying a boat alongside

mola A special blouse made by the Kuna Indians of the San Blas islands using intricate designs sewn in reverse appliqué

monkey fist A knot called a Turk's head formed on the end of a heaving line to aid the aim

mule Special 50-ton locomotives used to guide large ships through the Panama Canal

nautical mile A long distance measurement, equal to 1/60 of a degree on the equator. 1 nautical mile = 1.15 statute miles

norther A strong north wind

Ocean Cruising Club An international club administered from the UK for cruisers. Membership is open to those who have completed a continuous ocean passage of at least 1,000 miles, measured along the rhumb line, in a vessel of under 70 feet. Ocean Cruising Club gives out several annual and special awards for notable accomplishments in ocean sailing.

packing gland A stuffing box used around a propeller shaft at the point where it exits a boat's hull underwater. It is the most common method for preventing water from entering the hull while still allowing the propeller shaft to turn.

palapa Open-sided dwelling with a thatched roof made of dried palm leaves

panga Spanish: A flat bottomed fishing boat used in Mexico, usually powered by an outboard

parachute sea anchor a device external to the boat, attached to the bow used to stabilize a boat in heavy weather. It anchors not to the sea floor, but to the water itself, as a kind of brake. It pulls large amounts of water along as the boat moves in order to counter the effects of high winds and waves.

pay out Slacken or ease a rope so that it runs freely

pilot chart A chart of a major ocean area published, for the benefit of mariners, by the U.S. Naval Oceanographic Office in cooperation with the U.S. Weather Bureau. These charts contain information required in planning safe routes, including ocean currents, ice at sea, wind roses, storm tracks, isotherms, magnetic variation, and recommended routes or steamer tracks.

pitch-pole Be up-ended stern first, and completely overthrown by the sea

point of sail A sailing boat's course in relation to the wind direction

pooped If a sea breaks over the stern of a boat when she is running before the wind, she is said to be pooped.

Q flag Quarantine flag: an all-yellow flag displayed to indicate that the ship is in quarantine

reach To sail across the wind, i.e., with the wind cross the boat approximately at right angles to her

reef (1) Reduce the sail area by folding, rolling, or tying up parts of the sails (2) A chain of rocks lying submerged near the surface

rhumb line A path derived from a defined initial **bearing**. A rhumb line appears as a straight line on a **Mercator projection** map.

rode A line, as a rope or chain, used to attach an anchor to a boat

rogue wave (also known as freak waves, monster waves, killer waves, extreme waves and abnormal waves) Relatively large and spontaneous ocean surface waves that occur at sea and are a threat even to large ships and ocean liners. A wave whose height is more than twice the significant wave height (the mean of the largest third of waves in a wave record). Rogue waves are not necessarily the biggest waves found at sea; they are, rather, surprisingly large waves for a given sea state.

roller-furling A method of furling or reefing wherein a sail is rolled around a stay or rotating spar

running rigging All the movable parts of a ship's riggings, as distinct from the shrouds and stays that are permanently set up.

sahile Political or spiritual leader of an island in The San Blas Islands, Kuna Yala

sail to weather A point of sail hard on the wind, or sailing close-hauled with sails trimmed in tightly and sailing as close to the wind as possible without entering in irons

sampan A flat-bottomed skiff used in eastern Asia and usually propelled by two short oars or sometimes with a sail

seacock A controlling valve fitted to an underwater inlet

sheet A rope attached to the clew of a sail and used to trim it

short-tack To change directions for the tack at much more frequent and shorter intervals

shroud Wire ropes from a masthead to the ship's side to support a mast; upper and lower standing rigging

slip (1) A dock, hard or way (2) To let go a mooring chain

snubber A shock absorber, a secondary line set to absorb any stress or shock off of the main line (We commonly used a snubber on our anchor chain.)

SSB radio Single Side Band: Long-range radio used to communicate with other vessels and persons on land

stanchion A fixed, upright pillar support of iron, wood, or stainless steel used for guard rails, awnings, etc.

standing rigging Those parts of the rigging such as shrouds, stays, etc., that may be set up permanently

stays That part of the standing rigging supporting the masts in a fore-and-aft direction, and extending from the masthead forward and downward

tack To change the direction when sailing close-hauled by turning the bow to the wind and shifting the sails so as to fall off on the other side at about the same angle as before

tender A small vessel that supports a larger one

The Zone Nickname for the Panama Canal Zone used by Americans who live in the area and refer to themselves as "Zonies"

traveler track A metal ring, or fitting, positioned along a permanently mounted track and used to control the boom

tricolor A three-way red, white, and green navigation light mounted on the mast and used to provide information about the size, activity, and direction of travel of a sailboat

tuk-tuk An auto rickshaw or three-wheeler (tuk-tuk, trishaw, auto, rickshaw, tricycle, motor taxi, or baby taxi in popular parlance), a motor vehicle and a mode of transport for private use and as a vehicle for hire. We rode in these motorized carts, operated by a single individual, in parts of the Middle East, Africa, and Asia.

turnbuckle A device for adjusting the tension or length of ropes, cables, tie rods, and other tensioning systems

Valiant The name of the manufacturer of our 40-foot cutter- rigged offshore cruising sailboat, *Sanctuary*.

vee (or V) berth Berth in the bow of our boat and named after the shape of the berth due to the shape of the bow

VHF (Very High Frequency) Radio used on small boats for a wide variety of purposes including summoning rescue services, communicating with harbors, locks, bridges, or marinas. It operates in the VHF frequency range

watermaker A device used to obtain potable water by reverse osmosis of seawater. In boating circles, desalinators are often referred to as "watermakers"

winch A mechanical device used to pull in (wind up) or let out (wind out) or otherwise adjust the "tension" of a rope or wire rope

zarpe Spanish: An official departure permit

Sanctuary Layout

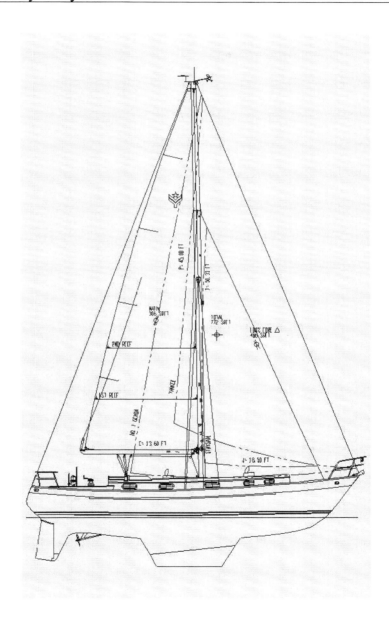

Sanctuary—Valiant 40

Hull ID #UNFO44701175-40T119T
Documentation #919404
Designer: Robert Perry—Seattle, WA
Builder: Uniflite 1975, Bellingham, WA
Production Sequence: 19th
LOA: 39'11" LWL: 34'0" Beam: 12'4" Draft: 6'
Displacement: 22,500 lbs. (Full: 28,000 lbs.)
Ballast: 7,700 lbs. (External lead glassed in)
Rigging Configuration: Cutter
Sail Area: 772 Square Feet
Hull Speed: 7.8 Knots (Fast Cruiser)

Sail Inventory:

Mainsail: Fully Battened Main with three reef points
Mainsail: Spare mainsail, non-battened
Yankee Jib: Roller Furling (on Profurl)
Genoa: 150% (with bag)
Staysail: (with on-deck bag)
Staysail/Lapper: Spare, with bag
Storm Staysail: (with bag)
Cruising Spinnaker: in dousing stocking, with bag

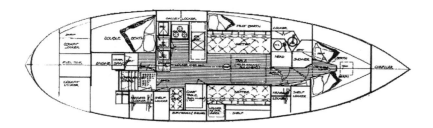

About Parkinson's Disease

Parkinson's disease is a chronic, degenerative neurological disorder that affects one in 100 people over age 60. While the average age at onset is 60, people have been diagnosed as young as 18. There is no objective test, or biomarker, for Parkinson's, so the rate of misdiagnosis can be relatively high—especially when the diagnosis is made by a non-specialist. Estimates of the number of people living with the disease therefore vary, but recent research indicates that at least one million people in the United States, and more than five million worldwide, have Parkinson's.

Parkinson's disease was first characterized extensively by an English physician, James Parkinson, in 1817. Today, we understand Parkinson's to be a disorder of the central nervous system that results from the loss of cells in various parts of the brain including a region called the substantia nigra. The substantia nigra cells produce dopamine, a chemical messenger responsible for transmitting signals within the brain that allow for coordination of movement. Loss of dopamine causes neurons to fire without normal control, leaving patients less able to direct or control their movement. Parkinson's is one of several diseases categorized by clinicians as movement disorders.

People are generally most familiar with the motor symptoms of Parkinson's disease, as they are the most evident signs of the disease from the outside. These symptoms, which also are called the "cardinal" symptoms of PD, are resting tremor, slowness of movement (bradykinesia), postural instability (balance problems), and rigidity. Other physical symptoms, such as gait problems and reduced facial expression, are also of note. These are due to the same discoordination of movement that causes the tremor and slowness.

There is increasing recognition of the importance of other symptoms of PD that are sometimes called "non-motor" or "dopamine-non-responsive" symptoms. While neither of these terms is ideal, these symptoms are common and can have a major impact on people with PD. For example, cognitive impairment, ranging from mild memory difficulties to dementia, and mood disorders, such as depression and anxiety, occur frequently. Also common are sleep difficulties, loss of sense of smell, speech and swallowing problems, unexplained pains, drooling, constipation, and low blood pressure when standing.

Parkinson's symptoms manifest differently in different patients. Many patients experience some symptoms and not others, and even the pace at which the disease worsens varies on an individual basis.

This information was provided by the Michael J. Fox Foundation for Parkinson's Research. To learn more about Parkinson's disease, or to contribute toward finding a cure, visit: http://www.michaeljfox.org/

Acknowledgements

I would like to thank Kurt Wilson, the editor of the *Register,* for his assistance in editing each chapter as it was published in serial form. He has since edited the entire manuscript. Thanks also to Jean Howze for additional editing.

The intern who told Jim to "go anyway" is Cathleen J. Miller, M.D. She is currently a Board Certified Neurologist with the Department of Neurology at Kaiser Permanente in Oregon. We owe her an enormous debt of gratitude and thanks.

Our journey would not have happened without the encouragement of our families, our friends, and countless strangers who became friends. Many of you are mentioned by name; many more are not. It would take another book to list you all. Please know that the contributions you made to our journey, and the kindnesses you showed us along the way, are never forgotten. We remember you with love and thankfulness. You allowed us to go anyway.

I also thank the one person without whom there would have been no sail around the world and no story: my friend, my partner, my love, my best critic, my biggest fan, my brave soul mate in the game of life, and the one who never gives up, Jim Foley.

About The Author

As clearly described in the first chapters of *Go Anyway*, Lyn Foley was not a sailor before the dream of offshore voyaging came into her life. She gained her skills on the often boisterous waters of San Francisco Bay, taking classes ranging from boat handling to celestial navigation. Only after taking a trial voyage (a challenging passage upwind from San Francisco to British Columbia) did she and Jim feel they were ready to attempt a longer voyage.

As a fabric artist and later, jewelry maker, her writing was at first limited to the newsletters sent out to friends as the voyage of *Sanctuary* progressed. She later contributed articles to various magazines.

Since returning from their voyage, Jim and Lyn settled in the small Texas town of Round Top where she learned the glass art of lampworking. She now designs and creates one-of-a-kind glass jewelry, which has been included in the collections of many galleries and is featured at art fairs throughout Texas. During this time she wrote this highly readable narrative, hoping to encourage both sailors and those with physical limitations to ignore the nay-sayers and reach for their dreams.

More than 23 years after being diagnosed with Parkinson's and despite ever worsening symptoms, Jim Foley still works at designing and creating silver jewelry. At the same time he is highly active in experimental testing to find ways to combat the symptoms of his disease.

In 2000 Lyn and Jim were recipients of the Ocean Cruising club Award of Merit which recognizes an outstanding voyage by an amateur sailor.

Visit www.LynFoley.com to see Lyn's glass work jewelry.

Visit www.GoAnyway.net to read more about *Sanctuary's* voyage around the world.

Made in the USA
San Bernardino, CA
28 October 2013